W. B. YEATS

A. Norman Jeffares, educated at Trinity College,
Dublin, and Oriel College, Oxford, has taught in the
Universities of Dublin, Groningen, Edinburgh,
Adelaide and Stirling. Though he has edited twenty-
four Restoration comedies and selections of William
Cowper and Walt Whitman, his main interest is in
Irish literature. Founder and Life President of the
International Association for the Study of Irish
Literatures, he has written on the work of many Irish
authors, including Swift, Farquhar, Goldsmith,
Sheridan, Maria Edgeworth, Charles Lever, George
Moore, W. B. Yeats and James Joyce.

He has a particular interest in Yeats's work. In
addition to the poet's widow and children, his sister
Lily and brother Jack, he has known many of Yeats's
friends and contemporaries, including Maud Gonne,
her daughter Iseult and son Sean MacBride, Lennox
Robinson, Harry Norman, W. J. Turner and Frank
O'Connor.

A former Chairman of Book Trust, Scotland,
President of International PEN Scotland, a member
of ACGB, Vice-Chairman of the Scottish Arts
Council and Vice-President of the Royal Society of
Edinburgh, he now lives at Fife Ness, where he is
writing his own Anecdotes, completing a third book of
poems and returning to an early interest in drawing
and painting.

Trinity College, Dublin: Drawings and Descriptions
W. B. Yeats: Man and Poet
Oliver Goldsmith
The Poetry of W. B. Yeats
George Moore
The Circus Animals: Essays on W. B. Yeats
A Commentary on the Collected Poems of W. B. Yeats
A Commentary on the Collected Plays of W. B. Yeats (with A. S.
Knowland)
Jonathan Swift
A History of Anglo-Irish Literature
Brought up in Dublin (poems)
Brought up to Leave (poems)
A New Commentary on the Poems of W. B. Yeats
A Pocket History of Irish Literature
Images of Imagination: Essays on Irish Writing
The Irish Literary Movement

Edited works include
Poems of W. B. Yeats
Selected Poems of W. B. Yeats
Selected Prose of W. B. Yeats
Selected Plays of W. B. Yeats
Selected Criticism of W. B. Yeats
Cowper: Selected Poems and Letters
W. B. Yeats: The Critical Heritage
Whitman: Selected Poems and Prose
Restoration Drama (4 vols)
Yeats, Sligo and Ireland
Poems of W. B. Yeats: A New Selection
Yeats's Poems
Yeats the European
W. B. Yeats: A Vision and Related Writings
The Gonne–Yeats Letters: Always Your Friend (with Anna
MacBride White)
Swift: The Selected Poems
Victorian Love Poems
Irish Love Poems
Irish Childhoods (with Antony Kamm)
W. B. Yeats: The Love Poems
Ireland's Women: Writings Past and Present (with Katie Donovan
and Brendan Kennelly)
James Joyce: The Poems in Verse and Prose (with Brendan
Kennelly)
The Love Poems of Ireland: Wonder and a Wild Desire
Oliver St John Gogarty: Poems and Plays

W. B. Yeats

A New Biography

A. Norman Jeffares

CONTINUUM
London and New York

Continuum

The Tower Building, 11 York Road, London SE1 7NX

370 Lexington Avenue, New York, NY 10017–6503

First published in Great Britain by Hutchinson 1988. Arena edition 1990

This revised edition published by Continuum 2001

British Library Cataloguing-in-Publication Data

A catalogue record for this book is available from the British Library.

ISBN 0–8264–5524–7 (paperback)

Library of Congress Cataloging-in-Publication Data

Jeffares, A. Norman (Alexander Norman), 1920–

W. B. Yeats, a new biography / A. Norman Jeffares.

p. cm.

Includes bibliographical references and index.

ISBN 0-8264-5524-7 (pbk.)

1. Yeats, W. B. (William Butler), 1865-1939. 2. Poets, Irish–19th
century–Biography. 3. Poets, Irish–20th century–Biography. I. Title.

PR5906 .J419 2001

821′.8–dc21

[B]

2001028179

Printed and bound in Great Britain by
The Guernsey Press Co. Ltd, Guernsey, Channel Islands

TO ALASDAIR, BRENDAN, COLIN,
SARAH AND WARWICK
FOR FRIENDSHIP AND MANY KINDNESSES

CONTENTS

ACKNOWLEDGEMENTS

The author wishes to thank A. P. Watt Ltd, acting on behalf of Michael B. Yeats, for permission to quote from W. B. Yeats's poems, plays and prose.

Every effort has been made to trace other copyright holders, and full acknowledgement will be made in future editions if the publisher is informed.

Poems (1895)

INTRODUCTION TO THE
CONTINUUM EDITION

This is a revised and expanded edition of a biography primarily intended as a narrative account of Yeats's life. To illuminate that life it draws where necessary upon his writings: published and unpublished poetry, the plays and the prose – *Autobiographies*, the fiction, the essays, *A Vision*, the Introductions, Prefaces and reviews, as well as letters, diaries and manuscripts. It tells the story of a continuous, arduous process that shaped Yeats's life as he made and remade himself out of the complexities and often contradictory elements in his character, in the process becoming a great poet.

Such is the continuous flow of information about and discussion of Yeats and his work that we now know a great deal about both, and various biographies are affected in different ways by this new material. To begin with, much of his own writing is being made available to readers. Allan Wade's selection of the *Letters* (1954) and other volumes of letters to various individuals are being superseded by the fine Clarendon Press edition of *The Collected Letters of W. B. Yeats* emerging under the general editorship of John Kelly. Volumes II and III have now been added to the first volume, which appeared in 1986. These superbly edited volumes have, at the time of writing, brought Yeats's correspondence up to 1904. In 1889 he had fallen in love with Maud Gonne, but her marriage of 1903 to John MacBride had by 1904 become a disaster. The highly charged friendship that inspired so many of his obsessional love poems to her can be charted from her point of view in *The Gonne–Yeats Letters: Always Your Friend*, edited by Anna MacBride White, Maud's granddaughter, and myself in 1992.

The contents of these various volumes of letters demonstrate the multiplicity of Yeats's interests, which go far beyond his virtually continuous occupation with writing. The letters present us with his explorations of Indian thought, theosophy, magic, occultism and spiritualism. They also reflect his deepening interest in politics; as his father had moved from the Unionism of orthodox Anglo-Irish landlordism to a belief in Home Rule, stimulated by his friendship with Isaac Butt, so the son's interest in Home Rule was to move to an increasing belief in nationalism.

In his *Memoirs*, Yeats described himself as 'a poor student', but the extent of his reading was remarkable. Despite his weak sight, while pursuing his study of magic and the occult as a young man he made himself well versed in translations of Irish legends, folklore and mythology, and in nineteenth-century Irish writing in English. (His interest in Swift and other eighteenth-century Irish writers came later.) Through a study of theosophy he came to Madame Blavatsky's *Isis Unveiled* (1875) and *The Secret Doctrine* (1888), while A. P. Sinnett's *The Occult World* (1881) and *Esoteric Buddhism* (1883) were other sources of ideas on spiritual and occult evolution. He discovered Blake with delight in his symbolism, editing him in co-operation with Edwin Ellis in three volumes in 1893 and writing an enthusiastic introduction to his own selection of Blake published the same year. Swedenborg and Boehme influenced him, and there were many other writers, such as Eliphas Levi and Cornelius Agrippa, who claimed his attention. Thanks to Warwick Gould, we now know how Joachim of Fiore held a place in this preoccupation, one which altered the views of Blake that he had formed in 1893.

This varied reading had practical outcomes. Knowledge of Irish literature underpinned the effort that went into the creation of influential Irish Literary Societies in London and Dublin. Essays, anthologies and reviews stemmed from it as he sought to make his way in London literary life and to earn the little money this work brought in. Similarly, his increasing knowledge of Rosicrucianism, magic and the occult, as well as the mysticism to which George Russell introduced him, reinforced his effective work as a mentor of the Order of the Golden Dawn.

To chart Yeats's reading in detail would be a long task. The books in his library have been listed (though the list is necessarily incomplete) and this cataloguing reveals something of his eclecticism.

He tended to find things he wanted in books and to seize on them, sometimes pencilling a line in the margin, sometimes writing a word that summed up some fact or image. This habit conveys something of his idiosyncratic form of study.

The early letters from London to Katharine Tynan have shown his desire for and need of friendship and social life, for sardonic observation and appreciation of the foibles of others. He wanted to know his contemporaries and assess them, something easily achieved in the closely knit society of Dublin in his youth, in the Dublin Hermetic Society, in the group that he met in the Tynan farmhouse, and in the circles that spread out from the Contemporary Club. Once John Butler Yeats moved his family to London again in 1887 there was the artistic and dramatic life which flourished in the suburb of Bedford Park to enjoy: the family had been there before, and returned again in 1888.

Yeats, however, was ambitious; he needed more than Bedford Park social life afforded, and among the members of the Rhymers Club, in the founding of which he took an active part, he found a kindred awareness of the influence exerted by literary reviews. He found other company in the Order of the Golden Dawn, such as Florence Farr, Annie Horniman and the eccentric MacGregor Mathers.

Yeats, perpetually discovering himself, was able to combine the contrasting pulls of opposite sides of his character. There was a solitary element (part of the writer's concentration) and there was a social and political one. The latter found expression, for instance, in his founding of Irish Literary Societies in London and Dublin in the 1890s, later in attempts to create a Celtic Mystical Order, and, in 1937, the founding of the Irish Academy of Letters. The 'doing' involved in these activities has interested Roy Foster, the first volume of whose compendious *W. B. Yeats: A Life* appeared in 1997. He has brought a historian's interest to bear on the effects of political and social change upon Yeats, who grew up in Victorian Ireland, his youth, as Foster puts it, spanning 'the exact period of crisis which inaugurated the decline of the Irish Protestant Ascendancy'.

The Yeats family had Home Rule views, but in the Contemporary Club in Dublin John Butler Yeats and his son had met many whose views were more nationalist. John O'Leary, the old Fenian, in particular, had a profound effect on the young poet, by then steeped in Shelley and Spenser; he lent him many of the books that shaped his political ideas as well as his literary ambitions. O'Leary got him to join the Young Ireland Society in 1885, hoping for a revival of Young Ireland-style politics. It was probably a year later that Yeats joined the Irish Republican Brotherhood (IRB) (his former membership of that organisation was one of the main reasons for his appointment to the Irish Free State Senate in 1922) and the Irish National Alliance.

The establishment of the Irish Literary Society in London in 1891 seemed to Yeats an opportunity to launch his plans for a Library of Ireland, to make legendary and national heroes known to a wider audience than that which had been reached by scholars and translators. But he was defeated by Sir Charles Gavan Duffy, who became head of the National Publishing Company. Duffy had himself earlier suggested a series of reprints, and did not want Yeats to give a neo-Fenian tone to the proposed list of books. Disillusionment at being outsmarted by the veteran, highly skilled politician made Yeats more combative and he realised he had created powerful enemies for himself. As a political propagandist he had not been successful, however much he was able to promote 'Celtic' literature in England. The London Irish Literary Society had, in effect, been taken over politically by T. W. Rolleston, while members of the one subsequently established in Dublin found Yeats unduly difficult in his fervent attempts to unite literature and nationalist politics. There was, however, a period in the 1890s when he saw himself (as Chairman of the Executive Committee of the '98 Centennial Association of Great Britain and France, set up to mark the centenary of the 1798 Revolution and to celebrate Wolfe Tone's part in it) playing a leading role in turning the Dublin Committee into something like an Irish Parliament attended by the four political parties – an optimistic and completely unrealistic ambition.

Maud Gonne's letters and his own accounts tell the significant story of how he was horrified by the Jubilee Riots in Dublin in 1897. He was exhausted by his political work and near a breakdown, from which he recovered after a spell in Sligo and his first long summer as Lady Gregory's guest at Coole Park in County Galway. He left the IRB in 1900, probably as a result of having seen political violence in action three years earlier, as well as experiencing disgust at the IRB's failure to deal effectively with Frank Hugh O'Donnell. This eccentric MP had intercepted money from the Transvaal representative in Europe intended to support Maud's activities (which included the plan of planting bombs on British troopships bound for South

Africa) and given it to the Irish Parliamentary Party (from whom Yeats got it back for the IRB). Maud also resigned at the same time. Both she and Yeats had argued at length against the IRB's failure to restrain O'Donnell. Maud may have agreed, temporarily at least, with her former French lover Millevoye's view, that the Irish revolutionaries were a set of *farceurs*. She – and Yeats – could not consider wasting time on an organisation which had successfully prevented Ireland making 'England's difficulty an opportunity.'

Much of his energy was also taken up with the disruption of the Order of the Golden Dawn, with getting rid of the notorious Aleister Crowley, with the exhausting task of reconstructing the Order so that its work could continue in a more orderly way. As well as reforming the Golden Dawn, he had formed the idea of creating a Celtic Order of Mysteries and locating it in a castle on an island in Lough Key, County Roscommon, and this involved much planning and discussion. He hoped to involve Maud in this, and, though she was interested and took some part in the planning, their friendship left him frustrated, the constant strain making him wonder if, like Lancelot, he had loved a queen 'beyond measure and exceeding long'.

Again we realise the interrelationships of the different aspects of his life: the political bound up with the intellectual, the intellectual linked with his obsession with Maud Gonne. The complications continued when he became involved in the creation of an Irish theatre – his experiences in the political arena and his enjoyment of controversy a preparation for 'Theatre business, management of men'. Now, however, he had found a close friend and confidant in Lady Gregory. Their friendship has been well described by John Kelly in ' "Friendship is all the House I have"; Lady Gregory and Yeats' (in *Lady Gregory, Fifty Years After*, edited by Ann Saddlemyer and Colin Smythe, 1987). Maud's letters show how she begrudged the time the Abbey and its controversies took from his poetry, but then she disliked Lady Gregory's increasing influence on him, realising that she was moderating his nationalism, and helping to diminish his revolutionary fervour. It was Lady Gregory who convinced him in 1898 that Maud's plan of inciting Kerry tenants to kill sheep and seize food was highly dangerous, for it would blunt morality by encouraging murder and theft, and, convinced by these arguments of hers, he began to dissuade Maud from advocating this irresponsible action.

For seven years after Olivia Shakespear had inducted him into the experience of sex in 1896 – only to find that Maud Gonne still occupied his thoughts – his abstention and continued preoccupation with Maud left him often ill through masturbation, 'when desire became an unendurable torture'. He still proposed to her, still hoped she would leave the world of politics for that of mystic truth.

While their political interest separated, their mutual interest in mysticism continued; it was only in 1898 that she told him of her affair with the French politician and journalist Millevoye, of the births of his and her children, stressing, however, her dislike of sexual love. All he achieved was the 'spiritual marriage'; and that did not last long, for Maud married MacBride in 1903.

There followed some unsatisfactory affairs – there was even a brief physical relationship with Maud in 1908 – and Yeats seemed the 'solitary man' of Woburn Buildings, the guest at English country houses, for whom long summers at Coole provided an orderly existence with ideal conditions for writing – and reading. But, as Lady Gregory realised, marriage would provide him with the stability of domestic family life. She had been horrified by the threatened possibility of his mistress Mabel Dickinson having a child, and relieved when the affair was ended by Yeats in an acrimonious meeting in 1913. She introduced him to various young women whom she thought suitable, but without success.

When Maud Gonne's husband was executed by a firing squad after the 1916 Rising Yeats proposed to her yet again, but was refused in the usual terms – 'Let us go on being close friends.' He then surprised her by asking if she would object to his proposing to her daughter Iseult. Maud was surprised, she told me, but did not object, nor, perhaps unexpectedly, did Lady Gregory object either, probably thinking Iseult would be malleable, and certainly a great improvement on Maud. Iseult enjoyed his friendship, indeed, as she described it to me, her flirtation with her mother's admirer of so many years, but finally she refused Yeats in 1917.

His marriage to Georgie Hyde Lees, which followed in October that year, transformed his life, but not without the complication of his troubled feelings of guilt about Iseult, his bafflement and self-examination about his past relationships with women – including Olivia Shakespear and his wife, and, especially, the long obsession with Maud Gonne.

Mrs Yeats's automatic writing provided the personal props he badly needed. *A Vision*, which resulted from the automatic writing, evolved into scaffolding in the poetry, with its cyclical view of history in the gyres, of human personality in the phases of the moon, and of the development of individual souls. Yeats paid his wife handsome, if brief, tribute in the poem 'Under Saturn' – how indeed could he forget the wisdom she had brought him, the domestic comfort she had created in their various houses, in Oxford, in Merrion Square and in Riversdale, and even under the starker conditions of living in and making functional the symbolic tower in Galway?

The 'wisdom' of 'Under Saturn' referred to the automatic writing and the subsequent 'sleeps' that were, joined with the poems associated with his *Per Amica Selentia Lunae* (1917), 'part of a religious system more or less logically worked out', the foundation of *A Vision*. It also implied Mrs Yeats's wide reading in magic and occultism as well as in European literature and philosophy. A long poem, 'The Gift of Harun Al-Rashid', pays further tribute to his gifted wife and the part she played in the shared activity that occupied so much of their time in the first years of their marriage.

The publication of transcriptions of the automatic script and the Sleeps and Dream notebooks under George Mills Harper's general editorship shows the extent of the married couple's work, something I realised in discussions with Mrs Yeats, who made the scripts available to me and told me how the writing had begun – and continued. (In the Bibliography I have commented on Brenda Maddox's use of them in her book *George's Ghosts* (1999).) Harper wrote a good account of the process in *The Making of Yeats's 'A Vision': A Study of the Automatic Script* (2 vols, 1987) and Virginia Moore, in *The Unicorn* (1954), studied how Yeats's beliefs changed and developed, examining the esoteric sources of many of his ideas and philosophical interests; some of the latter have been well handled in Donald T. Torchiana's *Yeats and Georgian Ireland* (1966).

Yet again the complexity and fullness of Yeats's life emerge from any reading of the scripts, just as, say, the notes to *A Vision* (1990) indicate the wide range of his reading, the ever-increasing scope of his references. There was, of course, the relaxation of reading detective stories; he lent some to the detectives guarding his home in the Civil War, to train them, he said, in the highest traditions of their profession. But he returned to Balzac frequently – he possessed 40 volumes of the *Comédie humaine* – regarding him as a great writer, a taste inculcated by his father's reading aloud *La Peau de chagrin* on a family holiday in 1874.

To mention the family is to recognise how much more we now know about the details of its life. William Murphy's generously full biography of John Butler Yeats, aptly entitled *Prodigal Father* (1978), has given us a life based upon an enthusiastic admiration of the originality of mind and conversational gifts of 'the father of the Yeatses'. Murphy has also written *Family Secrets: Yeats and His Relatives* (1995), the secrets probably relating to John Butler Yeats's epistolary affair with Rosa Butt, which the family did not wish to be disclosed. The book contains useful documentation of manuscript sources.

The father's fecklessness has been emphasised in such recent books as Bruce Arnold's *Jack Yeats* (1999), a brilliant study of W. B.'s artist brother. Gifford Lewis in *The Yeats Sisters and the Cuala* (1994) shows us the dangers of any facile acceptance of the Yeats/Pollexfen contrasts so beloved of John Butler Yeats, and she writes well about the close working relationships of W. B. and his sister Lollie ('very alike in their unpleasant qualities of self-absorption and self-righteousness'). Her criticism of 'the self-absorbed and improvident father' is similar to that of Bruce Arnold. A recent addition to our awareness of W. B. Yeats as a father is Michael B. Yeats's *Cast a Cold Eye: Memories of a Poet's Son and Politician* (1999).

Much specialised knowledge is available, perhaps the most impressive the two great variorum editions of the poems and the plays, which make it easier for readers to chart the many changes Yeats made in his texts over years of revision in different editions. The concordances by Stephen Parrish and others are equally valuable, as is the Cornell University Press Yeats MSS series, while Colin Smythe's bibliography is eagerly awaited, for it revises and expands, on a very large scale indeed, Wade's earlier work. The *Yeats Annual*, edited by Warwick Gould, contains a variety of contributions which add greatly to an understanding of the man and his work as well as his relationships with his contemporaries. There are many illuminating lives and studies, among them books dealing with AE, Florence Farr, the Fays, Oliver St John Gogarty, Maud Gonne, Constance Gore-Booth, Lady Gregory, Annie Horniman, George Moore, Lennox Robinson, Sean O'Casey, Olivia Shakespear, F. P. Sturm and J. M. Synge.

My first biography of Yeats, *W. B. Yeats: Man and Poet* (1949; 3rd edn, 1996), was founded not only upon reading but upon many conversations with people who knew Yeats intimately. I was most fortunate in knowing Mrs Yeats, Lily Yeats, Jack Yeats, Maud Gonne, Iseult Stuart, Lennox Robinson and many of Yeats's other friends. Mrs Yeats gave me access to the poet's papers, his MSS, TSS, diaries, journals, notebooks, letters and library. I was privileged to have had her frank comments on many aspects of her husband's life. She was a mine of information on all aspects of his writing. My admiration, respect and liking for her, always strong, have increased over the years.

In this present narrative life I have tried to appreciate the energy which went into Yeats's varied activities, to recognise his strategies in his deliberate progress towards gaining a lasting place in the literary world – and surprising it by his dynamic change of style after the publication of his *Collected Works* in 1908. His influence upon the creation of modern Ireland can now be seen more clearly; the practicality of his politics in the shaping of the Irish theatre can be understood; his generally constructive role as a senator can be weighed up – and the effect of all of these on his attitudes to European political movements after the First World War.

To return to his reading of Balzac is to recognise what he admired in him: his vigour. We can ourselves admire the vigour with which Yeats forged his way through the rhetorical oversimplification of the choice he put to his intellect: 'perfection of the life or of the work', and the pertinacity with which he pursued his boyish plan through his life, until he could assess what his twenties 'crammed with toil' and the subsequent crowded years of creation and controversy had achieved.

And what remains in our minds? Always, I think, the multiplicity of the man who began to write as a dreaming idealist, became a satiric sceptic and finally a conserver. He had learned to blend, out of contradictions, out of the antinomies of his own character, love and hatred, joy and bitterness, hope and despair.

Yeats's constant self-analysis and self-questioning and his preoccupation through so much of his life with human love and with the spirit world and the hereafter are factors which made him original in his searching, gave his rhetorical questions an impressive challenging power, for he faced the common human lot: evanescence of beauty, destruction and decay, the death of each individual. That certain end he faced bravely, his uncertainties hidden, partially, by the varying

masks, dignified and sometimes distant (originally adopted to overcome shyness), from which he became indistinguishable. They
enabled him to express with romantic emotion – curbed by an ironic
and unsentimental realism – love and passion, awareness of and
respect for tradition in his continuous search for unity, for an ultimate sense of tragic joy.

A. N. Jeffares
Fife Ness, 2001

ONE

1865–1881

William Butler Yeats was born in Dublin on 13 June 1865 at George's Ville No. 1, now 5 Sandymount Avenue – a characteristic nineteenth-century Dublin small red-brick suburban house, with a flight of granite steps leading to a hall door on the upper storey. The child was healthy, with, the doctor remarked, 'a fine *os frontis*'; he added reassuringly that he was so strong he could be left out all night on the window-sill and it would do him no harm.[1]

His father, John Butler Yeats, was reading for the Bar. He came from a family of Yorkshire origin, the earliest known Yeats, Jervis, having crossed sometime in the seventeenth century to Dublin, where for three generations the Yeatses were successful linen merchants. Benjamin, the grandson of Jervis, married Mary Butler, a member of a leading Anglo-Irish family, powerful and wealthy from medieval times, the heads of which were the successive Dukes of Ormonde. This marriage meant a good deal to the Yeatses, who subsequently used the Butler name frequently as a Christian name. Not only did Mary Butler contribute social status, however; she also brought the cachet of land – about 560 acres at Thomastown, County Kildare – and the income from this land was the more welcome when Benjamin's business failed. His wife also had a handsome pension from the War Office, so there was no financial problem involved in sending their son John, born in 1774, to Trinity College, Dublin. The family now left trade behind. After a distinguished career as an undergraduate John married Jane Taylor, the sister of an influential official at Dublin Castle, and in 1805 he became Rector of Drumcliffe in County Sligo where he remained until his death. He lived well and was popular locally. Several of his children stayed on in Sligo; he sent his eldest son William Butler and another, Thomas, to Trinity College.

William Butler Yeats (1806–62) entered the Church, becoming

a curate in County Down in 1831. He was a good horseman, his
rector remarking that he had hoped for a curate but they had sent
him a jockey. He married into the Corbet family, subsequently being
appointed Rector of Tullylish, near Portadown. Like Jonathan Swift
in his northern parish at the end of the seventeenth century, this
Yeats – an easygoing Evangelical – was uneasy in Northern Ireland,
disliking the temperament of the Presbyterians by whom he was
surrounded. He set about surrounding himself more closely with a
large family and by 1857 there were nine children, to whom he
offered an example of sympathy, affection and social refinement.
To his eldest son, John Butler Yeats, born at Tullylish in 1839,
he seemed 'the most agreeable of companions and the finest of
gentlemen'. He sent John Butler Yeats to a puritanical school at
Seaforth near Liverpool at the age of ten; after two years of this he
and his brothers William Butler (1843–99) and Robert Corbet
(?1842–57) were shipped to Atholl Academy in the Isle of Man, a
school run by a Calvinist Scot who firmly believed in flogging. At
the time there were two other Irish boys there, Charles Pollexfen
(1838–1923) and his brother George (1839–1910). These Pollexfens
came from Sligo; they were less academically inclined than the Yeats
brothers, remaining at the bottom of their classes. John Butler Yeats
was always at the top of his, while his younger brother Willie was
the most popular boy in the school. The Pollexfen brothers were
unresponsive, indeed downright disagreeable, though George did
reveal his storytelling talents in the dormitory at night. However,
they had what John Butler Yeats called magnetism and a primitivism
that came from their closeness to nature.

After enduring the Atholl Academy, John Butler Yeats went to
Trinity College, Dublin. Intended for the Church like his father
and grandfather, he read classics, but found he had no religious
belief and decided to become a barrister. His friends at College
included the Dowden brothers, John and Edward, and John
Todhunter, all three highly intelligent. As an undergraduate he did
not live in rooms in College but enjoyed staying at Sandymount
Castle, about three miles south-east of the centre of Dublin. This
was an eighteenth-century house gothicised with battlements, clois-
ters and a clock tower which had vistas over Dublin Bay. It was
owned by his uncle Robert Corbet, a sociable man and an enthusiastic gardener who kept ducks and swans on a pond, two eagles
chained on an island on it, and deer in his park. The Rev. William

Butler Yeats retired at fifty and came to live near the Castle, indeed died in it in 1862. John Butler Yeats then inherited from him a house in Dorset Street in Dublin and the income from the Kildare lands at Thomastown – then a little less than £400 net a year – and that was enough to marry on. After his graduation in 1862 he had won a prize for political economy and gone to stay with his old schoolfellow George Pollexfen in Sligo – where there were Yeats uncles and aunts to visit also. In Sligo he had met George's twenty-one-year-old sister Susan Mary, dark-haired and with large lustrous eyes, one blue and one brown. He later told his son that she married him 'because I was always there and the family helped'.[2]

Of course the family helped. The Pollexfens obviously saw in this young man – a landlord with a private income, intending to become a barrister – an excellent suitor. The Pollexfens themselves were ship-owners and mill-owners, prosperous and industrious, who though not on dining terms with the Sligo landowners regarded themselves as socially above neighbouring Protestant shopkeepers and farmers, unlike their less reserved and easier-going Middleton relatives.

These Sligo Pollexfens were descended from a Cornishman, the keeper of the forts at Berry Head, Torquay, who had married a Wexford woman, Mary Stephens; their son William ran away to sea and built up a fleet of merchant ships. In one of these, *The Dasher*, he sailed into Sligo and married the daughter of a widowed Pollexfen cousin from Jersey who had been brought to Sligo at the age of fifteen by William Middleton, a Sligo smuggler and sea-captain. Having married Elizabeth Middleton, William Pollexfen became a partner with her brother in the prosperous family firm, the milling company of Middleton and Pollexfen, to which he added the Sligo Steam Navigation Company.

John Butler Yeats was very taken with the Pollexfens, they seemed full of suppressed poetry as well as magnetism. But probably he hardly realised at first the full extent of their deeply sombre nature; family life with them was very different from that of the Yeatses. John Butler Yeats regarded his Yeats relatives in Sligo as clever and innocent: '*capricious* and *gentle* and *pure*'.[3] But later he described to his son Sundays in the Pollexfen household, when the family gathered in force and sat together, most of them (there were twelve children) in one room, 'all disliking each other, at any rate alien

mutually, in gloomy silence'.[4] Many years later he explained that he
had taken to the Pollexfens and married his wife because of their
genius for being dismal: 'I thought I would place myself under
prison rule and learn all the virtues.'[5] He saw his future wife's
individuality in her faults, he told her; these included sulking and
petulance – she had no sense of humour.

The marriage took place on 10 September 1863 and the young
couple began their married life in Dublin at George's Ville, buying
secondhand furniture for their six-roomed semi-detached house –
the poet was to call it a 'mean house' when he walked past in late
middle age (having earlier gone to see it when he was thirty-five), and
Robert Corbet addressed letters to his nephew from the splendour of
Sandymount Castle to 'The Quarry Hole', remembering it was built
on the site of a former quarry – but for a newly-married pair it must
have been pleasant enough. John Butler Yeats continued to use the
tower room in Sandymount Castle as a study, but despite the success
of his address as Auditor of the Law Students Debating Society,
delivered before a large and distinguished audience, any attractions
the law had originally possessed for him waned during the year and
a half he spent completing his terms. He was called to the Bar in
January 1866, found the courts tedious and enlivened his attendance
at them by drawing legal luminaries, not always in complimentary
fashion. This was not likely to aid his future career, but he had
always drawn well and now suddenly decided to become a professional artist. Oscar Wilde gave his decision artistic form, telling
how J.B.Y. announced at breakfast to his children that he was tired
of the law and would become a painter. To the question 'Could he
paint?' Wilde would reply, 'Not in the least, that was the beauty of
it.'[6]

Robert Corbet's finances failed and he developed palsy; he committed suicide by jumping off the Irish mailboat in 1873, and once
Sandymount Castle was sold the happiness of living near it had
vanished. This was a reason for John Butler Yeats's leaving Dublin,
but it also seemed sensible to start a new career where one was not
known; so, leaving his wife and children – Willie and Lily (Susan
Mary Yeats, born at Enniscrone near Sligo in August 1866) – with
her parents in their recently acquired large house, Merville, on the
outskirts of Sligo, he moved to London early in 1867 to enrol at
Heatherley's art school where he became friendly with John Trivett
Nettleship and Edwin J. Ellis. The three were later the leading

figures in an informal association known as 'The Brotherhood', all devoted to the idea that all that mattered was art.

Susan Yeats, with the children, joined her husband in July; they lived at 23 Fitzroy Road, Regent's Park, of which John Butler Yeats had taken a six-year lease. One of the poet's earliest memories was of boys playing in the street, among them a lad in uniform. When he asked who that lad was, the servant told him the boy was going to blow the town up; he went to sleep terrified. But his main memories were of Sligo, where he spent summer family holidays in 1868, in 1869 (the children stayed there that year till December), 1870 and 1871.

Susan Yeats, used to a well-to-do household as a girl, was later described by her eldest daughter as 'not at all good at housekeeping or child-minding'. She found her husband's inability to provide adequate money for the household in London depressing. She also particularly disliked his younger friend Edwin Ellis, who was insensitive in his reactions to others and particularly boorish in his attitude towards her. Indeed, John Todhunter described him to Edward Dowden as having 'estranged her husband from her'. The Pollexfens in Sligo had not approved of Susan's husband deserting the respectability and the likely financial rewards of the law for the unorthodoxy and uncertain returns of art, so when John Butler Yeats failed to exhibit at the Royal Academy, let alone sell a picture, they became decidedly and openly critical. In turn the artist identified in his wife's family an intense desire for property and money, a reverence for class which he abominated and a melancholia which he feared his children might have inherited.

There were now several more children to support – significantly none was given the Christian name of Pollexfen; they were Lollie (Elizabeth Corbet, b. 1868), Bobbie (Robert Corbet, 1870–73) and Jack (John Butler, b. 1871). While John Butler Yeats was generous and hospitable, he was also feckless. His habit of spending too long on his paintings and his reluctance to obtain commissions meant that still more mortgages were taken out on the Kildare lands. This diminished the sum the rents brought in – now down to about £220 a year – which if managed carefully might have sufficed for a reasonably comfortable life; however, prudent management of money was something of which the artist was incapable. After a summer holiday in Sligo in 1871, the family was in Fitzroy Road until July 1872 when they all returned to Sligo, where Mrs Yeats and the children were to stay with her parents in Merville for over two years. John Butler Yeats wrote in old age that he did not think his wife approved of a single one of his ideas or theories or opinions which were to her 'only foolishness'.[7] Back in London, however, he responded to her worried letters about the children, thinking the younger sons were not likely to be adversely affected by the Pollexfens, but telling her of his anxieties about the treatment Willie received from her family, particularly from his Pollexfen aunts.[8] He believed that Willie was intensely affectionate but 'from shyness, sensitiveness and nervousness, difficult to win and yet he is worth winning'.[9] He thought kindness, affection and gentleness were needed – but sensitiveness was 'so rare at Merville'. Old William Pollexfen, blue-eyed and bearded, was fierce and silent. A menacing figure of great physical strength who kept a hatchet by his bed to deal with burglars, who carried a revolver in his pocket to church in case of Fenian troubles, who hunted men with a horse-whip, he often roared at his grandchildren without meaning to be unkind, but nonetheless terrifying or humiliating them. The Yeats children liked him, admired him, but feared him and attempted to avoid him. They tried to see him only at mealtimes and then to sit on the same side of the table so that he would not be enraged by seeing them take too much sugar. 'He had an alarming way of stopping grumbling,' wrote Lily Yeats, 'and looking at us in silence while we carried two sugar spoons from the bowl to our plates.'[10] Willie confused him with God, thought of him in middle age whenever he read *King Lear* and wondered if the delight in passionate men in his own plays and poetry was more than memory of his grandfather. His grandmother, however, was sociable by nature, gentle, quiet, even-tempered and unselfish. Delicate ivory in complexion herself, she painted delicate water-colours and dispensed healing remedies and various charities. She made the rounds of the house when her husband was asleep 'to make certain there was no burglar in danger of the hatchet'.[11] The Pollexfen uncles and aunts, though fairly kind, were not very sympathetic; when they began to try to teach him to read – he did not know his alphabet at seven – they thought that he was mentally lacking. He seemed unsuccessful like his father, 'unsuccessful and therefore wicked'.[12]

*

Though Willie was unhappy in his grandparents' house at Sligo, there were some compensations: a large garden with ships' figureheads, places in which to hide away, two dogs with whom he chased rabbits and a pony to ride. There was a stable-boy, Johnny Healey, who read Orange ballads to him in the stable loft, and when there were rumours of a Fenian rising Willie thought he would like to die fighting the Fenians.

I was to build a very fast and beautiful ship and to have under my command a company of young men who were always to be in training like athletes and so become as brave and handsome as the young men in the story-books, and there was to be a big battle on the sea-shore near Rosses and I was to be killed.[13]

The artist's to-ing and fro-ing between London and Sligo went on. John Butler Yeats went to paint portraits at Muckross Abbey in February 1873, but his son Robert, a child of three, died suddenly of croup in Sligo the next month. Willie and Lily were soon happily drawing ships which imitated the ships in the harbour, flags flying at half-mast. Their father spent the summer in Sligo, returned to Muckross Abbey (it was, perhaps, typical of his fortunes that the day he presented the husband with a portrait of his wife, she left him for another man and the picture was rejected), and later painted the Cosby children at Stradbally Hall until the spring of 1874. He turned down commissions in Dublin and in the following October brought his family back to London, to 14 Edith Villas, North End, in West Kensington. A Pollexfen aunt summed up the family attitude to John Butler Yeats by telling Willie, 'You are going to London. Here you are somebody. There you will be nobody at all.'[14]

In Sligo he could see his grandfather's ships come up the bay or the river; his sailors treated the boy with deference, a ship's carpenter made and mended his toy boats and he thought no one could be so important as his grandfather. Yet during the very formative years that Willie spent at Merville – he was there from the age of seven years and one month to nine years and five months – he was deeply afraid of his Pollexfen uncles and aunts as well as of his formidable grandfather. In middle age he remembered 'little of childhood but its pain'.[15] There were, however, Middleton relatives who provided some alleviation of the Pollexfen regime. A Middleton cousin, George, lived at Rosses Point, down the Garavogue river from Sligo towards the sea, with whom Willie rowed and was taken sailing. On one of these yachting occasions:

... it had come on very rough. I had lain on deck between the mast and the bowsprit and a wave had burst over me and I had seen green water over my head. I was very proud and very wet. When we got into Rosses again, I was dressed up in an older boy's clothes so that the trousers came down below my boots, and a pilot gave me a little raw whiskey. I drove home on an outside car and was so pleased with the strange state in which I found myself that for all my uncle could do I cried to every passer-by that I was drunk, and went on crying it through the town and everywhere until I was put to bed by my grandmother and given something to drink that tasted of blackcurrants and so fell asleep.[16]

The Middletons – easygoing, without pride or reserve – were friendly with the country people and through them Willie heard many country stories and legends of fairies. He told a social club at Oxford in the early twenties that he first saw a fairy, a 'fay', as a child in Merville: it came down a moonbeam towards him, but retreated when he tried to speak to it. His cousin Lucy Middleton had second sight, and the family accepted the supernatural as a part of life.

The Yeats relatives were not like these homely practical Middletons, who enjoyed talking of their smuggling forebears. The ancestors discussed by the Yeats family were grander. Willie's great-aunt Micky was full of family history:

... there was a little James I cream-jug with the Yeats motto and crest, and on her dining-room mantelpiece a beautiful silver cup that had belonged to my great-great-grandfather, who had married a certain Mary Butler. It had upon it the Butler crest and had already been old at the date 1534, when the initials of some bride and bridegroom were engraved under the lip. All its history for generations was rolled up inside it upon a piece of paper yellow with age, until some caller took the paper to light his pipe.[17]

Conscious of past dignity though they were, the Yeatses seemed to Willie and Lily to be clever, gentle and quietly humorous. Lily stayed with her Yeats grandmother and aunts in Dublin: they were imaginative, demonstrative, full of laughter and affectionate. Inevitably she drew a contrast between their house and Merville, where 'Life was serious and silent, no merry talk at meals, no running to and fro'.[18] The Yeatses had come down in the world and thought the rising Pollexfens purse-proud. While the Pollexfens looked down on the superstitions of the peasants, they also criticised

English ways of life – yet they were more akin to these than to the social manners of the Yeats or Middleton families.

While the Pollexfen pressures on Willie were constant, he also had to experience his father's irruptions into Sligo life. John Butler Yeats could also be a terrifying figure, especially when his black-bearded face bulged over a fig on a bad tooth. Willie, who was devout, decided to follow his father's example and stay away from church; he must learn to read instead, said his father, who turned out to be an impatient teacher, flinging the reading-book at his son's head. However, he persevered into weekday lessons. Then came a dame school, and when his father heard that he was taught to sing:

> Little drops of water,
> Little grains of sand,
> Make the mighty ocean
> And the pleasant land

he wrote at once to the old woman, saying he was never to be taught to sing again. Willie was in fact tone-deaf. Less alarming were his father's readings of Chaucer; he told his children stories as they went for walks, versions of *The Merchant of Venice* or *Le Peau de Chagrin* blended with fantasies of his own. Then Willie was sent to lessons in spelling and grammar from an old gentlewoman, but he never learned to spell; to the end of his life he produced highly idiosyncratic versions of words, the best-known being 'he puts suggar on his pares'. He was hard to teach because he found it hard to attend to anything less interesting than his own thoughts; these were often disturbing, especially when he became aware of his conscience. Someone spoke to him of the voice of the conscience; he heard no articulate voice and began to think his soul was lost. After some wretched days he heard a whisper in his ear: 'What a tease you are!' At first it seemed as if an aunt who was present had spoken, but when he found she had not he was happy, thinking he had heard the voice of his conscience:

From that day the voice has come to me at moments of crisis, but now it is a voice in my head that is sudden and startling. It does not tell me what to do, but often reproves me. It will say perhaps, 'That is unjust' of some thought; and once when I complained that a prayer had not been heard, it said, 'You have been helped.'[19]

His father's unbelief set him thinking about the evidences of religion; he did not think he could live without it, and a great deal

of the rest of his life was occupied by a search for belief. He was
brought close to the fact of death when his brother Robert died in
1873 – his mother and a servant had heard the banshee crying the
night before – and two years later a baby sister, Jane Grace (b. 1875)
was to die in London. The facts of life were mingled with his
religious emotions, which were

... connected with clouds and cloudy glimpses of luminous sky, perhaps
because of some Bible picture of God's speaking to Abraham or the like.
At least I can remember the sight moving me to tears. One day I got a
decisive argument for belief. A cow was about to calve, and I went to the
field where the cow was with some farm-hands who carried a lantern, and
next day I heard that the cow had calved in the early morning. I asked
everybody how calves were born, and because nobody would tell me, made
up my mind that nobody knew. They were the gift of God, that much was
certain, but it was plain that nobody had ever dared to see them come, and
children must come in the same way. I made up my mind that when I was
a man I would wait up till calf or child had come. I was certain there would
be a cloud and a burst of light and God would bring the calf in the cloud
out of the light. That thought made me content until a boy of twelve or
thirteen, who had come on a visit for the day, sat beside me in a hay-loft
and explained all the mechanism of sex. He had learnt all about it from an
elder boy whose pathic he was (to use a term he would not have understood)
and his description, given, as I can see now, as if he were telling of any
other fact of physical life, made me miserable for weeks. After the first
impression wore off, I began to doubt if he had spoken truth, but one day
I discovered a passage in the encyclopaedia that, though I only partly
understood its long words, confirmed what he had said. I did not know
enough to be shocked at his relation to the elder boy, but it was the first
breaking of the dream of childhood.[20]

At first Willie and Lily liked the novelty of London. They were often
sent out by their father – who thought they needed more oxygen –
to walk from West Kensington to the National Gallery, with a penny
each with which they bought buns and rolls. They also visited the
Round Pond at Kensington Gardens, where Willie's Sligo-built
yacht *The Rose* was treated with some contempt by the owners of
larger boats. This provoked the artist into ordering for him an
expensive model of *The Sunbeam* (a famous yacht, celebrated in *The
Voyage in the Sunbeam* (1878) by Mrs (later Lady) Anne Brassey);
re-christened *The Moonbeam*, its arrival at the Round Pond led to
Willie's becoming Commodore of the Model Yacht Club. However,
he was often accused of moral degradation by his father, who taught

him lessons and shouted at him. Brother and sister began to hate London and yearn for Sligo; one day they shared their views near the drinking fountain at Holland Park, both very close to tears. Many years later Yeats remembered

... with wonder, for I had never known any one that cared for such mementoes, that I longed for a sod of earth from some field I knew, something of Sligo to hold in my hand. It was some old race instinct like that of a savage, for we had been brought up to laugh at all display of emotion. Yet it was our mother, who would have thought its display a vulgarity, who kept alive that love. She would spend hours listening to stories or telling stories of the pilots and fishing-people of Rosses Point, or of her own Sligo girlhood, and it was always assumed between her and us that Sligo was more beautiful than other places.[21]

The death of the baby in June 1875 was followed by that of John Butler Yeats's mother in Dublin. The family needed its Sligo holiday, but Susan Yeats stayed on there with the children until January 1877, with the exception of Willie; he was sent to join his father who was lodging with the Earle family near Burnham Beeches, having decided to study landscape – another somewhat impulsive action. Demonstrating his devotion to art if not financial success, he painted a pond from springtime on – the picture changing, as his young son observed, with the seasons, to be abandoned when he had painted the snow on its banks. Never could he bring himself to say any of his pictures was finished. Indeed, as the Dubliner Con Curran once remarked to Professor William Murphy, you had to look for the crucial moment in his work on a painting 'and snatch it from the easel when you thought it was right'. Apart from having to learn a lesson for his father for each evening, Willie found the time at Burnham Beeches an enjoyable adventure. There were the Earle children to play with, and he fished at daybreak, shot pigeons and roasted them on a string and wandered in the woods, thinking of Sligo and imagining seafaring adventures.[22]

In January 1877 the family was reunited again in their cramped quarters at Edith Villas, and Willie was sent to the Godolphin (now Godolphin and Latymer) School at Iffley Road, in Hammersmith. This was a traumatic experience of 'the rough manners of a cheap school'[23] which sharpened his sense of being different from his schoolfellows, who all pretended their parents were richer than they really were. He was an artist's son; it was not for him to think only of becoming well-off and living pleasantly; he was different. He remembered in *Reveries over Childhood and Youth* climbing to the top of a tree by the edge of the playing field and saying to himself, 'If when I grow up I am as clever among grown-up men as I am among these boys, I shall be a famous man.'[24] His schoolfellows all thought the same things; they got their political opinions from their fathers, who got them from their newspapers. It was the time of the Land War in Ireland and all Irishmen were lumped together. No subtle distinctions between Catholics, Southern Protestants, Northern Presbyterians – let alone historical differences between Irish, Old English, Cromwellians, or Anglo-Irish – plagued these sons of professional men 'who had failed or were at the outset of their career'.[25]

An insulting remark shocked Willie, basically somewhat timid, into fighting, ineffectively at first but later – under the insistent tutelage of a friend, Cyril Vesey, who shared his interest in moths and butterflies – he had improved sufficiently to win a battle with someone who had called him 'Mad Irishman'. This was his last fight but, after falling from a diving-board by accident, he learned to dive from greater heights than the other boys; also he took pride in not appearing to be out of breath after swimming underwater or running a race. In his last year at the school he was delighted to win a cup for running. He said later that the school was 'an obscene, bullying place, where a big boy would hit a small boy in the wind to see him double up, and where certain boys, too young for any emotion of sex, would sing the dirty songs of the street'.[26] But he thought it might have suited him more than a better school.

He found himself out of sympathy with his contemporaries' myths. Not for him pride in the English victories of Agincourt or Cressy, nor yet pride in the Irish defeats at Limerick or the Yellow Ford. He did not feel he belonged when he went on excursions with two other boys to such places as Coomb Wood, Richmond Park or Twyford Abbey. He was a stranger there; his world took shape in Sligo holidays, even on the way there in either the *Sligo* or the *Liverpool*, ships belonging to the Sligo Steamship Company owned by his Sligo grandfathers which maintained a weekly service between Sligo and Liverpool.

This was a romantic journey, a movement away from urban and industrial civilisation. As the ships came by the Donegal coast there was the excitement of men from Tory Island coming alongside with lobsters, talking Irish and blowing on a burning sod of turf to attract attention if it were night-time. And then came arrival in Sligo, framed by its mountains, Knocknarea and Ben Bulben, with the pleasure of being recognised and welcomed on Sligo Quay, with the rediscovery of relatives, of people believing in the supernatural, and of the pleasure of fishing for trout in the mountain streams and for pike by Castle Dargan, of living under the clear skies or great clouds tumbling in from the Atlantic.

There was no holiday in Sligo in 1878, perhaps because of shortage of money, but in the spring of 1879 John Butler Yeats took a two-year lease of 8 Woodstock Road in Bedford Park, the first English garden suburb designed as a home for painters, writers, composers and others interested in the arts. The family enjoyed the change from the inadequate space in Edith Villas; they liked Bedford Park's streets with their large trees and houses of timber and red brick. But despite a Micawberish belief that prosperity would soon come, proclaimed optimistically in a letter to the artist's friend Edward Dowden (whose own career was going well since his appointment to the chair of English Literature at Trinity College in 1867), no commissions were coming in. Moreover, only £50 had arrived from the Kildare lands for the half-year ending in March, £30 of which went to pay off debts and the remaining £20 to buy some furniture for the drawing room. Yet, somehow or other, there was money for a summer holiday at Branscombe in Devon which they all enjoyed. But by 1880 the butcher was owed over £26 and there was a fear he might supply no more meat. In 1881 more creditors were demanding money. Not surprisingly Mrs Yeats, often surly and morose, did not encourage her husband's hospitality. When he had invited the Dowdens for a long visit, she wrote to them without his knowledge to suggest that they might contribute the nominal amount of 15/- a week towards household expenses. Though John Butler Yeats pressed Dowden to come, saying his wife 'would not really like you to pay anything and most certainly I should not',[27] the visit was postponed. He couldn't invite the Dublin artist and friend of the family Sarah Purser and her brother to the house because of 'difficulties', obviously raised by his wife, who must have found the financial situation distressing, indeed alarming. Things were moving towards another crisis. Before taking the family for their summer holiday in Sligo in 1880, the artist told his wife there was no business to be found in either London or Dublin – though he was not able to bring himself to finish a painting of Eurydice

which both his friends Dowden and John Todhunter (who had
practised medicine in Dublin, became widely known for a public
lecture, later published as *The Theory of the Beautiful* (1872) and
moved to London in 1875 to devote himself to literature) wanted to
buy, nor could he finish a portrait of Dowden. That year Jack was
left to stay permanently with his grandparents in Sligo (though he
visited London at least once during that period), and at Easter 1881
Willie left the Godolphin School.

Rents from those Kildare lands which were not mortgaged virtually ceased to arrive; debts had swallowed the money (about £600)
brought in by the sale of the house in Dorset Street in Dublin and
money was owed to various friends. In a desperate bid to economise,
John Butler Yeats brought his family to Dublin in the late autumn,
having rented a studio for himself in York Street and having been
lent Balscadden Cottage – a long, low thatched house looking
north from cliffs near Howth harbour, on the northern side of the
peninsula which forms the northern arm of Dublin Bay. Six months
later they moved to Island View, nearer the harbour.

This enforced move from London turned out very well at first.
Mrs Yeats enjoyed being beside the sea and the then busy life of
the harbour; a fisherman's wife was engaged as a servant and she
and Mrs Yeats would 'tell each other stories that Homer might have
told, pleased with any moment of sudden intensity and laughing
together over any point of satire'.[28] The family atmosphere must
have become much easier, and Willie's relationship with his father
deepened as they took the train together from Howth into Dublin
and breakfasted in the studio where there were other visitors,
Dowden frequently among them. The artist would read passages
from the poets, and

... always from the play or poem at its most passionate moment ... He
did not care even for a fine lyric passage unless he felt some actual man
behind its elaboration of beauty, and he was always looking for the lineaments of some desirable, familiar life ... All must be an idealization of
speech, and at some moment of passionate action or somnambulistic
reverie.[29]

TWO

1881–1887

John Butler Yeats told Willie to enrol himself as a pupil at the High School, an Erasmus Smith foundation in Harcourt Street, a few minutes' walk from the studio in York Street. This was a great change from the Godolphin School. Here there was no bullying, no decorum, but an intelligent autocratic staff and some interesting pupils – among them Charles Johnson, Frederick James Gregg and William Kirkpatrick Magee (who later became known as the author and critic 'John Eglinton') who described Yeats as 'a kind of super-boy' immune from the ignominies of school discipline, who actually *liked* geometry and algebra. He told of Yeats concealing a crib inside his textbook in Greek and Latin classes and having difficulty in translating Demosthenes. Most of the boys worked extremely hard, for examinations opened doors into the future – into the civil service, or Guinness's brewery, or into Trinity College. Willie did not conform. He had his father's backing:

Sometimes we had essays to write; and though I never got a prize, for the essays were judged by handwriting and spelling, I caused a measure of scandal. I would be called up before some master and asked if I really believed such things, and that would make me angry, for I had written what I had believed all my life, what my father had told me, or a memory of the conversation of his friends. I was asked to write an essay on 'Men may rise on stepping-stones of their dead selves to higher things'. My father read the subject to my mother who had no interest in such matters. 'That is the way,' he said, 'boys are made insincere and false to themselves. Ideals make the blood thin, and take the human nature out of people.' He walked up and down the room in eloquent indignation, and told me not to write on such a subject at all, but upon Shakespeare's lines, 'To thine own self be true, and it must follow, as the night the day, thou canst not then be false to any man'. At another time, he would denounce the idea of duty: 'Imagine,' he would say, 'how the right sort of woman would despise a dutiful husband'; and he would tell us how my mother would scorn such a thing. Maybe there

were people among whom such ideas were natural, but they were the people
with whom one does not dine. All he said was, I now believe, right, but he
should have taken me away from school. He would have taught me nothing
but Greek and Latin, and I would now be a properly educated man, and
would not have to look in useless longing at books that have been, through
the poor mechanism of translation, the builders of my soul, nor face
authority with the timidity born of excuse and evasion. Evasion and excuse
were in the event as wise as the house-building instinct of the beaver.[1]

Willie blended his youthful interest in natural history – his earliest
surviving letter, written to his sister Lily when he was eleven, told
her about two crested newts he had in a glass jar – with reading
Darwin, Haeckel, Huxley and Wallace, and he was soon hotly
refuting 'Adam and Noah and the Seven Days'.[2] He continued his
habit of collecting beetles and moths, he explored the rock pools at
Howth, and he began to sleep out at night in a cave two hundred
feet above the sea; as he climbed a rocky ledge leading to it he would
imagine he was Manfred on a glacier, or Prince Athanase or Alastor.
When he thought of women they were modelled on poets' creations
– like the girl in *The Revolt of Islam*, they 'accompanied their lovers
through all manner of wild places, lawless women without homes
and without children'.[3]

He began to be troubled by the 'wonderful sensation' of sex; his
Memoirs described his first accidental masturbation at the age of
fifteen: from then on, he wrote, it was 'a continual struggle against
an experience that almost invariably left me with exhausted nerves'.[4]
In the autumn of 1882 he met a distant cousin about three years
older than himself, Laura Armstrong, who was then engaged to be
married, a flirtatious girl with what he called a 'wild dash of half
insane genius'.[5] He first saw her driving a dog-cart, her red hair
flowing in the wind; he found her very attractive. She corresponded
with him, signing her letters 'Vivien'; he was her 'Clarin'. Laura
wakened him from 'the metallic sleep of science' and he began to
write plays for her. She acted the title role in an amateur production
of his verse play, *Vivien and Time*, at a judge's house at Howth, and
he also wrote for her the part of the enchantress in *The Island of
Statues*. In 1884 she married. Later she appeared as Margaret
Leland, the wicked heroine of his novel *John Sherman* (1891).

John Butler Yeats, who regarded Laura as a most fascinating little
vixen and painted her portrait, had hoped his son would become a
scientist, but was nonetheless delighted by his sudden turning to

poetry. His own dramatic method of reciting or reading influenced Willie who did not understand scansion and spoke his lines aloud as he wrote them. He was now writing 'play after play', imitating Spenser and Shelley, and told Mary Cronin in a letter that he had very few poems under many hundred lines. Giving her a six-line poem, he commented flippantly – but prophetically – 'I'm afraid you will not care much for it – not being used to my peculiarities which will never be done justice to until they have become classics and are set for examinations.'[6]

At school Willie seemed unusual to his schoolfellows. His interest in collecting insects was remembered by some of his contemporaries, one of whom recorded his pursuit of a beetle which had escaped from a match-box, calling out to a master to prevent the others crushing it: 'Oh, stop them! Stop them! It's my bloody-nosed beetle.' He frequently played chess in class on a portable board held on his knee under his desk, particularly with his friend, Charles Johnson. Others recollected his dreamy nature and his ability to 'spout reams of poetry'; some resented what seemed his attitudinising and his ability to talk authoritatively about science and literature – one describing him as having something quietly repellent in his manner; yet others, his closest friends, realised there was an element of genius in him. John Eglinton described him as an unusually well-read young man with a conscious literary ambition:

> His chosen comrades thought at school
> He must grow a famous man;
> He thought the same and lived by rule,
> All his twenties crammed with toil;
> *'What then?' sang Plato's ghost, 'What then?'*[7]

Examinations loomed ahead, but Willie pursued his own interests; despite the headmaster's protests, he took French and German along with classics. George Wilkins, the headmaster's brother and like him a minor poet, took a poor view of Yeats as a student of classics; he had his crib, John Eglinton remembered, spread out inside his textbook when called upon to translate.

He left the High School in December 1883. John Butler Yeats wanted his son to enter Trinity College in accordance with what had become a family tradition, but he decided against this. There were several possible reasons for his decision: he might not be able to pass the entrance examination, notoriously easy though it was; he may well have been put off academic study by his dislike of the pragmatic and ironic attitudes of his father's friend Professor Dowden; and the family's acute shortage of money may also have swayed him. John Butler Yeats had moved the family yet again in early 1884 – away from Howth, which they all liked, to Ashfield Terrace in Terenure, a flat suburban area south of Dublin. He also moved his studio to St Stephen's Green, where he established his reputation as a conversationalist. His search for perfection, his painting and repainting, his not charging enough for his portraits meant that he did not impress likely well-to-do clients and so his financial situation grew even worse. The chronic shortage of money to meet bills and repay various loans continued, and a single oil-lamp 'for the sake of a necessary thrift' had to suffice the family every evening. But this caused problems; once Willie had finished his homework quietly,

> . . . he betook himself to the study of verse, murmuring over to himself the lines as he made them, at first quietly so as to disturb no-one – only his voice would grow louder and louder till at last it filled the room. Then his sisters would call out to him, 'Now, Willy, stop composing!' And he would meekly lower his voice. Alas, the murmuring would again become a shout. My daughters would again object, the evening always ending in his finding another lamp and retiring with it into the kitchen where he would murmur verses in any voice he liked to his heart's content.[8]

In May 1884 Willie enrolled as a student at the Metropolitan School of Art. During the period he was a student there, which lasted to April 1886, his range of social contacts expanded. He became friendly with another pupil, George Russell, and was fascinated by his visionary powers. Russell saw visions of unknown and beautiful beings in deserted places on the Dublin mountains and painted them. He never questioned their existence and his fellow students did not question his seeing them. His parents, who had come to Dublin from Lurgan in Northern Ireland, were earnestly evangelical and puritanical; they disapproved of his friendship with the artist's son, while the artist – with an inherited southern disdain for the narrow-minded and sectarian inhabitants of the north – regarded his son's friend as mediocre. The two youths used to recite their poems to each other in the kitchen of the Ashfield Terrace house long into the night. Russell's father, it is said, first met Yeats when he was roused in the small hours by what he thought was someone trying to break the upstairs windows of the house, but was in fact Yeats tossing up pebbles to wake his friend so that they could consider the final version of a poem they had been discussing earlier on their way back from the School of Art. As befitted art students, he and Russell affected loose red ties. They shared a distrust of Victorian attitudes; they doubted the reality of the world of matter; they believed in the subjective approach. Russell thought his paintings were complementary to Yeats's early poems, his first love in literature for which he never lost his affection. Willie, tall and thin, had grown a small black beard and wore narrow trousers reputed to have been his grandfather's, but his artificial stride – modelled upon memories of seeing *Hamlet* performed – and his absentmindedness, added to his habit of acting out what he had composed and speaking it aloud, made him appear decidedly unusual. He seemed to the Irish poetess and novelist Katharine Tynan, whom he met in June 1885, to live, breathe, eat, drink and sleep poetry.

A new interest, however, had entered his life which deeply disturbed his father – and his former headmaster. In his reaction against popular science, he found he wanted to believe in something; he desperately needed some religion, a need he had first felt as a child in Sligo. And reading A. P. Sinnett's *Esoteric Buddhism* (1884), given to him by his aunt Isabella Pollexfen, seems to have triggered off a search which was to occupy him all his life. In studying psychical research and mystical philosophy he began to break away from the influence of his father, whose sceptical attitude was countered by the son's increasingly keeping his new interests to himself when he was at home. Sinnett's books put forward Madame Blavatsky's claims to a spiritual authority given her by Masters who had existed in Tibet for thousands of years. Willie showed *Esoteric Buddhism* to George Russell and to his schoolfriend Charles Johnson who, more than Russell, shared his attitudes – indeed went beyond them in his enthusiasm for theosophy. Russell, though he joined the Theosophists five years later, was cautious at first. He did, however, find the ideas of Karma and particularly reincarnation more attractive than Christianity as an explanation of his own visions. He read Sinnett to gain spiritual understanding. But Yeats found the element of the marvellous attaching to Madame Blavatsky attractive. An early poem 'Anashuya and Vijaya' describes her Masters:

> ... who dwell on sacred Himalay –
> On the far Golden Peak – enormous shapes, ...
> Their hair along the mountains rolled and filled
> From year to year by the unnumbered nests
> Of aweless birds ... [9]

This poem also reflected a brief interest in Kálidása, the Indian romantic dramatist, from whose play *Sakuntala* came the name 'Anashuya'.

Yeats's main desire, however, was to explore the supernatural, and he and Charles Johnson, with five other youths, formed the Dublin Hermetic Society in June 1885; they rented a room in York Street and met there to discuss Oriental religion and theosophy. Yeats's influence as president can be seen in the title of the society, which indicated the members' interest in a philosophy kept secret or revealed in symbolism. Russell did not join, aiming at self-conquest, at moral attitudes. Yeats, however, thought the only permanent philosophy was that in poetry and was convinced that *Prometheus Unbound* (despite Dowden's telling him it was Godwin's *Political Justice* put into verse) contained such deep philosophical belief that it could make the poem a sacred book for the members. Perhaps affected by his father's scepticism, he adopted a somewhat more cautious approach than the enthusiastic Johnson. The headmaster of the High School, William Wilkins, who had regarded Yeats as 'the flighty poet', now asked Willie to use his influence on Johnson, a star pupil who was giving all his time to 'some sort of mysticism' and neglecting work for his examination. Willie was affronted at the idea that he should persuade his friend, now a committed Theosophist, to give up the pursuit of 'the most important of all the truths': and the rebuffed Wilkins later admitted that his former pupil was able to 'get about'.

Willie developed another crucial interest – in Irish politics, which stemmed from his attending meetings of the Contemporary Club with his father. This club – founded in 1885, its membership limited to fifty and later seventy-five members – had originated in meetings of friends organised by Charles Hubert Oldham, a Trinity College don in whose rooms the editorial policy of the new *Dublin University Review*, edited by T. W. Rolleston, was discussed. The Contemporary Club met to discuss social, political and literary questions of the day. Through Oldham Willie had met Douglas Hyde, 'still a college student who took snuff like those Mayo countrypeople whose songs and stories he was writing down',[10] and Katharine Tynan; and in the Contemporary Club he came into contact with many other Dublin intellectuals. The one who exercised most influence upon him was John O'Leary, the old Fenian leader who had returned to Dublin from exile in Paris at the beginning of 1885.

Willie shared his father's belief in the need for Home Rule: in the Contemporary Club he met many of his father's friends with similar ideas; but O'Leary's nationalistic views, romantic for his having suffered for them, were more positive. O'Leary had given up his medical studies to become a Fenian leader; arrested in 1865 for his part in the Fenian movement (which eventuated in a mismanaged rising in 1867) he had received a sentence of twenty years' penal servitude – commuted, after he had served five years of it, to fifteen years' exile outside Ireland. On his return to Ireland he was treated with universal respect. He was president of a Young Ireland society and Yeats began to speak in its debates, often pitting himself vainly against John F. Taylor, a distinguished barrister who was a fiercely savage orator with a superb talent for public performance. Yeats wished to become self-possessed, 'to be able to play with hostile minds'.[11] Harsh argument characterised conversation at the Contemporary Club, where unionist and nationalist could interrupt and insult one another without the traditional restraint of public speech. Yeats wrote in his *Autobiographies* that from the meetings of this society, and from the Irish books O'Leary lent or gave him, came all that he subsequently set his hand to. Willie was impressed by O'Leary's appearance; he was the handsomest old man he ever saw – something borne out by his father's fine painting of him now in the National Gallery in Dublin – he seemed wise, he was well-read, and given to uttering spontaneous outbursts of eloquence. And in turn he thought Yeats, 'Mr Yeets' as he called him, would be reckoned a genius, though this did not prevent him forcefully expressing his doubts in the small hours about some of the young man's accounts of 'blue manifestations in the Dublin hills': 'Great God in heaven, Mr Yeets, what do you mean?'

O'Leary was a good literary critic. While he had shared in the political sentiments of Thomas Davis and other writers in *The Nation* (1842–92) – the journal founded by Davis, Sir Charles Gavan Duffy and John Blake Dillon – he did not admire the style of their writings, particularly their popular poetry. Willie was developing his own strict views about the dangers of careless writing and admired O'Leary's stern principles. Through him he was introduced to a fresh view of Ireland, a new concept of Irish literature, of its patriotic expression in English in the work of such nineteenth-century poets as Thomas Davis, Jeremiah Joseph Callanan and James Clarence Mangan. He now began to meet Irish Catholic writers – notably Katharine Tynan, at whose home, Whitehall (a dairy farm at Clondalkin, south-west of Dublin) he was made welcome. She was sprightly and sympathetic. He confided his hopes and ambitions to her, as he began to publish: plays, poems and articles of his appeared in the *Dublin University Review* and, probably through Katharine Tynan introducing him to Father Moran, who edited the journal, in the *Irish Fireside* and the *Irish Monthly*. He had begun to notice that

Irish Catholics among whom had been born so many political martyrs had not the good taste, the household courtesy and decency of the Protestant Ireland I had known, yet Protestant Ireland seemed to think of nothing but getting on in the world. I thought we might bring the halves together if we had a national literature that made Ireland beautiful in the memory, and yet had been freed from provincialism by an exacting criticism, a European pose.[12]

Under the spell of conventional English Romanticism and swayed by his father's delight in drama, he wrote his first verse plays and poems, choosing Arcadian, Indian and Spanish subjects. His Arcadian play *The Island of Statues* was inspired by Spenser. The Indian poetry was written under the influence of Kálidása and the Brahmin Mohini Chatterjee, who had come to Dublin to help in the foundation of the Dublin Theosophical Lodge in late 1885 and early 1886; this developed out of the Hermetic Society, with Charles Johnson's enthusiasm as its driving force. Yeats and George Russell did not join it immediately, but became members in respectively a year's time and two or three years later. Some of Chatterjee's remarks affected Yeats deeply. One was that truth is a state of mind, not something to be conveyed from one mind to another; another stemmed from his quietism, and his advice given to someone who had asked 'Should we pray?' that before sleeping we should say: 'I have lived many lives, I have been a slave and a prince. Many a beloved has sat on my knees, and I have sat upon the knees of many a beloved. Everything that has been shall be again.' Yeats made the advice into a poem 'Kanva on Himself', archaic in its conventionally poetic use of 'thou', 'yore' and 'yonder', and reverted to it again in 'Mohini Chatterjee', written in 1929.

Chatterjee's description of Sankara particularly appealed to him: a system of metaphysical thought arising from a radical view of the *Upanishads* taken by Šankara Âchârya, a seventh-century Indian who emphasised inner realisation, disregard for action. However, Yeats did not share Russell's interest in the *Upanishads*; he was looking for traditional material which, he believed, the Indians and the pre-Christian Irish shared.

He had begun his twenties, 'crammed with toil', with the stuff of his poetry, many of the ideas he was to treat – in different ways – all his life. The advent of Laura Armstrong had set him to writing poetry, had sparked off his interest in love. Science had given way to mysticism, that persistent preoccupation which was to continue through his life, and now through O'Leary he discovered his distinctive role as an Irish writer.

Yeats experienced a good deal of excitement in exploring Irish poetry. He realised that most of the Irish poets who wrote in English wrote badly, but such romance clung around them that he told himself – and others – that most wrote well 'or all but well'. He was moved by reading bad verses describing the shore of Ireland seen by a returning, dying emigrant; they were written by a political exile who had died a few days after his return. He began to think personal utterance could provide as fine an escape from abstraction and rhetoric as drama, though his father, on whom he tried the idea, declared personal utterance was only egotism. Nevertheless he decided that he would henceforth write out of his own emotions; if he could be sincere and make his language natural without becoming discursive, indiscreet or prosaic, he would, he said, 'if good luck or bad luck make my life interesting, be a great poet . . .'[13]

While he pondered the value of Irish poets writing in English, while he began to write poetry about the scenery and folklore of Sligo that immediately achieved an identity of its own, he discovered a wealth of mythology in poetry in the Irish language which he began to read in translation. This was a stimulating discovery, a way of escaping from the shadow cast by English poetry, from Tennyson's

Arthuriad, Morris's Icelandic Saga material, Browning's Renaissance and Arnold's mixture of classicism and the dreamy English countryside. He had begun to be dissatisfied – as his father was – with Edward Dowden, whose courteous irony he may not have fully appreciated and whose academic attitudes he came to dislike. The Yeats family held Dowden in some contempt for not following his poetic bent but, as he explained to John Butler Yeats, if he gave up his professorship he would be obliged to work for his bread. However, Dowden encouraged the young man generously. In 1884 he had praised a play of his that John Butler Yeats had sent him and the artist was delighted, seeing in his son a capacity to voice the imaginative powers of the dour Pollexfens, 'the continual absorption in an idea – and that idea never one of the intellectual or reasoning faculty, but of the affections and desires and the senses'. He went on to create an image he was to repeat frequently: 'To give them a voice is like giving a voice to the sea-cliffs when what wild babblings must break forth.' His son later crystallised this saying of his father in his *Autobiographies*: 'We [the Yeatses] have ideas and no passions, but by marriage with a Pollexfen we have given a tongue to the sea cliffs. '[14]

Dowden privately preserved an open mind about the young poet's babblings, commenting in 1886 that Willie Yeats was hanging in the balance 'between genius and (to speak rudely) fool'. John Butler Yeats had been reassured when he read one of his son's poems to the Purser family and Sarah Purser – known as the wittiest woman in Dublin – said she would listen without sympathy. She did listen, however, and Yeats regarded his son's passports as made out; he was free to enter the kingdom of poetry. John Butler Yeats later recorded in a Memoir that, as a poor man, he did not want to proclaim to the world that he was bringing up his eldest son to be a poet. Willie's new nationalist friends were more sure of and more ready to proclaim the value of this 'new voice' which created beauty 'rapt and exalted, the very spirit of poetry'. He later imputed his turning his back on foreign themes to the effect of reading Standish James O'Grady (1846–1928), deciding as a result that the race meant more than the individual, and in this spirit began writing his first long poem, *The Wanderings of Oisin*, in 1886. O'Grady, like Douglas Hyde the son of a Church of Ireland rector, had come across books on Irish history and literature in a country house library on a wet day and, excited by what he found, wrote a *History of*

Ireland (2 vols, 1878 and 1880). This was a genteel but enthusiastic treatment of Irish mythological tales and the heroic deeds of the legendary hero Cuchulain and the Red Branch warriors. O'Grady followed this with a factual history of Ireland and then wrote various novels dealing with the adventures of Cuchulain and Finn as well as historical novels about the Tudor period in Ireland. An effective journalist, a leader writer on the Dublin *Daily Express* before becoming proprietor of the *Kilkenny Moderator*, he founded the *All Ireland Review* in 1900 and ran it until 1908. Yeats called him a 'Fenian Unionist' in 1898, and he certainly was a believer in Irish aristocracy – its last champion, according to George Russell – but with the proviso that it should be a working aristocracy; thus he was yet another writer to follow Maria Edgeworth in denouncing the evils of absentee landlordism. In *Toryism and the Tory Democracy* (1886) with its proposed coalition of landlords and peasants, he may perhaps have affected Yeats's later views. He exerted his main influence on younger writers, however, by showing them the treasure-house of Irish mythology, the legends and tales that were their largely unknown literary inheritance.

O'Grady himself did not know Irish, but Sir Samuel Ferguson (1810–1886), another Unionist, did. And Yeats's first essay, published in the *Irish Fireside* in October 1886, dealt enthusiastically with his work. In a longer version of it he was polemic, attacking Irish critics for failing Ireland's poets, for indifference to them – and here he specifically named Dowden. There is a highly significant passage in the longer version of the essay published in the November issue of the *Dublin University Review* where in praising Ferguson's *Deirdre* he remarks:

No one will deny excellence to the Idylls of the King; no one will say that Lord Tennyson's Girton girls do not look well in those old costumes of dead chivalry . . . But as Lord Tennyson's ideal women will never find a flawless sympathy outside the upper English middle class, so this Deirdre will never, maybe, win entire credence outside the limits – wide enough they are – of the Irish race.[15]

Ferguson – and O'Grady even more – had shown Yeats a way out of imitating the English romantics, had indicated a new exciting realm to explore. Ferguson seemed to Yeats the greatest poet Ireland had produced, the most central and most Celtic, the one man of his time who wrote heroic poetry 'like some aged sea-king sitting among the inland wheat and poppies – the savour of the sea about him and its strength'. He proclaimed that of all the many things the past bequeaths to the future the greatest are great legends, and asserted it was the duty of every Irish reader to study those of his own country 'till they are as familiar as his own hands, for in them is the Celtic heart'.

Yeats's new awareness of what having an Irish intellectual inheritance could mean was reinforced by his conversations with Douglas Hyde (1860–1949), who had lived in County Sligo until he was seven and after that at Frenchpark, County Roscommon, where he learned Irish from local people. When he did finally enter Trinity College in 1880 he was dreaming and writing poems in Irish – often nationalist in tenor – which appeared in *The Shamrock* and *The Irishman*. He was a member of the Contemporary Club, of the Dublin Young Ireland Society, of the Society for the Preservation of the Irish Language and of the Gaelic Union. He joined a Pan Celtic Society formed in 1888, and became the first president of the Gaelic League founded in 1893, holding this office until 1915 when he resigned because the League was becoming too political. His own personal aim was the same as that of the League, to keep the Irish language alive, and Yeats was impressed by his ability to absorb it, to convey the culture it contained, to be at home in Irish folklore and to write in English which was 'Gaelic in idiom and Tudor in vocabulary'. Hyde's aims, however, were centred on Irish and its preservation and were therefore different from those of Yeats, who knew no Irish and was aiming at an English-speaking audience. He assisted Yeats greatly when he was compiling *Fairy and Folk Tales of the Irish Peasantry* (1888) and read the proofs for him. He was Yeats's first source of informed information about Irish oral tradition and texts of Irish poetry and legend and helped him intermittently for many years.

Yeats worked at *The Wanderings of Oisin* from October 1886 to November 1887 – a particularly difficult period for the family. Matthew Yeats, who had acted as John Butler Yeats's agent, died in August 1885; a new agent succeeded him, and by October 1886 it was clear that not much was to be expected from the Kildare rents – indeed, John Butler Yeats was rapidly in debt to his new agent. He – and the tenants – welcomed the Ashbourne Act of 1885 which provided the funds for tenants to buy their lands from the landlords; these sums were to be repaid to the Irish Land Commission which was to administer the Act. John Butler Yeats was delighted to be rid of the complications, though he later regretted having had to sell land that had been, as his daughter Lollie put it in 1889, 'in the family for time out of mind. He I think feels it greatly. No wonder he is worried.'[16] The Land Commission paid him £500 less than he expected, and the balance of the transaction after debts were paid was a little over £1,000, which vanished at once in paying off other debts. When he had decided to sell, in 1886, he had hoped for a better result; he was not doing well out of his painting in Dublin so, characteristically, he decided to try London a second time and the family came together in May at 58 Eardley Crescent, near Earls Court, a shabby dark house that none of them liked with a garden of 'cat-haunted sooty gravel'. Before going there, Willie had stayed in lodgings and tried experiments in cheap living; after some time he was 'gaunt and nervous and able to do little work', plagued by coughs, colds and headaches. He found London 'hateful'.[17] So did his mother; that hot summer of 1887 Susan Yeats had her first stroke, and in December she suffered another while visiting a relative at Denby in Yorkshire. She left Denby in April 1888 for another house that John Butler Yeats had found in London for the family, 3 Blenheim Road in Bedford Park, and subsequently seldom left this house, dying there twelve years later. Her son described her in her last years as liberated 'at last from financial worry, having found perfect happiness feeding the birds at a London window.'

The social amenities of Bedford Park were excellent. John Butler Yeats joined the local club where he found apt audience for his original and stimulating conversation; John Todhunter, his old friend of Trinity days, was there, as were the Oxford historian York Powell and Elkin Mathews the publisher and artists such as Henry Marriott Paget and Joseph Nash. The club was a godsend to John Butler Yeats, for it was virtually impossible to entertain guests at home – when the Todhunters called, Willie borrowed three shillings from Todhunter and slipped out to buy tea, sugar, butter and marmalade to offer them hospitality. Willie paid for most of the household expenses out of the small sums he received for his contributions to periodicals, and Jack – now at art school – began to add his share. Lollie's diary conveys the chronic shortage of money dramatically. Food was short, and when any money did come in it had to pay off some of the bills; then new debts were immediately run up. It was very good news when Lily began to work in May

Morris's embroidery shop late in 1888, for which she was paid
10/- a week.

Willie had had a respite from the family troubles soon after the
move to Eardley Crescent in August 1887 when he went to stay
with his uncle George Pollexfen in Sligo. He wanted to finish *Oisin*,
which was – he wrote to Katharine Tynan in September – going
ahead famously; being in the country, he told her, helped him to
think. In October he wrote to her, this time from Charlemont – a
tall bare house overlooking Sligo harbour to which his grandparents
had moved in 1886 – to say he could not let her know when he
would come to stay at Whitehall because the entire third part of
Oisin had to be rewritten. But on 18 November he was to tell her
that the poem had come to an end. Finishing it in November 1887
was a great relief:

never has any poem given me such a trouble – making me sleepless a good
deal, it has kept me out of spirits and nervous – the thing always on my
mind – these several weeks back. It seems better now than when I was
working it out. I suppose my thinking so badly of it was mainly because of
colds and headaches mixing themselves up with the depression that comes
when one idea has been long in the mind, for now it seems one of my
successes. Two days ago it seemed the worst thing I ever wrote. A long
poem is like a fever – especially when I am by myself as I am down here.
This to me is the loneliest place in the world. Going for a walk is a continual
meeting with ghosts for Sligo for me has no flesh and blood attractions –
only memories and sentimentalities accumulated here as a child making it
more dear than any other place.[18]

After correcting the proofs of the first two parts of the poem in
September 1888, he wrote to Katharine Tynan that the third part
had most art:

... because I was in complete solitude – no one near me but old and
reticent people – when I wrote it. It was the greatest effort of all my things.
When I had finished I brought it round to read to my Uncle George
Pollexfen, and could hardly read so collapsed I was. My voice quite broken.
It really was a kind of vision it beset me day and night. Not that I ever wrote
more than a few lines in a day. But those few lines took me hours. And all
the rest of the time, I walked about the roads thinking of it.[19]

He went on to affirm that it is not inspiration that exhausts but art.
By art, he meant working over what he had written as well as the hard
work he had put into exploring his subject matter. *The Wanderings of
Oisin* came mainly from his reworking various translations: Nicholas

O'Kearney's translation of the 'Battle of Gabhra', Standish O'Grady's translation of 'The Lament of Oisin after the Fenians', Brian O'Looney's translation of Michael Comyn's 'The Lay of Oisin in the Land of Youth' (he also read the translation by David Comyn in *Gaelic Union Publications* (1880)), and John O'Daly's translation of 'The Dialogues of Oisin and Patrick'. He may have drawn on descriptions of paradises met in accounts by Charles Henry Foote, Crofton Croker and Gerald Griffin of various underwater and island paradises, and later included some of these in *Fairy and Folk Tales of the Irish Peasantry* (1888) and *Representative Irish Tales* (1891). Out of these sources he created a remarkable narrative poem which conveys sadness, weariness and an intense perception of beauty – and does so fluently, sensuously and most evocatively. It was a tour de force for a young man of twenty-three to have created it and to have expressed it with such a distinctive voice.

Oisin, the warrior son of Finn, gives St Patrick an account of the three hundred years he spent with Niamh, the daughter of the king of Tir-nan-Oge, the Land of the Young, who had come on her magical white horse to the land of men to seek his love. Together they visited the Land of the Young, then journeyed to the Island of the Living, hunting, fishing and making love for a hundred years before mounting the horse again to travel to the Island of Victories where Oisin struggled with a demon for a hundred years (a day's fighting was followed by three days' feasting). Next Oisin and Niamh spent a hundred years in the Island of Forgetfulness. On each island Oisin had been troubled by thoughts of his comrades, the Fianna, and each time this had prompted the lovers' departure. Finally he had returned to Ireland, warned by Niamh not to touch the ground. He had been about to return to his fairy bride, having found none of his companions, but then he had fallen from the horse when hurling a sack of sand two men could not lift, and now his years have suddenly descended on him. In this state he has been brought to Patrick, defiantly affirming that he will dwell with the Fianna – either in hell, as Patrick affirms, or at the Fianna's famous feasting. The subject allowed Yeats to introduce not only places and legends connected with Sligo and a good deal of unusual mythological detail obtained from the translations but also a degree of symbolism, for, he said, the three islands in the poem represent the three incompatible things man is always seeking: infinite feeling, infinite battle, infinite repose. And the poem shows the poet in love with the idea of love, ready for a goddess to carry him off. He had now found suitable subject matter and a highly individual manner in which to transmit the fascination of it:

> Caoilte, and Conan, and Finn were there,
> When we followed a deer with our baying hounds,
> With Bran, Sceolan, and Lomair,
> And passing the Firbolgs' burial-mounds
> Came to the cairn-heaped grassy hill
> Where passionate Maeve is stony-still;
> And found on the dove-grey edge of the sea
> A pearl-pale, high born lady, who rode
> On a horse with bridle of findrinny;
> And like a sunset were her lips,
> A stormy sunset o'er doomed ships;
> Her hair was of a citron tincture,
> And gathered in a silver cincture;
> Down to her feet white vesture flowed,
> And with the woven crimson glowed
> Of many a figured creature strange,
> And birds that on the seven seas range.
> For brooch 'twas bound with a bright sea-shell,
> And wavered like a summer rill,
> As her soft bosom rose and fell.[20]

THREE

1887–1891

Yeats divided the section of his autobiographies called *The Trembling of the Veil* into five sections and the first one he entitled 'Four Years: 1887–1891'. This was a period of preparation. At the time the family moved to London in 1887 he had been building up a social, intellectual, political and literary life of his own in Dublin where he was very content. Now he had to begin again in a London that he thought in 1887 just as dull and dirty as his earlier memory of it. It remained 'horrid' the next year, but the move to Bedford Park was to 'the least Londonish place hereabouts'.[1] He liked Bedford Park and the 'redbrick house with several mantelpieces of wood, copied from marble mantelpieces designed by the brothers Adam, a balcony and a little garden shadowed by a great horse-chestnut tree'.[2]

His social life began, as largely it had in Dublin, with his father's friends – York Powell, the Oxford don, replacing Dowden, the Dublin one. There was the artist J. T. Nettleship, about whose painting of a lion he wrote a poem, and Edwin Ellis, with whom he was to collaborate in editing Blake. But he soon adventured further into the literary world, visiting William Morris (whom he had met at the Contemporary Club in Dublin), now not far away at Kelmscott House in Hammersmith. There he attended the Sunday debates of the Socialist League and met Bernard Shaw, Sydney Cockerell, Henry Margers Hyndman and Prince Kropotkin the anarchist. The family intruded upon his attending French lessons at Kelmscott House; his father insisted he had to get his sisters into the class and so he soon left it, 'once more a figure in the comedy of domestic life'.[3] His bad pronunciation had amused Morris's son-in-law, H. Halliday Sparling, and Lily Yeats recorded in her diary how Willie 'divided it up into any amount of full stops where there weren't any so Madame said, "Mr Yeats, you don't read poetry like that, do you?" "Yes he does, yes he does," volunteered Mr Sparling, and in truth it was rather like his natural way of reading.'⁴

William Morris, burly, bad-tempered, reminiscent of his Sligo grandfather in this and other ways, soon became Yeats's 'chief of men'. His father had introduced him to *The Earthly Paradise* and *The Defence of Guenevere*; he enjoyed *The Man Who Never Laughed Again* and was later to describe Morris's prose romances as the only books he ever read slowly so that he would not arrive too quickly at the end. The best description of happiness he had known as a child was 'Golden Wings' with its description of an ancient castle 'midways of a walled garden'; he made this comment in an essay of 1902 subtitled 'The Happiest of the Poets'; in writing 'Four Years: 1887–1891' he thought that if an angel offered him the choice he would choose to live Morris's life, its poetry and all, rather than his own or anyone else's life. The houses in Bedford Park owed much to Morris in their interior design and decoration and Yeats was influenced by his medievalism. He brought his friends Katharine Tynan and George Russell to visit Morris and he made a new and useful friend, Ernest Rhys, at Kelmscott House.

A connection with William Henley, another impressive, strong-willed man, proved most profitable; he became one of the group who wrote for Henley's *Scots Observer* and later his *National Observer*. Henley rewrote some of his verse (notably 'A Cradle Song') which was disconcerting, and Yeats found him alarming but impressive, admiring his sincere vision and his dislike of Victorian ideas, especially logical realism. Henley made 'his young men' aware of the value of their work, being generous in his praise of good writing or 'the promise of it'. His Scottish judgment could 'neither sleep nor be softened, nor changed, nor turned aside'.⁵

At Henley's house in September 1888, Yeats met Oscar Wilde whom earlier he had heard lecturing in Dublin. He was deeply impressed by his fellow-Irishman's poise and self-possession, his capacity to speak in deliberate, perfectly ordered sentences. Wilde's charm – unlike that of Robert Louis Stevenson's cousin, R. A. M. Stevenson, another of Henley's writers – seemed acquired. He was characteristically kind; thinking Yeats on his own in London, he invited him to dinner on Christmas Day at his elegant house in Tite Street, Chelsea. Yeats remembered vaguely:

a white drawing-room with Whistler etchings, 'let into' white panels, and a dining-room all white, chairs, walls, mantelpiece, carpet, except for a diamond-shaped piece of red cloth in the middle of the table under a terra-cotta statuette, and, I think, a red-shaded lamp hanging from the ceiling to a little above the statuette.[6]

Yeats was made to feel inelegant by his host's glance at his extravagantly over-yellow shoes; he upset Wilde's eldest son Cyril by telling him a story about a giant and felt his own shapelessness, his lack of easy courtesy. Wilde praised him, however, comparing his art of storytelling with that of Homer. He was to praise *The Wanderings of Oisin* without qualification to him, describing the poem in a review of July 1889 as containing 'nobility of treatment and nobility of subject matter, delicacy of poetic instinct, and richness of imaginative resource'. William Morris was not so helpful; meeting Yeats by chance near Holborn Viaduct, he too praised *The Wanderings of Oisin* – 'you write my kind of poetry' – and promised to praise it in *The Commonweal* (something reported happily by Yeats in several letters to his friends) but didn't; he would have said more, Yeats remarked wryly in *Autobiographies*, 'had he not caught sight of a new ornamental cast-iron lamp-post and got very heated upon that subject'.[7]

After Christmas dinner, Wilde had read Yeats some of the proofs of his dialogue *The Decay of Lying* and though he wrote that neither then nor later did he care for anything in Wilde's writings but the wit, he must have been interested in Wilde's praise of art, which should depend upon masks, upon conscious attempts to mislead, rather than pursue sincerity or truth. Wilde put his ultimately subversive views in paradoxes: art is useless but it gives an age its character; indeed life imitates art. His own art of conversation had a flexibility, an easy freedom of language. After he finished reading from his proofs, he said, 'Ah, Yeats, we Irish are too poetical to be poets; we are a nation of brilliant failures.'[8] He also told him, when asked for literary gossip for a provincial newspaper that paid 'a few shillings a month', that writing literary gossip was no job for a gentleman.[9]

The whole concept of gentlemanliness mattered very much to the Anglo-Irish, particularly to the professional and the poorer elements among them – thus Yeats's father's constant argument that a gentleman is not concerned with getting on in the world. But the son, seeing his father put this theory into practice, realised clearly that money had to be found for living. He wrote to Katharine Tynan in February 1888 that he was trying to get some regular work to do, though this made his father sad for it might mean the end of his mental liberty. York Powell offered to recommend him for the sub-editorship of the *Manchester Courier* and he took some days to think it over. Though he was very attracted by the idea of regular employment, at last 'I told my father that I could not accept and he said, "You have taken a great weight off my mind".'[10]

He had a hand in the editing of *Poems and Ballads of Young Ireland* (1888), a collaborative anthology, 'got up by a dozen or so of us' (Rolleston, Hyde, Katharine Tynan and George Sigerson were involved), published by Gill in Dublin, in which four poems by Yeats were included. The first volume he edited himself, *Fairy and Folk Tales of the Irish Peasantry* (1888), had more than financial reward as its object; it had taken more than three months' reading to earn the twelve guineas he got for it, but the work made him more aware of what he called 'the tradition of Ireland'. In it he blended tales collected by Crofton Croker, Lady Wilde and William Carleton with some stories from the Irish by Douglas Hyde, and he included also poems by James Clarence Mangan, William Allingham and Sir Samuel Ferguson as well as some by himself. He edited out a good deal of the didacticism, scepticism and condescension he found in his authors' approaches to folklore and in places he rewrote them.

He made very effective use of this reading, deploying his knowledge into other books and articles as well as educating himself in Irish literature. For instance, he put to use the knowledge he had gained of Carleton in another collection, *Stories from Carleton* (1889), published by Walter Scott. And then he edited *Representative Irish Tales* (1891) for Putnams, a 2-volume edition which included Carleton and nine other Irish authors. He read 'innumerable' good and bad Irish novels in the process of selection and further equipped himself for future authoritative criticism of Irish writing. He certainly made full use of his material, employing the same format and some of the contents of *Fairy and Folk Tales* in *Irish Fairy Tales* (1892). Through this editing he was presenting Irish writing which was distinctive and seemed to him to have genuine literary merit.

*

Money, however, was badly needed and he found other ways of getting it. He stayed in York Powell's rooms at Oxford in August when he was copying out Caxton's edition of Aesop for Joseph Jacobs, who was editing it for the publisher David Nutt. The place seemed very beautiful to him after London: 'One almost expects the people to sing instead of speaking. It is all – the colleges I mean – like an opera.'[11] Later he finished the work in the British Museum. He wrote to Katharine Tynan that he was quite worn out; he often put off lifting the heavy volumes of the catalogue in the British Museum and later imputed this to being 'delicate'. He had been in a state of near collapse when he finished *The Wanderings of Oisin* in 1887 and in November 1888 he was attacked, as he recorded about a decade later, by 'lunar influences'; the next month he had one of his 'collapses' and didn't go out in the evenings as conversations left him exhausted. Obviously he was overworking: in the autumn of 1890 his doctor diagnosed a slight heart ailment and directed him, as he wrote to Katharine Tynan, 'to live more deliberately and leisurely'.[12]

He continued to be very worried about money. He had received very little of it for the six months' reading that went to the compiling of the fairy stories and the selections from Irish novelists – twelve guineas for the first and £20 for the second. Through O'Leary's influence, his work began to appear in *The Boston Pilot* and the *Providence Sunday Journal*. He wrote for *United Ireland* and contributed to *Poems and Ballads of Young Ireland* (1888), a joint effort of O'Leary's coterie; the *Leisure Hour* published him, and then *The Bookman*. Gradually he was beginning to be known in literary circles in London, and his correspondence shows how determined he was to achieve a reputation. He was obviously attracted to Morris and Henley, successful and forceful characters, a contrast to his father whose continuing inability to achieve recognition for his talent seemed the result of a lack of will power. This was an object lesson well learned; he wrote of it thirty years later, saying that he simply had had 'to escape this family drifting, innocent and helpless'.[13] Though resolute in his attempts to establish himself, the strain of doing so was considerable; he wrote many letters to his friends in Ireland and these, especially the ones to Katharine Tynan, reveal this tension clearly, particularly in their outbursts of dislike of London which was 'horrible' to him:

The fact that I can study some things I like here better than elsewhere is
the only redeeming fact. The mere presence of more cultivated people
too is a gain of course but nothing in the world can make amends for the
loss of green field & mountain slope & for the tranquil hours of one's
own country side. When one gets tired & so into bad spirits it seems an
especial misfortune to live here – it is like having so many years blotted out
of life.[14]

Out of this nostalgia for Sligo came, in 1888, 'The Lake Isle of
Innisfree', the most popular of his poems and the first one that had,
he thought, the rhythm of his own music in it. He sent the first
version – two verses – to Katharine Tynan, with whom he had
discussed Thoreau's *Walden*. In his teens he had been affected by
his father's reading him a passage from it, and had planned to live
in imitation of Thoreau on Innisfree, the heathery island, on Lough
Gill in Sligo, pursuing wisdom, 'having conquered bodily desire and
the inclination of my mind towards women and love'.[15] In his letter
to Katharine Tynan he alluded to a character in his 'tale', *John
Sherman* (1891), in connection with it:

Delayed by a crush in the Strand, he heard a faint trickling of water near
by; it came from a shop window where a little water-jet balanced a wooden
ball upon its point. The sound suggested a cataract with a long Gaelic
name, that leaped crying into the gate of the winds at Ballagh . . . He was
set dreaming a whole day by walking down one Sunday morning to the
borders of the Thames a few hundred yards from his house – and looking
at the osier-covered Chiswick eyot. It made him remember an old day-dream
of his. The source of the river that passed his garden at home was a certain
wood-bordered and islanded lake, whither in childhood he had often gone
blackberrying. At the further end was a little islet called Innisfree. Its rocky
centre, covered with many bushes, rose some forty feet above the lake.
Often when life and its difficulties had seemed to him like the lessons of
some elder boy given to a younger by mistake, it had seemed good to dream
of going away to that islet and building a wooden hut there and burning a
few years out rowing to and fro fishing, or lying on the island slopes by day,
and listening at night to the ripple of the water and the quivering of the
bushes – full always of unknown creatures – and going out at morning to
see the island's edge marked by the feet of birds.

The poem in its final form was made up of three stanzas: alliteration,
assonance, repetition, rhyming were all now completely at the service
of an atmospheric intensity, giving the sound a compelling cohesive-
ness:

I will arise and go now, and go to Innisfree,
And a small cabin build there, of clay and wattles made;
Nine bean rows will I have there, a hive for the honey bee,
And live alone in the bee-loud glade.

And I shall have some peace there, for peace comes dropping slow,
Dropping from the veils of the morning to where the cricket sings;
There midnight's all a glimmer, and noon a purple glow,
And evening full of the linnets' wings.

I will arise and go now, for always night and day
I hear lake water lapping with low sounds on the shore;
While I stand on the roadway or on the pavements grey,
I hear it in the deep heart's core.[15]

Despite his intense commitment to literary work, he continued to pursue his own brand of psychical research. This was not approved by Katharine Tynan, with whom he had attended a séance in Dublin in January 1888 – a famous occasion on which, nervously and violently disturbed and unable to remember a prayer, he had recited the opening lines of *Paradise Lost* while Katharine Tynan was saying a pater noster and an ave maria in the corner. He would not go to a séance for many years afterwards; but, having earlier kept away from the Dublin Lodge of the Theosophical Society, he was now very impressed by Madame Blavatsky. He had visited her in Norwood in 1887, and in 1888 joined the Esoteric Section of her lodge, which was concerned with occultism. He wanted more instruction in magic and became a member of the Recording Committee for Occult Research in December 1889; however, he was asked to resign from the Society in 1890. He was always longing for evidence and was too involved in experimentation for the taste of the other members. What he got from the Theosophists was a means of accepting and adapting theories of evolution and reincarnation which had the great benefit from his point of view of being based upon secret traditional doctrines. This linked it with his interest in Irish mythology and traditional folklore. What he got from Madame Blavatsky herself was an example of someone making their own philosophy out of many sources – something he was later to do when he wrote *A Vision*. He liked her, considering her a kind of Irish peasant woman with an air of humour and audacious power; he appreciated her passionate nature, her dislike of formalism and abstract idealism. Also he enjoyed her comments on his friend Charles Johnson who, contrary to her precepts enjoining chastity, married her niece. Madame Blavatsky had a romantic air about her, but she was very practical in her advice to Yeats when he read a speech ineffectively, taking his manuscript away from him and telling him to say his say.

Another 'figure of romance' was Samuel Liddell Mathers (1854–1918), who later called himself MacGregor Mathers, Comte de Glenstrae. Yeats first saw him in the British Museum, his gaunt face surmounting an athletic body. Mathers combined an interest in military affairs – he was a volunteer and had written a book on infantry campaigning – with occult study. He became a Freemason, joined a Rosicrucian Society and in 1887 published *The Kabbalah Unveiled*, then followed it with another book on the tarot cards and a translation of *The Key of Solomon the King*. It was at his invitation that Yeats was to join the Hermetic Order of the Golden Dawn in March 1890. The members of this society studied Rosicrucianism and ritual magic. The Isis Urania Temple of the Hermetic Order of the Golden Dawn had been founded in March 1888 by Dr William Wynn Westcott (a London coroner), Dr W. R. Woodman and Mathers; it was based on Westcott's translation of five rituals from a cypher manuscript 'discovered' by the Rev. A. F. A. Woodford in 1884. Westcott asked Mathers to amplify these rituals, and they created three ascending Orders. Westcott traced the Order back to Father Christian Rosenkreuz and, through him, even further back to older religious beliefs. The rituals now appear to have been pseudo-Masonic rites, blended with Ancient Egyptian and Kabbalistic texts; and the cypher manuscript – with its 'Fräulein Sprengel', who authorised Westcott to establish an English section of a German occult order of *Die Goldene Dämmerung* – something fabricated by Westcott. Yeats took it all very seriously and by January 1893 had become a full member of the Second Order, now called the RR et AC (Rosae Rubeae et Aureae Crucis). He was number 32 on the Roll and his initials were DEDI (*Demon est Deus Inversus*, the Devil is the converse of God) which probably came from Madame Blavatsky's teaching. She used the Latin words in *The Secret Doctrine* (1888) as the heading in Chapter XI, in Book I, Part II. The ideas of complementary contrariety, of opposition, in this chapter would obviously have appealed to Yeats (addressed in letters by Annie Horniman as 'My dear Demon'). After passing his Portal examination in 1893 (he underwent these rites and those for the 5=6 grades at Clipstone Street, where a ceremonial vault based upon the tomb of Father Rosenkreuz had been constructed), Yeats had to keep his status secret and this appealed to his delight in secrecy. The subjects he studied included astrological and alchemical symbolism, the ten Sephiroth and the twenty-two Paths of the Cabbalistic Tree of Life as well as the tarot trumps.

During his early twenties Yeats used to call on various women in London, friends with whom he could discuss ideas without having – as frequently happened in his talk with men – to argue with competing thoughts. The ideas that he shared were intellectual: he was shy, his early friendship with Laura Armstrong had probably flourished because she was safely engaged, and so he did not tell her he was in love with her. When one of his women friends suggested he should marry her, he was alarmed and disturbed. In London he wrote a great deal to Katharine Tynan whom he later called in his *Memoirs* 'a very plain woman'; one day he overheard someone saying that she was the kind of woman who might make herself very unhappy about a man and began to wonder if she was in love with him and if it was his duty to marry her: 'Sometimes when she was in Ireland, I in London would think it possible that I should, but if she came to stay, or I saw her in Ireland, it became impossible again.'

They were always great friends, he wrote; and he had no reason to believe she ever regarded him as other than a friend. Members of the Tynan family, however, thought he did once propose to her.[17] She had visited Blenheim Road twice in July 1889. He addressed her as 'Miss Tynan' in his letters until October of that year when he asked if he could use her Christian name. She became 'My dear Katey' after November, by which time she too was safely engaged, to Henry Hinkson whom she married in 1893. Yeats and she continued to be friends, but after 1892 they corresponded less frequently.

Women filled him with curiosity; his mind never seemed to escape from the disturbance of his senses. He wanted artistic, intellectual success; the pursuit of wisdom demanded asceticism. He dreamed of women modelled upon those in his favourite poets. Either brief tragedy ended their loves, or else they were lawless women without homes or children who accompanied their lovers 'through all manner of wild places'.[18] The Romantic poets, particularly Shelley, were a sanction for dreaming of a perfect love: 'Perhaps I should never marry in Church but I would love one woman all my life.' This was an alternative to the ascetic search for wisdom, the escape from sex offered by Innisfree – and, later in his life, by an imagined Byzantium – but the love he envisaged was influenced by Rossetti and Morris. The hero would offer hopeless devotion to his mistress. She was, however, to be a Shelleyan woman – heroic, lawless, beautiful – whom the poet would celebrate in 'the old high way of love'.

Yeats was twenty-three when what he later called 'the troubling of his life' began, with Maud Gonne driving up to the house in Bedford Park on 30 January 1889 with an introduction from John O'Leary:

I had never thought to see in a living woman so great beauty. It belonged to famous pictures, to poetry, to some legendary past. A complexion like the blossom of apples, and yet face and body had the beauty of lineaments which Blake calls the highest beauty because it changes least from youth to age, and a stature so great that she seemed of a divine race. Her movements were worthy of her form and I understood at last why the poet of antiquity, where we would but speak of face and form, sings, loving some lady, that she paces like a goddess.[19]

She seemed an incarnation of his ideal; what could he do but fall hopelessly in love with her? She had had a brief career as an actress, ended by illness. She was very self-willed, perhaps because of her upbringing – her mother died when she was five and a nurse and governesses looked after her and her sister while her father, a British Army officer, was posted overseas. Her own birth in Surrey, her London-born father's profession were no hindrance to her casting herself in the role of an Irish patriotic leader. She had spent some of her early childhood in Ireland, and had been affected by the cruelty of evictions there; she moved in anti-British circles in France, and was not at all averse to violence. Indeed she believed in war; she was ruthless, revolutionary – and beyond Yeats's reach. Independent means, independence of mind and a desire for action seemed to him to demonstrate her public talent. He dined with her almost every night she was in London, on her way back to Paris and her Boulangist friends. Enthralled and excited, he offered to write *The Countess Kathleen* for her, since she wanted a play in which she could act in Dublin. Her nationalism, like his own, had been shaped, he thought, by John O'Leary (who never took her activities very seriously), but he talked to her of his spiritual philosophy, his interest in the supernatural, his search for belief. He was in love, but he never meant to speak of love to her: '"What wife could she make," I thought, "what share could she have in the life of a student?"'[20]

He began work on *The Countess Kathleen* in February and in May read it to Florence Farr, who lived at Bedford Park. Yeats was very taken with her verse speaking as Amaryllis in John Todhunter's *A Sicilian Idyll*, which was performed in Bedford Park Clubhouse in May 1890.

She was an actress who had married Edward Emery, an actor, in 1884; he had left for America in 1888 as the marriage was not a success, and they were divorced in 1894. Shaw, with whom she had a close relationship in the early 1890s, described her as 'a young independent professional woman, who enjoyed, as such, an exceptional freedom of social intercourse in artistic circles in London'. She and Yeats became close friends. They shared an interest in mysticism and she also joined the Order of the Golden Dawn in 1890, but he was particularly interested in the help she could give him in producing the verse plays he intended to write.

In 1889 he was hard at work with his father's friend Edwin Ellis on their edition of *The Works of William Blake*, describing himself as 'now a prisoner with perpetual Blake – Blake – Blake'.[21] He copied *The Book of Thel* in Oxford; he and Ellis copied from the Blake manuscripts owned by the Linnells. Their 3-volume edition published in 1893 offered an explanation of Blake's symbolism, and they added a concordance of the mystical terms he used. Yeats's interest in the poet was deep; it was to inspire later critical articles and lead to a selection of Blake's poems published in 1906. There are echoes of Blake in several poems and he appears in the late poems 'An Acre of Grass' and 'Under Ben Bulben' as a highly symbolic figure.

Ernest Rhys, whom Yeats first met in 1887 – later to become famous as the editor of Dent's Everyman Library – had commissioned his work for the Camelot series; they became good friends and together formed the Rhymers' Club in January 1890. Having initially felt himself isolated in London, Yeats now wanted to meet poets who were his contemporaries; through this Club he came in contact with, among others, John Davidson, Ernest Dowson, A. S.

Hillier, Selwyn Image, Lionel Johnson, Richard Le Gallienne, Victor Plarr and Arthur Symons. He already knew Edwin Ellis, T. W. Rolleston and John Todhunter. Oscar Wilde sometimes came if the Club met in a private house, though the meetings were generally held in the Cheshire Cheese, an inn in Wine Office Court off Fleet Street, where the members read their poems aloud, talked criticism and drank a little wine. Yeats was later to say he learnt his trade here. He wanted the members to issue a manifesto but – like his fellow members of the Hermetic Society – they disliked affirmations of theory.

He had become sharply aware of his provincialism, his lack of 'the classical foundations of English literature and English culture'.[22] He was also well aware of the need to be known and his early letters frequently deal with reviewing: asking others to review his work, recording his reviews of them. Many members of the Cheshire Cheese were reviewers and Yeats's fear that unless the younger poets knew each other they would all become jealous of each other was alleviated somewhat as the Rhymers reviewed each other's work in, on the whole, favourable terms (something savagely commented upon by his old adversary J. F. Taylor in a letter to the *Freeman's Journal* of 7 September 1892: 'It is not an edifying spectacle to see A reviewing B, and B in turn reviews A, and both going into raptures of admiration'). Yeats realised the common situation and put it clearly to the members one night:

None of us can say who will succeed, or even who has or has not talent. The only thing certain about us is that we are too many.[23]

In July 1891 he was in Dublin and called on Maud Gonne at her hotel in Nassau Street. As she came through the door he was 'overwhelmed with emotion, an intoxication of pity'. She hinted at 'some unhappiness, some disillusionment'; he felt himself 'in love [with her] once more' and no longer fought against the feeling, no longer wondered what sort of wife she would make but thought of 'her need for protection and for peace'. He went off next day to Ballykilbeg House near Downpatrick in County Down, making fire balloons with Charles Johnson and his brother. A week later Maud wrote to him; she was sad, she had dreamed of some past where he and she had been brother and sister and had been sold into slavery. Back he rushed to Dublin and asked her to marry him; he sat holding her hand, speaking vehemently. After a while she drew her hand away. No, she told him, she would never marry: there were reasons, but using words 'that were not of a conventional ring', she asked for his friendship. They spent the next day upon the cliffs at Howth:

We dined at a little cottage near the Baily lighthouse, where her old nurse lived, and I overheard the old nurse asking if we were engaged to be married. At the day's end I found that I had spent ten shillings, which seemed to me a very great sum.[24]

He saw a lot of Maud in Dublin. After she returned to France she wrote to him of a deep personal grief: a child she had adopted three years before had died. (This was Georges, her son by the French Boulangist and journalist Lucien Millevoye, who was actually born on 11 January 1890 and died of meningitis on 29 July 1891.) Yeats went to meet her at Kingstown (now Dun Laoghaire) when she arrived in October on the mailboat which was carrying Parnell's body back to Ireland. She was dressed completely in black – in mourning for Parnell, people thought, though actually she was stricken with grief for the death of Georges and guilt that she had been away when the child first became ill. Yeats brought her for walks in the Dublin mountains, talked to her of his spiritual philosophy.

It was in October that he presented her with a vellum manuscript book entitled *The Flame of the Spirit*, which contained seven poems with space for more. These included a poem 'In Memory of Your Dream One July Night', and one written in August 1891 which called her 'No daughter of the Iron times', while another written in October is pessimistic about the likelihood of his marrying her:

> He who bade the white plains of the pole
> From the brooding years be apart;
> He has made the friend of your soul,
> Ah, he keeps for another your heart.

He knew nothing of her affair with Millevoye, nor of her real relationship to the dead child. He tried to comfort her, but it was George Russell's answer to her query about how soon a child was reborn and whether it might be reborn in the same family that impressed her. She told Yeats of the apparition of a woman dressed in grey; this person was invoked in a séance and confessed to having killed the child. Using symbols learned in the Golden Dawn, Yeats summoned up an image of the lady in grey who said she was a past

personality of Maud, who declared she must be evil and 'decided
to get rid of her'. In November 1891 Yeats persuaded Maud to join
the Order of the Golden Dawn. She passed four initiations, taking
the initials PIAL (Per Ignem ad Lucem, Through Fire to Light) by
which Yeats often alluded to her in his diaries. Soon she left the
Order, convinced it had links with Freemasonry, disliking Mathers
and thinking her fellow mystics drab and mediocre, a middle class
and very British lot – 'an awful set' who even invoked peace. Yeats,
however, continued to dream that he and she would devote their
lives to mystic truth: in 'a propaganda, secret and seeking out only
the most profound and subtle minds, that great beauty would be to
others, as it was always to me, symbolic and mysterious'.[25]

Meanwhile money continued to be very short indeed. Yeats wrote
to John O'Leary for the loan of £1 because he did not want to be
without 'the price of cabs etc.' when Maud Gonne returned to
London from Paris in late November or early December.[26] A few
days later he wrote again, to reassure O'Leary that Maud had
stipulated that she should pay her own share. This letter records
the welcome arrival of £10, a first instalment from Fisher Unwin
for *John Sherman*. This had followed on *Dhoya*, a story of the heroic
age, written at his father's suggestion that he should write a story
set partly in Sligo, partly in London. However, *Dhoya* was not what
J.B.Y. had in mind; he wanted a story about real people. *John
Sherman* resulted, which Yeats thought conveyed a typical Irish
feeling in Sherman's devotion to Ballah. He was modelled on Yeats's
cousin Henry Middleton who became a recluse in Sligo; he belonged
to 'the small gentry who in the west at any rate love their native
places without perhaps loving Ireland'. John Sherman is torn between artistic life and the temptation of achieving some security.
Differences between the Sherman and Howard families in the novel
reflect those between the Yeats and Pollexfen families. Howard the
curate was based on John Dowden the bishop, with something of
his brother the professor in him as well as of Charles Johnson. One
of the heroines, Mary Carton, owed much to Katharine Tynan and
the other, Margaret Leland, to Laura Armstrong. The shipping firm
for which Sherman works is modelled on the Pollexfens' Sligo
Steam Navigation Company. Yeats's letters as he was writing the
book keep recording his dislike of London; he was echoing William

Allingham's feeling for Ballyshannon and expressing his own attitude to Sligo; the novel contrasts artificial life in the city and natural life in the country. Allingham, he said in a review of his poems, would be best loved by those who shared his experience of childhood in some small western seaport town, for years the centre of their world, its enclosing mountains and quiet rivers a portion of their life for ever.

FOUR

1891–1894

The result of Yeats's immensely hard work and deliberate digging himself into the literary world of London was that his reputation as a writer was becoming established. *The Scots Observer* had published three of his poems in 1890; between then and 1892 *The National Observer* printed eleven, including the widely praised 'The Lake Isle of Innisfree'. The publication of his work in book form continued the process begun by *The Wanderings of Oisin* in 1889: it was reissued by Unwin in 1892, Yeats having borrowed money from John O'Leary to buy the remaining sheets from Routledge who had first issued it on a subscription basis. To the editions of Irish prose and *John Sherman and Dhoya* was added *The Countess Kathleen and Various Legends and Lyrics* (1892); eight of this volume's poems appeared in print for the first time, the rest having been published by various magazines. The play *The Countess Kathleen*, initially intended to impress Maud Gonne with his ability to write actable patriotic drama, also reflects Yeats's thought that Christian Ireland might provide better material for drama than the pagan legends which seemed to him more suited to epic and lyric; in his Preface he stressed that Ireland in the depths of time would 'probably draw her deepest literary inspiration from this double fountainhead if she ever, as is the hope of all her children, makes for herself a great distinctive poetic literature'. The play is set in a time of famine in Ireland when two merchants, agents of the devil, offer to buy the souls of the starving peasants for gold. The Countess Kathleen sacrifices her own possessions to buy food for the people so that they shall not sell their souls. The merchants then steal her gold and lie about the arrival of supplies by sea and land; she sells them her own soul in exchange for gold to feed the people and the return of the souls they have bought. She dies; but there is a battle between angels and devils and, after the angels have routed the devils, one of the angels reassures the bard Kevin that Kathleen is in heaven:

> The Light of Lights
> Looks always on the motive, not the deed,
> The Shadow of Shadows on the deed alone.[1]

The Countess owed something to Yeats's interpretation of Maud's character; after their meeting in London in 1891 he understood the story of the Countess selling her soul to save her starving people as a symbol of all souls who lose their peace or their fineness of soul or the beauty of their spirit in political service, and as a symbol of her own soul which seemed to him incapable of rest. Kathleen's 'sad resolve' in the play seems founded upon Maud Gonne's work on behalf of the poor and of evicted tenants in Donegal, Kathleen having heard

> A sound of wailing in unnumbered hovels,
> And I must go down, down, I know not where.[2]

Exhausted by her time in Donegal and threatened with tuberculosis, Maud Gonne was sent off to St Raphael to recover. There Yeats sent her 'A Dream of Death' which amused her greatly, seeing 'my epitaph he had written with much feeling'. Kevin the bard, to become Aleel in later versions of the play, is not unlike his creator, in despair in 1891 at Maud's refusal to marry him; he is 'alone in the hushed passion of romance'. Formerly obsessed with legends of the Fenians and the Red Branch kings, he cared little for the life of men but is now crazy, hopelessly in love with Kathleen, 'the sadness of the world upon her brow'. The merchants refuse the soul he offers them, since it is hers.

Many of the poems accompanying *The Countess Kathleen* bear ample witness to the effect of Yeats's falling in love. They are melancholic or wistful, as in 'The Pity of Love'. In 'When You are Old', brilliantly adapted from Ronsard's sonnet 'Quand Vous Serez Bien Vieille', there is an emphasis upon the poet's devotion; he has been the one man who 'loved the pilgrim soul in you' just as the lover in 'A Dream of Death' carves memorial words upon the beloved's grave; and the lover in 'The White Birds' yearns to escape out of the travail of human life with his beloved. This last poem was delivered to Maud three days after her request that Willie should write a poem about the seagulls that flew over them as they sat in the heather, resting on their walk around the cliff path at Howth the day after Yeats had first proposed to her. It has a Swinburnian flow, and a Pre-Raphaelite melancholia hangs about it, for the dream is doomed to failure:

> O would that we were, my beloved,
>   white birds on the foam of the sea,
> For we tire of the flame of the meteor
>   before it can pass by and flee;
> And the flame of the blue star of twilight,
>   hung low on the rim of the sky,
> Has awaked in our hearts, my beloved,
>   a sadness that may never die.
>
> A weariness comes from those dreamers,
>   dew dabbled, the lily and rose,
> Ah! dream not of them, my beloved,
>   the flame of the meteor that goes,
> Or the flame of the blue star that lingers
>   hung low in the fall of the dew:
> For I would we were changed to white birds
>   on the wandering foam – I and you.
>
> I am haunted by numberless islands,
>   and many a Danaan shore,
> Where Time would surely forget us,
>   and Sorrow come near us no more,
> Soon far from the rose and the lily,
>   and fret of the flames would we be,
> Were we only white birds, my beloved,
>   buoyed out on the foam of the sea.[3]

The love poems written to Maud which make use of the symbol of the rose marked a new development, an adventuring into the complex cave of Yeatsian symbolism, stalactites descending from the ceiling of Irish mythology, stalagmites built up with deeper, arcane magical meanings. It was a deliberate step. He felt he had to go beyond 'all those things "popular poets" write of'; that he had to become difficult or obscure *'And learn to chant a tongue men do not know'*.[4] The rose was a traditional symbol for love in English poetry and in Irish, but in the latter it stood for Ireland also – as in Aubrey De Vere's poetry or that of James Clarence Mangan, where the Dark Rosaleen personified Ireland – and Gaelic poetry used the image of

the Rose of Friday for the Rose of Austerity. Yeats employed the
image of the rose to symbolise Maud Gonne, to whom the Rose
poems were addressed, but also to suggest intellectual beauty –
differing, he put it, from that of Shelley and Spenser in that he
imagined it as suffering with men and not as something pursued
and seen from afar – spiritual and eternal beauty. And then there
was the secret meaning, the rose being the flower that blooms on
the sacrifice of the cross in Rosicrucian symbolism, of which Yeats
had learned as early as 1887 from his reading, as well as from his
conversations with MacGregor Mathers and his membership of the
Order of the Golden Dawn. In Rosicrucian symbolism the rose with
four leaves in conjunction with the cross forms a fifth element – a
mystic marriage of the masculine element, the cross, and the rose,
the feminine. The symbol, as well as conveying the nobleness of the
arts, also seems to have possessed for Yeats a quality that he was to
value increasingly, of tragic joy:

That shaping joy has kept the sorrow pure, as it had kept it were the emotion
love or hate, for the nobleness of the arts is in the mingling of contraries,
the extremity of sorrow, the extremity of joy, perfection of personality, the
perfection of its surrender, overflowing turbulent energy, and marmorean
stillness; and its red rose opens at the meeting of the two beams of the
cross, and at the trysting-place of mortal and immortal, time and eternity.[5]

There are four Rose poems in the volume. The opening poem links
the rose with his use of the Irish legends in some of the poems that
follow – 'Fergus and the Druid' in which the King gives up his
throne through love of Nessa, and 'Who Goes with Fergus?' which
in effect celebrates the power of poetry over action. 'Cuchulain's
fight with the Sea' – an extensively revised poem largely based on
a west of Ireland source recorded in Curtin's *Myths and Folklore of
Ireland*, on oral tradition, and on a ninth-century tale in *The Yellow
Book of Lecan* – tells the story of how Cuchulain's wife Emer sends
her son to the Red Branch camp with the injunction to reveal his
name only at the swordpoint to someone bound by the same oath,
with the result that Cuchulain, then living with his young mistress
Eithne Inguba, kills his own son and is finally deluded by the
chanting of King Conchubar's druids into vainly fighting a final
battle with 'the invulnerable tide'. 'The Rose of the World' introduces Homeric imagery, linking the story of the Sons of Usna –
Naoise and his brothers Ainle and Ardan – whose deaths were

brought about through Naoise's running away with Deirdre, King
Conchubar's intended bride – with Troy's 'high funeral
gleam'.

> Who dreamed that beauty passes like a dream?
> For these red lips with all their mournful pride,
> Mournful that no new wonder may betide,
> Troy passed away in one high funeral gleam,
> And Usna's children died.[6]

The poem was about the effect of Maud's 'lonely face'; the third
stanza was added to the original version (to George Russell's critical
indignation) by Yeats when anxious over the effect of rough mountain roads on Maud's wandering feet after they returned from a long
walk in the Dublin mountains. The Homeric imagery linked Maud
with Helen of Troy in 'The Sorrow of Love', while 'The Rose of
Peace' and 'The Rose of Battle' are complementary moods of faint
optimism and defeat respectively. But 'The Two Trees' must have
puzzled many readers, since few could then have known that the
holy tree growing in the beloved's own heart was the Sephirotic tree
of the Kabbala, the 'Tree of the Knowledge of Good and Evil',
which has two aspects – one benign, one malign. The beloved is
urged not to gaze in the bitter glass which the demons hold up
(probably representing abstract thought), ambushing the soul on its
way to truth. This idea may come from Blake's view that Art is the
Tree of Life, Science the Tree of Death; in an essay on him, Yeats
explained that Blake meant that men who sought their food among
the green leaves of the Tree of Life condemned none but the
unimaginative and the idle, and those who forget that even love and
death and old age are an imaginative art.

   This poem can stand without explanatory glossing, and there are
straightforward poems in the volume such as 'The Ballad of Father
Gilligan', a folk legend from Kerry, and 'The Lamentation of the
Old Pensioner' based on a conversation which took place on the
Two Rock mountain outside Dublin between George Russell and
an old peasant, not to mention 'The Lake of Innisfree'. None the
less, there was a need for the patriotic poet to defend himself, and
the volume's concluding poem 'To Ireland in the Coming Times'
does this with some self-confidence. Yeats wants to be seen in
the tradition of earlier patriotic Irish poets, Thomas Davis, James
Clarence Mangan, Samuel Ferguson:

Nor be I any less of them,
Because the red rose bordered hem
Of her whose history began
Before God made the angelic clan,
Trails all about the written page . . . [7]

His defence of obscurity, of his passion for the symbolism of the
mystical rose 'which has saddened my friends' is strong; Yeats is
adding a new dimension, that of mystery, the mystery he has found
in his occult studies to which he is giving symbolic poetic expression.
The poem, in part another indirect love poem, makes a direct
statement also: his kind of writing is no less a part of the long
struggle for Irish independence, an infusion of new universal life
into the old national mythology. Lionel Johnson, no doubt influenced
by Matthew Arnold's views of Celticism, when reviewing the volume
in *The Academy* proclaimed that the Renaissance of literature in
Ireland seemed to have begun, 'of literature, in the wide sense,
implying all that is disciplinary and severe in the acquisition of
knowledge, yet without injuring that delicate dreamy, Celtic spirit
which Celtic races never wholly lose'.

Yeats had ambitions going far beyond the limits of his own career;
he envisaged a remaking of Ireland's awareness of its own cultural
identity, something which his own often homesick exile in England
had taught him was a necessary part of an individual's and thus –
by extension – a nation's spiritual and intellectual development. He
was to use the word Celtic to convey in condensed form his own
belief in and yearning for a mythology at once romantic and heroic.

His ideas and ideals were for a literature that would combine
pagan and Christian elements in Irish thought; inherited emotions
and feelings needed reiteration. To give this literature a vital mythology, a national scope, to make it effective in regenerating a
proper national pride and self-respect needed, he realised, not only
enthusiasm but effective organisation: the audience for a reborn
Irish literature had to be created.

He had begun in September 1891 by organising, with John
O'Leary, an inaugural meeting of a Young Ireland League to unite
Irish literary societies. He plunged into more activity, for the time
seemed especially suitable – Irish politics being bedevilled by the
split in the Irish Parliamentary Party after Parnell's involvement in

the O'Shea divorce case and subsequent death in October. In December he held a meeting at Blenheim Road to plan an Irish Literary Society which would not only hold meetings but arrange for the publication and circulation of Irish books. He realised publication needed the support of subscribers – had not John O'Leary's help in finding them made the publication of *The Wanderings of Oisin* possible in 1889? He saw the membership of literary societies as a firm source of funds which would appeal to publishers, and began to plan a new Library of Ireland.

The literary movement began to achieve rapid momentum in 1892. In January it was decided to set up an Irish Literary Society in London: Gavan Duffy was asked to be President and Stopford Brooke one of the Vice-Presidents. An inaugural meeting was held in May, masterminded by Rolleston who became the Secretary; unlike Yeats at that time, he knew how to set up and administer a society. They disagreed about how any funds collected for an Irish Library were to be spent; Rolleston, a Trinity graduate whose appearance and manner had impressed Yeats at the Contemporary Club, wanted lectures, but Yeats thought wider audiences essential. Sent over to Ireland, Rolleston nearly allowed the Literary Society to be absorbed into a learned society instead, and Yeats himself crossed to Dublin in May 'in a passion' to found a National Literary Society in Ireland. This was planned out 'over a butter tub' and there ensued meetings, steering committees, acting committees, committees and sub-committees. It was a heady time: later Yeats described himself as being for the only time in his life a 'popular personage', his name widely known and the papers 'taking us up warmly'.[8]

Maud Gonne was to be involved. In addition to sharing his enthusiasm for creating a travelling theatre company – something they had discussed since 1889 – she was to get subscriptions from her Irish organisation in France, where she had been lecturing on Ireland in several cities. A sub-committee was set up to consult with her about her scheme to fund reading rooms and libraries in Ireland to which the National Literary Society would send lecturers, as well as providing small collections of Irish books.

While Yeats was working closely with John O'Leary on this National Literary Society in Dublin, Rolleston was equally closely involved with Gavan Duffy in London. Sir Charles Gavan Duffy (1816–1903) had considerable standing among Irish nationalists. In

1842, with Thomas Davis and John Blake Dillon, he had helped to start and was editor of the very influential paper *The Nation*. Tried for sedition and treason-felony and acquitted, he became an MP, then emigrated to Australia in 1856 where he became Prime Minister of Victoria in 1871. His *Ballad Poetry of Ireland* had made him a household word in Ireland. He returned to Europe in 1880 and wrote *Young Ireland 1840–1880*. Like Yeats, he had ideas about getting an Irish Library into being and came to Dublin in July to meet the provisional acting committee to discuss the publication of Irish books. Yeats rightly thought that Gavan Duffy's literary taste (rooted in the balladry and popular rhetoric of the Young Ireland period to which he was himself so inimical because of its didacticism and often careless composition) was likely to ruin any new library. The seventy-six-year-old Young Irelander seemed to the twenty-seven-year-old young man incapable of understanding the larger issues involved in recreating an Irish national awareness based upon the remote heroic past rather than on relatively recent politically-motivated literature. It was virtually inevitable that controversy erupted. Meetings were stormy, feelings ran very high indeed.

Yeats found Gavan Duffy's views supported by his enemy the barrister J. F. Taylor, an eloquent opponent; that was to be expected, but Dr Sigerson's support was a surprise. Like Hyde, the President of the National Literary Society, Sigerson – an influential Dublin doctor and scholar – seemed to Yeats not to reveal his inner thoughts; but then O'Leary rebuked Yeats for not keeping himself aloof from those he wished to influence. He had talked in public bars, talked late in many houses, shared his ideas with people who wanted authority. Gavan Duffy had the authority of age and established patriotic, political reputation; he came to Dublin with plans prepared for a publishing company of which he was to be chairman, in complete charge of the selection of books to be published. He had made public his proposals for a new Library of Ireland at the inaugural meeting of the Irish Literary Society in July. The in-fighting went on; a committee was proposed, but Rolleston pointed out in September that it was to be advisory only, that Gavan Duffy wanted complete control. He had, after all, suggested to the Young Irelanders in 1845 that they should institute a Library of Ireland and that venture had been successful. Yeats was being out-manoeuvred, and the crunch came in October when Rolleston and Gavan Duffy began negotiating with Fisher Unwin, Rolleston having told Duffy that Yeats had earlier put the idea of an Irish Library to the publisher. This enraged not only Yeats but John O'Leary. Yeats wrote to Edward Garnett, Unwin's reader, to remind him that negotiations had already begun between Unwin and himself: he told O'Leary he had put their case in a way that would stop 'the treacherous dealing' of Rolleston and Duffy. The publishing company proposed by Duffy did not eventuate, but the Irish Library was published by Unwin (twelve volumes appeared, but it did not nearly reach the sales originally hoped for) and Yeats's fall-back position of influencing Duffy's editorial policy through the Dublin and London Literary Societies was not effective. It was undoubtedly a great setback for his larger ambitions and Yeats never forgave Rolleston, though he blamed himself for having been over-impressed by him and for having talked too freely about his own plans.[9]

He had been deeply disturbed by the hostility he had aroused; it was a period of pain and disquiet. He was jealous of J. F. Taylor's influence over Maud Gonne; he objected to the inclusion of books of Irish oratory which Taylor selected for the country libraries in a way that seemed to reflect on Taylor's rhetoric. Maud and he quarrelled; she became ill with congestion of the lungs and Dr Sigerson, with whom he had also quarrelled, did not allow him to see her. He received disturbing reports from the eccentric woman who appointed herself a nurse. Maud's cousin Kay arrived and Maud was then carried to the train, despite Sigerson's protests, to travel to Paris to recover. Later the nurse circulated a story that Yeats had been Maud's lover, and that she had had an abortion.

Despite the defeats in his literary plans, the quarrel with Maud, the pressures of poverty that had prevented him from crossing to London and the loss of the lodgings he had been using in Dublin, 1893 was not altogether a depressing year for Yeats. The publication of *The Celtic Twilight* in the spring had clearly demonstrated his influential intellectual leadership and the Irish literary movement became largely labelled by the name of this book, a collection of essays which included some poems – the final one, 'Into the Twilight', originally having appeared as 'The Celtic Twilight' in *The National Observer*. The essays present stories of fairies or visionaries without any argument or speculation; they also describe people – such as Katharine Tynan's father, for instance, and George Russell

– as well as places in Sligo such as Drumcliffe and Rosses. The 1893 Preface states Yeats's desire 'to create a little world out of the beautiful, pleasant and significant things of this marred and clumsy world, and to show in a vision something of the face of Ireland to any of my own people who would look where I bid them'. He had written down accurately and candidly, he said, much that he had heard and seen, and had been at no pains to separate his own beliefs from those of the peasantry, 'but have rather let my men and women, dhouls and faeries, go their way unoffended or defended by any argument of mine'. These stories that Yeats recorded, the talk of 'henwives and queer old men', were part and parcel of the place he loved, and his early memories were filled with local tales which rested upon the country people's belief in the supernatural. As a result the book has an engaging quality of simplicity, an appreciation of the imaginative richness of his Catholic countrymen: 'in our land . . . there is no river or mountain that is not associated in the memory with some event or legend'.

Writing prose for Henley, he realised, had been his 'first discipline' in that art; practice in writing helped, and in these essays he was certainly writing in a more polished way than he had in his earlier pieces for the American journals. His own manner, perhaps influenced by that of Wilde, had changed too; he had begun to assume a more dignified, deliberate – and distant – manner. His beard had gone, though a moustache remained for a while, but the easygoing natural Willie Yeats of Dublin no longer remained: he had become Yeats or W. B. Yeats. His bad sight may have contributed to his seeming distant and detached. After a few minutes' reading his eyes became uncomfortable: he could see very little and described his left eye as practically useless; it had, he said, 'cornical cornea' in it and there was what he called 'stigmatism' in the right. What is remarkable is the vast amount of reading he achieved.

In February 1894 Yeats made his first visit to Paris, staying with the MacGregor Mathers on the Avenue Duquesne. His French was inadequate, but a visit to Verlaine went off well since Verlaine spoke English. Invited to 'coffee and cigarettes plentifully' in a letter signed 'Yours quite cheerfully', he found the poet at the top of a tenement house in the Rue St Jacques sitting in an easy chair, his leg swaddled in bandages; he asked Yeats if he knew Paris well and pointing to his leg said that Paris had scorched it, for he knew it 'well, too well' and 'lived in it like a fly in a pot of marmalade'. Yeats, who wrote up his visit for *The Savoy* in 1896, thought Verlaine's homely middle-aged mistress had given the room its character.

. . . her canaries in several cages hanging in the window, and her sentimental lithographs nailed here and there among the nude drawings and newspaper caricatures of her lover as various kinds of monkey, which he had pinned upon the wall.[10]

With an eye for oddity, he recorded the entrance of a slovenly, ragged man

. . . his trousers belted with a piece of rope and an opera hat upon his head . . . I think he must have acquired it very lately, for he kept constantly closing and opening it. Verlaine introduced him by saying, 'He is a poor man, but a good fellow, and is so like Louis XI to look at that we call him Louis XI.'[11]

Verlaine told Yeats to mention his name as an introduction to Mallarmé – on whom he called without success, as Mallarmé's daughter recorded in a letter to her father who had gone to lecture in England:

Il en est venue une autre [lettre] d'un espèce d'Anglais, qui est arrivée hier après-midi, voulant te voir et ne sachant pas un mot de français. Maman a mimé ton voyage et il a enfin saisi, puis s'est retiré.[12]

Despite his lack of French, he was 'slowly and laboriously' working his way through *Axël*, a symbolic drama by Villiers de l'Isle Adam; accompanied by Maud Gonne, who may have translated some of it for him, he attended one of the play's two performances on 26 February. Verlaine had recommended the perfect French of the author whom Arthur Symons had introduced to English readers in articles in 1887 and 1891, and was to include in *The Symbolist Movement in Literature* in 1899; the play meant that love was the only important thing in the world, said Verlaine, which Yeats thought a narrow interpretation. He wrote a review of the performance – which lasted from two o'clock in the afternoon until ten minutes to seven – for the April issue of *The Bookman*, sensibly suggesting heavy cutting of the second and third acts and recording that one fat old critic turned his back on the stage in the third to look at the pretty girls with his opera-glass. The play had a profound effect on Yeats. Lines he repeated from it fitted in with the poems he was writing at the time, later included in *The Wind Among the Reeds*; he summed up the conclusion, the suicide of the lovers who renounce the cloister, the active life of the world, the labouring life of the intellect and the passionate life of love; the infinite is alone worth attaining, and the infinite is the possession of the dead. Seldom, he wrote, has utmost pessimism found a more magnificent expression. *Axël* was a sign that young French writers were rejecting realism and returning by the path of symbolism to the only permanent things: imagination and poetry. And he was to repeat frequently some of the phrases of Villiers de l'Isle Adam, especially 'As for living our servants will do that for us.' The symbols became a part of him, he said, and for years to come dominated his thought.

He had come to Paris after writing *The Land of Heart's Desire* at Florence Farr's request; this was to let her niece Dorothy Paget (later a supporter of Bentley cars at Brooklands) act the part of a fairy child who tempts a married woman away from her humdrum life in a cottage to the fairy host. The play was produced from 29 March to 14 April in the Avenue Theatre – of which Florence Farr was now manageress – as a curtain-raiser for Todhunter's *The Comedy of Sighs*, which was a failure. It was succeeded by Shaw's very popular *Arms and the Man* and Florence Farr put on Yeats's play with it from 21 April to 12 May. Though it was not publicly known, the productions were financially supported by Miss Annie Horniman, another independently minded woman, proud of the fact that both her grandparents had kept shops. Her father, an MP, was the chairman of a firm of tea merchants in Manchester. She herself was very well-to-do and gave generous aid to various 'artistic pur-poses'. She was also a fellow member of the Order of the Golden Dawn, which she and Florence Farr had joined in 1890. As a student at the Slade she had been a friend of Moina, sister of Henri Bergson the philosopher, who married MacGregor Mathers. Miss Horniman supported the couple, first by giving him employment as curator of the Horniman Museum until 1891, and after that an allowance which ceased in 1896 when she became worried over his Jacobite politics, excessive drinking and general extravagance, and he quarrelled with her.

Apart from losing his glasses down a grating in the Strand on his way to the first performance – which he saw as a result in a kind of mist – Yeats enjoyed his first experience of having a play on stage; he went to nearly every performance. Oscar Wilde came to it and took the opportunity to congratulate him warmly on his story 'The Crucifixion of the Outcast'. George Moore, who didn't then know him, also came and later described Yeats in *Ave* as provoking

> ... a violent antipathy as he strode to and forth at the back of the dress circle, a long black cloak drooping from his shoulders, a soft black sombrero on his head, a voluminous silk tie flowing from his collar, loose black trousers dragging untidily over his long heavy feet – a man of such excessive appearance that I could not do otherwise – could I? – than mistake him for an Irish parody of the poetry that I had seen all my life strutting its rhythmic way in the alleys of the Luxembourg Gardens, preening its rhymes by the fountains, excessive in habit and gait.[13]

Yeats developed an equally violent antipathy to Shaw's 'inorganic, logical straightness' in *Arms and the Man*; Shaw was right, he said, to claim Samuel Butler as his master, for Butler was the first Englishman to make the discovery that it is possible to write with great effect 'without music, without style, either good or bad, to eliminate from the mind all emotional implication and to prefer plain water to every vintage, so much metropolitan lead and solder to any tendril of the vine'. Given the strength of this reaction to *Arms and the Man* – and notwithstanding his delight in the formidable man Shaw who could hit Yeats's enemies and the enemies of all he loved – it is not surprising that presently he had a nightmare that he 'was haunted by a sewing-machine, that clicked and shone, but the incredible thing was that the machine smiled, smiled perpetually'.[14]

He began to write a play, *The Shadowy Waters*, which as Jacqueline Genet has shown had many affinities with *Axël*: the contrast between the real world of corruption, treachery, robbery, and murder; there is an obsession with gold, a desire for debauchery, all contrasted with the heroes' lyricism. Both authors shared a dislike of science, an intense interest in the invisible – and both, as Yeats was to learn from Mallarmé, had spent their dreaming youth by the sea, with sailors' stories part of their heritage: dreams and imagination could divorce life and art; and both were part of the late-nineteenth-century poetic preoccupation with occultism. So *The Shadowy Waters* was a drama of escape, a spiritual quest which leads to death. Yeats himself escaped to Sligo to write it, staying with George Pollexfen most of the time from November 1894 to May 1895.

Uncle and nephew became close friends, sharing a belief in the supernatural. (George Pollexfen had become a member of the Golden Dawn in December 1893; in October 1895, he joined the Second Order.) Mary Battle, Pollexfen's servant, had second sight; she was affected in her dreams, Yeats thought, by the evocations he was making. He had the reputation locally 'of being a magician', of being carried five miles in the winking of an eye, of sending his cousin Lucy from her house at the First Rosses to the rocks of the Third in a similar time. He had sent her there in a vision, he wrote; and when he made a water evocation she saw mermaids in the night who soaked her with seawater. A servant in her house gave notice. He had used the symbol of water and names connected with the moon in the Kabbalistic system when George Pollexfen was delirious, suffering from blood poisoning from a bad vaccine administered in a smallpox scare. His uncle, who had been seeing red dancing figures, then saw a river flowing through the room sweeping the figures away. If they come back, said his nephew, banish them in the name of Gabriel, the moon archangel. This was not necessary, the uncle recovered. His main interest was astrology, in which he was more proficient than his nephew. He became sensitive to the Kabbalistic symbols. Yeats walked by the seashore at Rosses Point while George Pollexfen walked on the cliff or sandhills, Yeats imagining symbols and his uncle noticing what passed before his mind's eye. He became involved later in Yeats's plans for a Celtic Order of Mysteries, and the two were bound together in an attempt to trace traditions of belief older than those of European churches. They found the country people in Sligo full of visions and beliefs, Mary Battle particularly so, with her seeing figures coming from Knocknarea that seemed to be vastly superior to any contemporary people: 'There is no such race living now, none so finely proportioned.'[15]

As well as experimenting with symbols, Yeats had other things to write in addition to *The Shadowy Waters*. He was preparing the text of *Poems* (1895) in which he included many revised and rewritten versions of earlier poems, removing archaisms and generally tightening the texts. He was also rewriting *The Countess Cathleen* (from 1895 on '*Cathleen*' replaced '*Kathleen*') in the light of what he had learned from seeing *The Land of Heart's Desire* on the stage.

FIVE

1894–1897

The Land of Heart's Desire had impressed Olivia Shakespear, just as her appearance at a *Yellow Book* dinner in April 1894 had impressed Yeats. He had gone to the dinner with Arthur Waugh who reported that he could talk about the theory of poetry inside a bus 'which seriously alarmed two homely old ladies and scandalised a city man'. Olivia sat beside George Moore (who had Pearl Craigie on his other side) and opposite Yeats. Her great beauty suggested 'incomparable distinction' to him, her face having 'a perfectly Greek regularity', her hair 'very dark'; she was 'exquisitely dressed'. He was not introduced to her but found she was related to Lionel Johnson, who arranged a meeting between them in June 1894. Olivia Shakespear endorsed the letter: 'I shall be so glad to meet you.' Having admired *The Land of Heart's Desire*, she told him that she had decided, if she could not meet him, she would at least write to him. He told her – almost inevitably – of his incessant obsession with Maud Gonne, his sorrowful love. In his unpublished autobiography, now published as *Memoirs*, he wrote that he could not tell why Maud seemed to have turned from him, when he was putting his despair into *The Land of Heart's Desire*. She had been unwell when he was in Paris for February and he had not called on her at first. Their relations, he commented in his unpublished autobiography, were friendly enough but did not have their old intimacy. He did not know, of course, that she was then pregnant with a second child by Millevoye, Iseult, conceived for the sake of reincarnating the soul of the dead son Georges, later called Georgette, in the vault in Paris where he was buried in August 1891. Iseult was born on 6 August 1895.

Olivia, too, was unhappy. In December 1885 she had married Henry Hope Shakespear, fourteen years her senior, a solicitor who came as she did from a family with an Indian military background, though a less wealthy one than hers. He was interested in music, played the cello, sang and painted water-colours; but he seems to have been a dry stick, a dull man, and she later told Yeats that he had 'ceased to pay court to her' from the day of their marriage. They had one daughter, Dorothy, born in 1886, who was later to marry Ezra Pound. It was a loveless marriage.

Her novels – she wrote six between 1894 and 1910 – though not autobiographical, do show women trapped in marriage and resigned to the situation. This reflected her own attitude: she was unselfcentred and unselfish, deeply imaginative and sympathetic and, until she met Yeats, she seems to have simply accepted the fact of her unhappy loveless marriage, content to enjoy no more in life than 'leisure and the talk of her friends'. Yeats realised the profundity of her culture, her knowledge of French and Italian as well as English literature, her informed taste in art and music. Like him, she had had an early interest in Shelley – Lionel Johnson described her in 1884 as almost literally praying to him. She had just begun to write when Yeats met her, and he gave her literary advice in the letters he wrote to her from Sligo.

The high point of this visit was spending a few days at Lissadell, the Gore-Booths' big house outside Sligo. He recorded in his unpublished autobiography that he had broken the wall of long-settled habit: he was no longer of his grandfather's house, no longer of the merchant people of the town who did not mix socially with the county. He wrote twice to Lily to tell her about the visit and the Pollexfens (with the exception of George, who had always believed in his talent) began to think that maybe he had not – like his father – thrown away his life. Constance Gore-Booth, the elder daughter of the house and famous for her horsemanship, seemed in voice like Maud Gonne of whom, of course, he talked to her; the younger sister Eva, however, seemed more sympathetic and became his close friend. She too was told of his unhappy love, and so close did the friendship become that he almost said to her, acting on Blake's literary precedent, 'You pity me, therefore I love you.'[1] Almost . . . because he realised quite clearly that the great house 'would never accept so penniless a suitor' – and he was, after all, 'still deeply in love' with Maud Gonne.

He busied himself with controversy in the Dublin *Daily Express*, an argument with Dowden about Irish literature which was to become entangled with his own list of the thirty best Irish books. He was to build up a longer list in *The Bookman*, for which he wrote four articles (July-October 1895) on Irish national literature.[2] The first article omitted the Protestant 'Anglo-Irish' writers, Swift, Berkeley, Goldsmith and Burke, and in it Yeats attempted to diminish the influence of Thomas Moore and the Young Ireland authors, stressing less well-known writers such as Callanan, Carleton, Mitchel, Mangan and Sir Samuel Ferguson. The second article dealt with contemporary prose, the third with poetry (a better article than the one on prose, though through modesty he had to omit discussing himself, which was a sad lack in the total picture) and the fourth, more aggressive in tone, is an extended list of the best Irish books. Some of them were out of print (some on his list unfortunately still are) and the articles were intended to present a critical viewpoint, putting the literary movement into perspective: 'Only a little for English readers, and not at all for Irish peasants but almost wholly for the small beginning of that educated and national public which is our greatest need and perhaps our vainest hope'.[3] They were also intended as propaganda to encourage the publication and sale of Irish books. The last item on the list was Yeats's own *A Book of Irish Verse*, which had been published in March; it was compiled because he disliked existing anthologies. This disclaimer did not quite cover his aims; he wanted to distinguish between the poets of Young Ireland, Thomas Davis and those who wrote in *The Nation*, and such poets, less well known to the patriots, as Sir Samuel Ferguson and William Allingham. The latter possessed poetic sincerity: he was not afraid to attack the established heroes; he was sharp about Tom Moore, and found Thomas Davis often a little insincere and mechanical in his poetry.

When he returned to London he called – at his father's instigation – at Wilde's mother's house the day before Wilde's second trial to express sympathy and ask if he could be of help; he brought letters from various Irish writers. While he talked to Willie Wilde, Oscar was at a party at Ada Leverson's house, and Willie Wilde's wife came from it to say that Oscar had decided to go to gaol if necessary.

Yeats joined the Irish National Alliance (also known as the Irish National Brotherhood) at Rolleston's invitation, despite their relationship being strained. This was a secret organisation run by Dr Mark Ryan in London; it had broken away from the Irish Republican Brotherhood which Yeats had joined, probably in 1886. Like John O'Leary, he never took the oath but always regarded himself as an IRB man, thinking at first that he would be able to enlist the support of the organisation for his literary movement. He now found in Dr Mark Ryan a touching benevolence and an understanding of his literary aims, a view shared by Rolleston and Lionel Johnson whom Yeats brought to see Ryan.

Yeats was gradually growing disenchanted with Johnson, whose anecdotes about the great proved to be fabrications frequently retold and always in the same words. His drinking had become excessive and embarrassing – and was reputed to have led to his death when he fell off a stool in a bar and fractured his skull, though it seems the cause was that he had a cerebral haemorrhage the day before. Another member of the Rhymers' Club, Arthur Symons, proved a more congenial friend; he was most sympathetic and Yeats could talk freely to him, could express more of the thoughts that he had earlier felt able to discuss only with women (whose tea and toast saved precious pennies for his bus ride home to Blenheim Road). Symons had read him selections from Verlaine and Mallarmé and discussed the symbolists' techniques; he also conveyed his enthusiasm for Catullus; and Yeats later wrote that Symons had had a considerable effect on his theory and practice. Symons rented chambers in Fountain Court in the Middle Temple and sub-let two small rooms to Henry Havelock Ellis, who was living mainly in Cornwall; in his absence and with his agreement, Symons sub-let them to Yeats who stayed there from October 1895 to the beginning of March 1896. The chambers opened into those occupied by Symons:

If anybody rang at either door, one or other would look through a window in the connecting passage, and report. We would then decide whether one or both should receive the visitor, whether his door or mine should be opened, or whether both doors were to remain closed. I have never liked London, but London seemed less disagreeable when one could walk in quiet, empty places after dark, and upon a Sunday morning sit upon the margin of a fountain almost as alone as if in the country.[4]

It was a big step to leave home. From Blenheim Road his younger sister Lollie, with whom Willie had been quarrelling a good deal, wrote sardonically to Lily, on holiday in Sligo, 'W.B. has taken a room says he can live on 10/- a week, let him try.' Back home two weeks later, Lily recorded in her diary on 13 October 1895 that Willie had come home full of his new start and added 'very good thing, I think'. And it was. The household was gloomy, with John

Butler Yeats ill and depressed, Lollie quarrelsome and Mrs Yeats withdrawn into her own unhappiness, 'her mind gone'. The Pollexfen madness surfaced dramatically when her sister, now Agnes Gorman, escaped from a mental home and had to be recommitted. Yeats was to wonder later in his journal whether he had – and had always had – some nervous weakness inherited from his mother. It always alarmed him: 'Is it the root of madness?'[5]

There was, however, a compelling reason for the move into Fountain Court: back in London in May, he had met Olivia Shakespear again. The letters she had written to him in Sligo had given a sense of half conscious excitement; his, she told him later, were unconscious love letters. They began to meet in railway carriages, art galleries and in the house of her 'sponsor', Valentine Fox. She came to Blenheim Road in early October. 'Willie's latest admiration' was described by Lily as 'very pretty, young and nice'. Her beauty reminded him of Eva Gore-Booth's, which seemed delicate and gazelle-like. As if to justify himself, he misunderstood Olivia's talk of her 'pagan' ways, thinking she had many lovers and loathed her life. He equated her with her cousin Lionel Johnson:

Here is the same weakness, I thought; two souls so distinguished and contemplative that the common world seems empty. What is there left but sanctity, or some satisfying affection, or mere dissipation? – 'Folly the comforter,' some Elizabethan had called it. Her beauty, dark and still, had the nobility of defeated things, and how could it help but wring my heart? I took a fortnight to decide what I should do.[6]

During the fortnight after a conversation that was 'to decide so much in his life', in which she had obviously brought things to a head and declared her love for him, he was torn by doubt: he was poor; he would, perhaps, only add his tragedy to hers. He envisaged her returning to the evil life with which his imagination had endowed her, though he would in fact be her first lover – apart, that is, from her husband by whom she had had a child. On 14 September he wrote her a love poem, 'The Shadowy Horses', later to be entitled 'Michael Robartes bids his Beloved be at Peace' and later still Robartes was to become 'He'. His senses were excited and he had the honesty later to record his thought that if he could not get the woman he loved, 'it would be a comfort even but for a little while' to devote himself to another. Finally he asked her to leave home with him and she was 'gay and joyous'.[7]

Symons had known of the situation but not the identity of 'Diana Vernon', the name Yeats gave Olivia: he had, however, met her and called on her. At last she and her 'sponsor' were to come to tea in Fountain Court. Yeats, still thinking of Maud Gonne, went off to buy a cake but forgot his key and shut himself out; he found a man who climbed along the roof and in through an attic window and all was well. That evening, however, he talked to Symons from midnight till two or three o'clock in the morning about Maud Gonne – as if, perhaps, hoping to convince himself that he would never be able to win her, to free himself for Olivia. A few days later he got a wild letter from Maud asking if he was ill, had an accident happened? The day that he had Olivia Shakespear and the 'sponsor' to tea, he had walked into a room in Dublin where Maud was sitting with friends; she thought that he was really there, but, as no one else noticed him, knew it was his ghost and told him to return at midnight. This he did, clad in some outlandish garb, taking her soul away to wander round the cliffs at Howth to a place he remembered clearly (probably where they had walked and sat in the heather the day after his first proposal to her in 1891). All the old love for Maud had now returned and began to struggle with the new – for he had begun to think he was once more in love. But Olivia did not talk as well as when he first knew her; 'her mind seemed more burdened but she would show in her movements an unforeseen youth; she seemed to have gone back to her twentieth year'.[8] The mental and psychological burdens were considerable for her as well as Yeats. If she left her lawyer husband he might sue Yeats for damages in a divorce case and she could lose custody of her child, possibly lose her income and certainly upset her parents, especially her mother whom she loved deeply.

Apparently, the developing relationship was not hindered by Maud's letter and the two 'sponsors' (Yeats's may have been Florence Farr), described by Yeats as people of the world, advised them 'to live together without more ado'. Then Olivia, having tried to get a separation from her husband who became deeply distressed and ill, decided to give up the project, saying it would be kinder to deceive him than leave him. She helped Yeats to furnish the rooms he took in late February 1896 in 18 Woburn Buildings (now 5 Woburn Walk); they collected inexpensive furniture which could be thrown away later if he ever became prosperous. Just as he had been startled and a little shocked when Olivia gave him 'the long passionate kiss of love' – he so far knowing no other kind of kiss than a brother's – so he was embarrassed now by a discussion of the width of a bed in a Tottenham Court Road shop – every extra inch increased the expense (and probably they didn't buy it, since Yeats later owed Symons money for a bed). But there was worse embarrassment when she first came to him; nervous excitement made him impotent. Olivia, however, was kind and understanding:

The next day we met at the British Museum – we were studying together – and I wondered that there seemed no change in me or her. A week later she came to me again, and my nervous excitement was so painful that it seemed best but to sit over our tea and talk. I do not think we kissed each other except at the moment of her leaving. She understood instead of, as another would, changing like for dislike – was only troubled by my trouble. My nervousness did not return again and we had many days of happiness.[9]

He was, as usual, working extremely hard. Apart from his articles and reviews, *The Shadowy Waters* – which he thought he had finished by November 1894 – continued to occupy him, probably in 1896 and certainly in 1897 and 1899; it did not appear in print until 1900. Later he described it as having come into existence after years of strained emotion, living upon tiptoe. There was a good deal of Pre-Raphaelitism in Forgael's search for love 'of a beautiful kind/ That is not in the world'. The first never-finished version expressed terror caused by the barrier Yeats felt between himself and other people. One of Forgael's speeches indicates some of Yeats's current perplexities:

I can see nothing plain; all's mystery.
Yet sometimes there's a torch inside my head
That makes all clear, but when the light is gone
I have but images, analogies.[10]

Despite this work on *The Shadowy Waters* Yeats was deeply engaged in a difficult new project, writing a novel called *The Speckled Bird*. He was now getting better fees from magazines, but this projected novel had given him his first experience of an advance. Lawrence and Bullen, pleased with *The Celtic Twilight*, offered to pay him £2 a week for six months and his travel expenses to Ireland. The novel was to deal with mysticism, utilise his experiences in the Order of the Golden Dawn and draw upon his views of Maud Gonne, Florence Farr and Olivia Shakespear. In it he was tracing, through an autobiographical hero, vain efforts to combine artistic ideals with magic by the creation of a mystical brotherhood. This reflected his obsession with the need for mystical rites through which perception of the spirit could be reunited with natural beauty. The tensions were as great as those between asceticism and adoration of physical beauty. The novel showed the increasing complexity of his interests but it proved impossible to bring them into order, the novelist in him mocking the would-be adept. After these abortive efforts in 1897 and 1898, he returned to it again in 1899, 1900 and 1902, but never finished it. He would not show it to his father who, having found *The Shadowy Waters* absolutely unintelligible, was full of curiosity, indeed anxiety about the novel. He prophesied in the spring of 1896 that when the six months financed by Lawrence and Bullen had expired the novel would be only half begun, but then Willie would find himself at George Pollexfen's. In other places he would waste his energy 'in dreaming and projecting mighty plans'; he needed a friend to listen to the MS, to help with sympathy.[11]

In the summer of 1896 Yeats brought Arthur Symons on a visit to Ireland. Though sympathetic, he was not what was needed as a successor to John Butler Yeats, to John O'Leary or, to a lesser degree, to Edwin Ellis and to Lionel Johnson. Before leaving London, Yeats questioned Olivia Shakespear when she was in a state of semi-trance. He sought her advice about the way his writing seemed to have gone a long way from the emotions underlying the early poetry, the drama of *The Countess Cathleen* and the essays of *The Celtic Twilight*. His poetry had become elaborate and slow-moving, and so had his prose. He described the stories of *The Secret Rose* (1897) to John O'Leary as 'an honest attempt towards that aristocratic esoteric Irish literature, which has been my chief ambition. We have a literature for the people but nothing yet for the few.'[12] These stories were published in journals before being collected into book form. Some of them are linked to the poetry in their use of the rose as a symbol. There is, for instance, the old knight of 'Out of the Rose', his helmet decorated with a small rose made of rubies, a romantic, lonely, questing figure who prays to the Divine Rose of Intellectual Flame; as he is dying, he tells of his mission:

He had seen a great Rose of Fire, and a Voice out of the Rose had told him how men would turn from the light of their own hearts, and bow before external order and outer fixity, and that then the light would cease, and none escape the curse except the foolish good man who could not and the passionate wicked man who would not, think. Already, the Voice told him, the wayward light of the heart was shining out upon the world to keep it alive, with a less clear lustre, and that, as it paled, a strange infection was touching the stars and the hills and the grass and the trees with corruption, and that none of those who had seen clearly the truth of the ancient way, could enter into the Kingdom of God, which is in the Heart of the Rose, if they stayed on willingly in the infected world; and so they must prove their anger against the Powers of Corruption by dying in the service of the Rose of God.[13]

He is one of several figures in the stories who are at odds with society; a poor man in 'Where there is nothing there is God' is discovered by the monks who give him hospitality to be a saint; however, a wandering poet and satirist in 'The Crucifixion of the Outcast' is crucified by monks. The poet, too, has been affected by the rose; he has heard in his heart

. . . the rustling of the rose-bordered dress of her who is more subtle than Aengus the Subtle-hearted, and more full of the beauty of laughter than Conan the Bald, and more full of wisdom of tears than White-breasted Deirdre, and more lovely than a bursting dawn to them that are lost in the darkness.[14]

This story came from a translation of a medieval goliardic story by Kuno Meyer (which Yeats had reviewed in 1893: he was most efficient in using ideas or material from such reading in his own work) in which monks and religion itself are fiercely attacked. It fitted into the general theme of the stories of *The Secret Rose*, which was 'the war of the spiritual with the natural order', of the artist with society. The first story told of a poet asked by his princess, when enemies arrive, to complete his song before morning: before then, he says, he will pour out two verses that are in his heart. He is killed in the ensuing battle, but when the princess finds his severed head on a bush it sings this lyric, based 'on some old Gaelic legend' and consonant with many of the love poems written to Maud Gonne:

> Fasten your hair with a golden pin,
> And bind up every wandering tress;
> I bade my heart build these poor rhymes;
> It worked at them, day out, day in,
> Building a sorrowful loveliness
> Out of the battles of old times.

> You need but lift a pearl-pale hand,
> And bind up your long hair and sigh;
> And all men's hearts must burn and beat;
> And candle-like foam on the dim sand,
> And stars climbing the dew-dropping sky,
> Live but to light your passing feet.[15]

There are other elements in the stories: Cromwellian troopers leap to their deaths on Lugnagall; the story of Una Bhan, also from the seventeenth century, is the base for 'Proud Costello, MacDermot's Daughter, and the Bitter Tongue', while from the eighteenth century came Eoghan Rua O'Suilliabhain, the Irish wandering poet, partly a model for Yeats's character Red Hanrahan (originally called O'Sullivan the Red in poems of 1894 and 1896), who probably also derived from Yeats's reading in William Carleton about hedge schoolmasters; he had included 'The Hedge School' in his *Stories from Carleton* (1889) with its comment

> ... that hedge schoolmasters were a class of men from whom morality was not expected by the peasantry; for, strange to say, one of the strongest recommendations to the good opinion of the people, as far as their literary talents and qualifications were concerned, was an inordinate love of whisky and if to this could be added a slight touch of derangement, the character was complete.

Yeats's Hanrahan is a Gaelic poet, a womaniser (he has lost his school for this) and a lover of whiskey, who wants to be thought in league with the devil. 'The Poet, Owen Hanrahan, under a Bush of May', a poem included in the story 'The Curse of Hanrahan the Red', links him with Sligo scenery as does 'Red Hanrahan's Song about Ireland' in the story entitled 'Kathleen the Daughter of Hoolihan and Hanrahan the Red' in the 1894 and 1897 versions (it later became 'Hanrahan and Cathleen, the Daughter of Houlihan'). Here is the first version of the poem as it appeared in *The National Observer*, 4 August 1894:

> Veering, fleeting, fickle, the winds of Knocknarea,
> When in ragged vapour they mutter night and day,
> Veering, fleeting, fickle, our loves and angers meet:
> But we bend together and kiss the quiet feet
> Of Kathleen-Ny-Hoolihan.

Weak and worn and weary the waves of Cummen Strand,
When the wind comes blowing across the hilly land;
Weak and worn and weary our courage droops and dies
But our hearts are lighted from the flame in the eyes
Of Kathleen-Ny-Hoolihan.

Dark and dull and earthy the stream of Drumahair
When the wind is pelting out of the wintry air;
Dark and dull and earthy our souls and bodies be:
But pure as a tall candle before the Trinity
Our Kathleen-Ny-Hoolihan.

The poem changed considerably as Yeats rewrote it. Here is the
final version; it is a good example of his reworking a poem:

The old brown thorn-trees break in two high over Cummen Strand,
Under a bitter black wind that blows from the left hand;
Our courage breaks like an old tree in a black wind and dies,
But we have hidden in our hearts the flame out of the eyes
Of Cathleen, the daughter of Houlihan.

The wind has bundled up the clouds high over Knocknarea,
And thrown the thunder on the stones for all that Maeve can say.
Angers that are like noisy clouds have set our hearts abeat;
But we have all bent low and low and kissed the quiet feet
Of Cathleen, the daughter of Houlihan.

The yellow pool has overflowed high up on Clooth-na-Bare,
For the wet winds are blowing out of the clinging air;
Like heavy flooded waters our bodies and our blood;
But purer than a tall candle before the Holy Rood
Is Cathleen, the daughter of Houlihan.[16]

This poem was written to Maud Gonne, who incidentally recited it
to me with brio in 1945 when she was eighty, proclaiming it her
favourite among Willie's poems, having first read me 'When You
are Old', taking a book from a shelf as she was sitting by her fire:

When you are old and gray and full of sleep,
And nodding by the fire, take down this book
And slowly read and dream of the soft look
Your eyes had once, and of their shadows deep.[17]

The answer about his work that Yeats had received on asking Olivia
Shakespear whether he was to write an elaborate mysticism was
cryptic. He was too much under solar influence, he should live near

water and avoid woods 'which concentrate the solar power'. From MacGregor Mathers, Yeats had learned to equate solar with elaborate and rich work and lunar with all that was emotional, simple, traditional.

Yeats and Symons stayed in Sligo for a few days, Symons enjoying the scenery, the sea-faring people and even the dour George Pollexfen. Then they were the guests of Edward Martyn whom they had met in London through George Moore, the novelist, who was a friend of Symons. Both Moore and Martyn were Irish Catholic landlords and unlikely friends since Martyn was particularly pious and averse to women, Moore the opposite. Yeats had not expected the spaciousness and state of Tulira Castle, with its square tower and great yard where medieval soldiers had exercised. He angered Martyn greatly by invoking the lunar power in the waste room of the old tower which formed part of the castle where Martyn lived, since the waste room was over the chapel and Yeats's invocations might have obstructed the passage of prayer. After nine evenings of invocation, Yeats saw first a centaur and then a marvellous naked woman shooting an arrow at a star, the flesh tints of her body making human flesh seem unhealthy in contrast as she moved in brilliant light. The vision is described at some length in *Autobiographies* and the woman appears again in a later poem, 'Parnell's Funeral':

> Rich foliage that the starlight glittered through,
> A frenzied crowd, and where the branches sprang
> A beautiful seated boy; a sacred bow;
> A woman, and an arrow on a string;
> A pierced boy, image of a star laid low,
> That woman, the Great Mother imaging,
> Cut out his heart. Some master of design
> Stamped boy and tree upon Sicilian coin.[18]

Symons, who had not known of the invocations, read Yeats a poem at breakfast, the first he had written about a dream in which he had been visited by a woman of great beauty. Count Florimond de Basterot was also staying in the house (he used to come from Paris to spend his summers in his nearby house at Duras) and had dreamed of Neptune so vividly some nights before that he got out of bed and locked his door, since a locked door might be an obstacle to a dream so vivid. Yeats's invocations had been a form of prayer accompanied by an active desire for special results and at times he believed or half-believed that Lady Gregory – who came to call a few days after Symons had returned to London, where he was editing *The Savoy* – had come in answer to his invocations. They had met briefly before in London and now she invited him to stay at Coole Park, her nearby house, and began to collect stories of fairy belief for him before he arrived.

One of the stories in *The Secret Rose*, 'Rosa Alchemica', was written in late February 1896, before Yeats was urged in a series of letters written by George Russell in 1896 to join in a project aimed at showing the Irish people something of the mysticism of the ancient Celts:

... we are going to do great things over here, and by degrees you will find the mystics arising everywhere ... [19]

The gods have returned to Erin and have centred themselves in the sacred mountains and blow the fires through the country. They have been seen by several in vision, they will awaken the magical instinct everywhere, and the universal heart of the people will turn to the old druidic beliefs ... [20]

A Theosophical convention in New York had voted funds to prepare initiates for this new age, the dawn, as Russell put it, into which the Celtic Twilight was going to break: 'Let us be hopeful, confident, defiant!'

Yeats, however, realised that any attempt to revive 'the old beliefs' would be defying the Catholic Church. 'Rosa Alchemica' shows the likely result. The narrator, a secluded student of alchemy, longs for a world made of essences, life transmuted into art; he is interrupted by Michael Robartes, whom he had not seen for years 'and whose wild red hair, fierce eyes, sensitive, tremulous lips and rough clothes, made him look now, just as they used to do fifteen years before, something between a debauchee, a saint, and a peasant'.[21] Robartes urges the narrator to be initiated into the Order of the Alchemical Rose, which is dedicated not only to alchemy but to the worship of the old gods. The narrator falls into a trance in which he sees some of the old divinities:

I stopped before a door, on whose bronze panels were wrought great waves in whose shadow were faint suggestions of terrible faces. Those beyond it seemed to have heard our steps, for a voice cried: 'Is the work of the Incorruptible Fire at an end?' and immediately Michael Robartes answered: 'The perfect gold has come from the Athanor.' The door swung open and we were in a great circular room, and among men and women who were dancing slowly in crimson robes. Upon the ceiling was an immense rose wrought in mosaic, and about the walls, also in mosaic, a battle of gods and angels, the gods glimmering like rubies and sapphires, and the angels of the one greyness, because, as Michael Robartes whispered, they had renounced their divinity, and turned from the unfolding of their separate hearts, out of love for a God of humility and sorrow. Pillars supported the roof and made a kind of circular cloister, each pillar being a column of confused shapes, divinities, it seemed, of the winds, who rose as in a whirling dance of more than human vehemence, and playing upon pipes and cymbals; and from among these shapes were thrust out hands, and in these hands were censers. I was bid place my censer also in a hand and take my place and dance, and as I turned from the pillars towards the dancers, I saw that the floor was of a green stone, and that a pale Christ on a pale cross was wrought in the midst. I asked Robartes the meaning of this, and was told that they desired 'To trouble His unity with their multitudinous feet'. The dance wound in and out, tracing upon the floor the shapes of petals that copied the petals in the rose overhead, and to the sound of hidden instruments, which were perhaps of an antique pattern, for I have never heard the like; and every moment the dance was more passionate, until all the winds of the world seemed to have awakened under our feet. After a little I had grown weary, and stood under a pillar watching the coming and going of those flame-like figures; until gradually I sank into a half-dream, from which I was awakened by seeing the petals of the great rose, which had no longer the look of mosaic, falling slowly through the incense heavy air, and, as they fell, shaping into the likeness of living beings of an extraordinary beauty. Still faint and cloud-like, they began to dance, and as they danced took a more and more definite shape, so that I was able to distinguish beautiful Grecian faces and august Egyptian faces, and now and again to name a divinity by the staff in his hand or by a bird fluttering over his head; and soon every mortal foot danced by the white foot of an immortal; and in the troubled eyes that looked into untroubled shadowy eyes, I saw the brightness of uttermost desire, as though they had found at length, after unreckonable wandering, the lost love of their youth. Sometimes, but only for a moment, I saw a faint solitary figure with a veiled face, and carrying a faint torch, flit among the dancers, but like a dream within a dream, like a shadow of a shadow, and I knew, by an understanding born from a deeper fountain than thought, that it was Eros himself, and that his face was veiled because no man or woman from the beginning of the world has ever known what Love is or looked into his eyes; for Eros alone of divinities is altogether a spirit, and hides in passions not of his essence if he would commune with a mortal heart. So that if a man love nobly he knows Love through infinite pity, unspeakable trust, unending sympathy; and if ignobly, through unappeasable desire; but unveiled Love he never knows. While I thought these things, a voice cried to me from the crimson figures, 'Into the dance; there is none that can be spared out of the dance; into the dance; into the dance; that the gods may make them bodies out of the substance of our hearts'; and before I could answer, a mysterious wave of passion, that seemed like the soul of the dance moving within our souls, took hold of me, and I was swept, neither consenting nor refusing, into the midst. I was dancing with an immortal august woman, who had black lilies in her hair, and her dreamy gesture seemed laden with a wisdom more profound than the darkness that is between star and star, and with a love like the love that breathed upon the waters; and as we danced on and on, the incense drifted over us and round us, covering us away as in the heart of the world, and ages seemed to pass, and tempests to awake and perish in the folds of our robes and in her heavy hair.

Suddenly I remembered that her eyelids had never quivered and that her lilies had not dropped a black petal, or shaken from their places, and understood with a great horror that I danced with one who was more or less than human, and who was drinking up my soul as an ox drinks up a wayside pool, and I fell, and darkness passed over me.[22]

Robartes has thought that the local people will worship the pagan gods again, but the local fishermen – urged on by an old votary – break down the doors of the seaside temple and stone Robartes and his friends to death, the narrator escaping to become a pious Catholic. Yeats told Lady Gregory that Robartes was founded upon Russell. He is made to resemble Russell not only in appearance, but in his visionary faculty, his uncritical belief – he thought he had seen the new avatar – in his psychic experiences, in his enthusiasm for 'the old beliefs' and in his unawareness of how his own beliefs would be generally received. But Robartes is a magician, and he is more closely related to MacGregor Mathers in this, and in his interest in initiation ceremonies.

While Yeats expressed this reserve about Russell's visionary experiences in this story, Russell had been more open about his anxiety over his friend's activities in London, telling him to clear out of Arthur Symons's vicinity when he had heard in 1896 that Yeats was going to move into Fountain Court, and denouncing *The Savoy* as the organ of the incubi and the succubi, distrusting the doctrine of Art put forward by Symons and Yeats's apparent acquiescence in it. He was, however, reconciled to his friend when he read *The Secret Rose*, which was dedicated to him. Russell had not allowed for Yeats's vein of irony and detachment which had developed since the days of the Hermetic Society.

Two larger stories were intended for *The Secret Rose*, but Bullen, his publisher, disliked them, so they appeared in separate booklet form and later had 'Rosa Alchemica' added to them. The influence of Walter Pater appears in the elaborate style of 'Rosa Alchemica' and 'The Tables of the Law'. In 'The Tables of the Law' the narrator tells the story of Owen Aherne, a fellow student at Paris with Michael Robartes and himself. He is a spoiled priest, 'half monk, half soldier of fortune',[23] and an enthusiast for the writings and doctrines of Joachim of Fiore, whom Yeats read about in Renan, Pater, Wilde, Symonds and Ellis and about whom he also learned from Lionel Johnson, who was the model for Aherne in this story and provided Yeats with the Latin used in it. Aherne has a myth of his own, that the beautiful arts are sent into the world to destroy nations and ultimately all life. Like Joachim, he must assemble a sect to inaugurate the coming age of the Holy Spirit, learning their secret laws from what he writes on the empty ivory tablets in his private chapel. The story allows Yeats scope for his prose to be decorated with the names of Benvenuto Cellini, Guilio Clovio and Pietro Aretino. Aherne finally feels he has sinned against the Holy Spirit. The narrator flees in terror. 'The Adoration of the Magi' has the old Celtic gods still at large, 'going to and fro' (a phrase echoing Job 1:7 and 2:2) on the earth, an idea which Pater – writing on Pico della Mirandola – got from Heine's *Gods in Exile*. Yeats was himself convinced that a new cycle was beginning; he regarded his story as 'a half-prophecy of a very veiled kind'; in it the three old men are told to set out for Paris 'where a dying woman would give them secret names and thereby so transform the world that another Leda would open her knees to the swan, another Achilles beleaguer Troy':[24] these were images that were to recur in his poetry and prose. Thirty-eight years later, he paid tribute to the influence of Joachim of Fiore on his cyclic theory of history, in describing these stories as taking their images from the idea that 'civilization was about to reverse itself, or some new civilization to be born from all that our age had rejected, from all that my stories symbolized as a harlot, and take after its mother; because we had worshipped a single god it would worship many or receive from Joachim de Fiora's Holy Spirit a multitudinous influx.'[25]

These ideas, very much in the air at the end of the century, resulted in such apocalyptic poems as 'The Valley of the Black Pig', triggered off by some talk of MacGregor Mathers who had announced in 1893 or 1894 the imminence of wars on a vast scale.

It is linked with visions of Irish peasants about a battle routing the
enemies of Ireland; and Yeats wrote long notes on it, utilising his
reading in Rhys's *Celtic Heathendom* and Frazer's *The Golden Bough*.
He sets the poem in Sligo:

> The dew drops slowly; the dreams gather; unknown spears
> Suddenly hurtle before my dream-awakened eyes;
> And then the clash of fallen horsemen, and the cries
> Of unknown perishing armies beat about my ears.
> We, who are labouring by the cromlech on the shore,
> The gray cairn on the hill, when day sinks drowned in dew,
> Being weary of the world's empires, bow down to you,
> Master of the still stars, and of the flaming door.[26]

Yeats and Symons had interrupted their visit to Tulira in 1896 by
making an excursion to two of the Aran Islands, Inishmaan and
Inishmore, an exciting experience; they landed from a fishing-boat
to find themselves among a group of islanders, one of whom brought
them to the oldest man upon Inishmaan:

This old man, speaking very slowly, but with laughing eyes, had said, 'If
any gentleman has done a crime, we'll hide him. There was a gentleman
that killed his father, and I had hid him in my own house six months till he
got away to America.'[27]

In December Yeats went to Paris. There he met John Millington
Synge, who had grown up in Dublin and attended Trinity College
where among other subjects he had studied Irish. He had intended
to make a career as a musician, but gave up the idea in favour of
becoming a writer. He was twenty-five when they met, and Yeats
suggested his going to the Aran Islands (where a relative had been
a clergyman) to find his subject matter there. He introduced him to
Maud Gonne and persuaded him to join a Young Ireland Society
in Paris, from which Synge soon resigned because he disapproved
of its Fenian line. Yeats also met Dauthenday, the German poet,
and Strindberg, searching for the Philosophers' Stone; he met
followers of the eighteenth-century mystic Saint-Martin, taking
hashish with them and talking wildly. With Arthur Symons he went
to the first night of Alfred Jarry's *Ubu Roi*, a rowdy affair in which
they shouted to support the play, though afterwards Yeats was
saddened at objectivity displaying its power in comedy. But after
Mallarmé and Verlaine, Gustave Moreau and Puvis de Chavannes,
what more was possible, he asked: 'After us the Savage God'.[28]

The main purpose of Yeats's visit to Paris, of course, was to found
an Order of Celtic Mysteries. He had gone from Sligo in 1895 to
visit Douglas Hyde in Roscommon, where he explored Lough Key
in search of local memories of the tale of Tumaus Costello which
he was turning into a story, later included in *The Secret Rose*. The
boatman rowed him up the lake and they stopped to eat their
sandwiches at the Castle Rock, an island with a castle on it; the last
man who had lived there – for a fortnight – being Douglas Hyde's
father. The roof was sound, the windows unbroken.

The situation in the centre of the lake, that has little wood-grown islands,
is romantic, and at one end, and perhaps at the other too, there is a stone
platform where meditative persons might pace to and fro. I planned a
mystical Order which should buy or hire the castle, and keep it as a place
where its members could retire for a while for contemplation, and where
we might establish mysteries like those of Eleusis and Samothrace; and for
ten years to come my most impassioned thought was a vain attempt to find
philosophy and to create ritual for that Order.[29]

This idea became linked with his crusade for a new Irish literature;
he had an unshakable conviction that invisible gates would open

... as they opened for Blake, as they opened for Swedenborg, as they
opened for Boehme, and that this philosophy would find its manuals of
devotion in all imaginative literature, and set before Irishmen for special
manual an Irish literature which, though made by many minds, would seem
the work of a single mind, and turn our places of beauty or legendary
association into holy symbols.[30]

The philosophy Yeats sought was not to be altogether pagan; it was
to select its symbols from all the things that had moved men 'through
many, mainly Christian, centuries'. Out of this came his poem 'The
Secret Rose', published in *The Savoy* in September 1896, with its
blend of Christian, Rosicrucian, mystic, pagan and folklore elements.
This poem has an ending parallel to many of his references to a
coming apocalypse:

> When shall the stars be blown about the sky,
> Like the sparks blown out of a smithy, and die?
> Surely thine hour has come, thy great wind blows,
> Far-off, most secret, and inviolate Rose?

It is also, of course, a love poem, for in it he was also thinking of
Ireland and Maud Gonne:

A woman, of so shining loveliness,
That men threshed corn at midnight by a tress,
A little stolen tress.[31]

Meeting her in Paris, his hope revived again; she was sympathetic to this desire of his to create a Celtic Order of Mysteries. He helped her to found a Young Ireland Society in Paris, but politics were merely a means of meeting her. He used her clairvoyance to produce 'forms that would arise from both minds'. They worked through visions to create 'a symbolic fabric' at the centre of which were the four talismans of the Tuatha de Danaan – the sword, the stone, the spear and the cauldron – which related themselves in his mind with the suits of the tarot. And Blake's conception of the four-fold in man (which seemed to Yeats the foundation of Blake's symbolic system) may well have shaped these ideas as well. He was helped by MacGregor Mathers and also other members of the Golden Dawn. In 1897 he had discussed possible rituals with William Sharp who had been visiting Coole. Sharp, earlier a member of Rossetti's circle in London, had begun a double life, writing about Celtic spirituality under the name of Fiona Macleod, a persona he invented, a Highland lady living a remote life. Neither Yeats nor George Russell suspected that Fiona Macleod was a pseudonym; indeed when Sharp died in December 1905 his wife wrote to Yeats to say that her husband, and he only, 'was and wrote as, Fiona Macleod'. This work on the Celtic Order of Mysteries had continued in London in late 1897. In early 1898 Yeats was back in Paris again, in late April and early May, to discuss Celtic mysticism with both Maud and Mathers.

His affair with Olivia lasted only a year. Maud Gonne wrote to him early in 1897 to say that she was in London, would he dine with her? His trouble increased, he wrote nearly twenty years later: he had a struggle to earn his living, he was often preoccupied when Olivia came; then one morning instead of reading her love poetry – 'as was my way to bring the right mood round' – he wrote letters. She burst into tears and said, 'There is someone else in your heart.' It was 'the breaking between us for many years'.[32] 'The Lover Mourns for the Loss of Love', first published in 1898, puts the situation clearly:

> Pale brow, still hands, and dim hair,
> I had a beautiful friend,
> And dreamed that the old despair
> Might fade in love in the end;
> She looked in my heart one day,
> And saw your image was there,
> She has gone weeping away.[33]

He had found happiness and peace in the actuality of sex, but that was not enough. And the excuses he made to himself (in writing his autobiography in 1916) for not giving her 'the love that was her beauty's right' – that she was 'too near his soul, too salutary and wholesome to his inmost being' – *are* excuses. His regret, however, lasted through his life. The year 1896 was of deep significance to him; thirty years later, in December 1926, he was to write to Olivia and say 'one looks back to one's youth as to [a] cup that a mad man dying of thirst left half tasted. I wonder if you feel like that.'[34] 'The Empty Cup' was written then:

> A crazy man that found a cup,
> When all but dead of thirst,
> Hardly dared to wet his mouth
> Imagining, moon-accursed,
> That another mouthful
> And his beating heart would burst.
> October last I found it too
> But found it dry as bone,
> And for that reason am I crazed
> And my sleep is gone.[35]

The 'October last' referred to Yeats meeting Olivia in October 1926. Another poem in the series *A Man Young and Old*, 'The Mermaid', also referred to her:

> A mermaid found a swimming lad,
> Picked him for her own,
> Pressed her body to his body,
> Laughed; and plunging down
> Forgot in cruel happiness
> That even lovers drown.[36]

SIX

1897–1900

Yeats's relationship with Maud had become deeply entangled not only with his desire to create an Irish Order of Mysteries but with the nationalist politics into which he had entered, partly to impress her, but partly out of seeing himself, briefly, in the role of a leader. After 1891 he had hoped for a revival of the Young Ireland style of politics as a middle ground between the Irish Parliamentary Party and Fenianism, but he had decided to help the 'new movement', the Irish National Alliance. Maud Gonne had joined it; she wanted to collect funds for a Wolfe Tone memorial in America but could not get the authorisation she needed from the Dublin body. Yeats called a meeting in Woburn Buildings. (Rolleston had resigned and asked Yeats to send him back all his letters in case the police raided Yeats's rooms. A police report of 1899 was to describe Yeats as 'a literary enthusiast, more or less of a revolutionary, and an associate of Dr Mark Ryan'.) He made increasingly violent speeches at debates of the Irish Literary Society: he enjoyed the excitement of it all. And he formed what he called a grandiose plan. He was elected Chairman of the Executive Committee of the Centenary Association (to mark the centenary of Wolfe Tone and the Revolution of 1798) for Great Britain and France. The Dublin Committee was large and he thought it could be turned into something like an Irish Parliament which would be attended by the four Irish political parties. However, he had not fully realised the nature of his political associates and was later to find one of them, Frank Hugh O'Donnell, a dangerous enemy.

Danger came closer in 1897, the year of Queen Victoria's Diamond Jubilee. There were demonstrations in the streets; police protected the shopkeepers who had decorated their shopfronts for the occasion. Maud Gonne was persuaded to speak at a meeting in Dame Street organised by the labour leader James Connolly; she told the vast crowd that she had gone to St Michan's Church to decorate the graves of United Irishmen, leaders executed for taking part in the 1798 Revolution, and that she had been refused admission because it was Queen Victoria's Jubilee. Then she added, in a low voice, 'Must the graves of our dead go undecorated because Victoria has her Jubilee?' The crowd went wild and the political temperature mounted rapidly. Yeats and Maud Gonne left a meeting of the Council in the City Hall to walk to the National Club in Rutland (now Parnell) Square, where there was to be a magic lantern showing statistics of the evictions, persecutions and convictions in Victoria's reign. Crowds accompanied them; they were preceded by a mock funeral devised by Maud Gonne, a coffin with 'The British Empire' written on it; and then windows were smashed, to Maud's joyous excitement. Yeats knew she would not interfere; she thought that if one attempts to stop a crowd doing something illegal one may succeed, but may then seem certain to have done so to avoid personal danger. As they had tea at the National Club, an agitated man brought the news of a police baton charge. Yeats ordered the door to be locked and refused to let Maud go out until she explained what she meant to do, to which she replied, 'How do I know till I get out?' Regretting his rapidly cooling tea, he offered to go out himself, though as he had lost his voice at the earlier meeting this would hardly have been useful. That evening he went to all the Dublin newspaper offices to say that he was responsible for her not going out. These riots had a profound effect on him. Two hundred people were taken to hospital, and one old woman died after being injured in the police baton charge.[1]

Desperately trying to reduce his life to order, Yeats retreated to Sligo in the summer of 1897; George Pollexfen's restrictive regime might steamroller his habits into some shape. But then he went south to Galway, to Tulira Castle, then on to make his first long visit to Coole. Still tired from the effect of the Jubilee Riots and the rough and tumble of revolutionary politics, he was white, haggard and still voiceless. He had never been so sad and miserable. Since Olivia left him no other woman had come into his life, and for nearly seven years none did. It did not occur to him to seek another love affair; he would repeat to himself over and over again 'the last confession of Lancelot: "I have loved a queen beyond measure and exceeding long."' But he was tortured with sexual desire and disappointed love. Often as he walked in the woods at Coole 'it would have been a relief to have screamed aloud':

When desire became an unendurable torture, I would masturbate, and that, no matter how moderate I was, would make me ill.[2]

His nervous system was fraying; even dressing himself in the morning was an exhausting effort. But he was fortunate in being at Coole: 'Lady Gregory began to send me in cups of soup when I was called.'[3] This was typical of the care he was to receive from her. He was to write in his diary twelve years later – when he got a letter telling him Lady Gregory was dangerously ill – that he thought his mother was dying and his sister was asking him to come; then he remembered that his mother had died years before and that 'more than kin' was at stake; she was to him mother and friend, sister and brother.[4]

Coole provided something better than his uncle's hospitality with its regular walks to fixed destinations after luncheon and dinner, Yeats experiencing annoyance there that his uncle never treated him as quite a grown man, resenting the fact that if there was but one kidney with the bacon at breakfast he always took it without apology. He was, however, giving Yeats an allowance of a pound a week at this time. At Coole, not only was the house itself a delight with its library's shelves of leather and vellum mellowed by the passing centuries, with its walled gardens, its guardian row of beech trees, its flower-bordered gravel walk, its woods and swan-sheltering lake, but also the orderly life within it. The poet was surrounded by practical kindness: enjoying a programme of regular meals and outdoor exercise, he appreciated above all, after the stridencies of his immoderate and often unintellectual nationalists, the quiet, orderly peacefulness of the place.

Coole gave him more, however, than an opportunity for physical recovery. Lost, as he described himself, on the road of the chameleon, beset by a multiplicity of interests, he found psychological reinforcement in Lady Gregory's company. To him she seemed secure in her attitudes, the certainties of her aristocratic code, her blend of dignity and humility.

Born in 1852, she was thirteen years older than Yeats. She grew up in Roxborough, a big house in County Galway, in a large family of nine boys and seven girls (of whom she was the seventh), her

father, Dudley Persse, having married twice. She was not beautiful
and so did not seem to her overbearing family likely to marry. For
her plainness she compensated by giving self-effacing service to
others; she devoted herself to her brothers. By seventeen, however,
the forces which dominated her life had, she wrote in a draft of her
autobiography, taken possession of her: love of country (as a child
she had developed an interest in Young Ireland's ballads, poems
and songs); faith in the spiritual life (disturbed at the prospect of
everlasting hell, she had a religious experience at fifteen which made
her at peace with God); and delight in poetry and literature (amiable,
incompetent governesses had not damped her capacity to read
voraciously). Then in 1880, when she was twenty-eight, Sir William
Gregory married her. A neighbouring landlord, he was a widower
of sixty-one, a former governor of Ceylon. Through her marriage
she made many influential friends in London, and her husband
encouraged her in her writing, her first published work being an
essay on the Egyptian Arabi Bey and his Household. Arabi was one
of the Colonels in revolt, and Lady Gregory and Wilfrid Scawen
Blunt worked hard on his behalf when he was placed on trial in a
Khedival court; and both the Gregorys and the Blunts were to visit
him when he was exiled to Ceylon. Her friendship with Blunt
became a brief but intense love affair during which she wrote the
sonnet sequence he published in his *Love Lyrics and Songs of Proteus*
with the title 'A Woman's Sonnets', a farewell to their passion. She
later wrote four prison poems to him in 1888. They were temporarily
estranged, for his nationalistic views did not suit her view of Home
Rule for Ireland as Home Ruin.[5]

Sir William died in 1892 and she found each day sadder and
emptier. However, she was realistic. Fiercely opposed to Home Rule
in 1893, resigned to staying on in Coole and doing her best by it in
1894, she had come to realise very clearly by 1895 that the position
of Irish landlords was in jeopardy as democracy gained power. She
wanted to save 'the *home*, house and woods at least' for her only
child Robert, born in 1881.

Well aware of the failings of the landlords as a class through
reading Froude and editing her husband's autobiography (published
in 1894) and *Mr Gregory's Letter Box 1813–35* (published in 1898)
she was anxious to bring Robert up to do his social duty. She wanted
to be part of Ireland, to find a role for herself in what she realised
would be a changed society. Her views were moving towards Irish

nationalism, as Yeats's were towards a need to convert the educated classes to it. Both of them were out of sympathy with the rising Catholic middle class; both of them saw a need for an alliance of educated classes and country people. In *Dramatis Personae* Yeats wrote that:

When in later years her literary style became in my ears the best written by woman, she had made the people a part of her soul; a phrase of Aristotle's had become her motto: 'To think like a wise man, but to express oneself like the common people'.

Lady Gregory's interest in folklore had been strengthened when she met Yeats in the summer of 1896, and the following summer she brought him out with her, visiting cottages 'to gather folk-belief, tales of the faeries, and the like, and wrote down herself what we had gathered, considering that this work, in which one let others talk, and walked about the fields so much, would lie, to use a country phrase, "very light upon the mind"'.[6] It was better than agonising over his inability to make himself work on *The Speckled Bird*. He began to think that the Galway people possessed an ancient knowledge and this suited his attempts to achieve a philosophic unity as well as his desire to find actual evidence of the supernatural. Wanting to find the people gentle, even idealistic, she nevertheless concluded that Ireland 'is Pagan, not Xtian'[7] but neither she nor the peasants were pagans, Yeats thought, for 'Christianity begins to recognize the validity of experiences that preceded its truth and were, in some sense, shared by its founders'. Out of the process of recording the folk tales in which she wrote about two hundred thousand words – very good training if she ever wanted to become a secretary, she wryly remarked – she was forming the style in which she gave dignity to the material, that idiosyncratic, idiomatic, colloquial, studiedly simple style called Kiltartanese, after the village of Kiltartan near Coole. The revival of Yeats's interest in folk material showed him a way out of the over-involved, elaborate Paterian prose that he had been writing in *The Secret Rose*, so far removed from the simplicity of *The Celtic Twilight* and from the speech of the country people.

Yeats wrote that when he went to Coole the curtain had fallen upon the first act of his drama, his propaganda for a new kind of Irish literature, his editing, his articles, his speeches, the setting up of the

Irish Literary Societies in London and Dublin which had given a new generation of writers and critics opportunity to reassess the nature of Irish literature, to denounce past propaganda. Now he thought that if Ireland would not read literature it might listen to it.

I wanted a Theatre – I had wanted it for years, but knowing no way of getting money for a start in Ireland, had talked to Florence Farr, that accomplished speaker of verse, less accomplished actress, of some little London hall, where I could produce plays. I first spoke to Lady Gregory of my abandoned plan for an Irish Theatre, if I can call anything so hopeless a plan, in the grounds of a little country house at Duras, on the sea-coast, where Galway ends and Clare begins.[8]

Lady Gregory had brought him to visit her friend Count Florimond de Basterot and 'in his garden under his friendly eyes, the Irish National Theatre was born'.

At the time he had very obviously lost some of his energy and enthusiasm. He used a comparison:

. . . crows at nightfall return to the vast rookeries round Tulira Castle, whirling, counter-whirling, clamorous; excited, as it seems, by the sublime dance. It was the one unforgettable event of my first visit as of other visits there. And I was accustomed to say to Lady Gregory when it seemed that some play of mine must be first performed outside Ireland, or when it seemed, as it did once or twice, that I myself might find it impossible to live in Ireland: 'The crows of Tulira return to their trees in winter' or 'The crows return at nightfall', meaning that, after my death, my books would be a part of Irish literature. She, however, with her feeling for immediate action, for the present moment, disapproved of my London project. She offered to collect or give the money for the first Irish performances. My *Countess Cathleen* was ready, and either I or Lady Gregory spoke to Edward Martyn, who gave up a proposed German performance and became enthusiastic. Then came an unexpected difficulty. Dublin had two theatres, the Royal and the Gaiety, that had been granted patents, a system obsolete everywhere else. No performance, except for charity, could be given but at these two theatres; they were booked for the best months of the year by English travelling companies and in the worst months were expensive. We had to change the law, which we did with the assistance of an old friend of Lady Gregory's husband, Lecky the historian, representative in Parliament of Trinity College. The writing of letters, talks in the Lobby of the House of Commons, seemed to take up all our time.[9]

In the autumn, in better physical shape, Yeats continued to act as president of the '98 Association, writing speeches, chairing meetings of Irish supporters – and opponents (there were various warning

anonymous letters) – in England and Scotland. He accompanied
Maud Gonne, whose

> ... power over crowds was at its height, and some portion of the power
> came because she could still, even when pushing an abstract principle to
> what seemed to me an absurdity, keep her own mind free, and so when
> men and women did her bidding they did it not only because she was
> beautiful but because that beauty suggested joy and freedom ... Her
> beauty, backed by her great stature, could instantly affect an assembly, and
> not as often with our stage beauties, because obvious and florid, for it was
> incredibly distinguished, and if – as must be that it might seem that
> assembly's very self, fused, unified, and solitary – her face, like the face of
> some Greek statue, showed little thought, her whole body seemed a master
> work of long labouring thought, as though a Scopas had measured and
> calculated, consorted with Egyptian sages, and mathematicians out of
> Babylon, that he might outface even Artemisia's sepulchral image with a
> living norm.[10]

'The Lover pleads with his Friend for Old Friends' records some
of his feelings:

> Although you are in your shining days,
> And the tongues of the crowd
> And of new friends are glad with your praise,
> Be not unkind or proud,
> But think of your old friends the most:
> Time's bitter flood will rise,
> And your high beauty fall and be lost
> For all eyes but these eyes.[11]

Despite the excitement of the meetings he was later to describe this
period as the worst in his life, but he had learned much from his
earlier experience with the Literary Societies and become a more
efficient committee man, developing a suave manner for public
speech, however much he could lose his self-possession in conversations and agonise over doing so for hours afterwards. And he also
learned from these experiences in the '98 Association that the
Dublin Council had not the makings of an Irish Parliament: his
grandiose political project would not do.

Other projects, however, more than compensated for this
decision; he was far more interested in the work for an Order of
Celtic Mysteries, and now there was also the possibility of creating
an Irish theatre. In early 1898 he spent much time in London on
Celtic mysticism with members of the Golden Dawn and with

MacGregor Mathers in Paris in the late spring, Maud Gonne being involved in all this work. Then came the lobbying of MPs to have the theatrical licensing laws changed in Dublin. His summer was spent at Coole, the autumn with George Pollexfen in Sligo and then in November in Dublin. He had written to Lady Gregory in the previous autumn that Maud was very kind and friendly, but whether more than that he could not tell. He breakfasted with her one morning in the Nassau Hotel in early December and she asked him if he'd had a strange dream. He had dreamed that she had kissed him. She told him later, in the evening, that when she fell asleep the previous night she had seen a great spirit standing by her bed; he took her to a throng of spirits, and Yeats was among them. Her hand was put into his and she was told that they were married. After that she remembered nothing. He recorded in his unpublished autobiography that, 'Then and there for the first time with the bodily mouth, she kissed me.'[12] The next day she regretted speaking to him in that way, for, she said, she could never be his wife in reality. Then in response to his query if she loved anyone else she said, 'No' but told him there was someone else. Bit by bit she unravelled her past, things he had disbelieved before as malicious scandal. A poem 'He thinks of Those who have spoken Evil of his Beloved' expressed this:

> Half close your eyelids, loosen your hair,
> And dream about the great and their pride,
> They have spoken against you everywhere,
> But weigh this song with the great and their pride;
> I made it out of a mouthful of air;
> Their children's children shall say they lied.[13]

He learned of her offering her soul to the devil and feeling, as the clock struck twelve, that her prayer to get control of her own life had been answered. She had fallen in love with Lucien Millevoye when both of them were recovering from illness at the French town of Royan, and become his mistress, loving him but disliking sex which she thought only justified by having children. Their son had died in 1891. The idea had come to her (probably stimulated by conversation at AE's house in 1891) that the lost child might be reborn and she had gone back to Millevoye and Iseult was conceived in the vault under the memorial chapel and born in 1895. Since her birth Maud had lived apart from Millevoye, but thought herself necessary to him. In all that followed, Yeats wrote, he was careful to touch her as one might a sister. A few days later they shared a vision. She thought she was a stone statue through which flame passed; he felt himself becoming 'flame and mounting up through and looking out of the eyes of a great stone Minerva'.[14] She was emotional, would kiss him tenderly but declared marriage impossible, asserting her horror and terror of physical love. He wrote an incoherent letter to Lady Gregory, then in Venice; she came back at once, offered him money to travel, urged him not to leave Maud till she promised to marry him, but he said that he was too exhausted and told her he could do no more.

Lady Gregory and Maud were both staying at the Nassau Hotel in Dublin and Lady Gregory recorded in her diary for 18 December how Miss Gonne came to call on her in the evening and she was shocked by her appearance. Instead of the beauty she expected she

saw a death's head and what to say to her I knew not. She does not know I know anything so it was constrained. However, we got on amicably.[15]

This was the occasion, apparently, on which Lady Gregory asked Maud what her intentions were in regard to Willie and got the dusty answer that she and Yeats had more important things to think about.

Yeats spent Christmas with George Pollexfen in Sligo, having been heavily engaged in complex political negotiations with the Pan Celtic Association. On 31 January 1899, he made a short visit to Paris to ask Maud again to marry him. He was obviously distrait; he wrote to Synge from the Grand Hotel de la Haute-Loire, on the Boulevard Raspail, to say that he had forgotten the name of the man at whose house he was to speak that evening and the number of his house. George Pollexfen, sending his nephew a cheque for £7, had been 'in hopes you would have required more and for another purpose but suppose affairs did not culminate favourably'. He and his second-sighted servant Mary Battle thought that he was in great form at present 'but added that something that *you and I* had in mind would not come off this time'.[16] It didn't, and after Maud's refusal of his proposal Yeats returned to London in mid-February and busied himself with arrangements for the casting, rehearsals and performance of the Irish Literary Theatre plays.

*

The early poetry culminated in *The Wind Among the Reeds*, published
in 1899. It is poetry of dream and reverie, love poetry much of it in
a melancholy mode, reminiscent of Pre-Raphaelitism, blended with
Yeats's distillation of his reading in Irish legends, with an undercur-
rent of meaning to be suggested rather than made explicit by the
symbolism. It runs the risk of seeming enervated but it is evocative,
highly emotive in its deliberate and echoing repetitions:

> Had I the heavens' embroidered cloths,
> Enwrought with golden and silver light,
> The blue and the dim and the dark cloths
> Of night and light and the half light,
> I would spread the cloths under your feet:
> But I, being poor, have only my dreams;
> I have spread my dreams under your feet;
> Tread softly because you tread on my dreams.[17]

'The Autumn of the Body', a Pateresque essay, published the year
before with the title 'The Autumn of the Flesh', puts a *fin de siècle*
view, recording a belief that painting, music, science, politics and
religion have changed in many elaborate ways because of a growing
belief that nothing is known 'but the fading and flowering of the
world'. Man, Yeats asserted here, 'has wooed and won the world,
and has fallen weary, and not, I think, for a time but with a weariness that will not end until the last autumn, when the stars shall be
blown away like withered leaves'. He saw the arts as about to take
up 'the burdens' that have fallen from the shoulders of priests and
'lead us back upon our journey by filling our thoughts with the
essences of things and not with things'. He draws a contrast between
Flaubert's *The Temptation of St Anthony*, 'the last great dramatic
invention of the old romanticism', and Villiers de l'Isle Adam's
Axël, the first of the new. Maeterlinck has gone further, while in
England he cites Rossetti as beginning a new poetry and moves
to Arthur Symons interpreting Mallarmé's views as meaning
that poetry henceforth will be a poetry of essences, separated one
from another in little and intense poems. And, while not ruling out
the writing of long poems – indeed saying that they will be written
more and more 'as our new belief makes the world plastic under
our hands again' – he agrees with him, thinking such poetry will
result from 'an ever more arduous search for an almost disembodied
ecstasy'.[18]

In 'The Symbolism of Poetry' of 1900 he links symbolism with past poetry, misquoting Burns and then quoting one of his favourite passages by Nashe:

> Brightness falls from the air,
> Queens have died young and fair,
> Dust hath closed Helen's eye.

before going on to Shakespeare's *Timon of Athens*, to say that poetry flickers with the light of many symbols:

A little lyric evokes an emotion, and this emotion gathers others about it and melts into their being in the making of some great epic; and at last, needing an always less delicate body, or symbol, as it grows more powerful, it flows out, with all it has gathered, among the blind instincts of daily life, where it moves a power within powers, as one sees ring within ring in the stem of an old tree.[19]

He argues that besides emotional symbols there are symbols that 'evoke ideas alone or ideas mingled with emotions'. The 'intellect . . . decides where the reader shall ponder over the procession of the symbols, and if the symbols are merely emotional he gazes from amid the accidents and destinies of the world; but if the symbols are intellectual . . . he becomes . . . a part of pure intellect' and '. . . is himself mingled with the procession':

. . . if I watch a rushy pool in the moonlight, my emotion at its beauty is mixed with memories of the man that I have seen ploughing by its margin, or of the lovers I saw there a night ago; but if I look at the moon herself and remember any of her ancient names and meanings, I move among divine people, and things that have shaken off our mortality, the tower of ivory, the queen of waters, the shining stag among enchanted woods, the white hare sitting upon the hilltop, the fool of Faery with his shining cup full of dreams, and it may be 'make a friend of one of those images of wonder', and 'meet the Lord in the air'.[20]

He ended the essay by stating his belief that if people accepted the idea 'that poetry moves us because of its symbolism' the 'laws of art', . . . 'the hidden laws of the world, can alone bind the imagination'. 'Energetic rhythms' would be 'cast out', only 'wavering meditative organic rhythms' would be sought; the 'importance of form' could not be denied.

His own sense of form was, however, to change, just as his life was changing, and just as intellectual life was changing. The nineties were over; as he put it later, 'everybody got down off their stilts'.[21]

SEVEN

1900–1902

Yeats was always susceptible to – indeed he seems to have needed – the influence of strong figures. His Sligo grandfather's fierce ruling over the Pollexfen household and his father's strong views on art and literature once escaped, there had been other dominating figures to replace them: John O'Leary and his nationalism, William Morris and his interest in sagas as well as his literary Pre-Raphaelitism, W. E. Henley and his editorial skills had impinged on his personality and his progress as a writer.

From their first meeting on, Maud Gonne, herself in search of power, had exercised a potent sway over him. His youthful friendships with his contemporaries in Ireland, with George Russell and Katharine Tynan, were superseded by more sophisticated ones made in London, the influence of Arthur Symons replacing that of Lionel Johnson, while Florence Farr and Olivia Shakespear became much closer to him than Katharine Tynan had been in Ireland. But Lady Gregory's friendship was of more effect than any of these. In addition to providing him with order, peace and dignity at Coole where he could recharge his creative batteries in the summer months and also do a very great deal of writing, she supplied the stability of certain moral and social attitudes, her sterner conscience part of the patrician code of behaviour she had inherited; and her house was one that had, he wrote, enriched his soul out of measure, being a place where life moved without restraint through gracious forms.

This friendship was founded upon different needs. Yeats had lacked mothering in his youth, and he now got that, in middle age, at Coole. There was a regularity of life and the routine suited him, a typical day including reading after breakfast, a turn in the garden, writing from 11 till a late lunch, then fishing in the lake, afterwards reading and working at lighter tasks, then dinner and good conversation and a walk after dinner. He flourished in the comfort and the social confidence of Coole, where he enjoyed the role of being a poet with a patron who not only shared his ambitions for Ireland but offered him sympathy, encouragement and understanding. Lady Gregory hoped to be involved in the future of Ireland, to play a part – for she wanted to write – in the literary movement. Their collaboration was initially rooted in his interest in folklore which she sought to serve, but it soon grew into the creation of a national drama, a national theatre which was to give their friendship full and exciting scope. Their efforts were complementary.

Lady Gregory had what Yeats, often given to daydreaming, called a feeling for immediate action. When he had discussed his by then abandoned plans for a literary theatre in the suburbs of London with her that afternoon at Duras, she decided that Yeats, who had written *The Countess Cathleen*, Martyn who had written *The Heather Field* and *Maeve*, and she should form the Irish Literary Theatre. Since the original three knew little of theatre business George Moore was suggested as a co-director, along with Yeats and Martyn. Though Moore and Martyn were cousins and close friends, Yeats later described them as bound to each other by mutual contempt:

When I told Martyn that Moore had good points, he replied: 'I know Moore a good deal longer than you do. He has no good points.' And a week or so later Moore said: 'That man Martyn is the most selfish man alive. He thinks that I am damned and he doesn't care.'[1]

Martyn became worried about the orthodoxy of *The Countess Cathleen*, in which the Countess sells her soul for gold to save her starving people. An ecclesiastical authority whom he consulted disapproved of it: two other authorities consulted by Yeats and Lady Gregory did not disapprove. But Moore disapproved of a work of art being subjected to the attitudes of theologians. And Martyn disapproved of Moore's attitude. He decided to resign. Yeats talked him into changing his attitude. Everything seemed settled.

Frank Hugh O'Donnell, now a fierce enemy of Yeats, stirred the public pot with a pamphlet, *Souls for Gold*. Cardinal Logue thereupon condemned the play – without reading it. As a result, police were present when *The Countess Cathleen* and *The Heather Field* were performed in May 1899 in the Antient Concert Rooms in Dublin. Noisy protests at Yeats's play from one section of the audience were countered by cheers from another. An evil peasant in the first act tramples upon a Catholic shrine and this caused considerable discomfort in the audience. Yeats recognised afterwards that he had been mistaken in using traditional symbols without realising that such symbols possessed a reality of their own in Ireland.

He helped Moore to revise and recast Martyn's political satire, *The Tale of a Town*, at Tulira Castle, the play becoming in the process *The Bending of the Bough*. Martyn not having relished its being altered by the others, it was attributed to Moore when it was staged at the Gaiety Theatre in Dublin in 1900. In the summer of that year Yeats and Moore risked writing *Diarmuid and Grania* together at Coole. There was a good deal of argument before they agreed that Moore should handle construction, Yeats dialogue. At one stage in the collaboration (which Lady Gregory deplored and Yeats was later to blame when one of his own plays 'grew more and more incoherent' after months of work) Yeats wanted the dialogue translated into Irish, then translated back into English with Irish idioms. His own French, Moore asserted, would be better, and Lady Gregory could translate that into English for an Irish speaker to put into Irish so that Lady Gregory could English it again. Despite the inevitable quarrelling the play was actually finished by December, to be staged for a week in October 1901. The critics were not enthusiastic and nationalists positively disliked the play. Subsequently, however, Yeats recorded happily how the crowd from the gallery wanted to take the cab horse out of the shafts and drag him and Maud Gonne to some supper party after the performance.[2]

Yeats's interest in staging plays had developed further by 1901. Deeply impressed by scenery the young and then unknown Gordon Craig had created for a production of *Dido and Aeneas*, he attended the first performance of an Irish play by P. T. MacFhionnlaoich and two *tableaux vivants* by Alice Milligan, and was greatly taken with the acting of William Fay and his brother Frank. One an electrician, the other an accountant's clerk, they had been involved in amateur drama for ten years and had devised a method of acting which restricted movement and gesture – and not much of either – to whichever actor happened to be speaking. Yeats, then dominated by a desire to emphasize an obvious, all-pervading rhythm in plays as he had in his early poetry, found their acting much more attractive than that of the English players the Irish Literary Theatre had employed in its three years' existence. 'I had imagined such acting,' he wrote in *Samhain*, an occasional publication linked with the theatre, in 1902, 'though I had not seen it'. He had asked a dramatic company, he added (anticipating Beckett in this) 'to let me rehearse them in barrels that they might forget gesture and have their minds free to think of speech for a while'.[3] He thought the barrels could be on castors so that he could shove them about with a pole when the action required it. He came away from the Fays' performance with his head 'on fire', entranced by hearing genuine Dublin accents on the stage. The Fays' emphasis on dialogue fitted in well with the theories he was developing about the speaking of verse with the aid of Florence Farr.

As Aleel the poet, Florence Farr had been the only member of the cast of *The Countess Cathleen* to satisfy his ear. Dublin talked of her performance for years, he pronounced in *Autobiographies*:

And after five and thirty years I keep among my unforgettable memories the sense of coming disaster she put into the words:

> But now
> Two grey horned owls hooted above our heads.[4]

To accompany his lectures on verse-speaking, Florence Farr recited Yeats's poems to the accompaniment of the psaltery, an instrument similar to a lyre but with a trapezoidal sounding board which originated in the Near East and was popular in medieval Europe. Arnold Dolmetsch made one specially for her and Yeats; it contained all the chromatic intervals within the range of the speaking voice. Completely tone-deaf, Yeats was, however, conscious of tunes when making his poems; indeed he was surprised that George Russell used only two tunes when composing verses, saying that he himself did not often compose to a tune though he sometimes did, 'yet always to notes that could be written down and played on my friend's [Edward Martyn's] organ, or turned into something like a Gregorian hymn if one sang them in the ordinary way'.[5] Dolmetsch, however, thought Yeats did not recognise the inflection of his own voice, and had a short phrase of fairly indistinct tones which he used in reciting his poems. Maud Gonne once described him as 'booming and buzzing like a bumble bee' and that meant, she added, 'he is writing something'.[6]

His propagandist work continued; he reached a peak in his praise of Celticism when he took part in a controversy which he called a

stirring row while it lasted.[7] It was provoked by an article written by
John Eglinton (his former schoolfellow, W. K. Magee); afterwards
he began to use 'Irish' rather than 'Celtic' as a descriptive term.
Ireland could find in the beliefs and the emotions of her common
people, he declared, the habit of mind that created the religion of
the masses. She possessed in her written Gaelic literature, in her
tales of love and war, forms in which the imagination of Europe had
uttered itself 'before Greece shaped a tumult of legend into her
music of the arts'. These ideas were expressed in a later essay
produced for Lady Gregory's *Ideals in Ireland* (1901) in which he
quoted more from her work. She had collected a mass of folklore
which she allowed him to use in six long articles on folklore (in
which, adding material of his own, he advanced an essentially
mystical argument), her *Poets and Dreamers* was forthcoming and she
had greatly aided him in the writing of his play *Cathleen ni Houlihan*,
something she later thought he never fully acknowledged. This play
resulted from a dream of his, 'almost as distinct as a vision', of

> . . . a cottage where there was well-being and firelight and talk of a marriage
> and into the midst of the cottage there came an old woman in a long cloak.
> She was Ireland herself, that Cathleen ni Houlihan for whom so many
> songs have been sung and about whom so many stories have been told and
> for whose sake so many have gone to their death.[8]

He could not get down, he said later, out of 'that high window of
dramatic verse'; he had not got 'the country speech'. But Lady
Gregory had, and put his dream into 'the English of the West of
Ireland, the English of people who think in Irish'. Later she and
Douglas Hyde helped him in the writing of *Where There is Nothing*
and she largely rewrote it as *The Unicorn from the Stars* – it was
'almost altogether' her writing, Yeats told A. H. Bullen in a letter
of 12 February 1908. She also collaborated in *The Pot of Broth* and
The Hour-Glass, both folk plays, a genre in which she became very
much at home.

After he saw the rehearsals of Russell's *Deirdre*, a play with which
he was not in sympathy, he eventually agreed to let the Fays stage
Cathleen ni Houlihan, something suggested by Russell and Maud
Gonne, whose offer to play the part of Cathleen finally removed his
reservations. Both *Deirdre* and *Cathleen ni Houlihan* were performed
at St Teresa's Abstinence Association Hall in Dublin on 2 April
1902, Maud playing Cathleen to Yeats's immense satisfaction. He

had often described her appearance as that of a goddess and now 'her great height made Cathleen seem a divine being fallen into our mortal infirmity'.[9] His play had an electrifying effect. Stephen Gwynn, a distinguished Irish man of letters, went home having seen Maud Gonne stir the audience as he had never seen another stirred, and he asked himself whether such plays should be produced 'unless one was prepared for people to go out to shoot and be shot'.[10] And in old age Yeats was to ask himself the same question:

> Did that play of mine send out
> Certain men the English shot?[11]

Smarting over the way Moore and Yeats had treated *A Tale of a Town*, Martyn had withdrawn himself – and his financial support – from the Irish Literary Theatre. By 1902 Moore had also, as Yeats put it, dropped out of the movement. Their relationship had been exacerbated by another attempt at collaboration, their theme this time founded on events in the life of an eccentric anarchic visionary, an acquaintance of George Russell. They drafted a scenario for a play, but in August Yeats told Moore the collaboration was off, on the grounds that he had become the Inaugural President of the Irish National Theatre. (He knew that the Fays did not like working with Moore.) Moore responded with a wire to Yeats, then at Coole, to say he had written a novel on the scenario, to threaten an injunction if Yeats used it. Hearing from Russell that Moore had not written a novel but begun a play spurred Yeats, with the ready aid of Lady Gregory and Douglas Hyde, into writing *Where There is Nothing* in a fortnight, arranging to have it published in the *United Irishman* and – shades of the Duke of Wellington – writing to Russell, who was characteristically acting as mediator, 'Tell Moore to write his story and be hanged.'[12] He claimed that he had done this to save from 'a plagiarist' a subject that had 'seemed worth the keeping till a greater knowledge of the stage made an adequate treatment possible'.[13] But later, writing in *Autobiographies*, he thought that had he made Moore write a novel there might have been a third masterpiece to put beside *Muslin* and *The Lake*, but he was 'young, vain, self-righteous' and bent on proving himself 'a man of action'.[14]

Now increasingly immersed in writing plays, Yeats became involved as a protagonist in yet another quarrel, a highly dramatic row in the

Hermetic Order of the Golden Dawn. An initiate since March 1890 in the Isis Urania Temple, he had seen Wynn Westcott's influence waning; Westcott was now acting as the London representative of MacGregor Mathers, whom he had invited to join the Golden Dawn in 1887, and who composed the rituals of the Order, becoming one of its three Chiefs, and reorganising the Second Order with a bias towards magic. Mathers had moved to Paris in 1892 and founded another Temple there, the Ahathoor. He found it difficult to control the members of the Isis Urania Temple from Paris, and like many leaders of such groups became more eccentric and autocratic, demanding that his colleagues should obey his wishes. Some objected and in 1896 he had issued a manifesto demanding their submission. He expelled Annie Horniman that year for 'continued insubordination' to himself. Yeats seems to have remained friendly with him and his wife up to 1899; he had frequently consulted Mathers over the rituals of the Irish Order of Mysteries for the Castle of Heroes through which he hoped to keep Maud Gonne out of politics. Maud, after she left the Order of the Golden Dawn, had continued to dislike Mathers, and Yeats's friendship with him ended in 1900 when the quarrelling in the Golden Dawn came to a head, Mathers accusing Florence Farr, who had succeeded Westcott in 1897, of attempting to make a schism in the Order and alleging that Westcott's original communications with the Secret Chiefs which led to the foundation of the Order had been forged.

Yeats and Florence Farr became members of a committee set up by her to investigate these allegations. Mathers promptly refused to recognise it, indeed abolished it, telling Florence Farr he was removing her from office. Instead of coming from Paris when summoned by the Committee, he sent Aleister Crowley to London. Crowley, a sinister figure – though, when he chose, he could be an amiable *farceur* – had gone through the rituals of the Outer Order two years earlier, then was surrounded by human havoc in Scotland. Wanted for debt, under police observation and probably involved in a homosexual scandal, he had been refused admission to the Second Order in London, Yeats remarking that they did not think a mystical society was intended to be a reformatory. Crowley went to Paris where Mathers, self-styled Comte de Glenstrae, then admitted him, self-styled Laird of Boleskine and Abertaff, a full Zelator Minor. On 17 April Crowley broke into the Order's meeting rooms in London – the vault of the Adepti at 36 Blythe Road, Hammersmith

– accompanied by a Miss Elaine Simpson, and seized the rooms on the authority of Mathers. Florence Farr countered by calling a constable and having Crowley and his companion ejected. Two days later Yeats and a fellow adept, E. A. Hunter, talked to the landlord, had the locks changed and forbade Crowley to enter the rooms again. This time it was he who called for a constable, but again he was told to leave. He was described in a 'Statement by Fra, HES' as being 'in Highland dress, a black mask over his face and a plaid thrown over his head and shoulders, an enormous gold or gilt cross on his breast, and a dagger at his side'. Crowley next sent a message to the members of the Second Order threatening legal action, denying the account of 'the masked man' and suspending several members including Florence Farr, Hunter and Yeats. Mathers wrote to defend Crowley's mask as a symbolic device, a mask of Osiris. Since Mathers was obviously megalomaniac in his demands and aggressive actions, the Committee passed a resolution on 21 April to suspend him and some other members. At this meeting Yeats spoke about the history of the Order and introduced resolutions for reconstructing it. He now possessed enough knowledge of how to operate the formal business of committees to realise the confusion created by the utterly unbusinesslike habits of the members, and especially Florence Farr. On 25 April he wrote to Lady Gregory to tell her he had had to take the whole responsibility and make the necessary decisions. In arraigning Mathers, he had been carefully polite and was particularly pleased that nothing had been written or said 'which forgot the past and the honour that one owes even to a fallen idol'.[15] The subsequent case was settled out of court and Crowley, who had been 'bitter and violent and absurd', paid £5 costs.

Yeats hoped that they had now got, as he wrote to George Russell, 'a perfectly honest Order' with everyone working well for it.[16] He hoped he could return to writing *The Speckled Bird* – 'the new bits of which are really good' – but a new struggle developed: between Florence Farr and Annie Horniman, whom Yeats had invited to return to the Order and act as its Scribe. Florence Farr wanted to admit Zelators (members of the lowest of the ten Degrees of the Order) to her group which was studying the Egyptian Book of the Dead and the symbolism of the Tree of Life; but Annie Horniman did not approve of any movement away from traditional practice. The two women were poles apart in their attitudes, and they were both deeply interested in Yeats. Despite his attempts to reach a compromise beforehand, a Council meeting in February 1901 erupted into an unpleasant row about methods of holding elections and whether separate groups could legally exist within the Order. Not wanting the groups legalised, Yeats did not like the way the meeting went, and subsequently wrote four open letters to members of the Order during February, the first one the day after the stormy meeting. He did not want to be nominated as a member of the Executive Council; he had been upset by the treatment given to Miss Horniman (who had irritated everyone with her precise rectitude) and himself; but he did, however, offer to continue to instruct members in mystical philosophy. His second letter defended Miss Horniman's business capacity and objected to Florence Farr's changes in rituals as well as her proposal to admit candidates 'privately' to the Order. His third letter on the crisis contains his fear that a Resolution to be proposed by Florence Farr at the General Meeting might lead the way to black magic and to another major split. The wrangling continued with a letter from Robert Palmer Thomas (who had been removed from office by Yeats) attacking Yeats and Miss Horniman. At the General Meeting, on 26 February, they both resigned along with J. W. Brodie Innes who had failed to amend a Resolution put forward by Florence Farr's group, as Yeats had with another amendment. All three wrote yet another open letter. Then in March Yeats wrote 'Is the Order of RR & AC to remain a Magical Order?', following this up in May with 'A Postscript to Essay called "Is the Order of RR & AC to remain a Magical Order?"'

These two privately printed pamphlets go further than 'Magic', an essay published in *The Monthly Review* in September 1901, later included in *Ideas of Good and Evil* (1903). In it Yeats had been clear about his beliefs; he believed, he wrote, in the practice and philosophy of magic:

... in what I must call the evocation of spirits though I do not know what they are, in the power of creating magical illusions, in the visions of truth in the depths of the mind when the eyes are closed; and I believe in three doctrines, which have, as I think, been handed down from early times, and been the foundations of nearly all magical practices. These doctrines are:
1. That the borders of our mind are ever shifting, and that many minds can flow into one another, as it were, and create or reveal a single mind, a single energy.

2. That the borders of our memories are as shifting, and that our memories
   are a part of one great memory, the memory of Nature herself.
3. That this great mind and great memory can be evoked by symbols.[17]

The two pamphlets stressed Yeats's belief that the Order of the
Golden Dawn should be disciplined, its members obeying its laws
and bylaws, that examinations should be used for the grades, that
there should be respect for seniority, the highest Degrees having
due weight in the government of the Order, and that the oath taken
upon the Cross on Corpus Christi Day should be restored (an
emphasis upon the Christian elements in the Order). He felt a need
for the examinations as a ritualistic means for the members to tread
a symbolic path, to climb towards the light. Order and degree within
a hierarchical framework could aid the fathoming of evidence, the
obtaining of a mystical apprehension of ultimate truth. He feared
the fragmentation threatened by the 'carefully organized groups', by
'undesirable secret teaching', by irresponsible members unprepared
for 'that criticism which is the essence of all collective life': in short,
anarchic diversity. His search for unity led him to think traditional
symbols and formulae could act as powers in their own right; they
must remain a Magical Order; but experiments and research could
lead to black magic, 'an evil sorcery'. Adepts should receive power
from 'those who are above us' and that power, he affirmed, is 'forever
seeking the world'; it comes to a soul, consuming its mortality
because the soul has risen, 'into the path of the Lightning' of the
Supreme. The Order could have a missionary role, shaping life
through Adepts and teachers nearer the magical life. Apart from
being a religious belief of a kind, this was also a political recipe:
surrendering freedom could lead to becoming faithful servants of
the law; order could be achieved by art, by discipline.

The rigorous discipline and art of the poet was something he spelled
out in 'Adam's Curse', a poem recalling a meeting with Maud
Gonne after she had returned in May 1901 from a lecture tour in
America. Maud recalled Willie looking critically at her as she and
her sister Kathleen Pilcher (the 'beautiful mild woman' of the poem)
were sitting on a sofa, then telling Kathleen that he liked her dress
and that she was looking younger than ever, to which Kathleen
replied that it was hard work being beautiful 'which Willie turned
into his poem "Adam's Curse"':

We sat together at one summer's end,
That beautiful mild woman, your close friend,
And you and I, and talked of poetry.
I said, 'A line will take us hours maybe;
Yet if it does not seem a moment's thought,
Our stitching and unstitching has been naught.
Better go down upon your marrow-bones
And scrub a kitchen pavement, or break stones
Like an old pauper, in all kinds of weather;
For to articulate sweet sounds together
Is to work harder than all these, and yet
Be thought an idler by the noisy set
Of bankers, schoolmasters, and clergymen
The martyrs call the world.'

                              And thereupon
That beautiful mild woman for whose sake
There's many a one shall find out all heartache
On finding that her voice is sweet and low
Replied, 'To be born woman is to know –
Although they do not talk of it at school –
That we must labour to be beautiful.'

I said, 'It's certain there is no fine thing
Since Adam's fall but needs much labouring.
There have been lovers who thought love should be
So much compounded of high courtesy
That they would sigh and quote with learned looks
Precedents out of beautiful old books;
Yet now it seems an idle trade enough.'

We sat grown quiet at the name of love;
We saw the last embers of daylight die,
And in the trembling blue-green of the sky
A moon, worn as if it had been a shell
Washed by time's waters as they rose and fell
About the stars and broke in days and years.

I had a thought for no one's but your ears:
That you were beautiful, and that I strove
To love you in the old high way of love;
That it had all seemed happy, and yet we'd grown
As weary-hearted as that hollow moon.[18]

The day after the meeting that the poem describes he called on
Maud Gonne, to accompany her on her customary visit to the Lia
Fail (the Stone of Destiny in Westminster Abbey) and, as she
recounted in *A Servant of the Queen*, he said to her:

'You don't take care of yourself as Kathleen does, so she looks younger
than you; your face is worn and thin; but you will always be beautiful, more
beautiful than anyone I have known. You can't help that. Oh Maud, why
don't you marry me and give up this tragic struggle and live a peaceful life?
I could make such a beautiful life for you among artists and writers who
would understand you.'

'Willie, are you not tired of asking that question? How often have I told
you to thank the gods that I will not marry you. You would not be happy
with me.'

'I am not happy without you.'

'Oh yes, you are, because you make beautiful poetry out of what you call
your unhappiness and you are happy in that. Marriage would be such a dull
affair. Poets should never marry. The world should thank me for not
marrying you.'[19]

Later, in 1907, he was to write *Baile and Aillinn*, a tightly rhymed
'half lyrical half narrative' poem, crammed with references to Irish
mythology. Aillinn dies of a broken heart; so does Baile, his heart
'worn out'. Aengus, god of love, resolves the problem by turning the
lovers into immortal swans linked by a golden chain. There was no
such easy solution for the poet, though in the poem he claims that
he is not distressed by birds and rushes crying out their fill of lovely
and wise Deirdre, for she is neither wiser nor lovelier than his
beloved. But he does not want to be reminded of the lovers Baile
and Aillinn, happy without end, whose joys include being in the
cities where the Tuatha de Danaan found their talismans, the spear,
cauldron, sword and stone – a reminder to Maud Gonne of their
past visits to the Stone of Destiny in Westminster Abbey:

> never yet
> Has lover lived, but longed to wive
> Like them that are no more alive.[20]

Lady Gregory had seen the devastating effect, the strain of the
'mystic marriage' with Maud Gonne on Yeats. A draft for a lyric
probably written about 1897 reflects the effect of his frustration, his
obsessive unhappiness:

> O my beloved. How happy
> I was that day when you
> came here from the
> railway, and set your hair
> aright in my looking glass
> and then sat with me at
> my table, and lay resting
> in my big chair. I am
> like the children o my
> beloved and I play at
> marriage – I play
> with images of the life
> you will not give to me o
> my cruel one.[21]

Lady Gregory had pressed him not to leave Maud in 1898 until he had her promise of marriage, but though he had then declared himself exhausted he had, however, proposed to her in Paris in 1899 and did so yet again in London in 1900. Maud still had 'more important things to think about'. As usual, she was deeply involved in politics, busy plotting and arranging contacts between French Military Intelligence and the IRB – something which backfired when a French agent who had met Dr Ryan in London was passed on to O'Donnell and subsequently arrested. She had suggested to a Boer agent in Brussels a plan to plant bombs in the coal of British troopships en route to South Africa; the idea seemed too risky, but she did get £2,000 to aid revolutionary work in Ireland. Frank Hugh O'Donnell was suspected of diverting this money to the Irish Parliamentary Party; it was returned after Yeats spoke to John Dillon about it. Maud's credit in France was damaged. Some of the IRB decided O'Donnell should be murdered and, though his crazy enmity had pursued them both, Yeats and Maud Gonne eventually persuaded the IRB men out of the plan. They then got themselves out of the IRB, both somewhat shaken by the affair. She turned to the formation of Young Ireland Societies and joined in the Sinn Fein movement founded by Arthur Griffith, who had been a compositor and Rand miner before editing *The United Irishman*. (Griffith was reputed to have horsewhipped the Editor of the *Irish Figaro* for libelling Maud Gonne – to whom he always wrote as 'My Queen'.)

Yeats, already disturbed by the Dublin riots of 1897, had been told by Maud that she was inciting tenants in Kerry to kill the landlords and seize food. When he informed Lady Gregory of this in February 1898 he was given firm advice: that the famine in Kerry might have been exaggerated, but if it were real it should be dealt with differently. It was not for those who were 'above the people in means and education' to blunt the people's morality, to encourage them to murder and steal. He hadn't, he replied, thought of how the matter would affect the people, but only of Maud. And he decided to try to dissuade her from her plans.[22]

Lady Gregory's comments had already given momentum to his increasing detachment from violent revolutionary politics. He had, it is true, organised meetings and written to the press to protest against Queen Victoria's visit to Dublin in 1900 as a recruiting tour;[23] he had joined in demonstrations against it, rolling up red carpets laid in her honour, recording later that his nationalist activities had ruled out his being invited to dine at many Dublin tables, or to fish various trout streams. But he was compensated for such social losses by his long summers at Coole. Maud was frequently to remark that Irish writers who stayed there seemed less interested in the national struggle than in their own lack of money. Lady Gregory, when assuring Maud about her own intentions in regard to Yeats, had told her that she was only doing for him what she would do for her own son, that she felt for Yeats as if he were her son. She gave him advice on his rooms in Woburn Buildings ('Do you recommend me to have gas for lighting purposes or to keep it for cooking only?' he asked her, adding that the gas oven that Mrs Old, who looked after the rooms and cooked dinner for him, had had installed on her own initiative, would be a great comfort)[24] and she made them more comfortable, giving him a great blue curtain for his window, 'a feature of the room for twenty years', and the great leather armchair, in which Maud Gonne rested from time to time. She had supplied material for the articles on folklore that brought him in 'ten or fifteen pounds at a time'. And then one night when she and his other guests had gone, he found £20 behind his clock. He tried to return it, but she said he must take the money and give up journalism: 'the only wrong act that matters is not doing one's best work'. From time to time she gave him money; it was not, she said, to be thought a loan, but he could return it some day if he were well off. Because of his summers at Coole and the money she lent him he was able, he wrote in *Dramatis Personae*,

... through the greater part of my working life to write without thought of anything but the beauty or the utility of what I wrote. Until I was nearly fifty, my writing never brought me more than two hundred a year, and most often less, and I am not by nature economical.[25]

Unpublished poem by Yeats. He wrote these lines in a
vellum bound copy of *The Wind Among the Reeds*
(which he inscribed to Lady Gregory, on 14 April 1899.)

EIGHT

1902–1907

Looking back on 1902, Yeats wrote to Lady Gregory that it had been a very good year.[1] His intervention, with Douglas Hyde and George Moore, to save Tara – the site of the seat of the Irish High Kings – from being uprooted by labourers paid to find the Ark of the Covenant there had been successful. His eyesight again giving trouble, he had dictated portions of *The Speckled Bird*. He had, however, reached an agreement with Bullen, probably in 1901, that a book of essays should be substituted for the novel. These appeared as *Ideas of Good and Evil* in 1903. Bullen agreed, disturbed by the hostility to Yeats that he had experienced on a visit to Dublin.

Being freed from his contract to write the novel seems to have allowed more flexibility in replanning it, and his recent experiences in the Golden Dawn might offer him fresh material. The split in the Order now seemed healed and his play *Where There is Nothing* also made use of his Rosicrucian experiences. The hero Paul Ruttledge, like Martin Hearne, hero of the rewritten version of the play, called *The Unicorn from the Stars* (the title of which, *Monoceros de Astris*, was, he told his sister, a private symbol belonging to his mystical order – it was a temporary title, assumed upon completion of the Practicus Grade – and nobody knew what it came from; it meant the soul) is obviously founded upon aspects of Yeats himself in his Mosaic role, leading the members of the Golden Dawn through the wilderness, as we see from Martin's vision of the Mountain of Abiegnos, the mountain of inner spiritual struggle. In this play there is a shift from the physical, the armies of revolution and war, to the mental and spiritual.

He told Lady Gregory that she need not be troubled about his poetical faculty:

I was never so full of new thoughts for verse, though all thoughts quite unlike the old ones. My work has got far more masculine. It has more salt in it.[2]

He had been deeply influenced by reading Nietzsche, stimulated by his discussions with John Quinn, the Irish-American lawyer who visited Ireland in 1902. Quinn, the son of Irish Catholic immigrants, went to Washington as the secretary of a friend, a senator whose election campaign he had managed. By the age of twenty-three he had read law at Georgetown University in night courses, gone to Harvard and formed a New York law firm; by thirty-six he had his own firm. He was drawn to Jack Yeats's pictures by a note Lady Gregory had written on them, and he and Jack Yeats met her with Yeats, Hyde and Martyn at a *feis* at the grave of the Irish poet Raftery, over which Lady Gregory had had a new tombstone erected. Quinn went on to Coole, appreciating 'the magic in the air', the best talk and stories he had ever heard, especially from Yeats and Hyde. He was to prove the most generous of patrons to the Irish theatre, to Irish writers and artists, notably Yeats and his father. Himself a man, in Lady Gregory's words 'impetuous and masterful', he enjoyed Nietzsche in general, but it was Nietzsche's division of the soul's movements into Dionysiac and Apollonian that particularly impressed Yeats and he decided he had finished his own Dionysiac phase.

He wrote to George Russell that he was no longer in sympathy with 'The Autumn of the Body'; that the close of the previous century was full of a strange desire to get out of form, to get to some kind of disembodied beauty, and now the contrary impulse had come, he wanted to create form, to carry the realisation of beauty as far as possible. The Greeks, he added, 'said that the Dionysiac enthusiasm preceded the Apollonic and that the Dionysiac was sad and desirous but that the Apollonic was joyful and self-sufficient'.[3]

Some of this own increasing self-sufficiency, perhaps, could have been expected; after all, he was thirty-five at the turn of the century. A poem to Maud Gonne reflects the passing of time. He replies to one 'that is ever kind' who tells him that his 'well-belovèd's hair has threads of grey, And little shadows come about her eyes' so that all he needs is patience.

> Heart cries, 'No,
> I have not a crumb of comfort, not a grain
> Time can but make her beauty over again:
> Because of that great nobleness of hers
> The fire that stirs about her, when she stirs
> Burns but more clearly. O she had not these ways
> When all the wild summer was in her gaze.[4]

Another more freely written narrative poem, 'The Old Age of Queen Maeve', employs the rhythms of speech, more precisely and less adjectivally than his earlier treatments of Irish heroic material. It reveals Yeats moving away from high romance, for realism tempers his descriptions of the Queen of Connaught who aids the god Aengus, 'crossed in love', but asks this 'master of all lovers' after he and his sweetheart are together, 'O when will you grow weary?' Part of the poem is about the poet's reactions to Maud Gonne; his heart is unquiet; he compares his friend with Maeve:

> For there is no high story about queens
> In any ancient book but tells of you;
> And when I've heard how they grew old and died,
> Or fell into unhappiness, I've said,
> 'She will grow old and die, and she has wept!'
> And when I'd write it out anew, the words,
> Half crazy with the thought, She too has wept!
> Outrun the measure.[5]

Yeats's own high story, his striving to love Maud in the old high way of love, ended suddenly. Maud Gonne unexpectedly married John MacBride in Paris on 21 February 1903. She had praised his organisation of the Irish Brigade in the Boer War; he had accompanied her on her fund-raising tour in America; they had, however, little in common but their nationalist politics. His family was totally opposed to her; their nationalist friends, notably Arthur Griffith, warned them not to get married,[6] which Maud did, she said later, 'in a sudden impulse of anger'.

Yeats received what was to him the virtually incredible news when he was about to give a lecture. It was one of his best, but he never remembered what he said in it, and walked endlessly about the streets after it. An unpublished poem raged against her:

> My dear is angry, that of late
> I cry all base blood down
> As if she had not taught me hate
> By kisses by a clown.[7]

The poetry Yeats published after her marriage continued to pay tribute to her beauty; but it is love poetry of a new kind which now records the past: how the lady on the pedestal was lovely and how the poet had loved her. He records his loss in 'Old Memory' with its plaintive question:

> who would have thought
> It all, and more than it all, would come to naught
> And that dear words meant nothing?[8]

'Never Give all the Heart' records the fact that 'he gave all his heart and lost'.[9] He made some of the poems of *In the Seven Woods* walking about the woods in Coole, described lovingly in 1900 in the introductory lines to *The Shadowy Waters*, 'before the Big Wind of 1903 blew down so many trees, troubled the wild creatures and changed the look of things.' The look of his own life, too, had changed completely.

The affairs of the Irish National Theatre Society were turbulent. Loosely organised, it contained different pressure groups, one of which – led by Maud Gonne and Arthur Griffith – wanted Irish drama to forward their brand of nationalism. Maud, for instance, had vetoed Lady Gregory's *Twenty-Five* in 1902 on the grounds that it made the financial rewards of emigration too attractive. Padraic Colum's anti-recruiting play *The Saxon Shillin'* was rehearsed instead. But Willie Fay, who shared the desires of Yeats, Lady Gregory and Synge for a professionally-run national theatre, revised it into a form more suitable for staging. This led to accusations that Fay was trying to avoid upsetting Dublin Castle, the centre of British administration in Ireland.

The general situation was temporarily resolved early in 1903 when Russell, virtually the leader of the third group – largely working-class members who wanted an amateur theatre – suggested a democratic system of voting, in which plays and casting were to be settled by a three-quarter vote of all the members. Yeats then arranged a successful compromise. Colum withdrew his play and Lady Gregory revised hers. Various plays were repeated and in March Yeats's *The Hour-Glass* and Lady Gregory's *Twenty-Five* drew good audiences in Dublin; performances in London were warmly praised by the critics.

Yeats had hinted to Frank Fay in April 1902 that there was a possibility a wealthy friend might support the National Theatre Company. The letter to Fay was written by Miss Horniman, who often acted as Yeats's amanuensis when his sight was troublesome. In 1903, between March and October, she wrote Yeats four letters which contain diagrams blending tarot cards and astrological symbols. (Though an occultist and member of the Golden Dawn, she was, however, sceptical about Theosophy and Spiritualism.) He was 'Prince S', she 'Princess W', and in her first letter her system predicted that Yeats would experience new energy, she would find the transactions troublesome but 'work for love' would bring Divine Wisdom; in her second that he would enjoy the materialisation of his plans, gaining authority in dramatic affairs; in her third that his energy would lead to fame and power, though disappointment in friendship 'crowns all'; and, in her fourth, that some gift would cause quarrels and anger but would also bring good fortune and gain 'whilst away from home – self assertion is absolutely necessary'. She was reaching a decision to help the Irish company.

Meanwhile Yeats was continuing his commentary on the dramatic movement in occasional publications, the various issues of *Samhain* from 1901 and continuing to 1908, *Beltaine* from 1899 to 1900 and *The Arrow* of 1906. Essays he wrote in 1901, 'What is "Popular Poetry"?' and 'Ireland and the Arts', had stressed the plight of people more and those who cared for and were involved in the arts had to possess missionary zeal. The country people, he wrote in 'The Galway Plains', an essay of 1903 (prompted by Lady Gregory's *Poets and Dreamers*), were a community 'bound together by imaginative possessions, by stories and poems which have grown out of its own life and by a past of great passions which can still waken the heart to imaginative action'.[10] Essays on 'The Philosophy of Shelley's poetry' and on Morris, 'The Happiest of the Poets', reveal Yeats's own pursuit of moments of intensity, for the fusion of paganism and Christianity sought in earlier poems. Morris had a true vision because it was poetical. He knew, as Shelley knew

... by an act of faith, that the economists should take their measurements not from life as it is, but from the vision of men like him, from the vision of the world made perfect that is buried under all minds ... he was among the greatest of those who prepare the last reconciliation when the Cross shall blossom with roses.[11]

The fissile Rosicrucians, however, were far from reconciliation and though Yeats tried to mediate, there was another clash. The larger group, led by Dr Felkin, founded the Amoun Temple at the end of 1903 and gave the name Stella Matutina to their branch, which Yeats joined. Clashes continued in the theatre as well. In Dublin Yeats blocked two plays by James Cousins, *Sold* and *The Sword of Dermot*, regarding him as having no originality. In June a reading committee was formed, but split when Cousins offered *Sold* again. But then followed a more serious row, over Synge's *The Shadow of the Glen*, played in the Molesworth Hall with Yeats's *The King's Threshold*. The play was attacked as a slur on Irish womanhood and there were disturbances in the theatre, the extreme nationalists being affronted to such a degree that Maud and others resigned from the Theatre Society and supported the Cumann na nGaedhael Theatre Company which was rehearsing the plays of Cousins.

Yeats must have gone on his first lecture tour in North America with a feeling of relief to be out of the quarrelsome atmosphere surrounding him in both London and Dublin. John Quinn put a lot of thought and trouble into organising this tour for him. Yeats disembarked from the *Oceanic* in November 1903 finding Quinn's rooms in New York charming, feeling at home with the walls virtually covered with his brother Jack's pictures and Russell's as well as his own portrait by his father. Then came a hectic round of lecturing, mainly on 'The Intellectual Revival in Ireland', 'Heroic Literature', 'The Theatre' and 'Poetry'. He experienced the rigours of American reporting:

I had a long struggle with a woman reporter yesterday who wanted to print and probably will a number of indiscreet remarks of mine. Here is an example. 'What do you think of Kipling?' 'I shall say nothing whatever about Kipling if you please, I will say nothing about any living poet. If he would have the goodness to die I would have plenty to say. Good heavens, have you written that down?'
'Yes, it is the one Irish remark you have made.'
'You will please rub it out again.'
Thereupon we had a struggle of ten minutes and in spite of her promises I expect to see printed in large black letters 'Yeats desires Kipling's death'. I have sent an urgent message demanding a proof. I had been painfully

judicious for days, as the reporters had been Irish and asked about Ireland, but this woman asked about general literature and I was off my guard.[12]

Yeats 'lecturing on Speaking to the Psaltery in the wild and woolly West', a cartoon by his brother Jack B. Yeats, 15 December 1903

It was an extensive visit, including among other venues Yale, Smith College, Mount Holyoke, Amherst College, Trinity College, the University of Pennsylvania, the City College of New York, Wellesley College, Bryn Mawr, Vassar, Royal Victoria College (Montreal), Carnegie Hall, St Louis, Indianapolis, Purdue University, Notre Dame University, Indiana University, St Paul Seminary, the University of California at Berkeley, Stanford University, the University of Wisconsin, Beloit College, Queen's University (Kingston), the University of Toronto, Baltimore, Wells College Newark, Bridgeport and Connecticut. Yeats met leading Irish-Americans, talked to William James, lunched with President Roosevelt in Washington, and was given many receptions. He enjoyed some aspects of Irish America very much. In Chicago he was

entirely delighted by the big merry priests of Notre Dame – all Irish and proud as Lucifer of their success in getting Jews and Nonconformists to come to their college, and of the fact that they have no endowments. I did not succeed in my first lecture. I began of a sudden to think, while I was lecturing, that these Catholic students were so out of the world that my ideas must seem the thunder of a battle fought in some other star. The thought confused me and I spoke badly, so I asked if I might go to the literary classes and speak to the boys about poetry and read them some verses of my own. I did this both at Notre Dame and St Mary's, the girls' college near, and delighted them all. I gave four lectures in one day and sat up late telling ghost stories with the Fathers at night. I said when I was going away 'I have made a great litter on the floor' and pointed to torn-up papers, and one fat old priest said with a voice full of sincerity, 'I wish you were making it there for a month.' I think they were delighted to talk about Ireland and the faery – one priest, or rather a teaching brother, told me that nothing could heal the touch of the fool except the touch of the queen, and that she always wanted something in return, sometimes a good-looking young man to be her husband. He said the fool was ugly and deformed and always gave some deformity of body or mind. I think these big priests would be fine teachers, but I cannot think they would be more than that. They belong to an easygoing world that has passed away – more's the pity perhaps – but certainly I have been astonished at one thing, the general lack of religious prejudice I found on all sides here.[13]

He delighted in large audiences – several of about 2,000 in California – and, having made several hundred pounds, felt rich but tired out: 'O the weariness of another month here . . .'[14]

There was another weariness as well, being bombarded by requests for money from his sisters. They – and John Butler Yeats – had moved from Blenheim Road in 1902, to set up the Dun Emer Industries in Churchtown, about five miles south-west of Dublin, in collaboration with Evelyn Gleason, whose idea it was to establish an outlet for the work of Irish girls. It was a William Morris-like project: she was to manage the production of coverings, carpets and rugs, Lily Yeats to organise an embroidery section and Lollie to set up a printing press, its first book her brother's *In the Seven Woods* (1903). The venture was organised in a most unbusinesslike way which led to much subsequent disagreement. Apart from incompatibility and frequent friction over finance between Miss Gleason and the Yeats sisters, there was a constantly jangling relationship between Lollie and the editorial adviser to her press, her brother. He had interfered from the start, criticising some of the poems Russell had included in *The Nuts of Knowledge* which was to follow *In the Seven Woods*. Giving way, Russell remarked that the output of the press would be small if Yeats would not allow the printing of anything not on the level of a sacred book. Yeats confessed to Lady Gregory that he did not like the idea that the first money he had ever earned beyond the need of the moment should be expected to support his sisters' company. He could sacrifice a great deal for a cause but family duties 'just perhaps because they are thrust upon one' left him, he remarked, colder than they should.[15]

On returning to Ireland in March 1904 Yeats had a more serious disagreement with Russell (who had, incidentally, altered the rules of the Theatre Society to give the actors more control) over his having given former members of the Society permission to perform his *Deirdre* at a trade fair in St Louis in the summer. Yeats asked him to withdraw this permission on the grounds that he was not correct in giving it since the play belonged to the Society, and that he himself planned an American tour with the Theatre Society. Russell resigned, but in accepting his resignation Yeats wrote him a letter that mollified him somewhat:

I am nothing but an artist and my life is in written words and they get the most of my loves and hates, and so too I am reckless in mere speech that is not written. You are the other side of the penny, for you are admirably careful in speech, having set life before art, too much before it as I think for one who is, in spite of himself perhaps, an artist.[16]

While disliking his benevolent vagueness, his often uncritical encouragement of young writers, Yeats fully realised Russell's virtues, what he called his 'honest heart'. He needed his help in the exciting venture of turning the Theatre Society into a professional company that would operate in a permanent theatre. In April 1904, Annie Horniman wrote to Yeats to offer £5,000, part of the sum to provide an annual subsidy, part to pay for turning the Mechanics Institute on Abbey Street and an adjoining building on Marlborough Street into the Abbey Theatre. Officially she had been moved by a speech made by Yeats and by an article of his in *Samhain* about the hopes and plans he and his fellow dramatists shared. She could only afford to make a very little theatre and it must be simple, she wrote; they must do the rest to make a powerful and prosperous theatre with a high artistic ideal. She stipulated that there were to be no sixpenny seats in the new theatre, which upset the nationalist clubs. Maud Gonne was quick to tell Willie he was now considered lost to nationalism. The legal patentee of the new theatre had to be Irish, so Lady Gregory took this key position. Largely because of their competitive interest in the poet, she and Miss Horniman deeply disliked each other. Miss Horniman, too, was all for making Yeats comfortable; but as she disliked most things Irish she was at a decided disadvantage. A Quaker and a feminist, she described herself as a middle-aged middle-class dissenting spinster. She wore a dragon jewel of oxidised silver which she said was a likeness of herself. Though a most generous woman, she was very difficult indeed and had to be placated by Yeats on many occasions. She would obviously have been happy to marry him (hinting at this to his father in 1904), but he did not encourage her to do more than help his theatrical ambitions and act as his amanuensis when his eyesight was troublesome.

Work on the building of the Abbey began and this was not without drama. Part of the building had been a morgue, and workmen digging out rubbish there and finding human bones were convinced they had come across a murder. The caretaker, however, remembered that they had 'lost' a body about seven years before: 'When the time for the inquest came it couldn't be found.'

Russell's influence was needed to reorganise, yet again, the National Theatre, this time into a limited company with Yeats, Lady Gregory and Synge as the board of directors. 'I think,' Yeats wrote to Quinn, 'we have seen the end of democracy in the Theatre.'[17] He had agreed with Russell in the course of all the delicate negotiations:

Yes, of course I have no tact, and bully people. That is why I am leaving the whole matter to you. I can only threaten the body, but you can put the soul in uncomfortable places.[18]

The Society began its winter season with a capital of £40. Yeats stressed in *Samhain* the need for economy: plays had to be literary, stage management efficient and appropriate, and scenic art of a new kind. In an earlier issue of *Samhain*, he had asserted that the best plays worth getting were romantic and historical plays and plays about the life of artisans and country people. In time the poetical play could again be made a living dramatic form.

He was firmly committed to heroic verse plays himself. He had founded *The King's Threshold* (performed in 1903 with stage designs tactfully requested from Miss Horniman, and disliked by the company) upon an Old Irish prose romance, though some ideas were owed to Edwin Ellis – who had published a play *Sancan the*

Bard ten years earlier – to a Middle Irish tale, and to Lady Wilde's version of *Seanchan the Bard and the King of the Cats*, an amusing legend in Ossianic tradition. Yeats gave the poet Seanchan, who goes on hunger strike and dies, a moral victory over King Guaire and his courtiers who have refused him the old customary poet's right to sit 'at the great Council of the State'. This play introduces characters, the Mayor, First and Second Cripples, the servant Brian, a soldier, First and Second Girls, as foils to the King and his court, while Seanchan and his pupils do not conform to what is required of them. The Monk sees King and Church neglected but the Oldest Pupil defends the arts against new philistinism:

> If the Arts should perish
> The world that lacked them would be like a woman
> That, looking on the cloven lips of a hare,
> Brings forth a hare-lipped child.[19]

Seanchan rejects Fedelm's attempt to save him from his fasting; he resists both the King's blandishments and his threat to hang his pupils. But he dies and the Oldest Pupil affirms that

> some strange triumphant thought
> So filled his heart with joy that it has burst,
> Being grown too mighty for our frailty,
> And we who gaze grow like him and abhor
> The moments that come between us and that death
> You promised us.[20]

Here is an expression of the tragic joy, the 'final joy' Yeats thought an essential part of tragedy.

On Baile's Strand, on which he had been working since July 1901, which was first performed in the Abbey in December 1904, he pronounced the best dramatic verse he had written. The costumes designed by Miss Horniman included long red cloaks which Yeats said after the dress rehearsal had to go. Miss Horniman replied that this would spoil the colour scheme and mar the archaeological accuracy. 'Hang archaeology,' he retorted. 'It's effect we want on stage,' and told the actors to remove the cloaks. It was her last experience of designing for the Abbey.[21]

On Baile's Strand was similar in some ways to a poem of 1892, 'Cuchulain's Fight with the Sea', in which Cuchulain unwittingly kills his own son through the machinations of King Conchubar. In this play he adds the Fool and Blind Man as a kind of chorus, almost a peasant parody of the heroic action. He wrote a letter to Frank Fay about Cuchulain which shows that a good deal of his own character shaped that of the hero (who ages along with the poet throughout Yeats's career, though in the legendary tradition Cuchulain dies at twenty-seven):

About Cuchulain. You have Lady Gregory's work I know. Remember however that epic and folk literature can ignore time as drama cannot – Helen never ages, Cuchulain never ages. I have to recognise that he does, for he has a son who is old enough to fight him. I have also to make the refusal of the son's affection tragic by suggesting in Cuchulain's character a shadow of something a little proud, barren and restless, as if out of sheer strength of heart or from accident he had put affection away. He lives among young men but has himself outlived the illusions of youth. He is probably about 40, not less than 35 or 36 and not more than 45 or 46, certainly not an old man, and one understands from his talk about women that he does not love like a young man. Probably his very strength of character made him put off illusions and dreams (that make young men a woman's servant) and made him become quite early in life a deliberate lover, a man of pleasure who can never really surrender himself. He is a little hard, and leaves the people about him a little repelled – perhaps this young man's affection is what he had most need of. Without this thought the play had not had any deep tragedy. I write of him with difficulty, for when one creates a character one does it out of instinct and may be wrong when one analyses the instinct afterwards. It is as though the character embodied itself. The less one reasons the more living the character. I felt for instance that his boasting was necessary, and yet I did not reason it out. The touch of something hard, repellent yet alluring, self assertive yet self immolating, is not all but it must be there. He is the fool – wandering passive, houseless and almost loveless. Conchubar is reason that is blind because it can only reason because it is cold. Are they not the cold moon and the hot sun?[22]

Like Cuchulain, Yeats himself had put off dreams and illusion since by marrying MacBride Maud seemed to have brought her spiritual marriage with him to an end. He had a brief love affair with Florence Farr about 1904 – brief because, as he said later, 'she got bored'. They remained, however, very close friends. In July 1905, his mind full of Chaucer, he suggested to her a bicycle trip to follow the journey of the Canterbury pilgrims from Southwark and Greenwich to Canterbury through Rochester. 'I do not see why we should not go with some harmless person to keep up appearances.'[23] He could talk to her without reserve, could tell her anything. 'You cannot think,' he wrote to her in 1906, 'what a pleasure it is to be fond of somebody to whom one can talk – as a rule any sort of affection annihilates conversation, strikes one with a silence like that of Adam before he had even named the beasts.'[24] The second part of the sentence might have been a Pollexfen sentiment. Feelings in that family, his father wrote to him some years later, especially the affections and sympathies, were banned. There was, he added, one feeling accepted and allowed its sway, for married people might like each other, though even this was limited. They were never to give expression to this feeling, either in public or in private – he called it puritanism without religious ecstasy or exultation. But his son, in Yeatsian mood, continued his letter to Florence Farr with the remark that the best of life was to find an equal, to be 'moved and talkative, unrestrained, one's own self'.

He was writing to Olivia Shakespear again. The pattern was repeating itself, with praise of her latest novel again coming to her from the poet in the west of Ireland. 'Please write,' he ended a letter to her from Coole;[25] and he looked forward, in a letter from Dublin, to her reading the new book to him in London.[26] As ever she was kind and forgiving, and they became lovers again.

Maud Gonne, however, soon disturbed his thoughts and emotions. Her son Sean Seagan was born in Paris in January 1904, but MacBride – as Yeats had heard when on his lecture tour in America – had taken to drinking heavily. Maud told Yeats early in 1905 that she was going to sue for divorce, charging her husband with drunkenness, violence and a sexual assault on her eighteen-year-old half-sister (who was hastily married off to MacBride's forty-three-year-old brother in Ireland). Yeats was shaken and wrote to Lady Gregory that he could not bear the burden of this terrible case alone. MacBride denied the allegations, and until the case was heard in Paris in the summer Yeats was deeply anxious. Lady Gregory and John Quinn were also supportive of Maud's action. She was granted a legal separation with custody of Sean. Having become a Catholic, she would not remarry. The scandal caused much gossip in Dublin and when Maud, attended by Yeats, went to the Abbey in October 1906 she was hissed. Yeats castigated 'The daily spite of this unmannerly town' in 'The People' where his Phoenix reproves him for his complaint:

'The drunkards, pilferers of public funds,
All the dishonest crowd I had driven away,
When my luck changed and they dared meet my face,
Crawled from obscurity, and set upon me
Those I had served and some that I had fed;
Yet never have I, now nor any time,
Complained of the people.'[27]

She withdrew from most aspects of political life for twelve years after this. She was studying Irish, earning some money as a journalist and doing some painting as well as illustrating. She lived in Paris in the winters and in the summers on the Normandy coast at Colleville near Calvados in her ugly house Les Mouettes (to be demolished in the Second World War by the Germans to provide a field of fire against any Allied landing; when I was there in 1958 several old men remembered Maud as 'la belle Irlandaise' though they did not approve of her ménage). Iseult and Sean (custody of whom MacBride could have obtained if the child was in Ireland) made up the household, as well as a menagerie of dogs, cats, bantams and caged birds.

By 1906 George Russell felt that the old friendship between Yeats and himself had worn very thin. It had been strained when Yeats had successfully got James Starkey ('Seamus O'Sullivan', one of the younger poets encouraged by Russell) excluded from the publishing venture (it became Maunsel and Company) for which Joseph Hone was providing financial backing; he told Bullen that Russell would get all the bad poets in Dublin in print and what was already called 'the Twilight School' in Ireland would sap everyone's stability; he persuaded the nascent company to appoint Stephen Gwynn as literary adviser instead of Starkey. The relationship between Yeats and Russell was put to further strain over the refusal of the actress Maire Nic Shiubhlaigh to sign a contract. Yeats threatened her with a law-suit, to stress the need for contractual arrangements (he abandoned the idea because of a horoscope cast at his father's request by George Pollexfen, who was pleased with it but later found the wrong date of birth had been given to him). In the course of a long letter, Russell told Yeats that there was probably not one of the younger people of whom he had not made some stinging or contemptuous remark, adding that he had few or no friends in Dublin, to which Yeats replied that he desired the love of a very few people, his equals or his superiors:

The love of the rest would be a bond and an intrusion. These others will in time come to know that I am a fairly strong and capable man and that I have gathered the strong and capable about me, and all who love work better than idle talk will support me. It is a long fight but that is the sport of it.[28]

Though Russell was strong and capable himself, Yeats went on, he gathered the weak and not very capable about him, and they were a danger to all good work. He knew, he added, when Synge wrote his first play that he himself would never have the support of the nationalist clubs. In the face of a threatened secession from the company, he and Lady Gregory were resolute. By May, Maire Nic Shiubhlaigh and various members left to form Cluithcheori na hEireann (the Theatre of Ireland) with Edward Martyn as President and Padraic Colum, James Cousins, Patrick Pearse and Thomas Kettle on the board. (This group stayed in existence until 1916, its members then being more interested, according to Maire Nic Shiubhlaigh, in the Irish Volunteer Movement.) Russell gave the new company his blessing and his *Deirdre*.

He and Yeats became involved in another brouhaha when Yeats disapproved of another selection of Russell's poems, which Lollie had sought for the Dun Emer Press, accepted and set up without her brother's knowledge. Tempers ran high and Yeats's father, trying to pacify his turbulent offspring, wrote to Willie to ask if he had dropped affection from the circle of his needs, had he dropped love between man and woman. Is this, he asked shrewdly, the theory of the overman?

... if so your demi-godship is after all but a doctrinaire demi-godship. Your words are idle – and you are far more human than you think. You would be a philosopher and are really a poet.[29]

This particular quarrel with Lollie led to Willie's resignation as adviser to the Dun Emer Press, but later it, too, was patched up by Russell; and, though relations between brother and sister were seldom peaceful for long, both signed an agreement and there was a temporary and uneasy truce between them.

All of this combativeness seemed to many of his friends to stem from the effect of his American tour. Since Quinn had strengthened his interest in Nietzsche and the *Übermensch*, (he had known about the basis of Nietzsche's thought since 1896, when he had read three articles by Havelock Ellis on Nietzsche in *The Savoy*), he had aimed at toughness. On 13 June 1906, he had written firmly to Stephen Gwynn that he thought what Dublin wanted was some man who knew his own mind and had an intolerable tongue and a delight in enemies.[30] Annie Horniman, noticing the toughness and truculence, remarked that 'ever since he had been with Mr Quinn in America' he had got into the way of trying to avoid what he didn't like by simply ignoring what was said or written.

Much of what she said and wrote herself created difficulties. She disliked Willie Fay and made no bones about it, especially after she had given an annual grant in 1905 so that the Abbey's artists and managers could be paid. She rebuked Fay for not keeping discipline when the company was touring the north of England and Scotland (an understudy, selling the book of the play in Glasgow, having borrowed a low-cut dress from a chorus girl, demanded an extra sixpence for her autograph). She wanted to have him replaced as Stage Manager. Her complaint to Yeats was that she had been told not to interfere 'in a matter which I am financing'. Indeed she developed a distinctly proprietorial attitude to the theatre, emphasis-ing her financial role frequently, but tried a new form of interfering when Fay wanted Sara Allgood to play the title role in Yeats's *Deirdre*, the one-act play he had first drafted in 1905; she pushed Miss Darragh (Letitia Marion Dallas, an Irishwoman who acted on the London stage) at Yeats instead. No one in the company took to her; his father called her acting florid and stagey; and Willie Fay later described casting her as Deirdre as being like putting a Rolls Royce to run a race with a lot of hill ponies.

Deirdre was staged in late November 1906 with scenery designed and painted by Robert Gregory; it was a play Yeats revised frequently, learning much from seeing it on the stage. Oliver St John Gogarty, then in his late twenties, remembered Yeats reading it in mid-November:

He forgot himself and his face seemed tremulous as if an image of impalpable fire ... His lips are dark cherry red and his cheeks too take colour and his eyes actually glow black and then the voice gets all vibrating as he sways like a Druid with his whole soul chanting.[31]

Actresses who played Deirdre in subsequent productions were Maria Limerick, Sara Allgood, Maire O'Neill and Mrs Patrick Campbell. Yeats based the play on Lady Gregory's *Cuchulain of Muirthemne* (1902), a version made from several sources of the legend. He had praised this book of hers generously in the Intro-duction he wrote for it as 'the best that has come out of Ireland in my time', and indeed her handling of the story of Deirdre in

particular is very fine. Yeats regarded Deirdre as the Irish Helen
(with whom he linked Maud Gonne), Naoise as her Paris and
Conchubar as her Menelaus:

> One woman and two men: that is the quarrel
> That knows no mending.[32]

The play was effective in its compression of the action; tragic reverie
was achieved. The use of the musicians anticipates Yeats's later
interest in Japanese Nōh drama and the play gains from their comments, their intervention. The play is, in fact, more like a Nōh play
than the *Four Plays for Dancers*, deliberately based on the Nōh. The
heroic gesture, the moment of still truth at the centre of the action,
is captured when Naoise and Deirdre play chess, knowing they are
doomed, echoing the behaviour of Lugaidh Redstripe and his wife
who

> Sat at this chess-board, waiting for their end.
> They knew that there was nothing that could save them,
> And so played chess as they had any night
> For years, and waited for the stroke of sword.[33]

Deirdre herself, 'who might be some mild modern housewife but
for prophetic wisdom', attains her heroic stature in her breathtaking
apparent assent to Conchubar after Naoise has been murdered: 'In
good time / You'll stir me to more passion than he could', her regal
rebuttal of Conchubar's suspicion that she may have a knife and be
planning suicide:

> Have me searched
> If you would make so little of your queen.
> It may be that I have a knife hid here
> Under my dress. Bid one of these dark slaves
> To search me for it.[34]

The tension is finely created and when Conchubar tells her she can
make her farewells to Naiose's body she conveys to the musicians
her impending suicide and the tragic joy Yeats sought:

> Now strike the wire, and sing to it awhile,
> Knowing that all is happy and that you know
> Within what bride-bed I shall lie this night,
> And by what man, and lie close up to him,
> For the bed's narrow, and there outsleep the cock-crow.[35]

NINE

1907–1910

Controversy erupted at the first performance of Synge's *The Playboy of the Western World* on 26 January 1907. It made the second act largely inaudible, some of the audience blowing tin trumpets to express their disapproval of what Synge described as 'extravagant comedy'.[1] The disturbances went on. The play was regarded by nationalists as an insult to the people of the west of Ireland. It offended what has been described as the then current theory of Celtic impeccability, a feeling that Irish people should in general be presented in an ideal light. There was also a strong dislike of Yeats and Lady Gregory as well as of Synge – called, by a theatre employee, 'a bloody old snot' for writing such a play. Surprisingly, perhaps, the name of the English source of the theatre's finance, Miss Horniman, was not brought into this controversy. Yeats was in Scotland lecturing; when he returned to Dublin he and Lady Gregory brought in the police to keep order, another cause for outrage on the part of patriotic nationalists. The play was kept on for a week of tumult, and Yeats called a public meeting at the Abbey for 4 February. There he fought the case for the play in the teeth of the majority of those attending, reminding them that the author of *Cathleen ni Houlihan* was addressing them, and putting the issue squarely as one of freedom of speech, asserting the right of the theatre to put the play forward, the right of everyone to hear it and judge it, and the right not to have his hearing interfered with by anyone else.

Synge's play seems inoffensive enough now in all its exuberance of language and situation, its tragedy of the girl who loses her playboy, the only one in the western world, its true comedy of appearances affecting reality. And as for reality, had not Yeats on first meeting Synge in Paris in the autumn of 1896 urged him to go to the Aran Islands where the oldest man on Inishmaan that very

summer had told of the gentleman that killed his father, whom he
had hidden for six months 'till he got away to America'? Synge
thought that he had restored sex to Irish drama and that people
were so surprised by this that they saw the sex only,[2] while Yeats,
considering him a genius, thought the 'spontaneous dislike' of his
work an artificial frenzy, caused by the warping effect of sexual
abstinence and by the 'pomp and gallantry of journalism and its
right to govern the world'.[3]

While the protests crystallised Yeats's view that there was an
inevitable difference between the intellectual element in Irish life
and what he called the more brainless patriotic element, he recorded
in his journal that no man of all literary Dublin had dared to show
his face at the public debate but his own father who spoke with
sweetness and simplicity. In old age he recalled this incident, stream-
lining it into artistic shape:

> My father upon the Abbey stage, before him a raging crowd:
> 'This Land of Saints', and then as the applause died out,
> 'Of plaster Saints'; his beautiful mischievous head thrown back.[4]

What was particularly galling was that Russell, who had promised
to take the chair, refused to do so 'by a subterfuge'. For the moment
their differences seemed utterly irreconcilable, as Russell, who
disliked the tone of Synge's plays, savagely attacked Yeats and Synge
four days after the debate in *Sinn Fein* in *Britannia Rule the Wave*, a
parody of *Cathleen ni Houlihan*. With the death of John O'Leary in
March there vanished the man who had, for Yeats, imbued Irish
nationalism with intellectual dignity. 'There are things,' he had said,
'a man must not do to save a nation.'

Yeats's first visit to America had come as a relief, an escape and a
financially rewarding venture. Now came a greater relief, an escape
from the mud-slinging of Dublin into the clear sunshine of Italy,
and the aesthetically rewarding experience of seeing what aristocratic
patronage had achieved there in its generous encouragement of the
arts. Yeats accompanied Lady Gregory and her son Robert on a
tour which took in Florence, Urbino, Ferrara, Ravenna and Milan.
It had a profound effect upon him. Three or four years before, he
had been entranced by Castiglione's *The Book of the Courtier*, which
conveyed the cultured life of a Renaissance court, and from which

Lady Gregory had read out the famous commendations of Urbino; and now he could see the superb site, the perfectly proportioned palace on its windy hill, the works of art commissioned by the Duke whose patronage, like that of Duke Ercole of Ferrara and Cosimo de Medici, seemed to him a model of what independent taste could create.

The visit to Italy confirmed his increasing delight in discerning appreciation as opposed to the Dublin mob's emotional reception of the new art he and his friends were striving to bring into existence. The struggle consumed time and creative energy. On his return from Italy, Miss Horniman became increasingly difficult. The reciprocal dislike and ever-increasing distrust between her and Lady Gregory were freely communicated to the poet. Lady Gregory considered Yeats disgracefully subservient to Miss Horniman, who for her part regarded Lady Gregory as truly wicked. She wrote to Yeats that he was being made into a slave, his genius being put under a net in that precious garden of Coole Park, and he was only being let out when he was 'wanted to get something out of me'. In the Abbey one evening she and Sarah Purser could hardly be got out of the theatre, in eager converse in the Hall, agreeing that Lady Gregory was 'too stupid to be allowed to live'.[5]

The situation could hardly continue, and Miss Horniman brought it to a head by announcing that she would discontinue her subsidy to the Abbey in 1910, at the end of the period for which she had agreed to provide it. She decided to use an unexpected legacy to found a repertory theatre in Manchester, to which she invited Yeats to give his poetic plays. It probably seemed to her that, as he realised his own poetic drama was not getting the audience he had hoped in Dublin, it was a good psychological moment to capture him. But he told her he was not young enough to change his nationality, which is what she was, in effect, asking. If the Irish theatre failed, he wrote, he could return to lyric poetry, but he would write for his own people, 'whether in love or hate of them matters little – probably I shall not know which it is'. She realised she had lost: 'But what are my words against the wooing of the vampire Kathleen ni Houlihan'. She had a tilt at Mrs Patrick Campbell – and at Yeats as well: 'I believe she admires your poetical powers, & very likely she has taken a fancy to you too although you are much too old for a woman of forty who might well go in for someone young.'[6] She could herself still cause trouble; she had probably been largely responsible for an earlier situation in which Willie Fay issued an ultimatum that he must have control over the actors and actresses: this had led to his resignation and that of his brother in January 1908. Now, however, she also withdrew from any active role in the theatre beyond paying the subsidy, writing to Yeats that his wish that she should trouble him less would be fulfilled; she would be no less kind, but would not waste the rest of her life 'on a Lost Cause'.

Another departure from the Dublin scene was that of John Butler Yeats. Several Dubliners had put up money – an idea suggested by Hugh Lane and Sarah Harrison and strongly supported by his old friend Andrew Jameson – to pay for him to visit Italy, but on impulse he decided to spend this money on going to New York with Lily who was representing Dun Emer at an Irish exhibition there. 'Perpetually hopeful', he loved American life, casting a critical but appreciative eye over its foibles, its materialism and generosity. He never returned to Ireland, his situation in New York summed up neatly by a barrister: 'In Dublin it is hopeless insolvency. Here it is hopeful insolvency.' J.B.Y. wrote to Willie that this was rather neat 'and quite true, I think'.[7] His extended visit, hardly an exile, led to a flood of letters as he observed Dublin from a distance and commented on life, literature and art with originality and wit. He wrote magnificently lively letters to his family, especially to Lily, whose replies were sharply worthy of the family, and to Willie who began to come closer to appreciating his father's ideas, the better perhaps for the physical distance between them. The old man painted; as ever he failed to finish his paintings; as ever he drew superbly and, as ever, he talked incessantly, becoming as well known as a conversationalist in New York as he had been in Dublin.

There was change for the Yeats sisters too; they parted from Evelyn Gleason in 1908, changing the name of their enterprise from Dun Emer to the Cuala Industries, which included the Cuala Press, still Lollie's responsibility. The last Dun Emer book was Yeats's *Discoveries*, a book of essays praised by contemporaries for its prose style and seeming to *The Bookman*'s reviewer to demonstrate that Yeats had emerged from his land of dreams and discovered life. He writes that he wants his work 'to speak to vigorous and simple men, to emphasise the physical nature of beauty'.

About this time, between 1907 and 1908, the passionate devotion to Maud Gonne seems to have been rewarded, according to a journal,[8] and to a later poem 'His Memories' from the sequence *A Man Young and Old*:

> We should be hidden from their eyes
> Being but holy shows
> And bodies broken like a thorn
> Whereon the bleak north blows,
> To think of buried Hector
> And that none living knows.
>
> The women take so little stock
> In what I do or say,
> They'd sooner leave their cosseting
> To hear a jackass bray;
> My arms are like the twisted thorn
> And yet there beauty lay.
>
> The first of all the tribe lay there
> And did such pleasure take –
> She who had brought great Hector down
> And put all Troy to wreck –
> That she cried into this ear,
> 'Strike me if I shriek.'[9]

In 1907 Yeats was very busy preparing the eight volumes of his *Collected Works* which Bullen was to publish from his Shakespeare Head Press at Stratford-on-Avon in 1908, aided by a guarantee of £1,500 from Annie Horniman, which she gave, she wrote to Yeats, to show people, especially his 'twittering imitators in Ireland', his real status. He took a great deal of trouble over the edition and after some misunderstanding had arisen wrote to Bullen that one should never start on serious undertakings without a very careful business understanding – losing control of the Irish Library to Gavan Duffy had been a well-learned lesson. He withdrew from active work in the Abbey to devote himself for a year to making 'a final text' of all his books. But for this, he wrote in July 1907, he would never have consented to a collected edition at the time because an edition containing so much that was immature or inexperienced as there was in his already published works would do him a very great injury.[10] He was insistent that business matters should be arranged through the literary agent A. P. Watt.[11] Yeats and Bullen were at cross-purposes over several matters, particularly about the distribution in the edition of paintings or drawings of himself, which

Yeats wanted to have grouped together. Augustus John came to Coole in September and made many pencil and brush sketches to work up into an etching – 'all powerful ugly gypsy things'. John climbed to the top of the highest tree in Coole and carved a symbol there; no one else, not even Robert Gregory, could climb up to see what it was. Yeats's judgment was reserved: 'if one looked like any of his pictures the country women would take the clean clothes off the hedges when one passed, as they do at the sight of a tinker.'[12] John realised that his view of Yeats must seem brutal and unsympathetic to those who had vague and sentimental memories of the poet; he could not see any resemblance to 'the youthful Shelley in a lace collar', but he did recognise him as 'a robust virile and humorous personality', still the poet but far more interesting in his maturity than his immaturity.

Charles Shannon, on the other hand, commissioned by Quinn to paint the poet, produced something which seemed to him 'very charming but by an unlucky accident most damnably like Keats'.[13] His father, he thought, saw him through a mist of what he called domestic emotion. Mancini, an Italian painter living in Dublin, turned him into a joyous Latin, impudent, immoral and reckless, but John had made him a sheer tinker: drunken, unpleasant and disreputable, indeed 'a melancholy English bohemian, capable of everything except living joyously on the surface'. Alvin Langdon Coburn, the American photographer who came to England in 1904, made dramatic photographs of him, and John Singer Sargent did a charcoal drawing, 'a charming aerial sort of thing, very flattering as I think'.[14] Kathleen Bruce (Lady Kennet) made a bronze mask. Yeats was firm with Bullen: 'the one thing I will not have is sentimental representations of myself alone'.[15]

He was certainly not sentimental in the new love into which he projected himself in the spring of 1908. This was with Mabel Dickinson, whose snobbish brother Page L. Dickinson recreated in *The Dublin of Yesterday* (1929) much of the atmosphere of the United Arts Club which Yeats joined in May 1908, finding most of his social life in Dublin there. Dickinson tells the story of his having absentmindedly, one evening while immersed in talk, eaten two dinners in succession. The affair with Mabel Dickinson was primarily physical; the modern mystery of Rossetti's romantic women now tired him; he could only take pleasure, he said, in 'clear light, strong bodies'.[16] Mabel Dickinson had a strong body; she was a skilled masseuse: no mystery of a gothic kind about her. He wrote to her from Paris in 1908 to say that when he was last there ten years before he had hated all that was classic and severe; he wanted a twilight of religious mystery in everybody's eyes; he doubted if he would have liked her then. She was to be regarded, obviously, as the opposite of Maud, with her horror of sexual love. But Maud too was in Paris, and their spiritual marriage of 1898 was renewed – though its strains were now offset by the primarily physical relationship with Mabel Dickinson.

After he left Paris, Maud wrote to him on 26 June telling him that she thought a most wonderful thing had happened, the most wonderful she had met. If only they were strong enough to hold the doors open, she thought, they would obtain knowledge and life they had never dreamed of. These remarks followed on her advice that it would not be right for him to give up his London life completely, but that he should get free or partially free from the theatre. He must keep his writing before all else. She had hated his being in politics, even the politics she believed in, she wrote, because it took him from his writing. And the theatre was just as bad, for it brought him among jealousies, petty quarrels and little animosities. She urged him, in particular, not to attack Russell and his *Deirdre*. Even in such outer things she did not want there to be the least jar between them.[17] A month later, on 26 July, a letter described a 'wonderful' experience she had had the night before. She did not want to intrude upon his work on the play he was writing (probably *The Player Queen*), but she did want to know if the experience had affected him:

Last night all my houschold had retired at a quarter to 11 and I thought I would go to you astrally. It was not working hours for you & I thought by going to you I might even be able to leave with you some of my vitality & energy which would make working less of a toil next day – I had seen the day before when waking from sleep a curious somewhat Egyptian form floating over me (like in the picture of Blake of the soul leaving the body) – It was dressed in moth-like garments & had curious wings edged with gold in which it could fold itself up – I had thought it was myself, a body in which I could go out into the astral – at a quarter to 11 last night I put on this body & thought strongly of you & desired to go to you. We went somewhere in space I dont know where – I was conscious of starlight & of hearing the sea below us. You had taken the form I think of a great serpent, but I am not quite sure. I only saw your face distinctly & as I looked into your eyes (as I did the day in Paris you asked me what I was thinking of) & your lips touched mine. We melted into one another till we formed only *one being, a being greater than ourselves* who felt all & knew all with double intensity – the clock striking 11 broke the spell & as we separated it felt as if life was being drawn away from me through my chest with almost physical pain. I went again twice, each time it was the same – each time I was brought back by some slight noise in the house. Then I went upstairs to bed & I dreamed of you confused dreams of ordinary life. We were in Italy together (I think this was from some word in your letter which I had read again before sleeping). We were quite happy, & we talked of this wonderful spiritual vision I have described – you said it would tend to increase physical desire – This troubles me a little – for there was nothing physical in that union – Material union is but a pale shadow compared to it – write to me quickly & tell me if you know anything of this & what you think of it – & if I may come to you again like this. I shall not until I hear from you. My thought with you always.[18]

He pasted this letter, like the one of 26 June, into the notebook she had given him, recording that he had made an evocation and sought union with her on the night of 25 July.

In October he went to see Mrs Patrick Campbell play in his own *Deirdre*; she then played it in London in November: she had expressed an interest in *The Player Queen*, in being at his elbow when he wrote it. The worst stage for him, drafting a prose scenario, was carried out at Coole in the autumn; in late November he went to Paris, staying at the Hôtel de Passy where he read Balzac and visited the places in Balzac's novels. In his 'usual way' – he wrote to his father – he would read him all, and was at the twelfth or thirteenth of the forty volumes.[19] He was still occupied with redrafting and rewriting *The Player Queen* (and was to go on working on it until 1910; it was then laid aside until 1915 and finished in May 1917) in December, the month he began his journal, in which 'Every note must first have come as a casual thought, then it will be my life.'[20] In it he reveals his inner feelings freely; it is a frank and revealing portrayal of his emergence into self-knowledge, of his new efforts at self-control. He was developing the idea of the mask, a deliberate choice, an attitude. Warwick Gould has suggested that Balzac influenced this. Yeats read him intensely from February 1908 to October 1909 (by 1909 he had read 30 of the 40 volumes of the edition he possessed) and Fœdora in *Le Peau de Chagrin* may have

stimulated the idea. In the journal we see Yeats adopting the idea
of the mask as a social defence as well as a means of exploring, a
way of escaping from the exigencies of the reality into which his
new life of action led him in his desire to express not the traditional
poet but 'that forgotten thing the normal active man'. All happiness
seemed to him to depend upon having the energy 'to assume the
mask of some other self, that all joyous or creative life is a rebirth
as something not oneself, something created in a moment and
perpetually renewed in playing a game like that of a child where one
loses the infinite pain of self-realisation, a grotesque or solemn
painted face put on that one can hide from the terrors of judgment,
an imaginative Saturnalia that makes one forget reality.'[21]

Reality meant sleepless nights thinking of the time taken from
poetry. It meant a realisation that the worry of years, trying to do
too many different things, had upset his nervous system:

> All things can tempt me from this craft of verse:
> One time it was a woman's face, or worse –
> The seeming needs of my fool-driven land . . . [22]

He began to wonder whether he had always had some nervous
weakness inherited from his mother and records a curious breakdown when he could not employ his mind on any serious subject.
But then his sceptical side questions whether this is an indisposition
brought on by too much smoking, heightened by the nervous fear
of losing his inspiration. There were headaches, palpitations, won-
derings whether his talent would recover from the heterogeneous
labour of the last few years. He realised something of his 'petulant
combativeness', recording how he feared representatives of the
collective opinion and would rage stupidly and rudely. But what he
was experiencing was the difficulty of influencing men and women
of lesser vision, lesser energy:

The feeling is always the same: a consciousness of energy, of certainty, and
of transforming power stopped by a wall, by something one must either
submit to or rage against helplessly. It often alarms me; is it the root of
madness?[23]

The answer to his difficulty in concentrating lay in the discipline of
art. He tells himself he should exclude irritation from his conversation in the way he had learned to exclude it from his writings and
formal speech. He had had to subdue 'a kind of Jacobin rage' and
escaped from it by his sense of style. Is not one's art, he grieved,

made out of 'the struggle in the soul? Is not beauty victory over
oneself?'[24]

The obsession with Maud Gonne, previously shaped into poems of
defeatist devotion, now emerged in poems recording his passion in
the past tense. In *The Green Helmet* (1910) these were grouped under
the general title 'Raymond Lully and his wife Pernella' (the Lully
was later altered to Nicholas Flamel), probably because Yeats was
remembering that when Maud was initiated 'in the Hermetic
Students' he had begun to form plans of their lives being devoted
to mystic truth and he 'spoke to her of Nicholas Flamel and his
wife, Pernella'. In these poems he measures the waste of spirit his
love had involved, yet he excuses Maud because she is what she is.
The choice of an astrologer and his wife for the general title suggests
the spiritual marriage, but the poems praise Maud for having had
Helen's beauty,

> a kind
> That is not natural in an age like this.[25]

She has been like a goddess, possessing charm and sweetness but
strong and stern. While she believed that after her marriage and
during her long sojourn in France he had lost contact with crowds,
with ordinary people, and had become 'unaware of the forces
working for Ireland's freedom', he recorded in prose the thought
that she never could really understand his plans, his nature, his
ideas; but what did it matter, he thought, for much of his best work
had been done, and was still being done, in his attempts to explain
himself to her.

   This idea became the poem 'Words', probably provoked by their
interminable argument over his failure in her eyes to turn his art
into nationalist propaganda, her failure, in his, to understand his
purposes in striving for great art, in, for instance, fighting for the
art of Synge.

> I had this thought a while ago,
> 'My darling cannot understand
> What I have done, or what would do
> In this blind bitter land.'

> And I grew weary of the sun
> Until my thoughts cleared up again,
> Remembering that the best I have done
> Was done to make it plain;
>
> That every year I have cried, 'At length
> My darling understands it all,
> Because I have come into my strength,
> And words obey my call';
>
> That had she done so who can say
> What would have shaken from the sieve?
> I might have thrown poor words away
> And been content to live.[26]

This poetry relies upon the strength of its verbs; it is bare, undecorated and powerful in its acceptance of the past. Though, in effect,
it blames Maud for filling his days with misery and for rabble-
rousing, 'No Second Troy', linking her with Helen of Troy, praises
her nobility and beauty, 'high and solitary and most stern':

> Why, what could she have done, being what she is?
> Was there another Troy for her to burn?[27]

In his middle forties Yeats was dividing his life between London,
Dublin, Coole and France (he had even been taking lessons in
French again in Paris, and was to do so later in London). His
self-analysis was stimulated by changes in the ranks of his friends
and family. His mother had died when he was thirty-five but, like
most of her family, he had not been deeply affected. She had been
so long ill, he wrote to Mabel Dickinson eight years later, in May
1908, 'so long fading out of life, that the last fading out of all made
no noticeable change in our lives'.[28] When John O'Leary died in
1907, he had been living a somewhat withdrawn life consoled by
whiskey, and had become merely a symbolic figure in Yeats's mind,
his sayings to be recalled vividly later. John Butler Yeats was in New
York. What Lady Gregory had become to him he realised when she
was seriously ill in January 1909 and nearly died. He got a letter
from Robert and, not recognising the writing at first, thought his
mother was ill; then he remembered that she had died years ago
'and that more than kin was at stake. She has been to me mother,
friend, sister and brother.' He could not realise the world without
her, he wrote; the thought of losing her was 'like a conflagration in

the rafters'. And he concluded that 'Friendship is all the house I have.'[29] These thoughts produced the poem 'A Friend's Illness',[30] and in the diary he thought of Castiglione and a phrase that had often moved him: 'Never be it spoken without tears, the Duchess, too, is dead.'[31]

Synge, too, was gravely ill. He had been working on his version of the Deirdre legend and taken charge of the Abbey in 1908, but Yeats had to return to relieve him. He had undergone several operations and Yeats realised he was dying. A reserved man, he did not speak freely to Yeats, who saw him as a heroic figure, thinking his bad health had begun with the trouble over *The Playboy*. After his death on 24 March 1909 Yeats wrote frequently about him in his Journal, describing him as 'a drifting silent man, full of hidden passions'[32] who loved islands because their wild people seemed to embody the hidden dreams in which he appeared completely absorbed.

Yeats had to deal with Synge's family over his manuscripts; it was Lady Gregory's assumption that people would do what she wanted that led to the delays being sorted out. Yeats wrote an Introduction to Synge's works, an essay dealing with 'Synge and the Ireland of his Time', and later put some of the ideas his death had prompted into *The Death of Synge and other Passages from an old Diary* (1928).

After Synge's death Conal O'Riordan (whose pen name was Norreys Connell), who had experience as a stage manager, was appointed for some months to the Abbey, and this gave Yeats more time for *The Player Queen* which was causing him a lot of trouble. At the beginning of the year he had been working on *The Green Helmet* as well, a farcical treatment in ballad metre of a part of the Cuchulain legend, *The Feast of Bricriu*, which he had originally written in prose as *The Golden Helmet*, produced in the Abbey in March 1908. *The Green Helmet* was staged in the Abbey in 1910; in the play Cuchulain makes a heroic gesture, offering his head to the Red Man to cut off – it is an example of Yeats's delight in *sprezzatura*[33] – out of a kind of pure nobility, to right a wrong, to honour a guest, who 'played and paid with his head'. All is well, the Red Man appreciates Cuchulain's bravery:

> And I choose the laughing lip
> That shall not turn from laughing, whatever rise or fall,
> The heart that grows no bitterer although betrayed by all;
> The hand that loves to scatter; the life like a gambler's throw . . .[34]

In August there came a somewhat unheroic quarrel with John Quinn, whose mistress Dorothy Coates Yeats had met in Paris in 1908: they became friendly and Quinn had heard gossip about this from Dublin where Yeats had probably described the friendship indiscreetly, as well as getting an account from Miss Coates which depicted Willie, as William Murphy puts it, as 'a would-be seducer and herself as a staunch pillar of mistressly fidelity'. In New York John Butler Yeats tried hard to patch the quarrel up, but it was to last for five years.

Yeats continued to write and rewrite *The Player Queen* in the summer at Burren, a seaside place in Clare. The work had been alleviated by a few days in Paris where he met Sarah Purser, the Dublin artist and family friend, at Maud Gonne's and reported her comment, characteristically forthright, on Maud's cage full of canaries all singing together: 'What a noise! I'd like to have my lunch in the kitchen.' At Coole again he was writing philosophical statements in essay form to keep them separate from play writing. In November 1909 he dictated an amusing letter to his father about Mrs Campbell's reception of *The Player Queen*:

My dear Father: I'm here again in London, for the time. I came over to read my play to Mrs Campbell. She wrote to me to come at 1.15, lunch and read it afterwards (this was yesterday week). I went and word was sent down with apologies she wasn't yet ready. On towards two she and lunch appeared. After lunch she listened, much interrupted by the parrot, to Act I with great enthusiasm. I was just starting Act II when a musician arrived, to play some incidental music she was to speak through in some forthcoming performance. She said: 'This won't delay me long, not more than ten minutes,' and then began an immense interminable quarrel with the musician about his music. After an hour and a half of this I said 'I think I had better go and put off an invitation to dinner I had for to-night.' She begged me to do so – full of apologies. I went away and returned at 6.30 just as the musician left. I then started Act II. A deaf man sat there whose mission was, it seemed, to say irrelevant enthusiastic things to Mrs Campbell. I got through Act II well. Mrs Campbell still enthusiastic. Then there came in telephone messages and I was asked to stay to dinner and read it afterwards. At dinner there was young Campbell and his wife and two other relations of hers, probably poor ones. After dinner arrived Mrs Campbell's dressmaker, this would also take only a few minutes. Presently there was a mighty stir upstairs and somebody sent down in an excited way, like a messenger in a Greek Tragedy, to say that the dress was 6 inches too short in front.

At half past ten there was a consultation in the drawing room as to whether somebody shouldn't go up and knock at Mrs Campbell's door. It was decided that somebody should but everybody refused to be the one. I wanted to go home but I was told on no account must I do that. At half past 11 Mrs Campbell came down, full of apologies, it would only be a few minutes longer. At twelve young Campbell's wife, who is an American heiress, and therefore independent, announced that she was going home and did, taking her husband. I sat on with the relations, whose business it seems was to entertain me. We sighed together at the amount it would cost us in taxi cabs to get home. At half past twelve Mrs Campbell came in so tired that she had to lean on her daughter to get into the room. I said: 'This is absurd! You must go to your bed, and I must go home.' She said: 'No, I must hear the end of a play the same day as I hear the beginning.' I began to read. She did not know one word I was saying. She started to quarrel with me, because she supposed I had given a long speech which she wanted to a minor character and because of certain remarks which I applied to my heroine which she thought applied to her. She said at intervals, in an exasperated sleepy voice: 'No, I am not a slut and I do not like fools.' Finally I went home and I'm trying to find a halcyon day on which to read her the play again. I've even had to assure her by letter that it was not she but my heroine who liked fools.[35]

The same letter records something of his social life in London, where he was dining out a great deal. He sat beside the Prime Minister at a party given by Edmund Gosse, appreciating Asquith's range of reading, especially in poetry; but at the same party, warned in advance by Gosse to avoid politics, he told Lord Cromer, interested in virtually nothing else, that he looked on English politics as a child does at a racecourse, taking sides by the colour of the jockeys' coats, and added that he often changed sides in the middle of a race, a remark which dampened the conversation. From Sligo he had letters from Lily, on holiday there, but reporting on the hypochondriacal George Pollexfen's terminal illness. He had greeted his niece with the news that he thought he was going. Lily heard the banshee, which seemed 'a fitting thing' to her brother, who came to Sligo for the funeral.[36] Unlike that of Synge, a depressing occasion at the gloomy Mount Jerome cemetery in Dublin – 'none at that after some two or three but enemies or images of conventional gloom' – this was very touching, the church full of Catholics who had never been in a Protestant church before.[37] There was a Masonic service too:

> And Masons drove from miles away
> To scatter the Acacia spray
> Upon a melancholy man
> Who had ended where his breath began.[38]

Though they had corresponded on astrological matters Willie had not seen much of his uncle since he took to spending his summers in the comfort of Coole rather than in his uncle's more austere house, from which he took his uncle's material relating to the Golden Dawn and astrology all arranged in orderly fashion.

TEN

1910–1913

George Pollexfen's death meant a severing of the Yeatses' close links with Sligo, but while he was there for the funeral Willie imparted two items of news to Lily. He had heard from the Prime Minister in August that he was to receive a pension from the Civil List of £150 a year,[1] and there was a possibility that he might succeed Dowden in his chair of English at Trinity College, Dublin. The kind of Dublin malice which had greeted the appearance of the handsome vellum-bound *Collected Works* as a sign that Yeats's creative career was finished was now quick to dub him 'Pensioner Yeats'. He had, however, insisted that he would not be committed politically in any way by the grant, which was thought up by Edmund Gosse, with whom Yeats had become friendly in London and with whom he had joined the Academic Committee of the Royal Society of Literature in April. Lady Gregory had become involved in the matter of the pension, Gosse asking her to prepare material for a petition on Yeats's behalf, but this led to a misunderstanding between them in the summer. On 25 July Gosse surprisingly told her she had no right to interfere in the matter, writing her a letter 'beyond explanation or apology' in words used by Yeats in a letter to Gosse rebuking him for 'insolence to an old and dear friend'. This letter was not posted. Lady Gregory thought it a milk-and-water thing and gave it back to him. Gosse wrote to Yeats on 29 July to say the petition was with the Prime Minister; this was on the day Lady Gregory wrote to Birrell, the Chief Secretary for Ireland, with a draft petition, wondering what had called forth Gosse's extraordinary letter – unless he had gone out of his mind. The wires had obviously crossed. Gosse apologised, but Robert Gregory and Yeats did not give this letter to Lady Gregory as it seemed inadequate. Yeats wrote several letters to Gosse; none seems to have been posted; and in his journal he wrote many entries about the affair including a long letter to Robert Gregory, dated 2 August, in effect explaining himself to himself. He had moved from self-condemnation to self-justification. Lady Gregory and Robert, he realised, had expected him to act at once, in accordance with their accepted code of behaviour. Instead of that he was as an artist proud of belonging to a nobler world, of having 'chosen the slow, dangerous, laborious code of moral judgement'. Again he had been, he thought, too timid; and this difference which had occurred with Lady Gregory arose 'from unreconcilable attitudes towards life'. Life seemed to him the struggle against generalised thought. Lady Gregory was, after all, a writer of comedy, he decided; tragic art would have shaken her conventional standards; he consoled himself by thinking that she had always belonged to a political or merely social world, not the artist's world.[2] She did not forget his behaviour on this occasion (he called it 'the one serious quarrel' he had ever had with her); as at other times, she thought he fell short of the standards she expected. But she accepted him for what he was. In Sir Ian Hamilton's words she played up to him. He recorded how Yeats in the throes of composition in the previous summer at Coole was being thoroughly spoilt:

His bedroom was halfway down a passage on the first floor at the end of which was my room. All along the passage for some distance on either side of Yeats' door were laid thick rugs to prevent the slightest sound reaching the holy of holies – Yeats' bed. Down the passage every now and then would tiptoe a maid with a tray bearing (they told me) beef tea or arrowroot, though once I declare I distinctly smelt eggs and bacon. All suggestions that I could cheer him up a good deal if I went into his room and had a chat were met with horror.[3]

The academic world was different again from the artist's, yet it was one Yeats contemplated at times. In 1909 he had been unsuccessful in seeking a lectureship at University College, Dublin, but now his father, wildly excited at the possibility of his son succeeding Edward Dowden, wrote characteristically to warn him that the Trinity dons were 'a very astute people – like the Vatican their ideas are ignoble, but they make no mistakes in carrying them out'.[4] In 1906 Yeats had been reading Spenser for a selection for which he wrote an Introduction. In that year he had also been reading John Donne, Ben Jonson and various Jacobean dramatists. Now he was studying Chaucer and other medieval writers in the British Museum.

Dowden, whose ill-health had given rise for concern, suggested that the Trinity Board could make an arrangement by which Yeats need not lecture on such subjects as Old English; he did not, however, really favour Yeats as a successor since he was not a scholar. Robert Yelverton Tyrrell, one of the most distinguished Fellows, was putting him forward, another Fellow, Louis Claud Purser, Lollie's friend, supported the idea and Mahaffy, then Vice-Provost, was not averse to it. Yeats told him that his eyesight was bad, but Mahaffy – like Tyrrell a distinguished classicist – replied that that was no hindrance. There was no work to do in English – 'Dowden never did any,' a remark reported by Lily Yeats which Yeats's father described ironically as one of those things that endeared Mahaffy to all his friends and contemporaries. Literature, Mahaffy thought, was not a subject for tuition.[5] Dowden, however, asked for leave of absence, recovered his health and decided not to retire.

The Abbey was turning out well, though not without the usual accompaniment of argument and quarrelling. Yeats and his co-directors had put much hard work into it:

> My curse on plays
> That have to be set up in fifty ways,
> On the day's war with every knave and dolt,
> Theatre business, management of men . . .[6]

Management of women, too. Miss Horniman, who had a deep hatred of Irish nationalist politics, had been decidedly irritated when Shaw's *The Shewing-up of Blanco Posnet* was played in the Abbey in August 1909, thinking that this was a political act, the play having been banned in England. In February 1910, however, she offered to sell the theatre for a thousand pounds to the directors, Yeats and Lady Gregory, the purchase to be completed by the end of the year, until which time she would continue to pay the subsidy. During the course of the negotiations she was upset by some remarks made later by Shaw, and Yeats complained to Lady Gregory that Shaw, being a logician, could not understand life. 'It is as if a watch,' he wrote, 'were to try to understand a bullock.' Things were going well with no Martyn, no Moore, no Russell, no Fays, with Miss Horniman about to detach herself completely and thus leaving Lady Gregory and himself in undisputed command. He could free himself from some of the chores by appointing Lennox Robinson, a young dramatist from Cork, as Manager. He told him he liked his face, believed he had a dramatic future, was no older than Ibsen when he was taken from a chemist's shop to manage the Norwegian theatre and, like him, was not 'ignorant of the work he was sent to'.

Ignorant, however, of what to do when Edward VII died, Robinson kept the Abbey open. Other theatres closed. Miss Horniman sent a telegram to Dublin: to open on the day of the funeral would be political and stop her subsidy automatically. Robinson sent a telegram to Coole (Yeats being in France) to ask what he should do. 'Should close through courtesy' was Lady Gregory's reply, but it arrived too late – the telegraph boy had dawdled on his way to and from Coole. Miss Horniman wrote to the press, sent a telegram to require an apology from Lady Gregory, and considering the apology inadequate demanded Lennox Robinson's dismissal. Yeats returned to Dublin, refused to dismiss him and in December challenged through his lawyer Miss Horniman's right to have withheld the subsidy on the grounds that he had never taken political action in connection with the theatre and that there was no agreement to flout nationalist sentiment. Miss Horniman maintained that it was fully understood that the theatre could not be used politically. The case was arbitrated by C. P. Scott, Editor of the *Manchester Guardian*, who found that though she had acted in good faith Miss Horniman had not been justified in stopping her subsidy. Yeats and Lady Gregory wrote to say that if she could not accept the integrity of their actions they would not accept the money. She did not, and that was the end of it. She and Yeats met very rarely again. Her contribution to the creation of the theatre has been undervalued, both her financing its building and her providing the subsidy which made the Abbey, as Yeats put it in 1908, the first subsidised theatre in any English-speaking country, and enabled it to play what it thought worth playing and to whistle at the timid.

Money now had to be urgently collected for the Abbey – Yeats gave the proceeds of a number of lectures, Lady Gregory sought private donations from the well-to-do – and in 1911 after the Company had played successfully in London at the Court Theatre an American tour was arranged for four months on very good terms indeed. Yeats accompanied the players from 21 September to 18 October. This time he added to the ideas he had stressed in his earlier tour accounts of Synge's achievement and of Gordon Craig's ideas about scenery. His lectures were entitled 'The Theatre of Beauty' and 'The Twentieth Century Revival of Irish Poetry and Drama'. He stressed the Irishness of the Abbey's offering, its now being accepted as a part of Irish life and its having achieved so much in so short a time. For the *New York Times* he analysed the new middle-class Ireland that was coming into being.

There was a good deal of Irish-American opposition to the tour. It was agreed earlier that Yeats should stay for the players' first week in Boston and Lady Gregory should then take over. Yeats saw his father – now very happily installed in a boarding-house run by a Breton family, the Petipas sisters – but his visit was only for a night; this left no time to see John Quinn, conveniently, as they were still not on speaking terms. Earlier in the year Quinn had commissioned a self-portrait from John Butler Yeats in oils, for which he would pay whatever the artist asked; this generous commission was designed to allow the old man to clear off bills, pay for his return passage to Dublin and have some money over. Though he worked on the self-portrait till his death, it was never finished; it provided him with a fine excuse, a justification for staying on in New York since no time had been specified for its completion.

His letters continued to flow from New York; they were thought-ful, original and stimulating, so much so that Willie was to write to his father in 1912 with 'a great project', that he should write his autobiography; he might really do 'a wonderful book' and, he added, 'I think a profitable one'.[7] The suggestion was refused, but the correspondence continued, the artist philosophising upon the nature of art, literature, and human personality with a blend of tolerant wit and a sharp critical outlook. In 1913 Willie suggested a volume of criticism and philosophy extracted from his letters for the Cuala Press: this was published in 1917, selected by Ezra Pound, and received critical acclaim. Another volume, selected by Lennox Robinson, was published in 1920 and other selections have followed, all of them immensely readable.

Lady Gregory's part of the Abbey tour in 1911 was tougher than Yeats's. There were riots in the theatre in New York, though Theodore Roosevelt's presence calmed things down on the second night. The arrest of the players in Philadelphia caused a stir, generated useful publicity, and created public support for the Abbey in Dublin. Quinn, ever the efficient adviser and lawyer when he was needed, provided powerful and effective support. After the tour was over, Lady Gregory stayed with him in New York where they had a brief, passionate affair. Both were highly critical of Yeats at the time and commented freely to each other on his failings, Lady Gregory still angry over his former subservience to Annie Horniman. Yeats's hesitance in replying to Gosse about his insulting letter still rankled. Maud Gonne, who was convinced – erroneously – that Lady Gregory was in love with Yeats, had earlier been amused by the rivalry between the two patrons: 'Miss Horniman brought back Italian plaques to decorate the Abbey but Lady Gregory carried off Willie to visit the Italian towns where they were made.'

It was not hesitant men who aroused Lady Gregory's passion. Quinn, uninhibited in his approaches to women, had made her very happy, so much so that it all seemed 'a dream, a wonderful dream'.[8] Back in Coole in April, she praised something impetuous and masterful about him that had so satisfied her. In May, not unnaturally, she felt lonely and depressed but that, she wrote to him, was just paying for past happiness, that rapture of friendship 'that so possessed and satisfied me'.

There had obviously been a lot of suppressed grievances to be aired between Quinn and herself, but Quinn had not fully shared her condemnation of Yeats's spending the £15 he had earned in 1898 from 'The Prisoners of the Gods', the material for which Lady Gregory had given him, on visiting Maud Gonne in Belfast: 'no purpose served, no object to be gained, no work to do'. (She may, in any case, have been confused about this, as he had gone to Belfast with money received for an article 'Ireland Bewitched', published in the *Contemporary Review* in September 1899.) Quinn's private comment was that Lady Gregory didn't seem to understand that Yeats had gone off to Belfast because, being in love with Maud, he wanted to be with her. His relationship with Maud continued its complex course. He saw her in London in May 1909 and stayed with her in Normandy in 1910; there he wrote two poems about her, 'Against Unworthy Praise'[9] and 'Peace'[10] (and probably at the same time a poem to her daughter Iseult, 'To a Child dancing in the Wind'[11]), as well as beginning his essay 'Synge and the Ireland of his Time', stimulated by endless discussion with Maud about Ireland.

*

In London his friends included Florence Farr, Robert Bridges, W. T. Horton, Edmund Gosse and John Masefield, as well as the artists Althea Gyles (who designed the covers of several of his books, notably that of *The Wind Among the Reeds* (1899)), Pamela Coleman Smith, Charles Ricketts, Charles Shannon, William Rothenstein and T. Sturge Moore. He was also in close touch with Gordon Craig. At Woburn Buildings the Olds continued to look after him, Mrs Old cooking his meals, Mr Old doing some carpentry for him and the family taking his washing to Barnsbury to air it there, calling him 'Yeaty' among themselves. Their work was sometimes criticised. Annie Horniman had written him a characteristically blunt letter in 1907, for instance, telling him there were moths in his curtains, the books on the top shelves were absolutely filthy, the mattresses uncovered, the eiderdowns covering the blankets would be *filthy* very soon, the floors were littered with bits of paper and hadn't been washed down.[12] In 1908 she had complained that while looking for his keys she had opened drawers to find bits of fur rug in them which would mean his underclothes becoming moth-eaten, and she would have to annoy Mrs Old again with naphthalene. He had, however, she conceded, grown much tidier.[13]

John Masefield described Woburn Buildings and Yeats's rooms there in detail:

Forty years ago, that court of small houses was more romantic than it is today. At its western end in Upper Woburn Place, there were some interesting late Georgian houses behind planetrees, all long since destroyed and their site covered by the new hotel. In the early years of this century, the shadows of the planes upon the houses were ever very beautiful in the lamplight. A blind beggar always stood there, under the lamp, after dark, offering matches and shoe-laces upon a little wooden tray.

Number 18 was on the left of Woburn Buildings, as you went from Woburn Place towards Kings Cross. He always described it as 'next door to a lapidary's shop'. On the wood at the right of the door near the bell-pull was a small brass plate, with the name Yeats deeply engraven on it. The screw-holes of the screws which held it could be seen there fairly lately. I hope that someone has kept the plate.

On entering the house, you went along the hall to the stair, which led inwards, then curved, and brought you to the landing on which he lived. On this, the second floor, he had a biggish front sitting-room and a small back kitchen. On the floor above, he had corresponding rooms, in which he slept.

His sitting-room was papered with brown paper; the window was hung with dark curtains; brown baize at one time; later a dim blue.

On the wall to the right as you entered, there was, what?

Who can recollect what there was, forty years ago? Was there not a large painting of him, done by his father, some years before? Later, on that wall, there was the picture of *Memory Harbour*, painted by his brother. Were there not also bookcases on this wall? The window was over the front door; it looked out upon the court. On the wall to the left side of the window was there not a big black chalk or pencil drawing of him by his father, the original of the portrait reproduced as a frontispiece to the *Poems* (of 1899)?

The left side of the room had a fireplace in the centre. Over the mantelpiece hung a painting by his father illustrating a ballad by Blake, 'I thought Love lived in the hot sunshine'. There were also these things: Blake's first Dante engraving, *The Whirlwind of Lovers*; a little engraving of Blake's head; a print of Blake's *Ancient of Days*; and a little engraving from the *Job*. There were also two small pastels done by Yeats, of the Lake and hills near Coole; and a beautiful pencil drawing by Mr Cecil French, of a woman holding a rose between her lips.

To the left of the fireplace, a tall dark settle jutted out into the room. At its back were bookshelves which made as it were a screen to the door leading to the little kitchen. Behind this hung Beardsley's poster for the Florence Farr production of *The Land of Heart's Desire*.

To the right of the fireplace a small, dark divan ran along the wall to the outer wall of the house. Over this divan were a large photograph of a woman, and Blake's seventh Dante engraving, of Dante striking Bocca Degli Abbati's Head.

The table stood in the centre of the room during meals, and was then lifted to the side. At meal-times, it bore upon it a little curved metal gong or striker of an unusual oriental design (with some scarlet colour on it), which he struck to summon Mrs Old. After meals, the table bore dark glasses, brown or green, and a dull red-clay tobacco-jar (with an oriental dragon embossed on it), containing cigarettes. The chairs were dark; the effect of the room was sombre. After 1904–5, he added to the room a big, dark blue lectern, on which his Kelmscott Chaucer stood, between enormous candles in big blue wooden sconces. These candles stood about four feet and were as thick as a ship's oar. The dim dark blue of this lectern was the most noticeable colour in the room. He added curtains to match it.

This sitting-room has been described in detail because it was the most interesting room in London.

On Monday evenings, from eight until two or three in the morning, he was at home to his friends. It was the rule, that the last comer should always go down to let in the next comer. That curved stair, lit by a lamp at the curve, was trodden by all that made our world.[14]

Among those who visited him in Woburn Buildings were Sarojini Naidu and Rabindranath Tagore, to whose poems Yeats, always sympathetic to the spiritual – and vaguely philosophical – quality of Indian thought, wrote an Introduction in 1912. In Dublin he entertained on Sundays in the Nassau Hotel, where the talk was more likely to concentrate on Irish subjects. His other Irish meeting place, apart from Coole, was the Arts Club, whereas in England his social horizons continued to widen. He visited country houses in the easy Edwardian peace and prosperity, among them Reigate Priory and Taplow Court, and he commented after lunching with Margot Asquith at Downing Street that her house was interesting but full of uninteresting copies of famous paintings.

Lynton, Margate and 'The Prelude', Coleman's Hatch, Ashdown Forest were other places he visited with the Tuckers, whom he had met through Olivia Shakespear. Her brother Harry Tucker married Nelly (Edith Ellen) Hyde Lees, a widow since 1909, whose first husband William, born Hyde, had become Hyde Lees after being adopted by an uncle. He had married Nelly in 1889; they had a son Harold, who went to Eton and Wadham College, Oxford like his father before becoming a clergyman, and a daughter Bertha Georgie, known both as Georgie and 'Dobbs'. She attended several schools and was very well educated, being a good linguist by aptitude and very well read. She became a close friend of Olivia Shakespear's daughter Dorothy, and the Tucker family joined in the artistic, musical and cultural life Olivia had always generated about her.

Into this circle came Ezra Pound. Arriving in England in 1908, he had published *A Lume Spento*, poems largely Pre-Raphaelite in tone; he had read and admired Yeats as a student in America. Olivia and Dorothy brought him to Woburn Place. Yeats thought his first volume 'charming' but praised the next, *Personae* (1909) more warmly. To be praised by the man he called the greatest living poet was exciting, and Yeats, describing Pound, twenty years younger than himself, to Lady Gregory as 'this queer creature', thought him an authority on the troubadours and sensible about the right sort of music for poetry, better than Florence Farr, though he couldn't sing, sounding like 'something on a very bad old phonograph'.[15]

Another introduction followed in 1911. Georgie Hyde Lees was in the British Museum one morning and saw Yeats rush past her like a meteor; that afternoon when she and her mother were having tea with Olivia he arrived and she was introduced to him. They were to become increasingly friendly. Pound quickly reached an easy relationship with the older poet, dominating the conversation at his Monday evenings; though careful not to disturb the flow of Yeats's thought when he was recounting an anecdote, propounding a theory or reciting poetry, he could be disruptive and domineering. Yeats valued his criticism; he wrote to Lady Gregory that Pound helped him to get away from abstractions to what was concrete and definite; to discuss a poem with him was like getting her to put a sentence into dialect. Pound, now moving well away from his early style, was catching up with the latest phases, the experimental verse of T. E. Hulme and others to which he gave the name Imagism. He was trying, with difficulty, to practise what he preached to others: making it new. And this included rewriting the master: he made some alterations in five poems Yeats had written in Normandy in 1912 which went via Pound to *Poetry* (Chicago) at the request of Harriet Monroe. These were 'To a Child dancing in the Wind', 'The Mountain Tomb', 'The Realists', 'Fallen Majesty'[16] and 'A Memory of Youth'. The last two poems, about Maud, were still recording what had gone:

> We knew, though she'd not said a word,
> That even the best of love must die ... [17]

Though irritated by his impertinence in interfering with his *ipsissima verba*, Yeats found Pound's comments shrewd and stimulating; he could accept the forthrightness of his criticism, perhaps because of Pound's lack of knowledge of either an Irish or English background, his brashness, perhaps because of his insistence on the need for poetry to be something that could be said, perhaps because he found Pound's attention flattering. The friendship flourished.

Despite Olivia Shakespear's reservations about their friendship, Ezra and Dorothy kept up a close correspondence. Ezra had received the following letter from Olivia in September 1912, which indicates some of the problems conventional and unconventional attitudes created:

Dear Ezra

As I never have any opportunity of seeing you & discussing matters, I must write what I have got to say.

You told me you were prepared to see less of Dorothy this winter. I don't know if you wd rather leave it to me to say I don't think it advisable she should see so much of you etc. or whether you wd rather do it in your own

way – I suppose I cd trust you to do it? I don't want to put the onus of it
on your shoulders if you don't want me to – on the other hand, it seems to
be a sort of surgical operation with her before she can say anything to me
about you & of course, we *might* have a row over the business – for I don't
intend to give way about it – She has never mentioned you to me, & I don't
know if she still considers herself engaged to you – but as she obviously
can't marry you, she must be made [to] realize that she can't go on as
though you were her accepted lover – it's hardly *decent*!

There's another point too – which is the personal inconvenience & bother
to myself – I had all last winter, practically to keep 2 days a week for you
to come & see her, which was all very well whilst there was some chance
of yr marrying her, & I put up with it, but I really can't put up with it for
the remainder of our lives – it gets on my nerves.

The most serious thing about the whole business is that she isn't the
least likely – she can't in decency – 'transfer her affections' to anyone else
whilst you are always about – & you'll be doing her a great injury if you
stand in the way of her marrying – She must marry – She & I can't possibly
go on living this feminine life practically *à deux* for ever, & we haven't money
enough to separate – & should have less than we have now if her father
died – indeed, in the latter event I should probably marry again, & she wd
be very much de trop – raison de plus for her marrying.

You *ought* to go away – Englishmen don't understand yr American ways,
& any man who wanted to marry her wd be put off by the fact of yr
friendship (or whatever you call it) with her.

If you had £500 a year I should be delighted for *you* to marry her (no
nonsense about waiting 5 years etc.) but as you haven't, I'm obliged to say
all this – as her mother I can't see it any other way – I've seen too much
of girls wasting their lives on men who can't marry them, & they generally
end by being more or less compromised demivierges. I only *hope* you have
not talked about her to your friends. I trusted, perhaps wrongly, to your
honour in the matter – but I know that Mme Hueffer, for one, knows you
have an affair with somebody – Think all I have said well over before
answering – & remember you will gain nothing by being cheeky!

I shouldn't mind yr coming to see her once a week, but she can't go
about with you American fashion – not till she is 35 & has lost her looks.
Dear Ezra – I'm sorry for you – really – but you are a great trouble, & my
anxiety about her is always there. Tomorrow is her birthday, & all I can
feel is that I wish she had never been born. She chose her parents very
unwisely.[18]

They continued to see each other and their letters, apart from
revealing a great deal about the crowded social life and the intellectual liveliness of the life centred round Olivia, show the mixture of
respect and jocular affection with which they regarded Yeats, whom

they called the Eagle. In January 1913, for instance, Dorothy wrote
to Ezra:

The Eagle has been inspired. 'Every external weakness has a corresponding
inner strength.'[19]

A few of the poems in the Cuala Press edition of *The Green Helmet*
(1910) had shown a readiness to deal with public themes; the
Macmillan edition of 1912 added some fine poems which show a
sureness of touch, an eloquent ease in their new directness of speech
in personal poems. 'Friends', for instance, assesses the effect of
three women – Olivia Shakespear, Lady Gregory and Maud Gonne
– on Yeats's life.

He did not, however, write about Florence Farr, who suddenly
decided to go to Ceylon in 1912, where she became Principal of a
girls' school; she was to die of cancer in 1916. Yeats missed his easy
but often exasperated relationship with her.

'The Cold Heaven' describes feelings aroused in him by the cold
detached sky in winter; it conveys with rhetorical intensity of a new,
vibrant kind the poignancy of his sense of lonely responsibility for
past mistakes that continued to disturb him:

> Suddenly I saw the cold and rook-delighting heaven
> That seemed as though ice burned and was but the more ice,
> And thereupon imagination and heart were driven
> So wild that every casual thought of that and this
> Vanished, and left but memories, that should be out of season
> With the hot blood of youth, of love crossed long ago;
> And I took all the blame out of all sense and reason,
> Until I cried and trembled and rocked to and fro,
> Riddled with light. Ah! when the ghost begins to quicken,
> Confusion of the death-bed over, is it sent
> Out naked on the roads, as the books say, and stricken
> By the injustice of the skies for punishment?[20]

Poems Written in Discouragement (1913) revealed how his experience
of politics had toughened him as a commentator on the public
controversies that stirred his imagination. Three, in particular,
moved him deeply: those about Parnell, *The Playboy* and the refusal
by the Dublin Corporation of a building for Sir Hugh Lane's
collection. Lane, a nephew of Lady Gregory, had worked at
Colnaghi's in London and by his early twenties achieved a reputation as an art critic and most successful dealer. He had offered

his fine collection of mainly Impressionist paintings as a gift to
Dublin if they were properly housed. He favoured a bridge gallery
over the River Liffey designed by Sir Edwin Lutyens, whose being
an Englishman annoyed the patriots. 'To a Shade', written at Coole,
attacks the blind bitterness which has greeted Ireland's benefactors,
and links Lane with Parnell, whose ghost is told in 'To a Shade' to
return to Glasnevin Cemetery, 'For they are at their old tricks yet'.[21]
These men are of a 'passionate serving kind', their aim to enrich
their country, to create in succeeding generations 'loftier thought,
Sweeter emotion'. Parnell's death in 1891 Yeats later saw as one of
the Four Bells, deep tragic notes in Irish history, the first being the
Flight of the Earls in 1603; he heard the note of the Fourth that
morning when he went to meet Maud Gonne arriving in Ireland
from Holyhead at 6 am on the Mailboat – which was also bringing
back to Ireland what he thought much less of at the time, Parnell's
body.[22] Both Parnell and Lane had a common enemy, 'an old foul
mouth', William Martin Murphy – the proprietor of two papers, the
Irish Independent and the *Evening Herald* – whom Yeats regarded as
typical of the philistinism of the rising Catholic middle class of
Ireland which 'made its first public display during the nine years of
the Parnellite split, showing how base at moments of excitement
are minds without culture'.[23] Murphy, however, was not only an
anti-Parnellite; in addition to opposing in his newspapers Dublin
Corporation's housing the Lane collection in the way Lane
suggested, he had organised the great Dublin Lock-out in 1913 in
an attempt to break the Irish Transport and General Workers'
Union.

Yeats wrote several poems about the Lane gallery. In the main
one, 'To a Wealthy Man who promised a second Subscription to
the Dublin Municipal Gallery if it were proved the People wanted
Pictures', he was attacking not only Lord Ardilaun, the wealthy man
of the title, but 'the blind and ignorant town' with its patrons who
needed to learn how to lead taste, not to follow that of the Irish
crowd, contemptuously labelled Paudeen or Biddy, to learn of the
discriminating generosity of the Italian Renaissance patrons.[24]
He develops his scorn of middle-class materialistic Ireland in
'September 1913', contrasting it with those leaders of the past,
Edward Fitzgerald, Robert Emmet and Wolfe Tone who gave their
lives, the wild geese who chose exile and the more recent leader
John O'Leary, symbol of Yeats's youthful romantic concept of

Irish nationalism which was now, he thought, 'with O'Leary in the grave'.[25] Murphy had replied to 'To a wealthy man . . .' from, Yeats commented, 'Paudeen's point of view' and another poem, 'Paudeen', probably portrays Murphy in these lines:

> the fumbling wits, the obscure spite
> Of our old Paudeen in his shop . . . [26]

Yeats attacked the Lock-out in 'Dublin Fanaticism', a letter published in the *Irish Worker* on 1 November 1913. This charges the Dublin nationalist newspapers – the foremost being the *Irish Independent* – with a deliberate arousal of religious passion 'to break up the organisation of the workingman, with appealing to mob law day after day, with publishing the names of working men and their wives for purposes of intimidation'. He charged the unionist press with 'conniving at this conspiracy'. Conor Cruise O'Brien has pointed out that Yeats's intervention came when Murphy was supported by Archbishop Walsh, whose letter, published on 21 October, told the wives of the workers that if they allowed their children to go to the homes of English sympathisers (who wanted to save them from going hungry) then they could no longer be 'held worthy of the name of Catholic mothers'.[27] Yeats had himself felt the power of illiberal priests in the affair of *The Countess Cathleen*. And the thought behind the opening image of 'September 1913'

> What need you, being come to sense,
> But fumble in a greasy till
> And add the halfpence to the pence
> And prayer to shivering prayer, until
> You have dried the marrow from the bone?
> For men were born to pray and save:
> Romantic Ireland's dead and gone,
> It's with O'Leary in the grave.[28]

came from a speech he had made in July 1913 with potential subscribers to Lane's gallery in mind. 'I described Ireland,' he wrote to Lady Gregory, 'if the present intellectual movement failed, as a little greasy huxtering nation groping for halfpence in a greasy till but did not add except in thought "by the light of a holy candle".'[29] Touched by Yeats's article and a speech he made, George Russell felt all his old friendship and affection surging up and wrote to tell Yeats so.[30] Their friendship was renewed.

ELEVEN

1913–1916

Yeats had lost interest in the idea of an Irish Order of Mysteries at the time of Maud Gonne's marriage but he continued to use symbolic meditation, striving to ascend spiritually and to create more order in his own life. He was still involved in the Stella Matutina, and was to take the grade of Theoricus Adeptus Minor 5=6 in 1912 and to be advanced in October 1914 to the degree of 6=5 in a new ritual which involved his lying down in the coffin in the vault of the Order and hearing the ringing of thirty-six bells. He may even have proceeded to the grade of 7=4; a copy of the ritual for that Degree was among his papers.

The occult symbolism, however, no longer supplied the dynamic he had previously drawn from it and in 1911 he turned to spiritualism with increasing intensity. He wanted evidence that the soul survives the body's death, that there is another world; also he hoped to get guidance about his own life. As usual he wanted to believe, but as usual he was sceptical. His desire for experiment was strong and had led to his leaving the Theosophists. Madame Blavatsky, incidentally, like MacGregor Mathers, had disapproved strongly of spiritualism, but now he found that Julia's circle, established in Cambridge House – the Wimbledon home of the journalist W. T. Stead – recorded séances systematically in some detail, with the time, the place and the date as well as a record of the séances themselves. Stead had set up Julia's Bureau in Mowbray House in London in April 1909 to further the exchange of information between the dead and the living, Julia being Julia A. Ames, an American woman whose communication with Stead continued well after her death and was known through her *Letters from Julia* to him which appeared in book form as *After Death* (1897). Unimpressed by a sitting he attended there in May 1909, in Boston he was impressed by a medium known as Mrs Chenowith or Mrs C., the names given to Mrs Minnie Meserve Sonle by J. H. Hyslop, then in control of the American Society for Psychical Research. Stimulated by her, he approached spiritualism with fresh curiosity and energy in 1911. No need to recite *Paradise Lost* in panic now; since he had gone to a séance in London with Constance Gore-Booth sometime before her marriage in 1900, he found he was no longer frightened by the 'influences'. Now he would climb to the top storey of some house in Holloway or Soho and, as he put it in *Autobiographies*, pay his shilling and wait among servant girls for 'the wisdom of some fat old medium'.[1] He tried out Mrs Thomson whose control, Nelly, lived in her stomach and felt like a wet chicken. Her advice to Yeats was to wear a black beard and a white robe and become a yogi priest.

He attended more séances at Cambridge House when Mrs Etta Wreidt, an American, was the medium; she first came to England at Stead's invitation in 1911. Mrs Wreidt did not go into trance; she had a small metal telescopic trumpet through which voices were heard, and she conversed with her many controls. The voices used a variety of languages according to those of the sitters; these included Arabic, Croatian, Gaelic, Hindustani, Norwegian and Welsh. On 9 May 1912 Yeats recorded that a loud voice from the tin trumpet which was standing on its broad end in the middle of the room claimed to have come for 'Mr Gates'. It said, 'I have been with you from childhood. We want to use your hand and brain.' The spirit announced himself as Leo Africanus the writer and explorer.[2] Yeats was sceptical, but he recorded attending many séances in May and June in some of which Leo was truculent: he resented Yeats offering to help him – it was the other way round.

More promising at the time was the automatic writing of Elizabeth Radcliffe, a well-bred girl whom he met in the spring of 1912 – probably through Olivia Shakespear's friend Mrs Eva Fowler, an American married to a British Army officer. Miss Radcliffe's automatic writing, which he witnessed at Mrs Fowler's house (Daisy Meadow, near Brasted in Kent) embraced several languages – she herself knew only French and some Italian – and the spirits of dead people used her hand to give facts which she could not have known; notably about a London policeman Thomas Emerson who had committed suicide in 1850, his death not being reported in the press at the time. Yeats made enquiries of Scotland Yard, via Gosse to Edward Marsh, then Churchill's private secretary, to find out about him. Very excited about this writing, he carried out various experiments from 1912 to 1914 to test its genuineness; he kept detailed notes, asking questions mentally to see if Miss Radcliffe could receive them by telepathy and answer them. He wrote an essay, 'Preliminary Examination of the Script of ER', finished in October 1913, which remained unpublished at Miss Radcliffe's request.[3] He decided that he had clear evidence that departed spirits could communicate through a living mind and was convinced that he had proof of spirits keeping their identities after death. Her automatic writing seems to have ended in 1914, but before this her script had been accurate in a prophetic reply to a question about a crisis in his life – a question he also put to Leo at a séance on 23 June without getting a satisfactory answer.

The crisis had arisen in his relationship with Mabel Dickinson. She had sent him a telegram when he was at Coole, announcing that she was pregnant; this turned out to be a false alarm but Yeats thought himself deceived, that an attempt was being made to force him into marriage by 'an unmarried woman past her first youth'. A stormy meeting at the Victoria and Albert Museum on 6 June 1913 led to a violent scene at parting, and then to a truce. But the experience alarmed not only Yeats but Lady Gregory, who thought marriage was the answer lest some similar crisis disturb the poet's peace in the future.

The poems he was writing in 1913 were obviously affected by the example of Synge's poems and plays. Synge had written to him on 7 September 1908 to say that, as there had been a false poetic diction,

if verse is to remain a living thing it must be occupied when it likes with the whole of [the] poet's life and experience as it was with Villon and Herrick and Burns . . .

Pound's wish that Yeats would make it new was another factor influencing the harsh if comic tone of these poems where heroic romance gave way to a coarsening of phraseology – far, far from that of what had become the poetic diction of the Celtic twilight. This is realistic poetry now, with its mauling and biting, its lice and blood, its rummaging of rags and hair for fleas, its hunkers and its skelping of a lout, all linked to beggars and hermits. And one of these beggars wants to

> '. . . get a comfortable wife and house
> To rid me of the devil in my shoes,'
> *Beggar to beggar cried, being frenzy-struck,*
> 'And the worse devil that is between my thighs.'[4]

That devil no doubt prompted the treatment of Mabel Dickinson in 'Presences' (a poem written in 1915), though it did not affect the subsequent treatment of Iseult Gonne and her mother:

> One is a harlot, and one a child
> That never looked upon man with desire,
> And one, it may be, a queen.[5]

Maud had appeared in 'The Grey Rock': 'a woman none could please' who had dreamed of men and women like the gods at Slievenamon:

> And after, when her blood ran wild,
> Had ravelled her own story out,
> And said, 'In two or in three years
> I needs must marry some poor lout,'
> And having said it, burst in tears.

This was a poem, originally a new poetical thought which came from a half-dream or dream in January 1910, written before 1913, in which Yeats addresses his old dead friends of the Rhymers' Club, offering them an old story he had remade of the love of Aoife for a human – who has been unfaithful to her in rejecting her magic gift of invisibility and thus dying at the battle of Clontarf in 1014 – whose ghost she seeks to harry. Maud is compared with Aoife; but Yeats has kept his faith, even though he has lost his popularity with the revolutionaries,

> . . . the loud host before the sea,
> That think sword-strokes were better meant
> Than lover's music.[6]

In November 1913 *Poetry* (Chicago) had offered a prize of $250 for the best poem which it had published in the year and awarded this to Yeats for 'The Grey Rock'. He accepted £10 from the £50 to get Sturge Moore to design him a book-plate and suggested the remaining £40 should be given to a young American writer to whom it would give practical help and encouragement. He wrote another letter to suggest the money be given to Ezra Pound, who had demonstrated his vigorous creative mind.

'The Grey Rock' had been written with the members of the Rhymers' Club – the companions of the Cheshire Cheese – in mind, and Yeats's associations with the Beardsley period were further aroused when he went to visit Beardsley's sister Mabel, who was dying in hospital. 'Upon a dying Lady', seven poems written between January 1912 and July 1914 but not published until 1917 as Mabel Beardsley lingered on till 1916, record her bravery in the face of death. Yeats, reporting to Lady Gregory, was impressed by her gaiety: 'I wonder who will introduce me in heaven. It should be my brother but then they might not appreciate the introduction. They might not have good taste.'[7] 'Her Courage' imagines her soul flying to 'the predestined dancing-place'.[8] Mortality was in the air. Dowden died in April and hopes of being appointed to his chair were renewed, but the Board of Trinity College appointed an orthodox academic, Dr Wilbraham Trench, later described by Yeats as 'a man of known sobriety of manner and of mind'.

Such a phrase could hardly be applied to George Moore, the first two volumes of whose fictionalised memoirs *Hail and Farewell, Ave* and *Salve*, Yeats had treated with contempt as journalism. He had appeared in Moore's *Evelyn Innes* (1898) as Ulick Dean – a remote, mysterious, tall, thin young man with eyes giving a sombre ecstatic character to his face: they were 'large, dark, deeply set, singularly shaped, and they seemed to smoulder like fires in caves, leaping and sinking out of the darkness'. This character Moore altered in his revision of 1901 into a semblance of George Russell, dropping the College of Adepts and Rosicrucians about which the Yeats-Ulick had spoken at length. In the fictionalised memoirs, however, Yeats received sharper treatment: in *Ave* he became a Finnish sorcerer, a subaltern soul, a literary fop . . . a man of excessive appearance . . . a long black cloak drooping from his shoulders, a soft black sombrero on his head, a voluminous black silk tie flowing from his collar, loose black trousers dragging untidily over his long, heavy feet and he was like 'a rook, a crane, a Bible reader,' or 'a great umbrella forgotten by some picnic party'. The picture at first seemed to Yeats, surprisingly, 'not at all malicious'; later he began to resent it. It was, of course, a depiction of Yeats in the nineties: the Celt. And Yeats was trying hard to get well away from the image of himself he had projected then, declaring in 'A Coat' how very different he had become:

> I made my song a coat
> Covered with embroideries
> Out of old mythologies
> From heel to throat;
> But the fools caught it,
> Wore it in the world's eyes
> As though they'd wrought it.
> Song, let them take it,
> For there's more enterprise
> In walking naked.[9]

This poem arose from dislike of the poets whom George Russell praised and encouraged; James Stephens and Padraic Colum, however, were now admitted to have talent, but 'Seamus O'Sullivan' (Dr James Starkey), another member of AE's circle, continued the Celtic strain to Yeats's dislike. But while Yeats was moved by Katharine Tynan's *Twenty-Five Years: Reminiscences* (1913) in which she quoted (without his permission) many of his youthful letters – for this was a very vivid picture of the Dublin of his youth – George Moore's final volume of *Hail and Farewell, Vale* (1914), portions of which were published in the *English Review*, enraged him.

Here Moore sneered at his unrequited love for Maud Gonne as 'the common mistake of a boy'. He suggested that Lady Gregory had in her youth been a Protestant proselytiser, in Irish terms 'a souper' – a passage he altered to something nearly as offensive on threat of legal action. And he described Yeats, on returning from his second visit to America, 'with a paunch, a huge stick and an immense fur overcoat', as attacking the middle classes instead of talking 'as he used to do about the old stories come down from generation to generation'. But why, he demanded maliciously, should he denounce the class to which he himself belonged essentially: 'one side excellent mercantile millers and shipowners and on the other a portrait painter of rare talent'? This was a basis from which to attack Yeats's tracing his ancestry back to the Butler family; he repeated a story of Yeats having said at Russell's house that if he had his rights he would be Duke of Ormonde, to which Russell had replied that in any case he was overlooking his father. It was true that Yeats had become interested in family history, about which

Lily had become knowledgeable; he had been seeking out his coat of arms for a book-plate in 1909.[10]

His immediate answer to Moore came in two poems, the Introductory Rhymes[11] and the Closing Rhyme[12] in *Responsibilities*; the latter, 'that second Moore poem', – originally entitled 'Notoriety (suggested by a recent magazine article)' – appealed to Ezra Pound with its echoes of Ben Jonson and its final image from Erasmus. Yeats is glad to think of companions, notably at Coole, beyond the dull ass's hoof, and to reflect that undreamt accidents have made him

> Notorious, till all my priceless things
> Are but a post the passing dogs defile.

Dogs and asses – almost goats and monkeys! But the Introductory Rhymes speak directly to the ancestors, the 'Old fathers' elevated by their individuality beyond limitations of class, rooted deep in the past. Since Moore had mentioned the mercantile background, Yeats took up the challenge with the old Dublin merchant who had the privilege of remission of taxes, the 'ten and four' (which should have been the 'six and ten', but that, he wrote in a note, calling it this time the 'eight and six', was a trick of memory). This merchant was either the poet's great-great-grandfather (which is most likely) or that particular Yeats father or grandfather, Jervis Yeats, the first Yeats to come to Ireland. Then came the scholarly old rector, his paternal great-grandfather John Yeats, given an apparent whiff of nationalism by being Robert Emmet's friend. There were soldier ancestors as well, a Butler or an Armstrong (placed on the wrong side at the Battle of the Boyne in the first version of the poem, history rather than memory at fault here). And there were two sailors – his maternal great-grandfather, the William Middleton who dived after his hat in Biscay Bay, and his silent and fierce old maternal grandfather William Pollexfen.   All of them are apostrophised, asked to pardon the poet – nearly forty-nine now – who, all because of a barren passion's sake, has no child:

> nothing but a book,
> Nothing but that to prove your blood and mine.

The poem set the tone for the volume. Yeats was now well able to express scorn and anger, using bitter political rhetoric, as well as writing compassionate love poems and the contrasting poems about hermits and beggars. He was beginning to feel middle-aged: he had

digestive disorders and Ezra Pound, sharing Stone Cottage with
him, taught him to fence. In conjunction with the Swedish exercises
he had learned from Mabel Dickinson, this improved his health.
Ezra proved a pleasant companion; he read to him in the evenings,
listened to talk of spiritualism and went with him in the company of
several other poets to visit Wilfrid Scawen Blunt on his seventy-fifth
birthday. There were roasted peacocks at their celebratory meal,
which may have led to Yeats's lines

> What's riches to him
> That has made a great peacock
> With the pride of his eye?[13]

These were lines Pound was to recall in Canto LXXXIII as he
remembered Yeats composing verses in the winter in Stone Cottage
(where he acted as Yeats's secretary in the winter of 1913; Yeats
stayed there with him and Dorothy in the early part of 1915 and
1916):

> ... I recalled the noise in the chimney
> as it were the wind in the chimney
>   but was in reality Uncle William
> downstairs composing
> that had made a great Peeeeacock
>   in the proide ov his oiye
>   had made a great peeeeeeecock in the ...
> made a great peacock
>   in the proide of his oyyee
>
> proide ov his oy-ee
> as indeed he had, and perdurable
>
> a great peacock aere perennius
>   or as in the advice to the young man to
> breed and get married (or not)
>   as you choose to regard it
>
> at Stone Cottage in Sussex by the waste moor
> (or whatever) and the holly bush
>   who would not eat ham for dinner
> because peasants eat ham for dinner
>   despite the excellent quality
> and the pleasure of having it hot

> well those days are gone forever
>> and the traveling rug with the coon-skin tabs
> and his hearing nearly all Wordsworth
>> for the sake of his conscience but
> preferring Ennemosor on Witches
>
> did we ever get to the end of Doughty:
>> The Dawn in Britain
>>> perhaps not
>> (Summons withdrawn, sir.)
> (bein' aliens in prohibited area)[14]

Yeats went to America, his third visit, on the last day of January 1914. He stayed in the Algonquin on his arrival, to be visited, unexpectedly, by Dolly Sloan, the wife of John Sloan, a Northern Irish painter living in New York who had developed a strong friendship with John Butler Yeats. She told Willie his father was ill and was short of money: she was instantly bowed out of his room with 'Good day, Madam', for this was a family problem and had nothing to do with her. Nonetheless, her impetuous approach may have led Yeats to be gentler than usual with his father (who had written ten years before that he wished Willie did not sometimes treat him as if he were a black beetle). He stayed three days at the Petipas house and was taught some dancing there; he told his father that he had used some of his ideas in a lecture in London. His son's lecture in New York gave John Butler Yeats great pleasure, as did the £40 that Willie gave him in response to the news that he wanted $250 towards what he owed the Petipas sisters. John Quinn wrote a letter to suggest bygones should be bygones. Their friendship was re-established, to the great delight of Yeats's father who had constantly tried to heal the breach between them, and now described them as like two brothers. Quinn began to help Yeats to deal with the perennial problem of his father's finances. Willie would meet any deficit incurred as far as the Petipas sisters were concerned, Quinn would deal with them so that the artist did not handle any large lump sums of money, and the money necessary would be provided by Yeats selling Quinn his manuscripts on a regular basis.

Before the plan went into operation, there was a hiccup when John Butler Yeats, ambling over Sixth Avenue, was severely incapacitated by a cart which knocked him down. Lady Gregory, in New York in 1915, joined with Quinn in finding out his 'true financial position' and paid the Petipas bill with funds sent by Willie and money Quinn paid him for the manuscript of *Reveries over Childhood and Youth*. On hearing his bill was paid the artist characteristically ordered dinners for his friends and had three scotches.[15] Grateful for his son's generosity, he wrote to tell him that he had begun work on the self-portrait, 'a great burden' lifted from his shoulders. The confidential financial arrangement worked out well and allowed Yeats to pay for his father's living expenses until he died. However, the old man constantly rejected all attempts to get him to return to Ireland. Ycats was given a fine send-off on April the first, Quinn having selected and had *Nine Poems* privately printed to be presented at a farewell dinner. The tour's lecture fees enabled Yeats to repay Lady Gregory the £500 he now owed her: it had been a surprise to find how much the debt was and he was very pleased he could repay it. (He had offered to do so when he was in funds after his first lecture tour in the United States in 1903–4, but she had refused to accept anything on the grounds that he hadn't then made enough money to feel independent.) He was returning in time for Pound's wedding to Olivia Shakespear's daughter Dorothy. In May Yeats was in France. He and Maud Gonne accompanied Everard Feilding to Mirebeau, to investigate a miracle of a bleeding oleograph there. The Abbé Vachère, who owned it, allowed them to dip their handkerchiefs in the blood. Quinn gave advice from America: if Feilding knows his business, he wrote, an examination by a competent chemist will show if it is human blood or fake blood. Feilding brought his sample to the Lister Institute and the report was that it was not human blood, though it did not say what in fact it was. Yeats wrote an unpublished essay about it, dictating this to Maud. He was still pondering his discovery that the reflective part of séances was less convincing than the matter-of-fact part. As usual his scepticism warred constantly with his conclusions, which included the view that minds of some kind could speak or write through a medium in languages unknown to those present; that these minds knew the private affairs of sitters, had strange power over matter and could create luminous substances; that though their capacity for abstract reflection was slight they did possess practical wisdom. On 20 July 1915 Leo Africanus spoke at a séance at Mrs Wreidt's, prophesying that Yeats would now have roses after a period of thistles; he was to have much recognition and had done much that would be famous. Two days later Miss Scatcherd, a medium and a friend of W. T.

Stead, produced automatic writing at Woburn Buildings and in this Yeats was asked by Leo to write him a letter, giving his doubts about spiritual things, and then to write a reply as if from Leo, who would control him in his reply.

What was significant was the idea that Leo was Yeats's opposite, very unscrupulous, whereas the poet was over-cautious and conscientious. These letters made up a forty-page essay in manuscript entitled 'Leo Africanus', unpublished until 1982.[16] Yeats did some research and gives details of his life. Johannes Leo (Al'Hassan Ibn Mahommed Al Wezaz Al Fasi) was a Moor born c. 1494 who travelled widely and wrote in Arabic a description of Africa. Captured by Venetian pirates in 1520, he was presented to Pope Leo X as a slave; the Pope converted him to Christianity and he was then given the Pope's names Johannes Leo; an Italian version of his book was issued when he was at Rome. He renounced Christianity on his return to Africa, where he died in 1552. Was Leo the ghost of the traveller, or was he something Yeats or forces outside Yeats created? He was not convinced, he wrote, that in the letter was one sentence that had come from beyond his own imagination, no thought that had not occurred to him 'in some form or other for many years passed; if you have influenced me it has been less to arrange my thoughts'.[17] He had been conscious of no sudden illumination. Despite his fervent wish to believe, he kept up a sceptical detachment. There is an illuminating entry dated 23 November 1915 in Yeats's journal, which records that Madame Du Pratz said that she would die – 'disappear' – between 2 and 5 December next; this occurred when Pound and Sturge Moore were present. Beneath this entry Yeats inserted a sentence dated 23 January 1917: 'Now Clare Du Pratz is in excellent health.'

In the autumn of 1914 Yeats wrote to his father about the war; he thought that England was paying the price for having despised intellect. The war, he supposed, would end in a draw with everyone too poor to fight for another hundred years 'though not too poor to spend what is left of their substance preparing for it'.[18] By St Stephen's Day 1914 he had finished his memoirs, 'less an objective history than a reverie', which first appeared in a Cuala Press edition in 1915. The Macmillan edition of 1916 was the first of Yeats's books to have a cover design by Sturge Moore. Their relationship was fruitful; both expressed their views of the other's work freely but with respect and admiration, Yeats ready to accept Sturge Moore's departures from fact or text because these were justified artistically. Malcolm Easton has pointed out the influence of Ricketts on the design of *Reveries over Childhood and Youth*, and both Moore and Yeats – introduced to each other by Binyon in 1898 – greatly respected Ricketts and his work. Yeats was nervous about how his father would react to the chapter on Dowden, whom he considered an image of Victorian ideals and made to stand as a kind of Aunt Sally representing the whole of Dublin's ascendancy establishment. Another letter defended his treatment of Dowden as not hostile, merely a little unsympathetic; he had to picture him as unreal in order to contrast him with the real image of O'Leary. The result was a decidedly one-sided and ungracious view of Dowden. Where the book is most skilful is in its treatment of place – the contrasts between Sligo and London, and later Dublin – and of time, which is treated subjectively, since in the thirty-three sections of the book the autobiographer selects, connects and presents critical moments in his unfolding life. It is linked closely to the effect upon him of his grandfather and his father, and the fact that Yeats's first book was published at the time of William Pollexfen's death has a symbolic touch characteristic of what the book does as a whole, giving us the middle-aged poet's present view of what was significant in his youthful past. And while he regarded it as 'a sort of apologia for the Yeats family' in a letter written to Lily Yeats four days after he finished it, he seems to have been unaware of, or uncaring about, the feelings of his father who, after he had read the book, thought it was as bad to be a poet's father as an intimate friend of George Moore.[19] Willie saw himself as a young man escaping from, breaking away from his father's influence only when he began to study psychical research and mystical philosophy.

There seems to have been a remission in his investigations; in June 1914 he had written to Quinn that having got his thoughts in order and on paper he was recovering from his obsession with the supernatural. Nonetheless, he can hardly have welcomed a letter from W. T. Horton on 25 July saying that he had been troubled about him since he was at Yeats's last Monday evening: 'All this spiritism and spiritistic investigation leads to nothing.' Horton argued that telepathy, the powers of the hidden self, suggestion, hypnotism and self-hypnotism accounted for nearly everything in the way of automatism:

To see you on the floor among those papers searching for an automatic script, where one man finds a misquotation among them, while round you sit your guests, shocked me for it stood out as a terrible symbol. I saw you as the man with the muck rake in 'The Pilgrim's Progress' while above you your Beloved held the dazzling crown of your own Poetic Genius. But you would not look up & you went on with your grovelling.[20]

There was to be another row with Horton, who was incensed with Yeats in 1917 for omitting from *Ideas of Good and Evil* (1903) the section which dealt with Horton's work when the essay appeared as the introduction to *A Book of Images* (1898). Perhaps Ezra Pound's praise, in a review, of *Responsibilities* as a gaunter poetry, with a hard light, a hardness of outline with nobility as the core of Yeats's work,[21] encouraged him to continue work on *The Player Queen*, which was bound up with his thoughts about the antithetical self. The early attempts lacked simplicity and life and he escaped from the problems that the play, become allegorical, had caused him since 1908, by turning it into a farce. He intended it to be played in front of screens devised by Gordon Craig. The play has some mocking comedy, the scenes with the drunken poet Septimus an anti-romantic statement that the time for tragedy has passed. It is, of course, closely linked to Yeats's ideas about the mask, which were shaped as a result of introspective musing about how to achieve self-possession, and blended with those ideas of opposition and contrast present throughout his life.

Various poems written about Maud Gonne in 1914 and 1915 deal with the past-in-the-present. Yeats sees her as equal to Pallas Athene in 'A Thought from Propertius', a poem perhaps suggested by Ezra Pound's enthusiasm for Propertius;[22] avuncularly he teases Ezra by listing his girl friends in 'His Phoenix', boasting that he himself had known a phoenix in his youth 'so let them have their day'.[23] In 'Her Praise' he will, in an Irish phrase of which he was fond, 'manage the talk' until her name comes round.[24] And though he defends himself by his possession of an analytic mind as opposed to Maud's 'natural force', his regret in 'The People' that had he not devoted himself to Ireland, he might have lived in Italy, is answered by her reproof that despite her treatment by the dishonest crowd she had never complained of the people; and he is abashed.[25] Memories of the spiritual marriages of 1898 and 1908 no doubt prompted 'A Deep-Sworn Vow':

> Others because you did not keep
> That deep-sworn vow have been friends of mine.[26]

In 'Memory', those other friends though possessed of charm or beauty cannot compete with her.[27] In 'Presences', while Mabel Dickinson is regarded as a harlot, Maud remains a queen.[28] In 'On Woman' he has to live like Solomon, 'That Sheba led a dance'. He can, however, implore God to grant him in another life

> To find what once I had
> And know what once I have known.[29]

In 'Broken Dreams', compensation for 'Vague memories, nothing but memories' is the certainty that 'in the grave all, all, shall be renewed'.[30]

There was not much comfort in other moods. In 'The Hawk' he laments his failure to win an argument;[31] in 'Lines written in Dejection' he records the vanishing of old imagery;[32] in 'The Dawn' he would now be ignorant as the dawn that had seen fantastic things, Emain marking out the site of her palace, at Armagh, which became the capital of Ulster, the Babylonian astronomers, the fall of Phaeton;[33] but in 'The Fisherman' he creates a dream of a wise and simple man (in contrast to the reality of Ireland, scornfully presented as beating down wise men and great art) to whom he will write

> one
> Poem maybe as cold
> And passionate as the dawn.[34]

By 5 October 1915, however, he had written 'Ego Dominus Tuus', dated December 1915 when published in 1917. This poem was later published in 1918 with two essays, *Anima Hominis* and *Anima Mundi*, originally called *An Alphabet* but finally given a Virgilian title, *Per Amica Silentia Lunae*. He was to write to his father in May 1917 that the essays were a kind of prose backing to his poetry; in June he wrote that his father's thought resembled that in *An Alphabet*, but his own was part of a religious system more or less logically worked out. The setting of it all in order had helped his verse, he added, had given him a new framework and new patterns:

One goes on year after year gradually getting the disorder of one's mind in order and this is the real impulse to create. Till one has expressed a thing it is like an untidy, unswept, undusted corner of a room. When it is expressed one feels cleaner, and more elegant, as it were, but less profound so I suppose something is lost in expression.[35]

The ideas in 'Ego Dominus Tuus' are put in the form of a dialogue between Hic and Ille, Hic and Willie as Dublin had it; possibly the quip originated with Ezra Pound. The essay *Anima Hominis* deals largely with the self and the anti-self; the germination of the idea can be traced very early in Yeats's development. An early poem 'Life' first published in *The Dublin University Review* and later in *The Wanderings of Oisin and Other Poems* (1889), for instance, stated a germ of it:

> The child pursuing lizards in the grass,
> The sage, who deep in central nature delves,
> The preacher watching for the evil hour to pass,
> All these are souls who fly from their dread selves.

In a poem of 1892, Fergus gives up administering his kingdom to learn the druid's wisdom.[36] In the nineties when Yeats was studying Blake and Boehme, he met the idea of contraries in their writings. Observation of living characters also went to the making of the idea, with the contradictions in William Morris stressed. He thought of Synge when ill, writing of romantic daredevils; of Landor, calm in his noble prose, raging in private passion; of Keats imagining delights to make up for his lack of luxury; and, above all, of Wilde, who had told the youthful Yeats that nothing interested him but the mask. And there was obviously a deep contradiction in his own character to be observed, understood and poetically exploited. This kind of contradiction had emerged clearly in the novel *John Sherman*, but in the part of the journal written when Yeats was forty-four he appears shy, yet eager to achieve command of himself. The artist, he writes, loses grasp of the world but, setting out to find knowledge, he will become the most romantic of characters, playing with masks. Many entries reflect the tension caused by a conflict between the established poet and the incipient man of action. He was searching for confidence. The mask seemed more than face to him and eventually, after much inner doubting, much puzzling over his inability to rationalise any experience directly, he decided that all happiness depends upon having the energy to assume the mask of another self:

Active virtue as distinguished from the passive acceptance of a current code is therefore theatrical, consciously dramatic, the wearing of a mask. It is the condition of arduous full life. One constantly notices in very active natures a tendency to pose, or a preoccupation with the effect they are producing if the pose has become a second self.[37]

Capacity to play a part had developed in Yeats from youth onwards. The artificial stride adopted as an art student in imitation of Hamlet was succeeded by other attitudes; at an early meeting he told Maud he wanted to emulate, indeed to become an Irish Victor Hugo; when collecting material for *Fairy and Folk Tales of the Irish Peasantry* and for *Representative Irish Tales* his mind had drifted to the idea of the mask, believing that every passionate man is linked to another age, historical or imaginary, 'where alone he finds images that rouse his energy'. The thought of *Per Amica Silentia Lunae* was coming into his head when he began *The Player Queen* in 1907. Every character became an example of the finding or not finding of what he called the antithetical self. By 1909 he thought that masks could protect him against irritation, and against logic.

Where did it all come from, this use of masks, of a cover for change in personality? Blake had appealed to him enormously because of his contraries, but the clash was basically genetic, as Willie's father asserted frequently in his own obsession with differences between the Yeatses and Pollexfens. The first, he wrote to Lollie in 1911, would impel you to like your fellow creatures and live in gay harmony with them. The other impels you to dislike them and get into discomfortable relations with them. To Lily he wrote in 1916 – after his son had unexpectedly sent him a cheque via John Quinn – that

It may be endlessly debated whether Willie is a Pollexfen or a Yeats. The fact is he is both, one side of him not one bit like a Pollexfen and another side not a bit like a Yeats. It was like a Yeats to send this money and make no fuss about it. It was like a Pollexfen to have it to send.[38]

Contemplation of opposites led to some fine and memorable phrases in Yeats's prose, such as 'The poet finds and makes his mask in disappointment, the hero in defeat.' There is, too, this well-known passage:

We make out of the quarrel with others, rhetoric, but out of the quarrel with ourselves, poetry. Unlike the rhetoricians, who get a confident voice

from remembering the crowd they have won or may win, we sing amid an
uncertainty; and, smitten even in the presence of the most high beauty by
the knowledge of our solitude, our rhythm shudders.[39]

Poets are not sentimentalists, he declared roundly; the sentimentalists are

. . . practical men who believe in money, in position, in a marriage bell,
and whose understanding of happiness is to be so busy whether at work or
at play that all is forgotten but the momentary aim. They find their pleasure
in a cup that is filled from Lethe's wharf, and for the awakening, for the
vision, for the revelation of reality, tradition offers us a different word –
ecstasy.[40]

The essays gain by the infusion of the poet's personal life. In
lecturing on 'Friends of my Youth' on 9 March 1910 he said he
had no sympathy with the mid-Victorian thought, supported by
Tennyson, that a poet's life concerned nobody but himself. His life
was an experiment in living; those that come after, he affirmed, have
a right to know it. The lyric poet's life should be known, so that his
poetry is understood not as a rootless flower but as the speech of a
man.[41] Thus in *Per Amica Silentia Lunae* we have Yeats returning
home at night and going over all he has earlier said, in gloom and
disappointment, having 'overstated everything from a desire to vex
or startle, from hostility that is but fear',[42] or else with thoughts that
have been drowned by an undisciplined sympathy.

There is the account of his vision in Tulira Castle of the woman
shooting an arrow into the sky. There is an echo of his reading
Wordsworth, of whose intellect he had a poor opinion, describing
him as 'withering into eighty years, honoured and empty witted'.
There are accounts of how he used evocation, given sanction by a
reference to Goethe. Images should, he thought, be allowed to form
with all their associations before one criticises; being critical too
soon means that they don't form at all. Suspending will and intellect
would bring up from the subconscious anything of which you already
possess a fragment, and for a time he elaborated 'a symbolism of
natural objects' to give himself dreams or visions during sleep. The
exaltations and messages that came 'from bits of hawthorn or some
other plant' seemed the happiest and wisest moments of his life. He
came to believe in a great Memory passing before the mind's eye
'that one was to discover presently in some book one had never
read'. In the essays he discussed his current interests – in Dante,

in Henry More, in Balzac, in Swedenborg, in Stanislas de Guaita; and he introduced his readers to the idea of the Daimon. At this stage he asserted that spiritualists – and Plutarch – had it that a strange living man may win for Daimon an illustrious dead man; to which he added the thought that the Daimon comes not as like to like but seeking its own opposite. These ideas about the Daimon were not completely clear in his mind at this stage; the essays of *Per Amica Silentia Lunae* have a reverie-like quality about them and in their affirmations they are not unlike his father's generalising ideas. Yet he undercuts these affirmations with questions, so that he often leaves his options open.

Yeats's attitude to the war was made clear in 'A reason for keeping silent' which he contributed to Edith Wharton's *The Book of the Homeless* (1916). Later it was entitled 'On being asked for a War Poem':

> We have no gift to set a statesman right;
> He has had enough of meddling who can please
> A young girl in the indolence of her youth,
> Or an old man upon a winter's night.[43]

It was the only thing, he told Henry James earlier, that he had written or would write about the war.[44] He would keep, he added, the neighbourhood of the seven sleepers of Ephesus till the bloody frivolity was over. When supporting Joyce – in penury with his family in Zurich after leaving Trieste – for a grant from the Royal Literary Fund, he wrote to Gosse that it had never occurred to him that it was necessary to express sympathy with the 'cause of the Allies'. He would himself wish them victory; and Joyce, he thought, disliked politics and was probably trying to become absorbed in some piece of work till the evil hour had passed. Joyce, whose genius Yeats always praised, was granted £75.

They had first met in 1902. Joyce, opposed to the Literary Renaissance, which he was later to mock in *A Portrait of the Artist as a Young Man*, was a man of the city at whom Yeats directed his praise of the country.

'... The folk life, the country life, is nature with her abundance, but the art life, the town life, is the spirit which is sterile if it is not married to nature. The whole ugliness of the modern world has come from the spread of the towns and their ways of thought, and to bring back beauty we must marry the spirit and nature again. When the idea which comes from individual life marries the image that is born of the people, one gets great art, the art of Homer, and of Shakespeare, and of Chartres Cathedral.'

I looked at my young man. I thought, 'I have conquered him now,' but I was quite wrong. He merely said, 'Generalizations aren't made by poets; they are made by men of letters. They are no use.'

Presently he got up to go, and, as he was going out, he said, 'I am twenty. How old are you?' I told him, but I am afraid I said I was a year younger than I am. He said with a sigh, 'I thought as much. I have met you too late. You are too old.'

That was written as part of a potential Introduction for *Ideas of Good and Evil*. Did Joyce say 'too old for me to help you?' If he did, Yeats would probably have put his bad manners down to his background. When Joyce first went to Paris, Yeats was instructed by Lady Gregory to write and ask him to breakfast the morning he arrived in London 'if you can get up early enough'; he was to 'feed him and take care of him and give him dinner at Victoria before he goes, and help him on his way'. On the whole Joyce did not forgive those who helped him, though he did later attack his own attitude to Lady Gregory in *Ulysses*. The Yeats family – father, Lily and the poet – dispassionately praised his work in their different ways. Joyce surpassed any contemporary novelist in intensity, thought the poet, who later found in him an 'Irish cruelty and also our kind of strength'.[45]

In late 1915 he took up *The Player Queen* again. Obviously he wanted to write a full-length play, a tragedy, but so far he seemed to himself to have wasted the best writing of several years on it without success. Now, however, with his ideas on the self and anti-self clearer in his mind from his having formulated them in *Per Amica Silentia Lunae*, he took the bold step of turning the play into 'a wild comedy, almost a farce, with a tragic background – a story of a fantastic woman'. He had torn up hundreds of pages in his attempt to escape from allegory, he wrote; but over 1,100 folio pages remain – there were seventeen drafts in the early stages of the play's history; finally thirty-one were written before he completed the play in May 1917. (It was to be produced by the Stage Society in London in May 1919, by the Abbey in the following December.) It is most effective on the stage, and Septimus, a parody of the Romantic Poet, with his romantic self-pity and grandiose rhetoric, an impressive creation; his drunk scene shows Yeats a master of farce. The dance with the players as animals conveys Yeats's sense of grotesquerie admirably.

Out of the winters spent at Stone Cottage had come an exciting new stimulus to playwriting: the Nōh drama of Japan. While living there with Yeats Pound was himself working on the papers of Ernest Fenollosa, work which resulted in *The Classic Nōh Theatre of Japan* (1916); and Yeats believed that he had at last found a dramatic form that suited him, 'distinguished, indirect and symbolic, and having no need of mob or Press to pay its way – an aristocratic form'.[46] In the winter of 1916 he dictated *At the Hawk's Well* to Pound; this was the first of *Four Plays for Dancers*, those written subsequently being *The Only Jealousy of Emer*, *The Dreaming of the Bones* and *Calvary*. A Japanese dancer, Michio Ito, was in London learning classical and modern European dancing; he studied the movements of birds and animals in the London Zoo and, himself observed by Yeats, observed the hawks in particular; Yeats praised his genius of movement. But Ito knew very little about the Nōh and had been bored by it in Japan despite his uncle's enthusiasm for this esoteric art form.[47] He helped, however, by reading about its staging, and Edmund Dulac designed the masks and costumes for the play. *At the Hawk's Well* was performed twice in London in April 1916 – in Lady Cunard's drawing room, and two days later in Lady Islington's, Queen Alexandra being present – though as she was deaf it is doubtful what she made of it.

Here, then, was a select audience for an 'unpopular' drama founded upon the aristocratic theatre of Japan. Yeats described what seemed to him important in that tradition in his Introduction to Pound's *Certain Noble Plays of Japan*. He delighted in getting rid of scenery, substituting three performers who describe landscape or event, accompanying themselves with drum and gong and zither. And there was sanction for the use of masks. No actor's facial expression would get in the way of the poetry, and a stronger feeling for beautiful, appropriate language was required than in conventional, realistic European drama. Gesture must not rival speech, acting was to be simplified, scenery and costume to con-tribute to the whole effect. Yeats's characters, however, do not change in these plays; the main character fails to get what he or she wants and that is the end of it. The dancing sometimes fails to blend into the total action of the play and the chorus, unlike that of the Nōh, is on stage but not involved in the action, acting as a link between audience and stage, putting Yeats's views. He rejoiced in his freedom from 'the stupidity of an ordinary audience', knowing that the intensely poetic plays he was writing could hardly succeed in contemporary civilisation. As ever, he yearned for a society where all classes would share in a half-mythological half-philosophical folk-belief.

The war in which contemporary civilisation was doing its best to destroy itself impinged directly on the lives of Lady Gregory and Yeats after Sir Hugh Lane, having given his lifebelt to a woman passenger, went down on the *Lusitania* which was torpedoed by a U-boat in the Atlantic in May 1915. He left behind his collection of pictures, in the National Gallery in London, having bequeathed them to that Gallery in a new will he made in 1913, in 'momentary irritation' after the plans for a gallery in Dublin had been rejected amid bitter press comment. He subsequently became Director of the National Gallery in Dublin and in February 1915 wrote a codicil to his will, leaving the French pictures to the Municipal Gallery in Dublin (to which he had left them before writing his 1913 will). This codicil was not witnessed, and in 1918 the Trustees of the National Gallery in London made it clear they intended to stand on their legal right to retain the pictures. From 1916 on Lady Gregory fought a strong campaign throughout the rest of her life to get the pictures back to Dublin, and Yeats joined in with letters to the press and many meetings with political leaders in Ireland and England. The letter he wrote to the *Observer* (21 January 1917) shows his capacity to marshal his arguments clearly and cogently. Something of the great amount of frustration, of time and energy consumed in trying to carry out Lane's wishes about the disposition of his pictures can be seen in the frequent entries on the matter in Lady Gregory's *Journals*. In 1959 an agreement was eventually reached, sharing the pictures on a loan basis between London and Dublin.

Yeats's birthplace, 1 George's Ville, Sandymount Avenue, Dublin. Originally 3 Sandymount Avenue, it was later renumbered as 5 Sandymount Avenue. Photograph by A. Norman Jeffares, 1984.

W. B. Yeats when staying with his Pollexfen grandparents at their house, Merville, Sligo. Courtesy of Colin Smythe Ltd.

John O'Leary, oil on canvas by John Butler Yeats. W. B. Yeats described him as 'the handsomest old man I had ever seen'. Courtesy of the National Gallery of Ireland, Dublin.

Maud Gonne, a studio photograph by Chancellor, Dublin, c. 1889. Recalling their meeting that year, Yeats wrote, 'I had never thought to see in a living woman so great beauty.'

Olivia Shakespear, a photograph in the
Literary Yearbook (1897). In 'After Long
Silence', Yeats wrote:
                                    young
We loved each other and were ignorant.

Woburn
Buildings, off
Russell Square.
Number 18
(now Number 5,
Woburn Walk)
was Yeats's
London
residence from
1895 to 1919.
He rented the
first floor
initially, then the
one above as
well. Courtesy
of the Editors,
Yeats Annual.

W. B. Yeats in 1898,
by John Butler Yeats.
Pencil and wash with
white highlights on
paper. Courtesy of
the National Gallery
of Ireland, Dublin.

Florence Farr
(Mrs Edward Emery)
as a young woman.
Yeats first met her in 1894.

W. B. Yeats, a photograph by
G. C. Beresford. Courtesy of
Royal Holloway and New
Bedford College, University
of London.

Iseult Gonne, an undated oil
painting by AE (George Russell).
Courtesy of the National Gallery
of Ireland, Dublin and Colin
Smythe Ltd.

Lady Gregory, a photograph taken *c.*1912. Courtesy of Colin Smythe Ltd.

John Butler Yeats, self-portrait in old age. Charcoal and pencil on paper. Courtesy of the National Gallery of Ireland, Dublin.

W. B. Yeats.
Lithograph by
Ivan Opffer. On
the occasion of
Yeats's visit to
Stockholm to
receive the
Nobel Prize for
Literature in
1923. Courtesy
of the Editors,
Yeats Annual.

Yeats's last Irish
residence,
Riversdale,
Rathfarnham,
Co. Dublin.
Sketched in ink
by A. Norman
Jeffares in 1947
before the house
lost its entrance
porch; it was
later surrounded
by suburbia.

Michael and Anne Yeats at the Edmund Dulac memorial plaque to their father at Roquebrune Cemetery. They were attending the Princess Grace Memorial Library conference on 'Yeats the European' at Monaco, May 1987. Courtesy of the Editors, *Yeats Annual*.

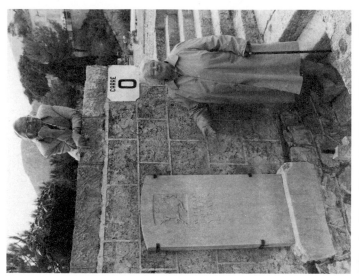

W. B. Yeats at Menton, 1938. A photograph by Nora Shackleton Heald, published in the *London Mercury*, March 1939.

TWELVE

1916–1917

Yeats was welcome in the English Establishment, so much so that Lady Cunard was able to tell him that he was to be offered a knighthood. He wrote to Lily about it, telling her that he had said, 'as I grow older I become more conservative and I do not know whether that is because my thoughts are deeper or my blood more chill, but I do not wish anyone to say of me "only for a ribbon he left us".'[1] But he had been left behind by the movement of Irish nationalism, a long way behind. Home Rule had been put off for the duration of the war; most Irishmen supported England in the war, recruiting was encouraged by John Redmond, leader of the Irish Party: about a hundred thousand Irishmen were serving in the British forces, thousands of them dying in France and elsewhere, notably in Gallipoli where the Dublin Fusiliers were slaughtered. Yeats did not know how serious the younger generation of revolutionaries were in their planning, but then in this he was like most of Ireland.

The Irish Republic was proclaimed on Easter Monday; the centre of Dublin was occupied by the Republicans, the Irish Volunteers of the IRB and members of the Citizen Army, probably about seven hundred in all. They held out from 24 to 29 April, during which time much of the centre of the city had been shelled and burnt out. Fifteen of the leaders were executed by firing-squad after courts-martial; they included Patrick Pearse, poet and schoolmaster, Thomas MacDonagh, critic and university lecturer, James Connolly, the labour leader, and John MacBride, Maud Gonne's estranged husband. Constance Markiewicz (Constance Gore-Booth had married Casimir Markiewicz, a Polish Count and landowner in the Ukraine, whom she met in Paris when they were both art students) was condemned to death but reprieved. Sir Roger Casement, who returned to Ireland in a German submarine, was arrested in the south-west and hanged in Pentonville Gaol on 3 August.

The executions turned the leaders into martyrs and made the defeat of the Easter Rising into a blood sacrifice that altered everything. Yeats, staying with William Rothenstein and his wife in Gloucester, heard the news with horror; innocent patriotic theorists, he thought, had devoted themselves to an abstract idea of sacrifice, the cult of blood, the belief that the nation needed to be redeemed by martyrdom, put forward by Pearse; and they were ready to die for their beliefs, knowing they were doomed. To Lady Gregory he wrote on 11 May that the Dublin tragedy was 'a great sorrow and anxiety'; he was trying to write a poem on the men executed – 'terrible beauty has been born again'. If the English Conservative Party had declared the Home Rule Bill would stand, he continued, there would have been no rebellion. He had no idea a public event could so move him and he was despondent about the future – the work of years overturned, the bringing together of classes and the freeing of Irish writing and criticism from politics.[2] He recorded his reactions in 'Easter 1916', privately printed in an edition of 25 copies in 1917 and then published in 1920. The poem retracts the contempt of 'September 1913', and sees what he had come to consider comedy

> All changed, changed utterly:
> A terrible beauty is born[3]

He sets the scene, economically, meeting the revolutionaries in the street, expressing his mocking scepticism afterwards at his club – he was now a member of the Stephen's Green Club – before naming some of the leaders and glossing them with compressed descriptions, all of them changed, transformed. Their devotion to a political cause had enchanted their hearts into stone. Was their death needless, he asks, seeing that England may keep faith over the Home Rule Bill. They have, however, changed utterly; they have become part of the long tradition of Ireland fighting to free itself of English rule, something deftly suggested by the line 'wherever green is worn', an echo of 'The Wearing of the Green' and 'Green on my Cape', songs inspired by the 1798 Revolution, 'A terrible beauty is born'. He returned to the effect of the rising in 1917 in two poems: 'Sixteen Dead Men'[4] linking the leaders more directly with leaders in the past, Lord Edward Fitzgerald and Wolfe Tone (against whom contemporary Ireland had been measured and found wanting in 'September 1913'), and 'The Rose Tree',[5] an echo of a ballad, 'Ireland's Liberty Tree', blended with Pearse's belief that bloodshed, 'cleansing and sanctifying', would redeem Ireland from what he saw as a position of slavery.

Two other poems, written in 1918 and 1919 respectively, reflect harsh views of Irish political life. 'The Leaders of the Crowd' contrasts the press, 'the abounding gutter', with Hippocrene, the fountain of the Muses in Helicon;[6] it was inspired by dislike of Arthur Griffith and the Sinn Fein press, Yeats sharply observing that political movements were held together more by what they hated than by what they loved. 'On a Political Prisoner' contrasts the youthful Constance Gore-Booth – whose assurance and arrogance he had admired, 'The beauty of her countryside / With all youth's lonely wildness stirred' – and what she, Constance Markiewicz, now in Holloway Gaol for the second time, had become now that

> A grey gull lost its fear and flew
> Down to her cell and there alit,
> And there endured her fingers' touch
> And from her fingers ate its bit.[7]

After Yeats reached his truce with Mabel Dickinson both Mrs Shakespear and Lady Gregory thought that he should marry – something his father and his sisters longed for, and to which he was not averse himself. Lady Gregory actively pursued the idea, bringing several suitable young women to visit him at Stone Cottage: Sloane Rangers of the time, they were good-looking, well-connected, well-to-do. He became friendly with one of them, but the possibility of marriage was something he discussed only with Georgie Hyde Lees. They had a lot in common. She was studying astrology, which he later described to her mother, Nelly Tucker, as 'a very flirtatious business'. Like many of his friends, she shared his interest in tarot cards. She was reading philosophy. She was attending séances with him and she was admitted – probably in 1914, with Yeats as sponsor – to the Stella Matutina section of the Golden Dawn, her motto being NEMO. Their friendship developed, and by November 1915 Mrs Tucker feared Yeats might propose to her daughter, who became involved in war work as a hospital cook and nursing assistant. She had confided to her cousin Grace that she intended to marry the poet. But with the execution of John MacBride, Maud had become a widow and matters changed.

Iseult Gonne came to London with messages from her mother. Maud, whose first reaction to the Easter Rising had been that tragic dignity had returned to Ireland, was sleeping badly, Iseult said; she was very sad and lonely. Yeats introduced Iseult to various fashionable friends; he wrote to Lady Gregory that Iseult was very distinguished, beautifully dressed, self-possessed. He thought that if he had had a normal life he might have had a daughter of her age.

He returned to France with her and stayed at Colleville: he proposed to Maud Gonne on 1 July, Lady Gregory having previously warned him that if she married him Maud would have to give up political life. In this she was thinking not only of the effect of such a marriage on him but on the Abbey, now dependent on donations from wealthy Irish Unionists who would not be so generous if her fellow-Director were to marry such a well-known revolutionary – one who was now deeply involved in moves to obtain amnesty for Irish political prisoners. But Yeats received the usual answer to his proposal from Maud, that his friendship was what she wanted. She was surprised when he asked her a week later if she would object if he were to propose to Iseult, replying that Iseult would not take him seriously (and Iseult told me she had proposed to him seven years before, when she was fifteen, to be informed there was too much Mars in her horoscope). She did, however, greatly enjoy flirting with her mother's rejected admirer during July and August; she read to him the young French Catholic poets, Claudel, Jammes and Péguy; he talked a great deal to her and impressed her by his agility and ease as a swimmer, his ability to 'swim for ages under water and reappear after a great distance'.

He had stayed on longer than he had intended, he wrote to Lady Gregory in August; he thought under the circumstances she would forgive him. Perhaps surprisingly, she thought Iseult sufficiently malleable to make him a wife. She would certainly be less difficult than Maud.

He returned to London for the winter, finished *Per Amica Silentia Lunae* – which he dedicated to Iseult – and began *The Dreaming of the Bones*, the most coherent of his *Plays for Dancers*. The first play had echoed Nōh in its use of folk tales and mythology: five centuries earlier Ze-Ami, the authority on Nōh, had used historical events, and figures as well from the rise and fall of the Heike family; now Yeats was to use contemporary events linked to the historical past.

He liked the Nōh convention of a Traveller, the *Waki*, asking his way with many questions. In *The Dreaming of the Bones*, the equivalent to the *Waki* of the Nōh is a young revolutionary who has fought in 1916 and is fleeing from Dublin to the west. He is the Traveller who can free from their curse the troubled, wandering spirits – the ghosts of Dermot MacMorrough, who had betrayed his country by inviting the Normans to Ireland in the twelfth century, and Devorgilla of Meath, with whom he had an adulterous relationship. The young man, representing Ireland, refuses to forgive them since their sclf-interested passion brought about seven centuries of alien rule in Ireland. The play shows, Yeats wrote to Stephen Gwynn in October 1918, that England once treated Ireland as Germany treated Belgium. Friends to whom he read the play in Gogarty's house in Dublin thought it 'marvellous'. He thought himself that it was 'only too powerful politically'. It was not published till 1919, not staged till 1931. He set the play in the stony area near the ruined Cistercian Abbey of Corcomroe in County Clare, linking not only the ghost lovers in the Nōh play *Nishikigi* but the Japanese feeling for place,[8] which reminded him of the awe Irish-speaking country people showed when some old building or holy well was mentioned. After all, he had originally wanted and 'had to put away an ambition to bring again to certain places their old sanctity or romance'.

There was a certain place which particularly appealed to him through its beauty and its link with oral tradition. This was the castle built, probably in the fourteenth century, by the de Burgo family at Ballylee, not far from Coole. He had described it in an essay of 1899 in which he told how a local beauty, Mary Hynes, was celebrated in a song made by Antony Raftery, the blind Irish poet, which was sung to him by an old woman who remembered both Mary Hynes and Raftery.[9] Robert Gregory urged Yeats to buy the castle, since 1783 part of the Gregory Estate: this was being split up into smaller holdings by the Congested Districts Board at the time and so Yeats began negotiations with them. The Chief Land Inspector reported that as the floors of the castle were gone and only a small proportion of the roof remained, its value as a residence was 'sentimental and therefore problematical'. Yeats wrote excitedly to Olivia Shakespear in November 1916, delighting in the fact that there was a sound cottage at the foot of the castle in which he could live, before the castle was roofed. 'If I get it,' he added, 'I shall plant fruit trees as soon as possible for the sake of the blossoms and because it will make me popular with the little boys who will eat my apples in the early mornings.'[10] He did get it, for £35, and was told he could take possession in April 1917.[11]

He wrote to his father in May from Coole Park to tell him the castle was a beautiful place; there were trout in the river under the window, and it would be an economy as he would need fewer rooms in London. (He had taken over the floor below his rooms in Woburn Buildings the year before.) John Butler Yeats was delighted:

It is all a symbol of the poetical life, a thirst for the soil, and you have it to the centre of the earth. It is in Ireland, another thirst instinctive, and therefore of the poet. And it is old, therefore again a poet's desire.

He liked the fact that it was reached by an old bridge, but reserved his real pleasure for a former landlord's exclamation: 'Hearing about this land purchase has been to me a *perfect holiday*. A leasehold is nothing – but a fee simple!'[12]

Olivia Shakespear was told of his plans. The architect, Professor William A. Scott, had been down from Dublin; the cottage could be repaired, extended and made comfortable for £200, while the castle could be restored at leisure, 'a couple of great rooms and for very little money'. Yeats was delighted at the prospect of living in the country.

Back he went to London from Coole to finish *The Dreaming of the Bones*, next to Dublin where Albert Power made a bust of him and then to Coole again, to start the builders off – a local builder, Raftery, having submitted an acceptable estimate. Yeats wrote to his father that he would make enough money to roof the castle by giving lectures and in August he was in Normandy preparing them. The household at Colleville now boasted in addition to the usual caged birds a mischievous monkey, a hysterical parrot which the monkey tried to pluck, a goat, seven rabbits, two dogs and the black Persian cat Minnaloushe, 'important and wise'. He went for long walks with Iseult, who was affectionate but seemed not to have the impulse to marry; he did not think she would change her mind. He told Maud, determined to go back to Ireland but refused permission to do so by the British authorities, that Iseult would be better in London than in Dublin, which provoked an angry outburst. She was in 'a joyous and self-forgetting condition of political hate' such as he had never encountered.[13] He felt restless in Normandy; he wanted to make some settlement in his life and had a mass of work to do in

Dublin and London. Iseult had always been something of a daughter
to him, he wrote to Lady Gregory, so he was less upset than he
might have been at her attitude.

Having obtained passports for the Gonne family he accompanied
the ménage, birds and animals and all, to London in mid-September.
On the journey Iseult was very depressed. Always moody, she went
off to weep by herself at Le Havre, crying because she was ashamed
at being selfish in not wanting him to marry and so break her
friendship with him. ('I need hardly say,' his letter to Lady Gregory
recounting these events went on, 'she had said nothing to me of
"not wanting".')[14] On the boat he told her that she must give him a
definite answer within a week; they would meet at a certain ABC
tea-shop in London. It was a last throw and he found the situation
a great strain. If she would not marry him, he told her, someone
else would – a friend of his who was 'strikingly beautiful in a barbaric
way'.[15] At Southampton the boat train was held up while Maud and
Iseult were searched as possible spies; on arrival in London they
were forbidden, under the Defence of the Realm Act, to land in
Ireland.

Iseult refused him. Thinking that she was going to Dublin, he
had written to Mrs Tucker from France and was invited to visit her
and Georgie. He was 'rather in a whirlpool', life was 'a good deal
at white heat' as he wrote to Lady Gregory, who received a succession
of extremely frank letters about the situation, seeking her counsel.
He decided that he would ask Georgie Hyde Lees to marry him –
something of which Olivia Shakespear warmly approved, though
she does not seem to have been taken into his confidence at this
stage. He wrote to Lady Gregory: 'Perhaps she is tired of the idea.
I shall however make it clear that I will still be friend and guardian
to Iseult.'[16]

His friend Denison Ross found a post for Iseult at the School of
Oriental Languages in London – Maud, who drew well, having
decided to take a flat in Chelsea for six months and study design.
When this assistant librarianship for Iseult was settled, Yeats wept
from happiness. However, both mother and daughter were a little
indignant with him over what they considered his prosaic marriage
plans. He wrote to the long-suffering Lady Gregory that it might
all seem cold and calculating, but he had come to his decision after
prayer and sleepless nights. Iseult seemed content; he had told her
he would not let anything break their friendship. But though he had

a great longing for order it was not to be so easily achieved, for Mrs Tucker was opposed to the marriage and since she knew Yeats had gone to Coole to get advice, she wrote to enlist Lady Gregory's help in breaking off what she regarded as an entirely undesirable engagement. The advice was, he wrote to Georgie Hyde Lees an hour after he had arrived at Coole, that they should get married as soon as possible, that it was the best thing that could have befallen him. Lady Gregory wrote what must have been a skilful and persuasive letter to Mrs Tucker to reassure her, and she agreed to the marriage. Then Yeats became emotionally disturbed, not least at some of what Lady Gregory must have put pretty plainly to him. He was particularly hurt by her remarking on his being married in the clothes he bought to court Iseult in. However, he was convinced that he would make Georgie happy and that in seeking to do this he would make himself happy also. And he very rightly added that she had great nobility of feeling. They were married on 20 October 1917 at the Harrow Road register office, with Ezra Pound as best man. His marriage transformed his life.

THIRTEEN

1917–1919

On 24 October, four days after his own marriage, Yeats – more miserable than he ever remembered being since Maud Gonne's marriage in 1903 – wrote a poem initially entitled 'The Lover Speaks'; it was about Iseult:

> A strange thing surely that my Heart, when love had come unsought
> Upon the Norman upland or in that poplar shade,
> Should find no burden but itself and yet should be worn out.
> It could not bear that burden and therefore it went mad.
>
> The south wind brought it longing, and the east wind despair,
> The west wind made it pitiful, and the north wind afraid.
> It feared to give its love a hurt with all the tempest there;
> It feared the hurt that she could give and therefore it went mad.
>
> I can exchange opinion with any neighbouring mind,
> I have as healthy flesh and blood as any rhymer's had,
> But O! my Heart could bear no more when the upland caught the wind;
> I ran, I ran, from my love's side because my Heart went mad.[1]

The misery produced another poem, 'The Heart Replies', written on 27 October; this one reflects the fact that he is married:

> The Heart behind its rib laughed out. 'You have called me mad,' it said,
> 'Because I made you turn away and run from that young child;
> How could she mate with fifty years that was so wildly bred?
> Let the cage bird and the cage bird mate and the wild bird mate in the wild.'
>
> 'You but imagine lies all day, O murderer,'
> I replied. 'And all those lies have but one end, poor wretches to betray;

I did not find in any cage the woman at my side.
O but her heart would break to learn my thoughts are far away.'

'Speak all your mind,' my Heart sang out, 'speak all your mind; who
   cares,
Now that your tongue cannot persuade the child till she mistake
Her childish gratitude for love and match your fifty years?
O let her choose a young man now and all for his wild sake.'[2]

Just before his marriage Yeats had begun to believe that he had
acted not, as he had thought, more for Iseult's sake than for his
own, but because his mind was 'unhinged' from strain. On 29
October he wrote to Lady Gregory from Ashdown Forest Hotel,
where he and his wife were staying on their honeymoon, that two
days before he had been in great gloom but the last two days he and
his wife – whom he called George, the name she was generally to
go by later – had been very happy. He hoped and believed she had
known nothing of his misery (which, of course, she had) and he
thought there had been something very like a miraculous
intervention:

I was saying to myself, 'I have betrayed three people;' then I thought, 'I
have lived all through this before.' Then George spoke of the sensation of
having lived through something before (she knew nothing of my thought).
Then she said she felt that something was to be written through her. She
got a piece of paper, and talking to me all the while so that her thoughts
would not affect what she wrote, wrote these words (which she did not
understand), 'with the bird' (Iseult) 'all is well at heart. Your action was
right for both but in London you mistook its meaning.'[3]

The strange thing was, he continued, that within half an hour after
the writing of the message his rheumatic pains, neuralgia and fatigue
had gone; he was extremely happy, and that sense of happiness had
lasted ever since. He should have said that when George had written
the sentence he asked mentally 'When shall I have peace of mind?'
and her hand wrote 'You will neither regret nor repine,' and he
thought he never would again.

Yeats was enormously excited by this experience. Of course, the
phenomenon of automatic writing was not new to him: had not
messages come to MacGregor Mathers through his wife Moina's
writing, and similarly to Dr Felkin through his wife? He knew of
others, too, who had had similar experiences: Lady Edith Lyttleton
and Mrs Travers-Smith (Edward Dowden's daughter Hester).

Moreover there was his own recent investigation of the automatic writing of Elizabeth Radcliffe, in the process of which he had developed a method of questioning. After a few days he applied this to his wife's automatic writing. She had originally attempted it as a means of diverting her husband's attention from his unhappiness, his worrying over 'personal' matters, mainly his relationships with the women in his life, and particularly with Iseult. But as he was to record in *A Packet for Ezra Pound*, written in 1928, his wife's attempt at automatic writing on 24 October had surprised him – the disjointed sentences in an almost illegible script seeming so exciting and sometimes so profound that he persuaded her to give an hour or so each day to the unknown writer. After half a dozen hours he offered to spend the rest of his life piecing together and explaining the scattered sentences, but this produced the answer 'No', followed by the statement, 'We have come to give you metaphors for poetry.'

The automatic script built upon beliefs already enunciated in the essay on Magic of 1901 and, as Yeats was to state in *A Packet for Ezra Pound*, upon the ideas of *Per Amica Silentia Lunae*:

I had just made a distinction between the perfection that is from a man's combat with himself and that which is from a combat with circumstance, and upon this simple distinction he [the Instructor responsible for the script] built up an elaborate classification of men according to their more or less complete expression of one type or the other. He supported his classification by a series of geometrical symbols and put these symbols in an order that answered the question in my essay as to whether some prophet could not prick upon the calendar the birth of a Napoleon or a Christ. A system of symbolism, strange to my wife and to myself, certainly awaited expression, and when I asked how long that would take I was told years. Sometimes when my mind strays back to those first days I remember that Browning's Paracelsus did not obtain the secret until he had written his spiritual history at the bidding of his Byzantine teacher, that before initiation Wilhelm Meister read his own history written by another, and I compare my 'Per Amica' to these histories.[4]

The automatic writing gave shape to thoughts which were to find their public expression in *A Vision* (1925; published first in 1926), a book initially mentioned in a letter to Lady Gregory of January 1918 as 'a very profound, very exciting mystical philosophy'.[5] The thoughts and imagery of *A Vision* underpin much of the poetry Yeats wrote after his marriage, giving it an air of assurance. This confidence, this sense of possessing a system of thought, a complete psychology, was what struck Virginia Woolf in 1930; she felt her own theories crude and jaunty beside his, realising the intricacy of his art – its meaning, seriousness and importance wholly engrossing 'this large active-minded immensely vitalised man'.

Yeats's marriage was itself consolidated not only in the common interest, the shared work and the sense of discovery that the automatic writing and its interpretation involved, but also by the content of the script which related to his often obsessional assessment of his relationships with Maud, Olivia Shakespear, Mabel Dickinson, Iseult and his wife. He still continued to reflect upon his own behaviour and attitudes in various emotional crises, but the ability to put questions and get answers – often elliptical, often full of reassuring common sense – diminished his sense of guilt and enabled him to achieve a certain detachment. It made him feel, he wrote to Lady Gregory, that for the first time he understood human life.

All this involved a great deal of work, and the sheer volume of the scripts Mrs Yeats preserved made an impressive sight. Professor Harper, who has selected some of them in two volumes (1987) and edited *A Vision* (1978), records 8,672 questions and 3,627 pages which survive, and that covers only the 450 sessions of the period between October 1917 and June 1921. Between March 1920 and March 1924, the communications transmitted through George Yeats's 'sleeps' amounted to 270 pages, covering 164 sessions. Yeats used a card filing system of 750 cards in an attempt to impose order on the material. There also exist in MSS dialogues he wrote for his invented characters Michael Robartes and Owen Aherne, which in effect are early versions of *A Vision*. The sessions of automatic writing were dated and timed, and occurred in the various places where the Yeatses stayed; these included Woburn Buildings, 'given little touches here and there' by George as well as some new furniture. However, Zeppelin raids made London unattractive, so they went to Stone Cottage where George, who to Yeats's surprise had become friendly with Iseult, invited her to stay for Christmas.[6] The communicators (or George) were adamant that no one else should be present at the sessions of automatic writing, which had continued intensely in November, dealing with the two basic elements in *A Vision*, one the cyclical theory of history, that posits periods of roughly two thousand years introduced by the coming of an Initiate or Messiah – an idea to be given startling force later, in January 1919, in 'The Second Coming':

> Turning and turning in the widening gyre
> The falcon cannot hear the falconer;
> Things fall apart; the centre cannot hold;
> Mere anarchy is loosed upon the world,
> The blood-dimmed tide is loosed, and everywhere
> The ceremony of innocence is drowned;
> The best lack all conviction, while the worst
> Are full of passionate intensity.
>
> Surely some revelation is at hand;
> Surely the Second Coming is at hand.
> The Second Coming! Hardly are those words out
> When a vast image out of *Spiritus Mundi*
> Troubles my sight: somewhere in sands of the desert
> A shape with lion body and the head of a man,
> A gaze blank and pitiless as the sun,
> Is moving its slow thighs, while all about it
> Reel shadows of the indignant desert birds.
> The darkness drops again; but now I know
> That twenty centuries of stony sleep
> Were vexed to nightmare by a rocking cradle,
> And what rough beast, its hour come round at last,
> Slouches towards Bethlehem to be born?[7]

The second idea embraced the twenty-eight phases of the moon as a means of understanding human personality – to appear in a then apparently obscure poem written in 1918, 'The Phases of the Moon'.[8]

It was partly a process of analysis – of clearing the subconscious – and partly a crystallisation of ideas that emerged in many poems. No wonder that by December Yeats was writing to Lady Gregory that George was 'a perfect wife, kind, wise, and unselfish'. She had made his life 'serene and full of order'.[9]

George's upbringing had prepared her for Yeats's mobility, for her family had frequently changed residences; she decided they would try living in Oxford, in rooms in Broad Street. She never knew whether she should be more surprised by the hats or by the minds of the dons' wives. If they were to live there every winter,

Yeats wrote to John Quinn, she thought she would be given to great extravagance out of a desire for contrast.[10]

An encouraging letter about living in Oxford came from Frank Pearce Sturm, a doctor, occultist and poet influenced and encouraged by Yeats, to whom he passed on his belief that Oxford was about to become the centre of a great revival of spiritual learning. He was deeply interested in the system of *A Vision*.[11]

Contrast was now emerging in the automatic script, as it had in Yeats's life. While continuing to cast philosophical material into arguments between Robartes and Aherne he was also finishing *The Only Jealousy of Emer*, a play about Cuchulain. Like many of his poems and plays about Irish mythology, this owed a good deal to what he read. Founded upon an Irish saga called *The Sickbed of Cuchulain and the Only Jealousy of Emer*, as well as on Lady Gregory's *Cuchulain of Muirthemne*, the play was probably also influenced by translations and treatments by Eugene O'Curry and George Sigerson. But this was no mere rehandling of old tales; for it was part of his own personal saga, Cuchulain (himself) emotionally affected by the goddess Fand (Maud Gonne), wife of the god of the sea Manannan Maclir, by Eithne Inguba, Cuchulain's young mistress (Iseult), and by Emer, his wife (George, with possibly something of Lady Gregory's character thrown in). He found it difficult to resolve the play's symbolism, but the automatic script referred to Bricriu's withered arm, Bricriu of the Sidhe being the changeling put in Cuchulain's place, a maker of trouble. The meaning of the play is also intimately bound up with the idea of the mask, of the anti-self, as well as with Yeats's frustrated love for Maud, who is like the fairy mistress who lives on the life of her lovers. She seeks the love of men, but if they refuse her she is enslaved to them; whereas if they consent they become totally hers. Cuchulain is saved by Emer's sacrifice; he enjoys Eithne's love, but he does not forget the woman of the Sidhe.

On 23 January 1918 Robert Gregory was killed on the north Italian front; he was shot down in error by an Italian pilot, but this was not known at the time by either Gregory's family or by Yeats. At Lady Gregory's prompting, Yeats wrote 'A Note of Appreciation' published in the *Observer* on 17 February. This develops the ideas he put first in a letter of 8 February to John Quinn, that Robert Gregory was the most accomplished man he had ever known – he could do more things well than any other – and his paintings had majesty, austerity and sweetness. In 'The New Faces', a poem of 1912, he had looked forward to Coole's future once he and Lady Gregory were dead:

> Let the new faces play what tricks they will
> In the old rooms; night can outbalance day,
> Our shadows rove the garden gravel still,
> The living seem more shadowy than they.[12]

This may reflect his feeling about what would happen to Coole 'slowly perfecting itself and the life within it in ever increasing intensity of labour' and then probably sinking away 'through courteous incompetence, or rather sheer weakness of will, for ability has not failed in young Gregory'.[13] Yeats probably shared Hugh Lane's opinion that Robert Gregory would not work unless he needed money. Now, however, he tempered this view: 'though he often seemed led away from his work by some other gift his attitude to life and art never lost intensity – he was never the amateur'. He wrote to Lady Gregory that he was trying a poem in manner like one that Spenser wrote for Sir Philip Sidney ('A Pastoral Elegy upon the Death of Sir Philip Sidney, Knight, etc.'); this was 'Shepherd and Goatherd', a not very successful pastoral elegy completed in March. It includes some ideas which were part of what can be called *A Vision*'s thought, often owed to the automatic writing, such as the dreaming back (originally, however, explored in the essay 'Swedenborg, Mediums and the Desolate Places') which he envisages for Gregory:

> Jaunting, journeying
> To his own dayspring,
> He unpacks the loaded pern
> Of all 'twas pain or joy to learn,
> Of all that he had made.

The poem is more of a tribute to Lady Gregory than to Robert, who

> . . . had gathered up no gear,
> Set carpenters to work on no wide table,
> On no long bench nor lofty milking-shed
> As others will, when first they take possession,
> But left the house as in his father's time
> As though he knew himself, as it were, a cuckoo,
> No settled man.[14]

Robert Gregory had hardly been master in Coole; he and his wife
Margaret (they were married on 26 September 1907) felt that they
were treated like children, and he told her of his sense that Yeats
had usurped his position. A schoolboy of sixteen when Yeats made
the first of his long summer visits to Coole – Robert's wife remarked
that while the sedum was in flower, he was sure to be there – Robert
found when he returned from Oxford in vacations that Yeats was at
the centre of Coole's social life – he continued to sit at the head of
the table, occupy one of the two master bedrooms and give advice
about the estate. Robert and Margaret had believed that Lady
Gregory's legal right to live at Coole ended when Robert became
twenty-one in 1902, but she herself thought her husband's will had
given her the right to do so in her lifetime. Determined to clear the
debts with which she found the estate was encumbered, by the time
she ended her trusteeship she gave up the annuity Sir William had
left her and broke the entail set up in 1840. All was sacrificed to
give Robert financial freedom; all her efforts were designed to keep
house and estate viable for him, but there was misunderstanding
about the position and, while she was happy to look after her
grandchildren, Robert and Margaret chose to live largely in London
and in France. As Colin Smythe has pointed out, within a fortnight
of Robert's death Lady Gregory offered to leave Coole immediately,
but the offer was not taken up.[15] She had not wanted the responsibility of keeping it up with, as she put it in 1921:

> . . . its anxieties and loneliness, with the burden of keeping it in order and
> paying its taxes and rates and labour, more than my income will cover, and
> that I must sell treasures for or earn. I shrink from having my last years
> cumbered with thought of management and money.[16]

But it seemed her duty, and she felt she had to take on the increased
responsibility so that her grandson Richard could inherit and keep
the place. The irony was, of course, that he did not want to live in
Coole, and did not feel he could tell her that.

In the spring of 1918 Yeats brought his wife to Ireland. After Dublin,
where the Yeats sisters took to George and welcomed her warmly,
they visited Wicklow, staying at Glendalough and Glenmalure. At
Glendalough Yeats wrote 'Solomon to Sheba', a poem about their
marriage, which refers to their shared secret knowledge:

'There's not a man or woman
Born under the skies
Dare match in learning with us two,
And all day long we have found
There's not a thing but love can make
The world a narrow pound.'[17]

Another poem written in 1918, 'Solomon and the Witch',[18] also used this Solomon and Sheba imagery for poet and wife (no matter that he had used it of Maud Gonne in a poem of 1914, 'On Woman'[19]); in this Sheba cries out in a strange tongue, her utterance interpreted by Solomon as the crowing of the cockerel who thinks Chance and Choice are one, the suggestion being that when a perfect union takes place between them the world ends or time comes to a stop. Like so many others written subsequently, this poem is bound up with the thought of *A Vision*. Chance and Choice had appeared in his poetry as early as *The Island of Statues* (of 1885), and the symbolism was explained in the notes to his play *Calvary* (1921) (founded upon Oscar Wilde's story *The Doer of Good*) in a story of 'an old Arab' told by Aherne:

. . . Kusta ben Luki has taught us to divide all things into Chance and Choice; one can think about the world and about man, or anything else until all has vanished but these two things, for they are indeed the first cause of the animate and inanimate world. They exist in God for if they did not He would not have freedom, He would be bound by His own Choice. In God alone, indeed, can they be united, yet each be perfect and without limit or hindrance. If I should throw from the dice-box there would be but six possible sides on each of the dice, but when God throws He uses dice that have all numbers and all sides. Some worship His Choice; that is easy; to know that He has willed for some unknown purpose all that happens is pleasant; but I have spent my life in worshipping His Chance, and that moment when I understand the immensity of His Chance is the moment when I am nearest Him . . .[20]

In 'Solomon to Sheba' Yeats was echoing his 1910 diary, where he put his view that true love is a discipline; it requires so much wisdom, he added, that the love of Solomon and Sheba must have been lasting:

Each divines the secret self of the other, and refusing to believe in the mere daily self, creates a mirror where the lover or the beloved sees an image to copy in daily life; for love also creates the Mask.[21]

In 'Solomon and the Witch', there is realism in Solomon's reflection
that

> 'Maybe the bride-bed brings despair,
> For each an imagined image brings
> And finds a real image there . . .'

Despite his stating that the world ends when the two unite, Sheba
remarks that the world remains and Solomon concedes that

> 'Maybe an image is too strong
> Or maybe is not strong enough.'

To which Sheba replies:

> 'The night has fallen; not a sound
> In the forbidden sacred grove
> Unless a petal hit the ground,
> Nor any human sight within it
> But the crushed grass where we have lain;
> And the moon is wilder every minute.
> O! Solomon! let us try again.'

The moon was wild in another poem written in March 1918, 'Under
the Round Tower';[22] this is set in the Glendalough graveyard with its
slender pencil-shaped round tower, within which and on the top of
which – according to a beggar's dreams – the sun and moon, golden
king and silver lady, symbols of man and woman in the *Stories of Red
Hanrahan*, prance and sing. They stand for Yeats and his wife.

There was no dreaming, however, about the poet's own tower in
the west on which Raftery the builder was working; its golden king
wanted his silver lady to see it. And there was Coole to visit, where
formidable old friend and forthright young wife could take each
other's measure. Luckily Lady Gregory approved of George,
although Margaret Gregory received both the Yeatses rather rudely
on their visit of 1918. Yeats recorded in a notebook in October 1921
that one night she had, as usual, contradicted everything he said at
dinner and instead of avoiding argument as he had before he 'turned
on her'. He had come down to dinner 'in the highest spirits with
this wicked intention' and after dinner he went upstairs in the same
frame of mind. George told him he had behaved badly, 'but had so
much sympathy with me, that we omitted our usual precaution
against conception' and from then on they expected a child.[23]

Lady Gregory lent them Ballinamantane House near Gort so that they could supervise the alterations to Ballylee Castle. They bought the contents of an old mill – beams, three-inch planks and paving-stones – and Yeats wrote a poem, later shortened and revised into 'To be carved on a Stone at Thoor Ballylee':

> I, the poet William Yeats,
> With old mill boards and sea-green slates,
> And smithy work from the Gort forge,
> Restored this tower for my wife George;
> And may these characters remain
> When all is ruin once again.[24]

By mid-June Yeats had finished 'In Memory of Major Robert Gregory', linking him with the tower and with other dead friends: Lionel Johnson, John Synge, George Pollexfen:

> Always we'd have the new friend meet the old
> And we are hurt if either friend seem cold,
> And there is salt to lengthen out the smart
> In the affections of our heart . . .

Robert Gregory had loved Ballylee:

> the old storm-broken trees
> That cast their shadows upon road and bridge;
> The tower set on the stream's edge;
> The ford where drinking cattle make a stir
> Nightly, and startled by that sound
> The water-hen must change her ground.

The poem, carefully rhymed in its stanzas *aa bb c dd c*, is a dignified and authoritative elegy, gaining strength from its repeated description of Gregory: 'Soldier, scholar, horseman, he'.[25] But 'An Irish Airman foresees his Death' is perhaps a greater tribute for its compression of Gregory's life with its skilful repetition, its poise and balance:

> A lonely impulse of delight
> Drove to this tumult in the clouds;
> I balanced all, brought all to mind,
> The years to come seemed waste of breath,
> A waste of breath the years behind
> In balance with this life, this death.[26]

While the Yeatses were out of London Maud and her children, Minnaloushe the cat, the dogs and the birds all lived in Woburn

Buildings. Maud crossed to Ireland in disguise in February and came to Galway, to offer condolences to Lady Gregory and to call on Willie and George at Ballylee. Her reaction to the marriage, as reported to John Quinn by Arthur Symons, had been amusement: 'Wish you had heard Maud laugh at Yeats's marriage – a good woman of 25 – rich of course – who has to look after him; she might either become his slave or run away from him after a certain length of time.' But Lily Yeats told Quinn that Maud as well as Lady Gregory seemed pleased; after all, she remarked, they both had had their 'whack' of Willie. Maud rented 73 Stephen's Green in Dublin but was arrested in May, suspected of being involved in a 'German plot'. She was moved to England to Holloway Gaol where, along with Constance Markiewicz and Kathleen Clarke, she was to be held indefinitely.

After a few final weeks in Galway – virtually camping in Ballylee in September – the Yeatses returned to Dublin, Yeats wanting their child to be born in Ireland. They found it impossible to get any furnished accommodation, but Maud then offered them 73 Stephen's Green at a nominal rent. In November, Mrs Yeats, who was pregnant, became seriously ill with pneumonia which had developed after influenza.

Maud, too, was ill in prison and Yeats had written to influential friends about her condition. A Harley Street doctor diagnosed a return of her tuberculosis and, after Quinn sent telegrams to Lord Northcliffe's assistant and to T. P. O'Connor, the Irish MP, she was released from Holloway (where she had been for five and a half months) and sent to a nursing home. After five days there she went back to Woburn Buildings, then evaded detectives and, disguised as a nurse, returned to Dublin where she went at once to 73 Stephen's Green. However, Yeats, without consulting his wife, refused to let her in, fearing the effects which any pursuit of Maud by police or military might have on George's health. A violent quarrel ensued, letters flew, he was accused of lack of patriotic feeling, of cowardice: but friendship was soon re-established. The Yeatses found various lodgings in Dublin and Maud returned to 73 Stephen's Green, where Yeats visited her at her 'At Homes' and, as Cecil Salkeld recorded, there was now no constraint between them; she received Yeats with 'the gay good humour characteristic of her'.

The summer and autumn produced several poems. 'Two Songs

of a Fool' reflects Yeats's continuing concern about Iseult, the tame
hare of this poem and several others, Mrs Yeats being the speckled
cat:

> I slept on my three-legged stool by the fire,
> The speckled cat slept on my knee;
> We never thought to enquire
> Where the brown hare might be . . .[27]

'To a Young Beauty' warned Iseult about the Bohemian company
she was keeping:

> Dear fellow-artist, why so free
> With every sort of company,
> With every Jack and Jill?[28]

This poem shows his appreciation of Donne, whom he had read in
Grierson's edition in 1912: 'the intricacy and subtleties of his
imagination are the length and depth of the furrow made by his
passion':[29]

> There is not a fool can call me friend,
> And I may dine at journey's end
> With Landor and with Donne.[30]

'An Image from a Past Life', set at Ballylee, was written in September
and explained at length in Yeats's notes to the poem, as being
about an 'Overshadower' or 'Ideal Form' (possibly an expansion of
Tagore's poem 'In the Dusky Path of a Dream', where he seeks the
love of a former life). However, Yeats permits the woman in his
poem, not the man, to see the Overshadower. Images, he says, pass
from one mind to another with ease and probably from the portion
of the mind that is outside consciousness, the second mind seeing
what the first has already seen. The poem reverts to 'nineties
language when 'She' describes 'the sweetheart from another life'
and 'He' fails to assuage her fear.[31]

In Dublin on 23 November he wrote 'Demon and Beast', a poem
which though determinist, escapes into a moment of happiness – an
escape, as Peter Ure suggested, from the demon of hatred and the
beast of desire. The poem develops the idea of turning or spinning
in gyres or gyrations, reflecting some of the geometrical diagrams
that were emerging in the automatic writing as symbols of the
beginning, development and destruction of periods of history. This
poem shows Yeats's freedom in handling apparently disparate sub-

jects, brought together by his imaginative thought; in it he combines
images of portraits in the National Gallery of Ireland with gulls and
a duck on the lake in Stephen's Green:

> For aimless joy had made me stop
> Beside the little lake
> To watch a white gull take
> A bit of bread thrown up into the air;
> Now gyring down and perning there
> He splashed where an absurd
> Portly green-pated bird
> Shook off the water from his back;
> Being no more demoniac
> A stupid happy creature
> Could rouse my whole nature.[32]

He blends this moment of sweetness with an account of the monks
of the Thebaid and their ecstatic fasting, something of which he
had read in Flaubert's *La Tentation de Saint Antoine*, the *Lausiac History*
of Palladius and two books[33] by an Anglo-Irish clergyman, the Rev
J. O. Hannay (who, as George A. Birmingham, wrote novels now
underestimated, both serious and comic) before moving to an oracular
question, 'What had the Caesars but their thrones?' This perhaps is
to be explained in terms of *A Vision* and linked with another poem,
'The Saint and the Hunchback',[34] as meaning that the Caesars had
no check upon their power whereas Christianity, as exemplified by the
monks of Thebaid, provided a curb in the subjugation of the flesh, in
renunciation, the Christian idea of God a contrast to the praise of the
body created in the handiwork of Phidias or Scopas.

The kind of communication between minds suggested in the
notes to 'An Image from a Past Life'[35] can also be experienced,
Yeats suggested, in dreams. 'Towards Break of Day' records two
dreams he and his wife dreamed on the same night when they were
staying at the Powerscourt Arms Hotel at Enniskerry, Co. Wicklow,
in December. He dreamed of a waterfall on Ben Bulben, she of 'the
marvellous stag of Arthur' in the 'Tale of King Arthur' told by Sir
Thomas Malory. Here is the poem:

> Was it the double of my dream
> The woman that by me lay
> Dreamed, or did we halve a dream
> Under the first cold gleam of day?

> I thought: 'There is a waterfall
> Upon Ben Bulben side
> That all my childhood counted dear;
> Were I to travel far and wide
> I could not find a thing so dear.'
> My memories had magnified
> So many times childish delight.
>
> I would have touched it like a child
> But knew my finger could but have touched
> Cold stone and water. I grew wild,
> Even accusing Heaven because
> It had set down among its laws:
> Nothing that we love over-much
> Is ponderable to our touch.
>
> I dreamed towards break of day,
> The cold blown spray in my nostril.
> But she that beside me lay
> Had watched in bitterer sleep
> The marvellous stag of Arthur,
> That lofty white stag, leap
> From mountain steep to steep.[36]

And here is what was written in the automatic script on 7 January. After the word 'Dreams' came 'I gave you dream each – now I give you two more in one – at castle?' There followed a condensation of the poem – probably, Professor Harper suggests, before it was written (it was first published in the following November):

> Hand and eye
> waterfall & stag
> Hand – eye
> waterfall
> touch – desire to grasp
> eye – desire to see
> possessive hand – desiring eye.[37]

This particular sitting was remarkable for a diagram drawn during it which links 'Towards Break of Day'[38] with 'Another Song of a Fool'[39] and 'The Double Vision of Michael Robartes'; the rough drawing is of the last poem's 'grey rock of Cashel' with 'Cormac's ruined house' surmounting it, the setting for the images of the girl now dead who dreams of dancing between a Sphinx and a Buddha:

> O little did they care who danced between,
> And little she by whom her dance was seen.[40]

She is part of his dreams, and they include Helen, Homer's paragon 'Who never gave the burning town a thought'. The drawing also includes the symbols of 'Another Song of a Fool', butterfly, hands, eye, schoolmaster's birch and book. It is possible that the third stanza's images of roses and meat are also intended in the drawing of the bird and a circle below it, enclosing a cross above the signature of Thomas, the communicator. Here is the poem:

> This great purple butterfly,
> In the prison of my hands,
> Has a learning in his eye
> Not a poor fool understands.
>
> Once he lived a schoolmaster
> With a stark, denying look;
> A string of scholars went in fear
> Of his great birch and his great book.
>
> Like the clangour of a bell,
> Sweet and harsh, harsh and sweet,
> That is how he learnt so well
> To take the roses for his meat.[41]

This poem relates to another, earlier poem, 'Tom O'Roughley', written on 16 February 1918, in which the fool proclaims that

> 'An aimless joy is a pure joy . . .
> 'And wisdom is a butterfly
> And not a gloomy bird of prey.'[42]

The automatic script (sometimes called 'the system'), in answer to the query 'Why have you made this drawing?', replies:

You are empty – drained dry – the true moment for vision – a new influx must come this time from the past – you are drained dry from looking into the future & exhausted by the present – passivity is dangerous in the present & future – so go to the past – A historical & spiritual past – the church the castle on the hill . . . go to the hill
Castle
I know the place – your name is foreign – Cormac . . . she can look at it from below & if I want her up up she will go.[43]

Professor Harper suggests that this and further references to Cashel may have been George's method of getting Yeats to leave Dublin, where he stayed too busy to please her, and she was trying (he suggests) to lure him to Cashel by suggesting the castle would stimulate a poem based upon complementary dreams. This is probably correct; she had earlier thought Powerscourt more peaceful than Dublin. In Dublin he began to talk about 'the system' to a private audience at the Arts Club. He was disturbed by the way the Sinn Fein movement and its press were developing under Arthur Griffith, a feeling expressed in 1918 in 'The Leaders of the Crowd':

> They must to keep their certainty accuse
> All that are different of a base intent;
> Pull down established honour; hawk for news
> Whatever their loose fantasy invent
> And murmur it with bated breath, as though
> The abounding gutter had been Helicon
> Or calumny a song.[44]

Maud was affected by this, he thought, and in 'On a Political Prisoner', a poem written between 10 and 29 January 1919 on Con Markiewicz ('I'm writing one on Con,' he told his wife, 'to avoid writing one on Maud'), he developed his idea that the leaders of the crowd murmur the inventions of their loose fantasy as though 'The abounding gutter had been Helicon'. Now he wonders if Con Markiewicz recalls the years before her mind

> Became a bitter, an abstract thing,
> Her thoughts some popular enmity:
> Blind and leader of the blind
> Drinking the foul ditch where they lie?

He draws a poignant contrast between the prisoner in her cell taming a seagull and his memories of her as

> The beauty of her country-side
> With all youth's lonely wildness stirred,
> She seemed to have grown clean and sweet
> Like any rock-bred, sea-borne bird . . .[45]

The effect of hate, political and intellectual, occupied his thoughts even in 'A Prayer for my Daughter',[46] for Anne Butler Yeats, born in Dublin on 24 February 1919. The poem begun two days later was finished at Thoor Ballylee in June – an atmospheric poem, full of foreboding for all its appreciation of courtesy, radical innocence, custom and ceremony:

> I have walked and prayed for this young child an hour
> And heard the sea-wind scream upon the tower,
> And under the arches of the bridge, and scream
> In the elms above the flooded stream;
> Imagining in excited reverie
> That the future years had come,
> Dancing to a frenzied drum,
> Out of the murderous innocence of the sea.

While wishing his daughter beauty, he has reservations; the over-beautiful can be unwise in their choice of company, an idea which leads him to think of Helen of Troy, of Aphrodite and of their choice of mates. Contemplation of what damage such women or goddesses could inflict, in their undoing of Amalthea's horn of plenty, led to an appreciation of his wife:

> Hearts are not had as a gift but hearts are earned
> By those that are not entirely beautiful;
> Yet many, that have played the fool
> For beauty's very self, has charm made wise,
> And many a poor man that has roved,
> Loved and thought himself beloved,
> From a glad kindness cannot take his eyes.

But while he extends various wishes for his daughter, he touches on his own mind (perhaps influenced to these thoughts by the automatic writing) which

> ... because the minds that I have loved,
> The sort of beauty that I have approved,
> Prosper but little, has dried up of late ...

He contemplates the effect of hate, then turns in particular to the intellectual hate that dominates Maud and writes a devastating indictment of her:

> An intellectual hatred is the worst,
> So let her think opinions are accursed.
> Have I not seen the loveliest woman born
> Out of the mouth of Plenty's horn,
> Because of her opinionated mind
> Barter that horn and every good

> By quiet natures understood
> For an old bellows full of angry wind?

This question of hatred is complex. In 1903 Maud had taught him hate by kisses to a clown, but there was more to it than the classic reversal of *amo* into *odi*. His art came from resolving a struggle in his soul; he could escape from rage as a writer by his sense of style – ecstasy something achieved out of emotions arising from a love of what is hated. Courtesy requires discipline – it may be the discipline of the mask – but it brings its rewards, primal unity, a state of self-delight. Some of these ideas stem from the contraries he had earlier found in Blake, and the positive ones come from his reading in the Neo-Platonists, Proclus, and Plotinus reached through Ficino's translation – itself translated by Taylor (a copy of which was owned by Mrs Yeats) and later by Stephen MacKenna (first read most appreciatively by Yeats in 1920). Beauty, physical beauty, could enable the soul to recognise its own divine beauty, an idea of Pietro Bembo that Yeats had found in Castiglione's *The Book of the Courtier*. Echoes of that book which had such an appeal for him probably lie behind the prayer for his daughter's happiness. When all hatred is driven out, he proclaims, the soul recovers radical innocence

> And learns at last that it is self-delighting,
> Self-appeasing, self-affrighting,
> And that its own sweet will is Heaven's will . . .

This state can resist outer pressures and avoid the dangers of abstraction, of hatred:

> She can, though every face should scowl
> And every windy quarter howl
> Or every bellows burst, be happy still.

This idea had already been put in a poem to Iseult Gonne, 'Michael Robartes and the Dancer', where 'He' explains a picture of a knight rescuing a maiden from a dragon ('Saint George and the Dragon', ascribed to Bordone, in the National Gallery of Ireland) as showing the maiden being at the mercy of the half-dead dragon of her thoughts. 'He' suggests that opinion, or education, is useless; her lover's wage is what she sees in her looking-glass: 'All must come to sight and touch.' 'She' is perplexed; school has not suggested such ideas, which 'He' supports by reference to a Latin text (Joseph

M. Hassett has suggested that this is Ficino's translation of Plotinus[47]):

> ... blest souls are not composite,
> And that all beautiful women may
> Live in uncomposite blessedness,
> And lead us to the like – if they
> Will banish every thought ...[48]

And concentrate on being beautiful, for feminine beauty frees the soul imprisoned in the body.

During a visit to England in May 1919, Yeats saw *The Player Queen* produced by the Stage Society at the King's Hall, Covent Garden; it was later repeated at the Abbey in December, with Arthur Shields as Septimus the poet. In June he gave up the rooms in Woburn Buildings, his London dwelling since 1896. What was worrying him in April 1919, as he wrote to George Russell, was that Ireland had a lunatic faculty, an automatic reaction which made it oppose everything England affirmed, and this habit of taking the opposite side killed thought, led to mob rhetoric and incurred the risk of Marxian revolution – the spear-head, as he put it, of materialism 'and leading to inevitable murder.'[49]

The summer went well at Ballylee. The ground-floor room of the castle with its wide window over the river, its arched door leading to the thatched hall between castle and cottage, was attractive and Yeats wrote there as well as on the river bank where he watched an otter fishing for trout, Anne in a seventeenth-century cradle, his wife painting the wooden ceilings of their spectacular property. But Ballylee was too damp for winter occupation, Dublin too political and London unattractive in many ways, so they moved in October 1919 to 4 Broad Street, Oxford, a house with a lease renewable every six months.

FOURTEEN

1919–1923

Installed in Oxford Yeats thought he would earn a roof for the castle, the second and third floors of which were open to the weather. Lily and Lollie agreed to look after Anne, a tenant was found for Broad Street and on 13 January 1920 Yeats and his wife sailed for the United States on the *Carmania*, the visit lasting till 29 May.

John Quinn reported to Pound that Yeats seemed devoted to his wife, she seemed interested in and devoted to him 'and the old man beamed upon both of them'. John Butler Yeats was indeed delighted with his new daughter-in-law, with her endless kindness and sympathy and with the fact that she was, as he put it to Lily, not without the salt of malice; relaying her remark that Mrs Ford, a collector of the famous and a very wealthy woman (whom he and his daughters thought stingy), smelt of whisky: 'In these prohibition days,' he went on, 'there are men who would kiss any woman for the sake of that smell though George thinks that Mrs Ford even with that addition would not tempt anyone.'[1] George got to know him and John Quinn well (she approved of him and American architecture but not much else American – except, of course Ezra Pound whom she liked and whose work she admired increasingly), and in February the artist drew a charmingly cheerful pencil sketch of her. She thought his refusal of his son's invitation to return to Ireland with them – something strongly desired by Quinn – came from a wish not to be a burden on his children in his old age. Having guaranteed his living expenses in New York, Yeats did not want to press his father in case he would seem motivated by saving money in doing so.

Although the J. B. Pond Lyceum Lecture Bureau which arranged much of the tour became bankrupt, the lecture tour was financially rewarding. It included visits to Toronto; Montreal; Northampton,

Massachusetts; Yale; Washington; Pittsburgh; Oberlin College; Chicago; Oak Park, Illinois; Salt Lake City; Portland, Oregon; Berkeley; San Francisco; Los Angeles; Hollywood; Pasadena; Santa Barbara; New Orleans; San Antonio; Georgetown, Austin, Waco, Dallas, Sherman, all in Texas; Kirksville, Missouri; Boston. Ezra Pound commented that Yeats would have made enough 'to buy a few shingles for his phallic symbol on the bogs. Ballyphallus or whatever he calls it with the river on the first floor.'

One of the high points of the tour was a meeting with Junzo Sato, then Japanese Consul at Portland, Oregon. He had read Yeats's poetry in Japan and now heard him lecture; he brought him a present wrapped in embroidered silk:

He untied the silk cord that bound it and brought out a sword which had been for 500 years in his family. It had been made 550 years ago and he showed me the maker's name upon the hilt.[2]

Yeats fetched George, thinking they might find a way of refusing the gift. When she came, he said to Sato that the sword should surely remain in his family, to which Sato replied, 'My family have many swords.' Yeats later wrote to 'put him under a vow' to tell him when his first child was born, so that he could leave the sword back to his family in his will. In 1980 I met Junzo Sato, a slight frail figure, in Tokyo, when he described in detail Yeats's delight, sixty years before, in the age of the ceremonial sword and the inherited craftsmanship that had gone to its making, celebrated later in '*My Table*':

> Chaucer had not drawn breath
> When it was forged. In Sato's house,
> Curved like new moon, moon-luminous,
> It lay five hundred years.[3]

Another meeting Yeats had was with de Valera, collecting funds among the Irish-Americans, who seemed 'a living argument rather than a living man'; both Yeats and Quinn seized on his persistence. This quality, backed by a devotion to abstract principle, was later to disturb Yeats deeply, though he did find de Valera more human on a subsequent meeting.

In the summer of 1919 he had seriously pondered accepting an invitation to lecture at the University of Tokyo for two years. It would be pleasant, he thought, to get away from the tumult of war; but would he return to find a grass-grown city? Would he mind if

Sinn Fein was using his tower as a store for arms? During his stay in America he decided not to go to Japan and towards the end of the lecture tour he wrote to Lady Gregory to enquire about conditions in County Galway: would cattle-driving mean there would be no milk to be had for Anne? Guerilla warfare – begun by the murder of two members of the Royal Irish Constabulary at Soloheadbeg on the day the first Dail was meeting in the Mansion House in Dublin – had developed into a vicious cycle of murders and reprisals by 1920. The RIC had been increased in number by the intake of men recruited in England (eventually about 7,000 in all), who became known as the Black and Tans after the name of the Scarteen Hunt because of their uniforms, a mixture of khaki and police uniforms. Former army officers were also recruited in England (there were nearly 1,000 of them by the end of 1920) and known as Auxiliaries. Terrorist measures were adopted by the Black and Tans; Lady Gregory wrote a series of devastating articles about them in *The Nation*, an English weekly journal, in 1920, and her *Journals 1916–1920* convey a sense of the fear caused by the horrors perpetrated in her part of the country.

On their return from America in May, the Yeatses had a short spell in Ezra Pound's flat in Church Street, Kensington. Then came the enjoyment of 4 Broad Street, the seventeenth-century house in Oxford that now had the furniture from Woburn Buildings installed – its peacefulness, perhaps paradoxically, heightened by a green parrot and Anne 'staggering about full of destructiveness'. There was plenty of good company: John Masefield and Robert Bridges lived on Boar's Hill and Lily, on a visit, walked there with her brother. Yeats enjoyed visiting Lady Ottoline and Philip Morrell at Garsington, the manor house with its

> ... gardens where the peacock strays
> With delicate feet upon old terraces.[4]

There were visits from Sturge Moore and his wife and from Dulac.

George's cousin Grace Spurway, an undergraduate at Saint Hugh's, came to tea, asked a question after a monologue by the poet and was not invited back again, meeting George occasionally in a tea-room.[5] Undergraduates were asked to Monday 'At Homes', among them Charles Morgan, William Force Stead and L. A. G.

Strong, who later wrote enthusiastically about Yeats's encouragement, finding him perceptive and sensitive to the shyness of younger people. Among the older members of the university he formed a close friendship with Maurice Bowra – well recorded in Bowra's autobiography – whose view of Yeats's poetry appeared in *The Heritage of Symbolism* (1943).

Other dons were aware of his presence in a city not yet overcrowded and over-affected by 'the man who made the motors', as Yeats was later to describe William Morris. Percy Simpson invited Yeats to dinner in Oriel. 'He so enjoyed it,' he once remarked to me, 'the setting, the silver, the ritual; pity I never asked him again.'

Maud asked him to return to Ireland to help with Iseult's marital difficulties in August. After her relationship with Ezra Pound in London, Iseult had a close friendship with Lennox Robinson in Dublin and then married Francis Stuart in 1920. She picked him, Yeats wrote to Olivia Shakespear, 'by what seemed half chance, half a mere desire to escape from an impossible life, and when he seemed almost imbecile to his own relations.'[6] He was then eighteen years old.

Another problem which arose in August was his father's future. The Petipas sisters had sold their boarding-house; the money Quinn held in the trust account was down, in September, to $71, and the boarding-house bills were mounting. Quinn urged Yeats to install the artist in a warm, comfortable room in Dublin, to which he received in reply a telegram agreeing to the contents of his letter. This was not what Quinn had wanted and eventually a letter written in George's hand and signed by Yeats went to the old man, saying he should return to Dublin where a studio would be provided.[7] This met with a refusal, accepted by Yeats with, 'It is for you to decide. I can say no more.' He told his father, however, that he might have to arrange another lecture tour (so much would be 'taken from life and work') in the winter of the following year if the money ran out; this – a psychological error – potentially extended the artist's stay yet further.[8] Meanwhile there was his own physical problem of recovering from an operation performed with his 'usual exuberant gaiety' by Gogarty in Dublin for the removal of his tonsils; there had been a haemorrhage; and literary talk before and after the operation with discussion of dying speeches – Yeats looking about for a good model, having always contended that 'a model is necessary to style'.[9] The operation had been preceded by a visit to Maud, who was staying in a cottage in Glenmalure with her son and Cecil Salkeld. There Yeats wrote 'On a Picture of a Black Centaur by Edmund Dulac'.[10] *Michael Robartes and the Dancer* was published by the Cuala Press when he was in Dublin. This volume included the four poems on the Easter Rising as well as the then magnificently mysterious poems linked to *A Vision*'s thought. But the strain of poetry exhibited in 'The Second Coming', 'Demon and Beast' and 'A Prayer for my Daughter' developed further when he returned to Oxford. There, in November, he wrote the atmospheric 'All Souls' Night':

> Midnight has come, and the great Christ Church Bell
> And many a lesser bell sound through the room;
> And it is All Souls' Night,
> And two long glasses brimmed with muscatel
> Bubble upon the table. A ghost may come . . .[11]

In the poem he describes his own marvellous thought, which he holds tight 'Till meditation master all its parts'. This is the framework for his evocation of three recently dead friends: W. T. Horton, Florence Farr and MacGregor Mathers. In writing on Mabel Beardsley and Robert Gregory, he had discovered the attraction of trying to sum up character, to capture the essence of the dead in some intensely remembered action, speech or gesture. He could not write of the living for publication except in the most cursory way, he wrote to Lollie; he could not write of anyone, let alone the family, if he had to think of any point of view but his own and making it just in his own eyes. But the living could be treated in a different yet discreet way. This was the time when visitors to Broad Street were assessed in terms of *A Vision*'s twenty-eight phases, and placed in whichever one seemed appropriate to them according to their natures as the Yeatses saw them. Yeats and his wife would often mutter a number cryptically to each other, seldom disagreeing about the guest's phase. The poet did, however, tell L. A. G. Strong that initially they had both put him in the wrong phase.

Ambushes and atrocities multiplied throughout Ireland as emotions were roused by such events as the death in November 1920 of Terence MacSwiney, Lord Mayor of Cork, after seventy days of hunger strike in Brixton Gaol; by the murders on a bloody Sunday of fourteen British undercover intelligence officers in Dublin; by the crowd at a football match in Croke Park being fired

on and by the shooting of IRA leaders in Dublin Castle on the same
day. A company of Auxiliaries burnt the centre of Cork in December;
the following May, the IRA were to burn the Custom House in
Dublin. Invited to speak at the Oxford Union on 17 February 1921,
Yeats made a passionate attack on the English policy of countering
the IRA by the terrorisation, the 'horrible things done to ordinary
law-abiding people by these maddened men', the Black and Tans
and the Auxiliaries. He exempted from his attack the British troops
who had been longer in Ireland, their nerves severely tried, for such
things – with a few exceptions – had not happened where they had
been in charge. English law, he pointed out, had broken down in
Ireland, but the law had not; though not himself a Sinn Feiner, he
thought Sinn Fein justice was real justice. He did not know which
lay heaviest on his heart, the tragedy of Ireland or the tragedy of
England. The speech had its effect, the motion 'That this House
would welcome complete Self Government in Ireland, and
condemns reprisals' being carried by 219 votes to 129.

The horrors in the area of Gort, relayed to him by Lady Gregory,
inspired 'Reprisals',[12] published in *The Nation* in 1921, addressed
to Robert Gregory's ghost:

> Half-drunk or whole-mad soldiery
> Are murdering your tenants there.
> Men that revere your father yet
> Are shot at on the open plain.
> Where may new-married women sit
> And suckle children now? Armed men
> May murder them in passing by
> Nor law nor parliament take heed.

At Oxford Yeats completed 'Four Years'; this was the first book of
The Trembling of the Veil, another excursion into autobiography – he
was publishing them in the *London Mercury*, then they were to appear
as a Cuala edition; Werner Laurie had offered him £500 for the
right to issue this section subsequently in a privately printed edition
for which Yeats was to supply copy by June 1922, the advance being
earmarked in his mind to clear J.B.Y.'s bills and finance his return
to Dublin. This volume of autobiography showed the effect of *A
Vision's* ideas. For instance, Wilde, Henley and Morris were thought
of as copying or trying to copy the image which was always opposite
to the natural self or the natural world. Wilde's charm was acquired,

a mask he wore when it pleased him; he lived an imaginary life, performing a play which was the opposite of all he had known in early childhood or youth; he could not endure the sedentary toil of creative art and so remained a man of action. Morris was given the same treatment. His dream world was the antithesis of daily life; more joyous than any contemporary intellectual, he created new forms of melancholy; given to violent outbursts of temper, he wrote romances in which characters faced crises with calm confidence. Lacking that asset, the youthful Yeats was abashed before Wilde 'as wit and man of the world alone'. Morris reminded him of his fierce Pollexfen grandfather. Henley appealed through his certainty and arrogance, the sense of violence he distilled. These three men were dominating, a contrast to John Butler Yeats, and Henley was 'quite plainly not upon the side of our parents'.

John Butler Yeats, incidentally, had been writing to Quinn on 14 October 1920 about Swift and Wilde as devotees of extremes – the one fighting against himself, the other made rotten by his absorption in beauty. Joyce, he went on, got from Dante the terrible hardness of which Wilde had so little and Swift too much. When he read his son's 'Four Years' in *The Dial* of July 1921, he was deeply upset by the family being described as 'enraged' when Willie came back to Bedford Park from his copying chores in Oxford in 1888, seeing the phase as 'one of your dramatis personae.' He was convinced that had his son not 'left him' for Lady Gregory and her friends and associates he would have loved and adored concrete life, and told him so; to Lollie he wrote that he was sure Willie had no malice towards the family and wanted 'to tell histories'.[13] The autobiographer told his sister that the word 'enraged' might be changed to 'troubled' in the Cuala edition – provided it did not upset the type too much.

By September he was writing stern letters to his father after the old man refused to come home, saying he had become ill through nervous tension brought on by Quinn's insistence on his returning. A passage booked for 5 October was now altered to 5 November, but John Butler Yeats secretly had this moved on to 3 December and then, finally, said he would not leave. It was energy, he said to a friend with some justice, that kept him in New York. In vain did his son tell him that Quinn was overworked and worried – he had been deeply involved in what he described as the financial reign of terror which had set in during December 1920. And Quinn was deeply enmeshed in the legal battles to protect Joyce's right to publish *Ulysses* in complete form. He wrote in some justified exasperation that he had 'Old Man Yeats' on his back, Arthur Symons as well whose wife was exorbitantly extravagant, and his Irish friends kept asking him to do things – not to mention Pound and later Eliot for whom he was to negotiate the publication of *The Waste Land* in the United States. No wonder Yeats told his father that Quinn's feeling of responsibility for him made him extremely angry; he told Quinn in a letter of 30 September that his father's inability to return to Ireland was caused by his infirmity of will, though Quinn considered it strength of will, sheer stubbornness. Their early quarrels, he wrote, had been caused by his father regarding the qualities which he thought necessary for achieving success in art or life as egotism, selfishness or brutality. He was reliving the difficult days of Bedford Park again; his father exasperated him and, paradoxically, brought out in him the Pollexfen strain. In March the year before John Butler Yeats had explained the dual nature of his son to Quinn (who had thought St John Ervine unbalanced in his comments on the poet in two articles published in the *North American Review* in February and March) by saying there was a good deal of his mother in 'Willie'. She was not sympathetic; she was not concerned about the feelings of others, being unaware of them, living on an island of her own. Yet simple people who did not know sympathetic discourse and its ways of courtesy knew she was not thinking of herself:

I used to tell her that if I had been lost for years and then suddenly presented myself she would have merely asked 'Have you had your dinner?' All this is very like Willie.

Willie, however, had his worries. When they returned from America lack of progress on the restoration of Ballylee was frustrating, and since the bulk of the funds from the lecture tour were earmarked for getting it finished money seems to have been tight. They rented Michin's Cottage in Shillingford in April 1921, the slight discomfort offset by making 'a pot of money'[14] out of letting Broad Street; thence they moved to Cuttlebrook House in Thame in June. George had had a miscarriage in 1920 and there was now some anxiety about her pregnancy, but she gave birth to a son on 22 August in Thame. Writing to John Quinn to ask him to be godfather along with Lennox Robinson, Yeats reported that she and the child were well, the doctor saying that the baby had a beautiful head. 'All I can say,' Yeats wrote, 'is that he is better looking than a new-born canary (I had four hatch out in my bedroom a little while ago) and nothing like as good-looking as the same bird when it gets its first feathers.'[15]

The Yeats name would not die out now – Yeats's father was immensely pleased at the news – though the baby (registered as William Michael but christened Michael Butler) had a serious operation in Dublin in September, followed by another in London in October after the family had returned to Oxford. In the spring Yeats had been reading Mrs Strong's *Apotheosis and the After Life*, searching out 'signs of the whirling gyres of the historical cones'; later came Trollope. Apart from reading he was busy with his memoirs which made him – he wrote to Olivia Shakespear in August – feel clean, as if he had bathed and put on clean linen. He was characterising Douglas Hyde, AE, Standish O'Grady, Lionel Johnson and 'the verdigris green sectaries' who had wrecked the literary movement for a time, then Wilde and the *Savoy* period. He told her he could return to poetry with a renewed simplicity.[16] He had written poems in the spring which he had earlier described to her as simple and passionate, a lament for lost peace and hope. These were entitled 'Thoughts upon the Present State of the World' when they first appeared in *The Dial* in September, and later became 'Nineteen Hundred and Nineteen'.[17] For Yeats the world ultimately meant Ireland and the poems were inevitably based on the state of things in Ireland.

The first section of the poem, however, places events in Ireland in historical perspective. Yeats had been reading Thucydides; many ingenious lovely things had gone in the destruction of Athens:

> There stood
> Amid the ornamental bronze and stone
> An ancient image made of olive wood –
> And gone are Phidias' famous ivories
> And all the golden grasshoppers and bees.

He sketches in the Edwardian and early Georgian peace with its impeccable law, the amelioration brought about by public opinion, an army a thing for show; but all has changed:

> Now days are dragon-ridden, the nightmare
> Rides upon sleep: a drunken soldiery
> Can leave the mother, murdered at her door,

> To crawl in her own blood, and go scot-free;
> The night can sweat with terror . . .

He comes to one of his resonant cries of despair:

> But is there any comfort to be found?
> Man is in love and loves what vanishes,
> What more is there to say?

Again, the thought of *A Vision* is there; the second section deals with the effect of the Platonic year, the third with the futility of past dreams. The fourth section records the new bitterness; the fifth, with a powerful echo of Blake, turns to mockery, while the sixth, with its vision of violence and witchcraft, draws upon past tradition about the dance of the daughters of Herodias, a witch queen who called sorcerers to Sabbaths. In a headnote to an early poem, 'The Hosting of the Sidhe',[18] Yeats wrote that Sidhe is the Gaelic for wind and the Sidhe (or faeries) journeyed in winds like the daughters of Herodias in the Middle Ages. He may have been remembering Heine's *Atta Troll* and Arthur Symons's poem 'The Dance of the Daughters of Herodias', but the poem shifts to the Irish evil spirit Robert, son of Art, who was the fourteenth-century incubus of Dame Alice Kyteler of Kilkenny who had been married four times. It was reputed that she poisoned her first three husbands and deprived the fourth of his senses by philtres and incantations. The Bishop of Ossory – Richard de Ledrede, a Franciscan friar – held an inquest in 1324 and found that there was a band of sorcerers in the city of Kilkenny headed by Dame Alice. Yeats got his information about this scandal from various sources. The sacrifice of 'bronzed peacock feathers, red combs of her cocks', for instance, probably came from Holinshed's *Historie of Ireland* (1577), but in addition to MS accounts in the British Museum of the proceedings against Dame Alice and her confederates, Yeats also read Carrigan's *History of the Diocese of Ossory* as well as the account of the trial in the *Transactions of the Ossory Archaeological Society*. Probably he also read the chapter on Dame Alice in St John D. Seymour's *Irish Witchcraft and Demonology* (1913). Why did he develop this train of thought? His note on the poem in *The Dial* of September 1921 said, 'The country people see at times certain apparitions whom they name now "fallen angels", now "ancient inhabitants of the country" and describe as riding at whiles "with flowers upon the heads of the horses".' He assumed that now the times had become worse these horsemen were giving way to worse. But what may have triggered off his interest in the doings of the people of Kilkenny was a curious episode in the automatic writing which had occurred on 23 February 1918, when a spirit wrote that her name was Ann[e] Hyde, Duchess of Ormonde; she had married her husband James in July 1681 and had come to give the Yeatses her 'dear love'. Two days later George dreamed of her; her child had lived only three days and she herself had died young. Yeats looked her up in Burke's *Peerage*; after confusing her with another Anne Hyde – the daughter of Edward Hyde, the Lord Chancellor and Earl of Clarendon, and wife of James II – he turned to the *Dictionary of National Biography*, Clarendon's *Diary* and Carte's biography of James Butler, who became Duke of Ormonde in 1680. His wife Anne, who had the courtesy title of Countess of Ossory, had died unexpectedly in 1677, having had a miscarriage. It appeared from the automatic script that she and the child that never lived wished to reincarnate. More communication ensued in July; a query from Yeats as to why Anne Hyde had chosen them as her son's parents, and later a script suggesting that their child could be in some way connected with an avatar or avatars. The word came from George Russell's vision of 1896, of a child rising above Ben Bulben: this vision linked the ancient gods of Ireland, magic, forerunners and spiritual revelation. The avatar would be fifth from 'the work'. Yeats took this to mean his child would be the fifth in line from the Rev. John Yeats, rector of Drumcliff, fifth of those who had lived in the shadow of Ben Bulben.[19]

That a daughter – christened Anne Butler after the Countess – rather than a son was born to the Yeatses in February 1919 was excused by the communicator Thomas. Sex could not be influenced by the communicators, but a second child could be envisaged. On 19 June 1919 a communicator suggested that Yeats should study the Hyde papers in various museums and write Anne's history; she was buried in a church near Kilkenny. The Yeatses went there in July 1919 to visit St Canice's Cathedral and search for local information. The impressive size of Kilkenny Castle, the Butler seat, flanked by the river and dominating the city, presumably impressed Yeats, but their expedition was disappointing; they did not discover Anne Hyde's burial place.

In October 1921 Yeats wrote an entry in a notebook relating to the disclosures about Anne Hyde made in the automatic script. The likelihood of their son, born two months before, being a sole avatar was not indicated in the automatic script, but Yeats obviously found the idea of avatars of great interest because of his belief that the revelation of a subjective avatar, of a new civilisation, would be by shock – something indicated in 'The Second Coming'[20] and returned to in a session of the automatic writing in November 1919.

The Irish situation was conducive to such thinking. In July 1921 de Valera and other leaders of Sinn Fein and the IRA – among them Arthur Griffith and Michael Collins – agreed a truce with British representatives in Ireland. By 6 December the Anglo-Irish Treaty was signed in London, creating the Irish Free State with a constitutional status akin to that of Canada. By late December Yeats was in deep gloom; though he expected the Treaty to be ratified by the Dail, as it was to be, by a small majority, he feared the bitterness that could follow; all could be blood and misery. The Treaty had left open the question of what 'Ireland' meant. Six counties were given the choice of opting out of the Irish Free State. (A Boundary Commission was to adjust the border, and some of the Irish delegates who had signed the Treaty expected that two counties, Tyrone and Fermanagh, would be transferred to the Free State because of their predominantly Catholic and nationalist populations – vainly, as it turned out, when the Commission met in 1924.) Despite his forebodings – there was a chance, he thought, that the extreme party might carry the country – Yeats decided that he would like to live in Dublin. George was enthusiastic for the move.

If chaos ensued, he wrote to Olivia Shakespear, they would abandon Ballylee to the owls and rats and live in some far land. If England and Ireland were divided 'beyond all hope of remedy' the children could not be brought up in Ireland to inherit bitterness, nor in England either where, being Irish by family, fame and tradition, they would live in an unnatural condition and grow sour and argumentative.[21]

By mid-February he became more cheerful. He found consolation in the fact that his father who had died on 3 February of a brief illness – 'a tired heart' – brought on by a long walk in the cold, had not survived into infirmity but died in his sleep. (J.B.Y.'s last letter to Lily, written on 1 February 1922, characteristically discussing the differences between Pollexfen and Yeats temperaments, proclaimed that his 'insistence on the fact that money was of small account compared to spiritual and artistic matters has borne its fruit and I am content'.) Yeats regretted, however, that his father had not lived to see his son established in Dublin.This had happened because George (who could stand Oxford no longer) had gone to Ireland and bought, at a very low price, 82 Merrion Square – the kind of large dignified house that his father, had he been successful, might have been expected to own in Dublin's most prestigious square ('to Dublin what Berkeley Square is to London', he told Olivia), then occupied largely by members of the professions.[22] Yeats himself recalled a ballad naming the Square as Wellington's birthplace (though Wellington himself had no idea where he was born). Now he felt 'very grand', delighted that his children would grow up in a spacious home – something he had lacked after he left Sligo: indeed he had been fearing something like the Ashfield Terrace house into which they had all been crammed in his later schooldays in Dublin. Two rooms in Ballylee Castle were nearly finished, so they went to Ireland in March, letting Broad Street till July. Finding Ballylee delightful after the uncertainties of Dublin, Yeats finished *The Trembling of the Veil* there, having gone to an Irish Race conference in Paris; he had been nominated as a delegate by the Ard Fheis of Sinn Fein, a first sign that he would not be without honour in the new country. Other honours were to follow.

Political tensions between those who supported the Treaty and those who opposed it increased. In June the British government, following the murder in London of Sir Henry Wilson, a Field Marshal and a unionist, put pressure on Michael Collins to attack the anti-Treaty forces who were occupying the Four Courts in Dublin. Civil war had now broken out; part of the centre of Dublin was again in ruins. Collins pursued the fighting with energy, recapturing Cork, but was himself killed in an ambush in County Cork in August. His death followed on that of Arthur Griffith from a heart attack brought on by overwork; the new leaders, William Cosgrave, Kevin O'Higgins, Ernest Blythe and Richard Mulcahy, using an Emergency Powers Bill, decided that any republicans taken in arms would be shot. In return, the anti-Treaty republicans decided that any members of the Dail who had voted for the Emergency Powers Act would be shot on sight. In the violent atmosphere before the Civil War began Yeats had noticed that everyone spoke with caution, not knowing who would be master tomorrow. But despite some minor alarms all was relatively quiet at

Ballylee, quieter still when there were no railways running, no
newspapers, no posts. Often, he wrote to Olivia, they sat all day in
the garden – George gardening, he himself writing and Michael
asleep under a tree.[23] He was correcting proofs and writing 'Meditations in Time of Civil War'[24] which captures the atmosphere of
the time:

> We are closed in, and the key is turned
> On our uncertainty; somewhere
> A man is killed, or a house burned,
> Yet no clear fact to be discerned . . .

Both sides visited the tower:

> An affable Irregular,
> A heavily-built Falstaffian man,
> Comes cracking jokes of civil war
> As though to die by gunshot were
> The finest play under the sun.
>
> A brown Lieutenant and his men,
> Half dressed in national uniform,
> Stand at my door, and I complain
> Of the foul weather, hail and rain,
> A pear-tree broken by the storm.
>
> I count those feathered balls of soot
> The moor-hen guides upon the stream,
> To silence the envy in my thought;
> And turn towards my chamber, caught
> In the cold snows of a dream.

The poem moves from a contemplation of ancestral houses, a
pondering whether glory can be inherited, whether greatness van-
ishes along with the violence that went to the making of great houses,
the creation in stone of

> The sweetness that all longed for night and day,
> The gentleness none there had ever known . . .

His own house, Ballylee Castle, now called Thoor Ballylee (from
the Irish *túr*, a tower; he wrote to Olivia Shakespear that it would
keep people from suspecting them of a deer park and modern gothic)
is described in the second and third poems, and the fourth moves

to wonder how his descendants will live: will the vigour – the flower of the poem – be transmitted to them? He knows, however,

>whatever flourish and decline
>These stones remain their monument and mine.

Nevertheless, he was thinking of the present as well as the future. In June he wrote to Olivia Shakespear that he was tired and in a rage at being old:

>... I am all I ever was and much more but an enemy has bound me and twisted me so I can plan and think as I never could, but no longer achieve all I plan and think ...[25]

At Ballylee the republicans blew up the ancient bridge one midnight: 'They forbade us to leave the house, but were otherwise polite, even saying at last "Good-night, thank you", as though we had given them the bridge.'[26] The neighbourhood became quite peaceful as no bridges were left, but the river at Ballylee was dammed by the debris of the bridge and the kitchen was two feet under water the day the family left for Dublin. They had planned to return to stay with Lady Gregory while superintending the finishing of another tower room, but this plan was abandoned as somebody had shot the builder and he was in hospital.

In November came the *Later Poems* and *Plays in Prose and Verse*, for which Charles Ricketts had designed the binding, a unicorn and fountain for the end papers. Yeats and his wife were delighted; he thought that young people find an identity between an author's imagination and paper and book-cover, and was pleased with the idea that young readers would come to his work in this 'serviceable and perfect' form.[27]

On a visit to London to lecture, Yeats dined with T. S. Eliot and with Dulac, to whom he wrote on his return to Dublin telling him he had become a Senator. Gogarty, who had urged his appointment on the government (he had been a friend of Griffith and became a Senator himself), had brought the news to 82 Merrion Square when Yeats was in London; getting no answer, he had chalked 'Senator W. B. Yeats' on the letterbox and next day phoned Mrs Yeats, telling her that her husband's quondam membership of the IRB (which she neither knew of nor had guessed at) was the reason for his appointment, not primarily his poetry nor his work for the Abbey, though he later praised President Cosgrave for recognising the value of Yeats's distinction, his potential contribution to the new state.

Yeats was delighted. 'I feel I have become a personage,'[28] he wrote to Olivia Shakespear, having received an honorary degree from Queen's University, Belfast and from Trinity College, Dublin as well. The latter was a pleasant renewal of the family's link since his father, grandfather and great-grandfather had been graduates (and his son and his son's son have become graduates in their turn). And it was the family friend Louis Claud Purser who looked after the social arrangements; he was sometimes appealed to on points of classical knowledge, and had corrected Yeats's proofs upon occasion. There was, however, a family division when Yeats was a Senator, since his brother, who had returned from England to live in Ireland (at Greystones, County Wicklow) in 1910, supported the anti-Treaty forces. Yeats was proud of his brother's paintings as John Butler Yeats had been, thinking his painter son had 'the poetic mind' and would become a great artist. Family feeling reasserted itself and the brothers resumed their relationship in which they accepted each other without being – as Jack once put it to me as he did a lightning sketch of a horse kicking free of an outside car – 'closely in touch very often'. Jack was in many ways very self-contained though sociable; he concentrated on a few friends.

Yeats took the new kind of work in the Senate very seriously; a week after his first appearance, he described it as:

... a new technique which I am learning is silence – I have only spoken once and then but six sentences and shall not speak again perhaps till I am (if I shall ever be) at ease with it ... At the Senate house I have for near neighbours two senators, one of whom has had his house bombed for being senator, and one is under sentence of death because he owns the *Freeman's Journal*. For all that we are a dull (and as President Cosgrave has pointed out with evident content) well-dressed crowd. I shall speak very little but probably intrigue a great deal to get some old projects into action.[29]

Later he was to write to Olivia and others of two bullet holes in the windows of the house and of his armed guard, there to protect him, who had challenged him on his own stairs. He gave his guards detective stories 'to train them in the highest tradition of their profession'. In January 1923 Maud Gonne was arrested and imprisoned, and he wrote to Iseult to offer to help 'with the authorities' in getting warm blankets for her. Maud had written to him to say that if he did not denounce the government she would renounce his society for ever. Being a Senator had other, more menacing dangers. Some had their houses burned down. Gogarty, in addition, was kidnapped from his house and brought to another house by armed men, from whom he escaped by jumping into the Liffey and swimming to safety. Later Yeats was present when he released two swans upon the river, having pledged them to the Liffey as an offering should he escape; he wrote a Preface for Gogarty's ensuing book of poems, *An Offering of Swans*.

It was a time of great fulfilment: long a bachelor, he was now married with a son to carry on the Yeats name; long poor and unsettled, he was now rooted in Ireland, owning his castle in the west and his fine town house in Dublin; long deeply committed to Irish politics, he had now come – via the Contemporary Club, the Young Ireland Society, the IRB and the presidency of the '98 Association – to a position where he could join in the creation of the institutions of the new state, where the people he met were like coral insects 'but with some design in our heads of the ultimate island'.[30]

As a Senator he was to have a considerable influence in areas where he possessed expertise; he reserved himself, he wrote to Quinn, for the things he understood. These were the Irish Manuscripts Committee, the preservation of historic buildings, the Irish National Gallery and Museum and, particularly, copyright as well as the matter of a new coinage – he chaired the committee which selected the excellent designs.

He continued to press for the return of the Lane pictures to Ireland, making several visits to London for this purpose, and he planned an Irish Academy of Letters. He was impressed by his father's friend Andrew Jameson, of the distillery firm; he thought that the few able men among the elected Senators had been nominated by Ministers:

In its early days some old banker or lawyer would dominate the House, leaning upon the back of the chair in front, always speaking with undisturbed self-possession as at some table in a board room. My imagination sets up against him some typical elected man, emotional as a youthful chimpanzee, hot and vague, always disturbed, always hating something or other.[31]

He found it difficult, however, to reach any ease of conversation with the government Ministers; though several of them used to visit 82 Merrion Square he felt that he could never know them; their minds knew no play that his mind could play at. He could not resist some irony in his Senate speeches, which he composed carefully, walking up and down in his study, shaping and reshaping them, then dictating them to his wife when they sounded right to him – often 'breaking into laughter over some witty phrase, or mischievous illustration of a point'. The Head Usher in the House remembered his 'mellifluous and slightly ironic tone' as he occasionally intervened in a debate. When he sought to persuade earnestly, 'his voice became strong and his manner firm, and all touches of the faint underlying humour vanished'. Mr Kelly was himself not unironic in describing Yeats's manner 'to his inferiors . . . bland, kindly and inoffensively condescending, which, added to his somewhat bemused look, usually evoked responsive feelings of protective affection, which, not unlikely, caused the Senator some inward amusement.'[32]

FIFTEEN

1923–1927

There was even greater fulfilment for the poet whom many had thought finished when he published his *Collected Works* in 1908, the year he had written 'All things can tempt me from this craft of verse',[1] for he was awarded the Nobel Prize for Literature in 1923. Bertie Smyllie, the editor of *The Irish Times*, recounted how he gave him the news that for the first time an Irish poet had won the prize

... which amounted to quite a considerable sum, I think between seven and eight thousand pounds. I was rather friendly with Yeats at the time, and it was fairly late in the evening, getting on to eleven o'clock I suppose, and I rang him up at his house, hoping that he didn't know the news. He came to the phone himself – he *didn't* know the news. I said, 'Mr Yeats, I've got very good news for you, a very great honour has been conferred upon you,' and I was rather enthusiastic and gushing at the time, and I said, 'This is a great honour not only for you but for the country,' and I could tell that he was getting slightly impatient to know what it was all about, so I said, 'You've been awarded the Nobel Prize, a very great honour to you and a very great honour to Ireland,' and to my amazement the only question he asked was, 'How much, Smyllie, how much is it?'[2]

Various reporters called; by half past twelve the Yeatses were alone. They searched for a bottle of wine to celebrate, couldn't find one so cooked some sausages instead. Yeats decided that they should go to Stockholm for him to receive the prize on 10 December; he found the ceremony impressive and thought as he examined his medal, which shows a young man listening to a muse who has a great lyre in her hand and is young and beautiful, that he was good-looking once like that young man, 'but my unpractised verse was full of infirmity, my Muse old as it were; and now I am old and rheumatic, and nothing to look at, but my Muse is young.' Like the angels in Swedenborg's vision, she seemed to be moving perpetually 'towards the day spring of her youth'. It was the first time he had seen a Court and he was most impressed by the reception at the Palace, waiting in a long gallery surrounded by black-coated civilians, grey- and silver-clad guards many wearing the chains of the three Swedish Orders: 'men of learning, men of letters, men of science, much of the intellect of Sweden'. 'Where else could a like assembly be gathered,' he wondered; and before the evening ended he felt moved 'as if by some religious ceremony, though to a different end, for here it is Life herself that is praised'.[3] Some years later he was delighted to hear that the Swedish Royal Family said he had the manners of a courtier and that they had liked him better than any previous Nobel Prize winner.

He lectured to the Swedish Royal Academy on the Irish theatre, saying that when the King gave him his medal and diploma two forms should have stood on either side of him – an old woman, Lady Gregory, sinking into the infirmity of age, and the ghost of a young man, John Synge. They would have been pleased to be there because their work, like his own, 'delighted in history and tradition'. Then came a visit to the great new Town Hall; no work comparable in method or achievement, he thought, had been accomplished since the Italian cities felt the excitement of the Renaissance; the building expressed 'subordination, design, a sense of human need'.

The Royal Theatre staged his *Cathleen ni Houlihan* and Goldsmith's *She Stoops to Conquer*, and then the week in Stockholm had ended; it was to be encapsulated in *The Bounty of Sweden*, an eloquent sort of 'bread and butter letter' to Sweden. The prize money was welcome and he reassured Quinn that none of it would be spent on Ballylee. He invested £6,000 and kept £500 to pay off the debt on the Merrion Square house or to pay for Lily Yeats's expenses; she was seriously ill with tuberculosis and he had gone to London in July to arrange her stay in a nursing home. The rest of the £7,500 had gone on the trip to Sweden and on finishing the furnishing of the house, as well as buying something he had always wanted: the nucleus of a reference library. He bought the *Encyclopaedia Britannica*, the *Cambridge Histories (Ancient, Medieval, Modern)*, an edition of Gibbon's *Decline and Fall*, as well as art books.

The Nobel Prize had brought Yeats 'an immense correspondence' from all over the world, but his main work in 1924 was the completion of *A Vision*, which Werner Laurie was to publish; he was also revising

and rewriting parts of various volumes of his work for the Macmillan
Uniform Edition, in which his *Essays* were published in March. In
July *The Cat and the Moon and Certain Poems* was published by Cuala,
the play, written shortly after his marriage, intended as the equivalent
to a Japanese *kiogen* – a farce in colloquial language centring on a
holy well visited by a lame man on a blind man's back in search of
a cure. It was prompted by St Colman's Well, near Thoor Ballylee,
and by a local story; the symbolism is highly, indeed over, compressed, the musicians' song 'The Cat and the Moon' having the
cat suggesting man and the moon as the opposite he seeks perpetually; the lame man taking the blind man on his back suggests –
'doubtless', as Yeats's note put it – man becoming one with his
opposite.

A note to the play gave Yeats scope to mythologise his marriage.[4]
In this the Caliph Harun Al-Rashid presents Kusta Ben Luka with
a new bride; 'she had, to the great surprise of her friends, fallen in
love with the elderly philosopher'. In another tradition Kusta had
'bought her from a passing merchant'. There were other stories,
but general agreement that he was 'warned in a dream' to accept
the Caliph's gift, and 'a few days after his marriage his wife began
to talk in her sleep', telling him all the things he had spent his life
vainly searching for, in the great library of the Caliph and in the
conversation of wise men. This in-joking resulted in 'The Gift of
Harun Al-Rashid', written in 1923, in which Yeats pays tribute to
his wife's part in *A Vision* and to her beauty:

> All, all those gyres and cubes and midnight things
> Are but a new expression of her body
> Drunk with the bitter sweetness of her youth.

He can proclaim his delight with a fine flourish:

> And now my utmost mystery is out.
> A woman's beauty is a storm-tossed banner;
> Under it wisdom stands, and I alone –
> Of all Arabia's lovers I alone –
> Nor dazzled by the embroidery, nor lost
> In the confusion of its night-dark folds,
> Can hear the armed man speak.[5]

Another adventure of the system's ideas went into a poem 'Leda
and the Swan',[6] explained in a note as originally written for *The Irish
Statesman*, a largely political review, at the request of the Editor,

George Russell (who decided against publishing it, diplomatically saying his conservative readers would misunderstand it). It was meant as a comment on politics – that the soil which produced the philosophers, encyclopaedists and the French Revolution was now exhausted and some movement heralded by a violent annunciation would come from above. It takes the rape of Leda the human by the father of the gods for metaphor, with its subsequent effect upon human history, Leda's daughter Helen causing the fall of Troy. Scholars and critics have occupied themselves with likely sources for the imagery, suggesting, *inter alia*, Spenser's *Prothalamion* and his *Faery Queene*, Dryden's 'Alexander's Feast', Todhunter's *Helena in Troas* and Gogarty's 'To the Liffey with Swans'. The visual imagery may be owed to an Etruscan bas-relief in the British Museum according to Charles Madge, but Yeats possessed a coloured photographic copy of Michelangelo's picture of the rape at Venice, and he probably saw the statue of Leda and the Swan, formerly at Markree Castle, Collooney in County Sligo. (It was later in a garden north of Sligo when I saw it, but was reputed in 1986 to have been bought by a dealer.) Whatever the sources, Yeats gave the poem the stamp of his style, his capacity to compress, to intensify, to interrogate the reader by his probing, awestruck questions which are really affirmations of his own highly individual thought:

> Being so caught up,
> So mastered by the brute blood of the air,
> Did she put on his knowledge with his power
> Before the indifferent beak could let her drop?

'Leda and the Swan' first appeared in *To-Morrow*, a review established for a brief life of two issues by a group of younger writers, including F. R. Higgins and Francis and Iseult Stuart, whom Yeats wanted to help; he wrote an unsigned leading article, proclaiming the immortality of the soul, counting among atheists bad writers and bishops of all denominations, dismissing demagogues, calling the soul back to its ancient sovereignty, declaring 'it can do whatever it please'. Yeats himself must almost have had a feeling of omnipotence during 1924 as he worked on, steadily getting the system into order, with the pleasant interruptions of receiving an honorary degree from the University of Aberdeen in 1923 and enjoying the celebration of the Tailteann games which took place in August after the Dublin Horse Show. This was the period of his wearing a top-hat, being a man of influence if not power and possessing, as he thought, a mysterious knowledge that *A Vision* would reveal. But it was the last year his health was to be unimpaired. One of his eyes had become virtually useless; he was growing a little deaf, and his body had filled out too much for his liking. On the regular walks he substituted for his Swedish exercises he found he was suffering from loss of breath. His blood pressure was too high. To the doctor asking if he had been over-excited, he replied that he had lived a life of excitement; it was time for a rest from Dublin life, a change of scene. With his wife he took a long holiday, the longest he had ever had, lasting from November 1924 to February 1925, in Sicily, in Capri and in Rome.

The illness accentuated his sense of increasing age; he was now 'a sixty-year-old smiling public man'.[7] But age was a thing to rage at and the public man was, after all, still a poet capable of passionate expression of public and private matters. The full flowering of his poetry became obvious in *The Tower* (1928), which contained some magnificent poems establishing Yeats as a most powerful poet who could use the speech of ordinary men with supremely evocative rhetorical skill, still capable of consummate artistry, still capable of putting old ideas in new ways.

Some of the poems in the volume had been written years before and Yeats had kept them back for obvious reasons. 'I don't want them,' he once said to his wife, 'to know too much about me.' Thus the volume included 'The New Faces' of 1912 and 'Owen Aherne and His Dancers' of 1917. Some poems had first appeared in various journals, others in *Seven Poems and a Fragment* (1922), *The Cat and the Moon* (1924) and *October Blast* (1927). To the broad effects of 'Nineteen Hundred and Nineteen' and 'Meditations in Time of Civil War', he now added 'The Tower',[8] finished in October 1925, which was to set the note of many future poems about the tension between ageing body and exuberant imagination. The first section suggests that he should

> bid the Muse go pack,
> Choose Plato and Plotinus for a friend
> Until imagination, ear and eye,
> Can be content with argument and deal
> In abstract things; or be derided by
> A sort of battered kettle at the heel.

This poem uses actual figures from the neighbourhood of the tower, Mrs French and Mary Hynes as well as the tower's previous inhabitants and one of his imagined characters, Hanrahan, hedge schoolmaster turned poet. They are given existence through intensified attention to concentrated moments of their lives; he asks if they, too, raged about old age. The section ends with a heartfelt cry:

> Does the imagination dwell the most
> Upon a woman won or woman lost?
> If on the lost, admit you turned aside
> From a great labyrinth out of pride,
> Cowardice, some silly over-subtle thought
> Or anything called conscience once;
> And that if memory recur, the sun's
> Under eclipse and the day blotted out.

In the second section he had extended the local lore (the subject of his 1900 essay, 'Dust hath closed Helen's Eye') about the peasant girl Mary Hynes, celebrated by the blind Irish poet Raftery – a link with Helen and the blind poet Homer and, by implication, with Maud Gonne and his own poetry – by discovering the anecdote about a lady of a local big house, Mrs French, in *Recollections of Jonah Barrington* which Mrs Yeats was reading to him at the time he wrote the poem. His interest in Sir Jonah Barrington was symptomatic of his recognition of his roots in the Anglo-Irish world of the eighteenth century – the one Irish century without confusion, as he remarked – and its authors whom he had either not known or, for his nationalist purposes, ignored when he was exploring the world of Irish legend and mythology in his youth, something recognised in his reference in the third section to

> The people of Burke and of Grattan
> That gave, though free to refuse –

Barrington was part of the society that had flourished in the high peak of the Anglo-Irish ascendancy, the period of Grattan's Parliament, of the building in Dublin of elegant town houses – Powerscourt, Belvedere, Clonmell and Alborough – of Fitzwilliam, Merrion and Mountjoy Squares and of fine public buildings – the Parliament House and Trinity College, the Viceregal Lodge, and the Custom House and the Four Courts which graced the Liffey's quays. It was an age of high achievement in artefacts – in furniture, silverware, Waterford glass, plasterwork, book-binding. Painting had developed rapidly in the latter half of the eighteenth century, the theatres had flourished and oratory cast its spells in the Courts and in the Parliament in Dublin.

Yeats began to explore the eighteenth-century Anglo-Irish writers with zest. Captain Dermot MacManus, a well-read man with an excellent library, whom he described as 'a revolutionary soldier', had introduced him to Bishop Berkeley's works and Lennox Robinson gave him a 2-volume edition of Berkeley. Edmund Burke was a suitable statesman for a Senator of Yeats's kind to study, for he supplied a gradualist, conserving attitude. His view in *Reflections* that the state was 'a tree, not a mechanism to be pulled in pieces and put up again but an oak tree that had grown through centuries' was one quoted by Yeats in the Senate, a symbol he had used earlier in speeches in 1893 and 1903–4. Though Swift was eventually to mean much more to him, by 30 November 1925 when he made a speech at the Irish Literary Society on 'The Child and the State', he was sufficiently at home with both Berkeley and Burke to see how their attitudes, their Anglo-Irish culture, could be useful in the shaping of the new, the predominantly Catholic Ireland of his time; though he had earlier disregarded them as part of the English system, he now saw them as non-English, as Irish innovators.

He liked to use both men as part of the Anglo-Irish tradition; at a dinner in Trinity College in 1927, for instance, he announced that 'Berkeley was the first to say the world is a vision; Burke was the first to say a nation is a tree.' He summed them up in one of the fine sweeping affirmative generalisations he enjoyed: 'And those two sayings are a foundation of modern thought'.

He returned from his continental holiday in fine fettle, though by April when he went to London to see politicians in connection with the Lane pictures – he now stayed at the Savile Club – he suspected that George and Lady Gregory had conspired to send him off because he had been writing too much verse and reading too much philosophy. Though by the third section of 'The Tower' he had declared his faith:

> I mock Plotinus' thought
> And cry in Plato's teeth,
> Death and Life were not
> Till man made up the whole,
> Made lock, stock and barrel
> Out of his bitter soul . . .

The poem ends on a quiet, masterly dying cadence of sound, for, in the Irish phrase, he intends to make his soul,

> Compelling it to study
> In a learned school
> Till the wreck of body,
> Slow decay of blood,
> Testy delirium
> Or dull decrepitude,
> Or what worse evil come –
> The death of friends, or death
> Of every brilliant eye
> That made a catch in the breath –
> Seem but the clouds of the sky
> When the horizon fades;
> Or a bird's sleepy cry
> Among the deepening shades

Life was not all study in the spring of 1925. He wrote 'The Three Monuments' – referring to the statues in Dublin streets of Nelson, Daniel O'Connell and Parnell, to whose private lives he was to allude challengingly in the course of the speech he made in the Senate on 11 June, opposing the government's measure to outlaw bills making divorce legal in the twenty-six counties. This speech became notorious for, regarding the Bill as an infringement of the rights of the Protestant minority, Yeats had prepared it very carefully, wanting to stress that though Protestants were a minority they were no less part of Ireland than the Catholic majority. Differences existed; there was no reason not to be aware of them, indeed not to be proud of them. The peroration was itself a proud one, stressing the patriotic role of the Anglo-Irish:

We against whom you have done this thing are no petty people. We are one of the great stocks of Europe. We are the people of Burke; we are the people of Grattan; we are the people of Swift, the people of Emmet, the people of Parnell. We have created the most of the modern literature of this country. We have created the best of its political intelligence.[9]

There was a visit to Mürren in the autumn of 1925 and then came Milan, a place he had disliked in 1907 and still did. Once *A Vision* was completed he had allowed himself to read philosophy, which might have interfered with its ideas. There must have been a feeling of vacuum after the proofs were finally corrected and the hard work of years in print, the book being published on 15 January 1926.

After it came out, there was anti-climax. It reminded him, he wrote to Olivia, of the stones he used to drop as a child into a very deep well – the splash far-off and very faint. The only review, he told her, was by AE. In it his old friend, recording how he had followed Yeats's mind since he was a boy, objected to the apparent rejection of free will, that Yeats would have him believe that a great wheel turns ceaselessly and that he and all others drop into inevitable groove after groove, that his will was only free to accept or rebel but not to alter what was fated. But he was appreciative of the book's cold beauty, aware of the system's bewildering complexity but coherent metaphysical structure, and suggested that an impish humour informed the portraits of men and women chosen as typical of their phases, as well as recording his likely reservations about Yeats's interpretation of historical ages. He concluded that almost any of its crammed pages would need a volume to elucidate its meanings and proffered the idea that it might be discussed feverishly by commentators a century hence, might even come to be regarded as the greatest of Yeats's works; he was glad it was written.[10]

Yeats was now thinking a good deal about education, and was influenced by Gentile's *The Reform of Education* which he read in Dino Bigongiari's translation of 1923. On his Italian holiday in 1925 he had discussed Gentile with Joseph Hone, the Irish publisher and biographer, who spent a morning in bookshops in Rome with Mrs Yeats looking for books which could have influenced the Fascist revolution. Mrs Yeats translated and summarised some of these for him. Later he read Gentile's *Teoria Generale dello Spirito come Atto puro*, translated by Wildon Carr. He had read Croce's *Philosophy of Vico* in 1924 and began to study his *Philosophy of the Practical* in 1926, having been led to him by lectures on his *Estetica* given by Douglas Ainslie in London. But there was more to his interest in education than theory; he became a friend of the Minister of Education, Joseph O'Neill, and his wife, and learned a lot about Irish schooling from them. He was disturbed by the state of school buildings in Ireland – insanitary, out of repair, badly heated, too small – but even more by what he heard from school-teachers of the anarchy and violence of young people. All over the world during the Great War young people became anarchic and violent, he said in a speech on 'The Child and the State', but

... in Ireland it is worse than elsewhere, for we have in a sense been at war for generations and of late that war has taken the form of burning and destruction under the eyes of the children. They respect nothing, one teacher said to me. 'I cannot take them through Stephen's Green because they would pull up the plants.' Go anywhere in Ireland and you will hear the same complaint. The children, everyone will tell you are individually intelligent and friendly, yet have so little sense of their duty to community and neighbour that if they meet an empty house in a lonely place they will smash all the windows.

He realised lessons on civic duty were not the answer but saw as the remedy teaching religion, civic duty and history as all but inseparable:

Every child in growing from infancy to maturity should pass in imagination through the history of its own race and through something of the history of the world, and the most powerful part in that history is played by religion. Let the child go its own way when maturity comes, but it is our business that it has something of that whole inheritance ...[11]

In February 1926 he visited St Otteran's School in Waterford to see the Montessori principles (about which he was well-informed) in action, as well as those of the Parents National Educational Union. He was most impressed and praised the school on several occasions. The visit led to a magnificent poem, 'Among School Children', an impassioned reflection upon the nature of human life.[12] A draft in his white vellum notebook outlined the topic, the thought that life will waste schoolchildren, 'perhaps that no possible life can fulfil our dreams or even their teacher's hope. Bring in the old thought that life prepares for what never happens.' He sets the scene of the poem casually, conversationally, perhaps ironically:

> I walk through the long schoolroom questioning;
> A kind old nun in a white hood replies;
> The children learn to cipher and to sing,
> To study reading-books and histories,
> To cut and sew, be neat in everything
> In the best modern way – the children's eyes
> In momentary wonder stare upon
> A sixty-year-old smiling public man.

He dreams of Maud telling him of some experience 'That changed some childish day to tragedy'; he wonders if she was like the children he sees:

> And thereupon my heart is driven wild:
> She stands before me as a living child.

Then he moves to thoughts of her appearance and his, wonders how a youthful mother would feel seeing her child sixty years old. The poem, influenced considerably by the ideas of Gentile, takes off into contemplation of Plato, Aristotle and Pythagoras who became 'Old clothes upon old sticks to scare a bird'. The poem was, he wrote to Olivia Shakespear, a fragment of his last curse on old age; it meant that even the greatest men are 'owls, scarecrows' by the time they achieve fame. The poem's end is a contemplation of life beyond the apparent limitations and restrictions of normal experience, an affirmation of human possibilities:

> Labour is blossoming or dancing where
> The body is not bruised to pleasure soul,
> Nor beauty born out of its own despair,
> Nor blear-eyed wisdom out of midnight oil.
> O chestnut tree, great-rooted blossomer,
> Are you the leaf, the blossom or the bole?
> O body swayed to music, O brightening glance,
> How can we know the dancer from the dance?

His attitudes to education were generous, aimed at helping children to self-fulfilment. He regarded the child itself as the proper end of education, pondering how often European education had drifted into error. For several centuries religion's systems were regarded as more important than children; and he deplored the modern habit of regarding the nation as more important than the child and subordinating the child to the idea of the nation. In the words of his contemporary at the High School, John Eglinton, Yeats himself had enjoyed an enviable immunity from the various ignominies of school discipline; his father's educational views had aimed at spontaneous development. The mind, he believed, should be free to create, not at the mercy of any imposed abstraction, while recognising its human limitations.

The limitations imposed by age found expression in 'Sailing to Byzantium',[13] the opening poem in *The Tower*, provoked by seeing a pair of lovers – 'the young in one another's arms'; it is a powerful poem, arising out of a personal mood, as the first draft MS showed:

> All that men know, or think they know, being young,
> Cry that my tale is told, my story sung.

Gradually the autobiographical element was generalised as version succeeded version. The directness of

> I therefore travel to Byzantium
> Among these sun-brown pleasant mariners
> Another dozen days and we shall come
> Under the jetty and the marble stair

alters to a stress on the age of Byzantium. The mariners bring him to a city

> Where all is ancient, singing at the oars
> That I may look in the great church's dome
> On gold-embedded saints and emperors
> After the mirroring waters and the foam
> Where the dark fins a moment rise
> Of fish that carry souls to paradise.

Ageing poet and ancient city are listed here subtly in the final version of the poem. The birds of sensual life in Ireland give way to the image of the artifice of eternity, the golden bird (probably a childhood memory of the Emperor's nightingale, on the cover of Hans Andersen's tales):

> Of hammered gold and gold enamelling
> To keep a drowsy Emperor awake;
> Or set upon a golden bough to sing
> To lords and ladies of Byzantium
> Or what is past, or passing, or to come.

What Byzantium meant to Yeats is made clear in *A Vision* where he wrote:

I think if I could be given a month of Antiquity and leave to spend it where I chose, I would spend it in Byzantium a little before Justinian opened St Sophia and closed the Academy of Plato. I think I could find in some little wine shop some philosophical worker in mosaic who could answer all my questions, the supernatural descending nearer to him than to Plotinus even, for the pride of his delicate skill would make what was an instrument of power to Princes and Clerics, and a murderous madness in the mob, show as a lovely flexible presence like that of a perfect human body.

I think that in early Byzantium, and maybe never before or since in recorded history, religious, aesthetic and practical life were one, that architect and artificers – though not, it may be, poets, for language had been the instrument of controversy and must have grown abstract – spoke to the multitude and the few alike. The painter and the mosaic worker, the worker in gold and silver, the illuminator of Sacred Books, were almost impersonal, almost perhaps without the consciousness of individual design, absorbed in their subject-matter and that the vision of a whole people. They could copy out of old Gospel books those pictures that seemed as sacred as the text, and yet weave all into a vast design, the work of many that seemed the work of one, that made building, picture, pattern, metal-work of rail and lamp, seem but a single image; and this vision, this proclamation of their invisible master, had the Greek nobility, Satan always the still half divine Serpent, never the horned scarecrow of the didactic Middle Ages.[14]

Always ready to fight for his causes, Yeats faced a replay of national-ism's antagonistic attitudes to art when O'Casey's play *The Plough and the Stars* was staged at the Abbey in February 1927. He – largely by lecturing – and Lady Gregory – largely by appealing to wealthy friends – had raised funds for the theatre in England before the Treaty was signed: after that, they felt that support should not be sought outside Ireland. The Irish government, however, influenced by Ernest Blythe – then Minister of Finance – decided to give an annual subsidy to the theatre; this was £800 in 1925 and sub-sequently £1,050. (The Directors henceforth included a government nominee.) While Yeats, Lady Gregory and Lennox Robinson were enthusiastic about *The Plough and the Stars* George O'Brien, the government's nominee, had strong reservations about the prosti-tute's language in Act II, fearing that this must put the subsidy at risk. These antipathies were overcome, as were those of the cast to the coarser elements in the play, which dealt with the Easter Rising in a way which was to madden diehard nationalists by its presentation of non-heroic sides of that action. The theatre was packed for the play, but on the fourth night the hissing and moaning which had greeted the second and third nights erupted into violence. Yeats called for silence, but could not be heard; he had anticipated the demonstration and left the theatre earlier to give a text of what he intended to say to *The Irish Times*:

You have disgraced yourselves again. Is this to be an ever-recurring cel-ebration of the arrival of Irish genius? Synge first, and then O'Casey! The news of the happenings of the past few minutes will go from country to country. Dublin has once more rocked the cradle of genius. From such a scene in this theatre went forth the fame of Synge. Equally the fame of O'Casey is born here tonight. This is his apotheosis.[15]

In April he had an attack of measles (as well as a mild rupture caused by his Swedish exercises) but by May he was at Ballylee, his health improving there. He was writing poetry and 'as always happens', he wrote to Olivia, no matter how he began, it became love poetry before he was finished with it. In April he had been reading philosophy – Whitehead's *Science and the Modern World* in Dublin, followed by Spengler's *Decline of the West* and Plotinus in MacKenna's translation at the tower. He recorded the visit there of an old piper turned beggar through paralysis, who lamented the fall of the great houses burned out or left empty: 'The gentry have kept the shoes on my feet, and the coat on my back and the shilling in my pocket – never once in all the forty and five years that I have been upon the road have I asked a penny of a farmer.'[16] Yeats responded with five shillings and the old beggar headed off for the nearest town – to drink away the five shillings, the poet fancied.

The love poetry of 1926 and 1927, ten of the eleven poems of *A Man Young and Old*, recorded the past in relatively disguised form, 'the wild regrets, for youth and love, of an old man':[17] the effect of Maud; his heart's agony; Olivia's effect on him; his memory of the 'first of all the tribe' in his arms; his laughter at the friends of his youth; the blossoming of love 'When we had all the summer-time/ And she had all the spring'; the secrets of the old; his wildness.[18]

The eleventh poem is 'From "Oedipus at Colonus"'. Yeats had been intermittently interested in translating Sophocles from 1904 onwards. Gogarty made him a rough translation of *Oedipus* in 1904 and there was an idea of staging *Oedipus* in the Abbey in 1910 to show the theatre's freedom from the power of the Lord Chamberlain, who had forbidden the play in England. In the winter of 1911–12 a visitor to Dublin, Dr Rynd of Norwich Cathedral Chapter, read the Greek text aloud while Yeats turned Jebb's version into 'speakable English'. He did not go on because the censorship was withdrawn in England, but several years later his wife found the manuscript and persuaded him to work on it again. This time he used Paul Masqueray's translation of Sophocles into French.

King Oedipus was produced at the Abbey on 6 December, 'bare, hard and natural like a saga' as Yeats described it to Olivia Shakespear. He had again enlisted Gogarty's help, getting him to chant the Greek of the play aloud to him as he wrote. 'The one thing I kept in mind,' he wrote in the preface, 'was that a word unfitted for living speech, out of its natural order, or unnecessary to our modern technique, would check emotion and tire attention.' The translation is extraordinarily effective. The play, like his version

of *Oedipus at Colonus*, catches the spirit of the original and entirely
justifies Yeats's view that when Oedipus at Colonus went into the
Wood of the Furies, he felt the same creeping in his flesh that an
Irish countryman feels in 'certain haunted woods in Galway and
Sligo'.[19] He worked on Sophocles' *Oedipus at Colonus* at the same
time; it was first staged at the Abbey on 12 September 1927. In it
he wanted to be more idiomatic and modern and less literal.

Work on the Oedipus plays slowed up work on his *Autobiographies*,
this part intended to deal with the period from 1900 to 1926 – a
'last great effort'. Other matters also interrupted his creativity,
however: in May he had been appointed Chairman of the Senate
Committee to decide upon a new Irish coinage; this sat between
1926 and 1928 and his report, made up of his own opinions and
impressions, is full of vitality and common sense; here is section VII
of it:

As certain of the beasts represent our most important industry, they were
submitted to the Minister of Agriculture and his experts, and we awaited
the results with alarm. I have not been to Chartres Cathedral for years, but
remember somewhere outside the great door figures of angels or saints,
whose spiritual dignity and architectural effect depend upon bodies much
longer in proportion to the length of their heads than a man's body ever
was. The artist who must fill a given space and suggest some spiritual
quality or rhythmical movement finds it necessary to suppress or exaggerate.
Art, as some French critic has said, is appropriate exaggeration. The expert
on horse-flesh, or bull-flesh or swine-flesh, on the other hand, is bound to
see his subject inanimate and isolated. The coins have suffered less than
we feared. The horse, as first drawn, was more alive than the later version,
for when the hind legs were brought more under the body and the head
lowered, in obedience to technical opinion, it lost muscular tension; we
passed from the open country to the show-ground. But, on the other hand,
it is something to know that we have upon our half-crown a representation
of an Irish hunter, perfect in all its points, and can add the horseman's
pleasure to that of the children and the artists. The first bull had to go,
though one of the finest of all the designs, because it might have upset,
considered as an ideal, the eugenics of the farmyard, but the new bull is as
fine, in a different way. I sigh, however, over the pig, though I admit that
the state of the market for pig's cheeks made the old design impossible. A
design is like a musical composition, alter some detail and all has to be
altered. With the round cheeks of the pig went the lifted head, the look of
insolence and of wisdom, and the comfortable round bodies of the little
pigs. We have instead querulous and harassed animals, better merchandise
but less living.[20]

After a painful bout of arthritis in January 1927, followed by influenza in February, he fought a battle in the Senate over the Copyright Bill in March eventuating in a 'long impassioned speech'. He went on correcting *Oedipus at Colonus*.

In June there followed the tranquillity of the tower; he and George were there on their own with no companion but a large white dog, its face 'like the Prince Consort or a mid-Victorian statue – capable of error but not of sin'.[21] The mixture of reading philosophy and writing verse continued: Hegel and love poems, this time a series of poems to be grouped later as *A Woman Young and Old*. Into this peacefulness came news of the assassination on 10 July of Kevin O'Higgins, the Minister for Justice – shot at Booterstown, a Dublin suburb, on his way to Mass. He and his wife had become friends of the Yeatses and Yeats admired the strength of O'Higgins, who had argued for the executions of those captured with arms in their possession in the Civil War, seventy-seven in all. O'Higgins had said that, 'Nobody can expect to live who has done what I have', a phrase that Yeats was frequently to cite: the murder was 'no mere public event', he wrote to Olivia. It triggered off two poems, 'Blood and the Moon'[22] written in August, and 'Death',[23] written in September:

> Nor dread nor hope attend
> A dying animal;
> A man awaits his end
> Dreading and hoping all;
> Many times he died,
> Many times rose again.
> A great man in his pride
> Confronting murderous men
> Casts derision upon
> Supersession of breath;
> He knows death to the bone –
> Man has created death.

Constance Markiewicz, who had been on the opposite side to O'Higgins in the Civil War, died in August 1927, her sister Eva the year before. Yeats began a poem on the sisters in September and was still working on it in November: they were among 'the dear memories' of his youth and the poem, 'In Memory of Eva Gore-Booth and Con Markiewicz',[24] is an elegy for lost beauty, lost youth, the lost battle with time as well as a condemnation of the

choices the sisters made about their lives.[25] This is a magnificently
evocative poem, based on his memories of staying at the great gaunt
limestone house, Lissadell, as a young man:

> The light of evening, Lissadell,
> Great windows open to the south,
> Two girls in silk kimonos, both
> Beautiful, one a gazelle.
> But a raving autumn shears
> Blossom from the summer's wreath;
> The older is condemned to death,
> Pardoned, drags out lonely years
> Conspiring among the ignorant.
> I know not what the younger dreams –
> Some vague Utopia – and she seems,
> When withered old and skeleton-gaunt,
> An image of such politics.
> Many a time I think to seek
> One or the other out and speak
> Of that old Georgian mansion, mix
> Pictures of the mind, recall
> That table and the talk of youth,
> Two girls in silk kimonos, both
> Beautiful, one a gazelle.
>
> Dear shadows, now you know it all,
> All the folly of a fight
> With a common wrong or right.
> The innocent and the beautiful
> Have no enemy but time;
> Arise and bid me strike a match
> And strike another till time catch;
> Should the conflagration climb,
> Run till all the sages know.
> We the great gazebo built,
> They convicted us of guilt;
> Bid me strike a match and blow.

SIXTEEN

1927–1932

In October 1927 Yeats was offered £300 for the use of sixteen or more pages of verse for six months by William Edwin Rudge who owned the Fountain Press, a private press in New York. He decided to give him *A Woman Young and Old*, 'Blood and the Moon' and 'A Dialogue of Self and Soul'. Writing to Olivia Shakespear in the first week of October, he recorded that *Oedipus at Colonus* seemed to be haunted by the barking of a phantom dog, telling her how writing the new poems was interrupting the revision of *A Vision* and confirming his opinion that to a serious studious mind only two topics could be of the least interest – sex and the dead. He thought he would die later in October; he 'hardly expected to recover' when a cold turned into congestion of the lungs, with a high temperature and delirium.[1] He was advised to seek sunshine and by early November Mrs Yeats had arranged for them to travel to Algeciras where, in the garden of the Hôtel Reina Cristina, he went on working, though now conscious of how tired he had been. He was revising the proofs of *The Tower* (1928), rewriting some poems and writing down ideas for others as well as writing new ones, wanting to finish the book for Rudge before some doctor got at him. 'At Algeciras – a Meditation upon Death' records the setting, and his sombre mood:

> The heron-billed pale cattle-birds
> That feed on some foul parasite
> Of the Moroccan flocks and herds
> Cross the narrow Straits to light
> In the rich midnight of the garden trees
> Till the dawn break upon those mingled seas.
>
> Often at evening when a boy
> Would I carry to a friend –
> Hoping more substantial joy

Did an older mind commend –
Not such as are in Newton's metaphor,
But actual shells of Rosses' level shore.

Greater glory in the sun,
An evening chill upon the air,
Bid imagination run
Much on the Great Questioner;
What He can question, what if questioned I
Can with a fitting confidence reply.[2]

His lung had not recovered and it began to bleed at Seville where
they moved for the sake of more sunshine and heat. After ten days
there, Mrs Yeats decided better medical advice could be found in
France and they moved again, this time to the Hotel St George at
Cannes. The advice was stern: he was to live between bed and
couch, downstairs to lunch was effort enough. He was exhausted by
the overwork of years; he was not to read too much (this annoyed
him because he had read all the good detective stories and was
enjoying Wyndham Lewis's *Time and Western Man*, with which he
found himself in fundamental agreement), not to allow himself to
be excited; it would take three or four months before he might be
able to work a little. He was depressed at first, then consoled himself;
he had always found it very hard to work, and now he could permit
himself a good conscience.

Yeats was delighted by Sturge Moore's strongly defined representation of Ballylee on the cover of *The Tower* which was published in
February 1928, regarding it as 'most rich, grave and beautiful'
and 'admirably like the place'. Reviewers recognised the volume's
achievement. 'An imaginative and prosodic beauty that brings one
the pure and impersonal joy of art' was the description given by *The
Times Literary Supplement*; Yeats was 'what we moderns mean by a
great poet' according to *The Criterion*; while the *New Republic*'s
reviewer, Theodore Spencer, drew attention to the poems' air of
authority obtained by reference to a system outside themselves, and
to their richness of tone which made them echo and re-echo in the
mind, in a proper marriage of thought and emotion.

Emotion without the bitterness of memory was something that
Yeats – convalescing, told to walk slowly, even to turn his head

slowly so his thoughts would slacken – was anticipating now that he and George had planned changes in their life. They had moved to Rapallo in mid-February, attracted by the presence there of Ezra and Dorothy Pound. They decided to take a flat and spend from August to April in it, either keeping the top floor of 82 Merrion Square and letting the rest of it or selling it and getting a smaller house or flat in Dublin. The children would go to school in Switzerland. The one work Yeats would keep on would be his Directorship of the Abbey; his term of office in the Senate was due to end in September and, though he would miss the £360 a year this brought in, living in Italy would be cheaper and he would be out of Irish bitterness. Already, he wrote to Olivia Shakespear, new poems were floating in his head.

He began to write 'A Packet for Ezra Pound' and to read philosophy again, corresponding with Sturge Moore about it. Rooms were found in Rapallo, via Americhe 12–8, for the next winter, and they returned to Ireland via Switzerland on 18 April. He gave Olivia Shakespear an amusing account of his medical condition:

Two Dublin doctors have sat upon me; the Cannes man said, 'Lungs and nervous breakdown can be neglected, nothing matters but blood pressure' and gave me a white pill. The Monte Carlo man said, 'Blood pressure and lungs can be neglected, nothing matters but nervous breakdown,' and gave me a brown pill. The Dublin men say, 'Blood pressure and nervous breakdown can be neglected, nothing matters but lungs,' and have given me a black pill . . .[3]

Once home, Irish bitterness was not to be escaped. Yeats dictated a letter to Sean O'Casey about *The Silver Tassie* – which the Abbey Directors decided to reject. O'Casey, furious, communicated the letter to the *Observer*. Yeats recorded the Abbey's debt to O'Casey's previous plays in generous terms:

You were interested in the Irish Civil War, and at every moment of those plays wrote out of your own amusement with life or your sense of its tragedy; you were excited, and we all caught your excitement; you were exasperated almost beyond endurance by what you had seen or heard, as a man is by what happens under his window, and you moved us as Swift moved his contemporaries.[4]

But he went on to say that O'Casey was not interested in the Great War, he had no experience of it, and he was therefore writing out of his opinions. This was direct enough, and it chimed with Yeats's

own attitudes to that war as 'bloody frivolity' but it was not tactful
– nor was the comment which followed, which put its query in a
somewhat superior way: 'Do you suppose for one moment that
Shakespeare educated Hamlet and King Lear by telling them what
he thought and believed?' He saw Hamlet and Lear educating
Shakespeare. And the advice to O'Casey to find a new theme was
hardly kind, since – newly married and with a child about to be born
on 30 April – he needed not only some encouragement but some
reward for his work. But then Yeats was not to be swayed by personal
considerations in making artistic judgments. The *Catholic Bulletin*
was perhaps more to the point than its writer realised in calling
Yeats 'the Proud Pollexfen' when recalling his previous proclamation
of the apotheosis of O'Casey. Perhaps the fact that he was ill had
affected the tone of the letter, sensible in many of its judgments –
'Put the dogmatism of the letter down to splenetic age,' he ended
up. Lady Gregory had shown surprising insensitivity in sending on
to O'Casey not only his letter, but a note to her about how O'Casey
could withdraw the play if he agreed with the criticism or, if not,
offer it to a London management. O'Casey published the letters of
the Abbey Directors in the *Observer* on 3 June. Yeats asked the
Society of Authors to take action against the paper; he insisted on
the views of Walter Starkie (another Director, who had been away)
being included when *The Irish Statesman* published the other correspondence on 9 June. With the benefit of hindsight it might have
been wiser to have staged the play, but Yeats thought that when it
was published their views would be understood. The tragedy was,
he told Lady Gregory, that O'Casey was 'now out of our saga'.

The row with O'Casey and late hours had sent his blood pressure
up again. He was afraid he might not be able to finish the revision
of *A Vision* and so, trying hard to overcome fatigue, he was overworking. Mrs Yeats had realised she had a semi-invalid to deal with, and
the sale of the Merrion Square house in May was symbolic of the
change. Yeats was exhausted after a trip to London and when he
made his last speech in the Senate it was of three sentences followed
by a minute of great pain. This reconciled him to leaving and he
was cheered by the Chairman, Lord Glenavy, telling him the Senate
would re-elect him whenever he liked. He doubted it, but was
pleased that Glenavy should think so. Mrs Yeats had wanted him
to leave the Senate earlier; in late 1925 she had written to Tom
McGreevy to say that her husband was full of verse that never got

time to be written. She thought that for him 'to spend hours listening to rubbish in and out of the Senate and going to committees and being visited by fishermen's associations . . . and miaows and bow-wows of all sorts mostly mongrel is a bit too much'.

He stayed at a hotel in Howth in July while Mrs Yeats got ready a flat in 72 Fitzwilliam Square, looking over the square, with blue walls and ceilings and gold-coloured curtains. But though he liked the flat he found life in Dublin exhausting; he was involved in fighting the introduction of censorship and by October longed to get away to the seashore and the palms of Rapallo, 'Ezra to quarrel with, and the Rapallo cats to feed after nightfall'.[5] Once there in November he enjoyed the sunshine, the arrival of books and furniture – some from Ireland, some made for them in Genoa – and feeling much better than he did at home. He settled into a routine of writing in the mornings – finishing 'A Packet for Ezra Pound' – and taking a walk in the afternoons. Rapallo seemed like the little town described in the 'Ode on a Grecian Urn'.

The result of throwing off all burdens – 'no more opinions, no more politics, no more practical tasks',[6] he wrote optimistically to Olivia Shakespear – was that he wrote lyrics and never wrote, as he told Lady Gregory, 'with greater ease', completing eleven lyrics in two months. These poems were published as *Words for Music Perhaps*, 'all praise of joyous life', the product of 'exultant weeks' at Rapallo where the winter weather, cold but dry, suited him. He recovered quickly from a tiring visit to Rome in January and he enjoyed the company of Ezra Pound's friends, among them George Antheil the musician (whose work Basil Bunting, 'one of Ezra's more savage disciples', was there to write up), who was pressed into writing music for *Fighting the Waves* (a new version of *The Only Jealousy of Emer*). Another he met was Gerhard Hauptmann, the dramatist, who envied Yeats being two years younger than himself, though Yeats envied the German his ability to swim in the sea and drink several bottles of champagne a day.

Letters written in the early spring of 1929 to Olivia Shakespear and Lady Gregory indicated the happiness he experienced in finding idleness a duty. By April he announced to Olivia that he had finished nineteen lyrics, and that he was well and more cheerful than he had been for years. He returned to Dublin, visiting London for a fortnight on the way, looking up old friends; as well as Olivia he saw Sturge Moore, Charles Ricketts and Lady Ottoline Morrell; and he met Wyndham Lewis, to whom he had written from Rapallo, discussing his work. Both men approached each other cautiously, their sympathy for each other such that they did not want, according to Yeats, to discover any fundamental difference.

In Dublin he spent most of the summer in the Fitzwilliam Square flat. He was still revising *A Vision*, but thought he would have a poetic rebirth, all kinds of images coming into his mind as he wrote about his cones and gyres. He visited Coole, finding Lady Gregory very frail; he promised her a poem on the house and drafted 'Coole Park, 1929'[7] in prose:

Describe house in first stanza. Here Synge came, Hugh Lane, Shaw Taylor, many names. I too in my timid youth. Coming and going like migratory birds. Then address the swallows fluttering in their dream like circles. Speak of the rarity of the circumstances that bring together such concords of men. Each man more than himself through whom an unknown life speaks. A circle ever returning into itself.

The poem provides its vignettes economically. Yeats is included among the others as 'one that ruffled in a manly pose/For all his timid heart'. The visitors who 'came like swallows and like swallows went' were kept, as he was, by Lady Gregory's powerful character to their first intent. Two lines he wrote but omitted from the final version make this clear:

> She taught that straight line that sets a man
> Above the crooked journey of the sun.

The image of the swallows, probably taken from Pythagoras, has hints of the swallow as an image of indolence, and Lady Gregory, as he recorded in *Autobiographies*, never lost her sense of feudal responsibility, 'not of duty as the word is generally understood, but of burdens laid on her by her station and her character, a choice constantly renewed in solitude'.[8] He finished this elevated and eloquent tribute while at Coole in September: a memorial in advance, it ends in prophecy of what actually happened to the house. Lady Gregory rented it back from the Forestry Department which had taken over house, garden, fields and woods. After her death the Department sold it; the purchaser stripped the roof of its lead, and it was finally pulled down in 1941.

> Here, traveller, scholar, poet, take your stand
> When all those rooms and passages are gone,
> When nettles wave upon a shapeless mound
> And saplings root among the broken stone,
> And dedicate – eyes bent upon the ground,
> Back turned upon the brightness of the sun
> And all the sensuality of the shade –
> A moment's memory to that laurelled head.

Before finishing it, he had stayed for a few days in July at Glendalough, visiting the Stuarts at Laragh Castle nearby; in Dublin there was the excitement of seeing a production by Ninette de Valois of *Fighting the Waves* at the Abbey, his 'greatest success on the stage since *Cathleen ni Houlihan*', he told Olivia, the production a great event with the politicians, the Governor General and the American Ambassador present to admire the play with its masks by Hildo van Krop, its music by George Antheil and its choreography by Ninette de Valois. The theatre was packed night after night.[9]

Another excitement was contemplating the tempting offer of a year's professorship in Japan, before Mrs Yeats returned from bringing the children from Switzerland. As he expected, she was firm in her views and he was both relieved and disappointed. It would have been an adventure in old age to wander about Japanese temples among the hills. His Irish wandering embraced Coole again and it was the last time the family stayed at Ballylee, which was too damp for Yeats's rheumatism and generally inconvenient, as they did not have a car and Mrs Yeats had to bicycle four miles to Gort for provisions. Back in Dublin he found himself yearning for the quiet of Rapallo, and set out for London on 23 October to spend nearly a month there on the way to Italy.

In the course of this stay in London – where he saw Shaw's *The Apple Cart*, a play he hated – he caught a severe cold and coughed up blood again. After a few days in bed he left for Rapallo where, despite a feeling of sleepiness, he wrote a haunting poem for *Words for Music Perhaps*, 'After Long Silence',[10] about his friendship with Olivia Shakespear. He had shown her the prose draft of it in London:

> Subject
> Your hair is white
> My hair is white
> Come let us talk of love
> What other theme do we know

> When we were young
> We were in love with one another
> And therefore ignorant

The poem shows his skill at work, intensifying, endowing with eloquence, employing repetition with a casual ease to emphasise the poem's affirmations:

> Speech after long silence; it is right,
> All other lovers being estranged or dead,
> Unfriendly lamplight hid under its shade,
> The curtains drawn upon unfriendly night,
> That we descant and yet again descant
> Upon the supreme theme of Art and Song:
> Bodily decrepitude is wisdom; young
> We loved each other and were ignorant.

His health deteriorated at the end of the year. His temperature rose in the evenings, he had a kind of nervous collapse, he hastily wrote a will and then collapsed into the rigours of what a specialist from Genoa diagnosed as Malta fever. This left him enfeebled; he spent most of nine weeks in bed and in March 1930 walking even a few hundred yards brought on stage fright. He had grown a beard, which Ezra Pound, meeting him in the open air in a café (because he was afraid of being infected), admired so much that he said Yeats should be sent as Minister to Austria, the only place that would perfectly appreciate the beard. Mrs Yeats having decided he needed mountain air, he began to recover very quickly when they moved to Portofino Vetto, fifteen hundred feet up, overlooking the bay of Santa Margherita; he could see the vast tranquil sea and the coast with its sunlit houses as far as Genoa. Consecutive thought still tired him, but during the fortnight's stay on the mountain-top he was reading Swift's *Diary to Stella* as well as detective stories.

When he came down to Rapallo there was the pleasure of a visit from John Masefield who designed a model brigantine to cheer him up; he made *The George and Willie* in Oxford and it graced Yeats's study in Fitzwilliam Square. Mountain air had helped him so that he felt able to work on *A Vision* for about an hour in the mornings, as well as reading Swift and making entries on him in a manuscript book and enjoying the arrival of Michael and Anne to whom he read *The Ancient Mariner*, *The Lays of Ancient Rome*, 'How they brought the Good News from Ghent to Aix', 'The Pied Piper' and *The Lay*

of the Last Minstrel. The Italian sunshine of June was followed by a
long sea voyage to London and, after a few days in Dublin, he sat
for a portrait painted in the open air by Augustus John at Renvyle
in August. Then came a visit to Coole and one to Rosses Point with
the family before the return to Dublin. His blood pressure was up,
but by 23 October he had finished his play on Swift, *The Words upon
the Window-Pane*, which he had been writing at Coole; it went into
rehearsal, to be produced at the Abbey on 17 November. Before
that he had made visits to Masefield in Oxford, to May Morris at
Kelmscott, and met Virginia Woolf at Garsington where Walter de
la Mare was another visitor.

On his return to Dublin the Swift play was a greater success than
he hoped, 'beautifully acted', particularly by May Craig who played
the demanding role of Mrs Henderson the medium. Yeats set his
play in Dublin and just as *Fighting the Waves* had proved that he
retained his capacity to write an entirely poetic play, so *The Words
upon the Window-Pane* demonstrated his ability to handle realism, to
provide suitable material for the Abbey actors who had developed
their style to suit the plays of the Cork realists, Lennox Robinson,
T. C. Murray and the down-to-earth Dublin dialogue of O'Casey's
tragic-comedy – and to match this realism to his own esoteric
thought. For his Swift play is not only a convincing portrayal of
Dubliners attending a séance but a dramatic manifestation of his
idea that the dead dream back – one he had earlier explored in the
poem 'Shepherd and Goatherd' and in his Nōh-style play *The
Dreaming of the Bones* as well as in *A Vision*.
    The starting point for the play was Yeats discovering lines cut on
a bedroom window in Fairfield, Gogarty's Dublin home where he
had stayed years before:

> Mary Kilpatrick – very young
> Ugly face and pleasant tongue.

In the play, comment on Swift and his relationships with Stella and
Vanessa comes from Dr Trench and John Corbct, a young Irishman
working for a Cambridge doctorate. He recognises the lines on the
window-pane in the eighteenth-century house as part of a poem
Stella wrote for Swift's fifty-fourth birthday:

> You taught how I might youth prolong
> By knowing what is right and wrong;
> How from my heart to bring supplies
> Of lustre to my fading eyes . . .

Corbet hopes to prove that 'in Swift's day men of intellect reached the height of their power . . . that everything great in Ireland and in our character, in what remains of our architecture, comes from that day; that we have kept its seal longer than England'. In the Introduction he wrote for the play Yeats expounded these ideas: modern Ireland could be shaped by paying attention to Swift's morality, his insistence upon distinguishing between right and wrong. The Introduction links Swift with Molyneux, whose *Case of Ireland Stated* (1698) had championed the Irish parliament's independence; he was reading Swift 'for months together, Burke and Berkeley less often but always with excitement, and Goldsmith lures and waits'. He was returning to the Anglo-Irish intellectual inheritance he had shunned in his youth – Goldsmith and Burke as too English, Swift because he was not romantic. (Berkeley he had not read seriously before 1922–23.) It seemed to him that as he collected material for his thought and work, he was looking for some identification of his own beliefs with those of Ireland, seeking an image of 'the modern mind's discovery of itself . . . in that one Irish century that escaped from darkness and confusion'.

Swift created Ireland's political nationality, he thought, through the *Drapier Letters*, and Berkeley – publishing 'to know whether other men have the same ideas as we Irishmen' – had fought the Salamis of the Irish intellect before he was twenty-five. He traced an Irish hatred of abstraction in various works of Swift, Berkeley, Goldsmith and Burke. They are the characters of the poem 'Blood and the Moon',[11] whom he linked to his symbolic tower; from walls like its walls had risen 'a bloody, arrogant power', but it was 'half dead at the top'. (The tower was never completely restored and one room at the top was empty, a flat concrete roof was used instead of an ornate one designed by Lutyens.) The image echoes Swift's seeing a tree withered and decayed in its uppermost branches and saying 'I shall be like that tree, I shall die at top.' He declared that his winding stair at Ballylee was an ancestral stair:

> That Goldsmith and the Dean, Berkeley and Burke have travelled
>   there.

Swift beating on his breast in sibylline frenzy blind
Because the heart in his blood-sodden breast had dragged him down
    into mankind,
Goldsmith deliberately sipping at the honey-pot of his mind,

And haughtier-headed Burke that proved the State a tree,
That this unconquerable labyrinth of the birds, century after century,
Cast but dead leaves to mathematical equality;

And God-appointed Berkeley that proved all things a dream,
That this pragmatical, preposterous pig of a world, its farrow that so
    solid seem,
Must vanish on the instant if the mind but change its theme;

Saeva Indignatio and the labourer's hire,
The strength that gives our blood and state magnanimity of its own
    desire;
Everything that is not God consumed with intellectual fire.

He was to return to the idea that these men were the founders of
Irish thought, notably in his Introduction to J. M. Hone and M. M.
Rossi, *Bishop Berkeley, his Life, Writings and Philosophy* (1931):

Born in such a community, Berkeley with his belief in perception, that
abstract ideas are mere words, Swift with his love of perfect nature, of the
Houyhnhnms, his disbelief in Newton's system and every sort of machine,
Goldsmith and his delight in the particulars of common life that shocked
his contemporaries, Burke with his conviction that all States not grown
slowly like a forest tree are tyrannies, found in England the opposite that
stung their thought into expression and made it lucid.

He put an 'overstatement . . . yet with its measure of truth' into the
mouth of his 'enthusiastic Cambridge student'[12] to the effect that
Swift foresaw 'the ruin to come, Democracy, Rousseau, the French
Revolution; that is why he hated the common run of men – "I hate
lawyers, I hate doctors," he said, "though I love Dr So-and-so and
Judge So-and-so" – that is why he wrote *Gulliver*, that is why he
wore out his brain, that is why he felt *saeva indignatio*, that is why
he sleeps under the greatest epitaph in history.' Yeats himself had
made an excellent translation of the Latin epitaph:

> Swift has sailed into his rest;
> Savage indignation there
> Cannot lacerate his breast.
> Imitate him if you dare,

World-besotted traveller; he
Served human liberty.[13]

But in *The Words upon the Window-Pane* he takes the Swift of
'Blood and the Moon' and shows him dreading madness, reliving in
Swedenborgian manner what was described in *A Vision* as the
passionate or tragic moments in his life; refusing to marry Vanessa,
agonising over whether he had wronged Stella; afraid of solitude, a
soul in agony.

While the Swift was in rehearsal, Yeats wrote to Lady Gregory
telling her he would dedicate it to her, and telling her also that he
had been offered membership of the Athenaeum. 'A greater honour
than a knighthood and less expensive than a peerage,' Rothenstein
informed him; but he jibbed at the cost as he didn't think he
was often enough in London to justify the expense. Rothenstein
described him with enthusiasm as dressed in a crimson shirt and a
flowing coloured tie, now 'brown skinned under his crown of white
hair, his dark eyes aslant, broad-shouldered and ample of form –
he once so pale and lanky'. His health had improved, but Lady
Gregory, now in her late seventies, had become frail and so he
decided to stay in Dublin for the winter and to spend time with her
at Coole. The flat in Rapallo was let to Ezra Pound's father and –
partially to keep out of the excitement of life in the centre of Dublin
– a furnished house, South Hill, was rented from February to May
1931 on Killiney Hill, about ten miles south of Dublin, with a view
over Killiney Bay.

Yeats was in deep need of quiet for work on an Edition de Luxe
of his works which Macmillan proposed to publish; he was to have
his unpublished material ready by the autumn – this would include
the revised version of *A Vision*, *Wheels and Butterflies* (plays and
essays), *Byzantium* (this was a new book of verse, which emerged as
The Winding Stair and Other Poems (1933)), new Hanrahan stories,
the Cuala diaries and the versions of the Sophocles plays. 'Months
of rewriting. What happiness!'[14] When he wrote to give Olivia
the news about the Edition de Luxe he mentioned finishing *The
Resurrection*, describing it as 'young men talking, the apostles in the
next room overwhelmed by the crucifixion'. The play went through
several manuscript and printed versions, being performed at the

Abbey in 1934. It contains 'Two Songs from a Play' which linked
the Christian story to classical mythology, to the Virgilian prophecy
in the *Eclogues*, and expounded *A Vision*'s ideas about the effect
of Christ, who controlled irrational force, miracle substituted for
reason:

> Odour of blood when Christ was slain
> Made all Platonic tolerance vain
> And vain all Doric discipline.

And man is praised for creating, heroically, despite the fact that all
things pass away (an idea also put in *Autobiographies*: why should we
believe that religion can never bring round its antithesis?):

> Everything that man esteems
> Endures a moment or a day.
> Love's pleasure drives his love away,
> The painter's brush consumes his dreams;
> The herald's cry, the soldier's tread
> Exhaust his glory and his might:
> Whatever flames upon the night
> Man's own resinous heart has fed.[15]

The play is close to the 'Dove or Swan' section of *A Vision* and to
'The Second Coming', and in the Introduction to *Wheels and Butterflies* Yeats traces his preoccupation with cyclical events back to his
youth, to *The Wanderings of Oisin* and to the idea of an incarnation
heralding a new age.

The idea that young men are discussing the crucifixion is significant, as is a remark in another letter to Olivia of February 1931 that
he was writing very much for young men between twenty and thirty,
thinking of himself at that age wanting to feel that poets had seen
into the mystery of life though they had not told of it. Young men
might not read *A Vision*, but would be pleased it existed. He realised
he had created a myth and a myth could be believed in – though
one only assented to philosophy. He wanted to be in tune with the
new generation of younger Irish writers, as the later Preface to
Wheels and Butterflies (1934) showed. He encouraged Frank
O'Connor, Sean O'Faolain and Liam O'Flaherty whose work he
particularly admired; their realism he praised publicly. Very conscious of age now, he decided the Abbey needed younger leadership
and so F. R. Higgins became a Director.

In May 1931 Yeats had to rescue the Cuala industries from

financial difficulties. Later that month he went to Oxford to receive
an honorary D.Litt. Maurice Bowra had put his name forward
and recorded later how the colour of the Sheldonian Theatre (its
stonework not then restored) of old ivory and old books had appealed
to Yeats, who was pleased by the large attendance (a debate on
the proposed abolition of Divinity Moderations was to follow the
conferring) and by the dinner Bowra gave for him in the Senior
Common Room in Wadham College. When he went away Yeats
said with some justice to John Sparrow, one of the guests, that 'no
Emperor does himself so well as an Oxford don'. Sparrow enjoyed
a two-hour conversation with him, packed with ideas and arresting
phrases echoing round an Oxford hotel – 'The tragedy of sexual
intercourse is the perpetual virginity of the soul' or 'Damn Bertrand
Russell. He's a proletarian. He has a wicked and vulgar spirit. I
suppose if you had so many ancestors at that date [Hume's] in the
peerage you can't help your behaviour being that of the public
house.'[16]

In London most of the material for the Edition de Luxe was
delivered to Macmillans, Yeats depositing six of the seven volumes
on Harold Macmillan's floor. Back in Dublin in July he worked on
Berkeley with Mario Rossi, a young Italian scholar who had come
to Ireland to collaborate with Joseph Hone in a study of Berkeley.
Rossi, ebullient and warm-hearted, later became Reader in Italian
at the University of Edinburgh and had vivid memories of Yeats's
kindness to him and of his curiosity about Italian philosophy, particularly that of Croce and Gentile. In no one had he found a more
eager interest in metaphysics. Yeats, he wrote to Hone, did not feel
philosophy as an abstruse speculation, was not interested in its
difficulties, but wanted to 'connect thing and image, to prove that
the poet's expression goes further than usual vision, reaches –
beyond sensation and word – the intimate transempirical nature of
the world, to assure himself that the poet's way of dealing with
reality is in fact a metaphysical description of it'.[17]

This was a fruitful friendship and one Mrs Yeats regarded more
favourably than the relationship with the Indian, Shri Purohit Swami,
whom Yeats had met in London and for whose *An Indian Monk*
(1932) he wrote an Introduction. She resented encroachments upon
Yeats's time; his poetry was what mattered. Lady Gregory's visits to
Dublin she found not a little trying, for the old lady was somewhat
exigent, and she wrote in very understandable exasperation to

Dorothy Pound in August 1931, 'Christ how she repeats herself now ... She'll tell you the same saga quite literally three times in less than an hour, and repeat it again the next day, and the day after that too ...'[18]

Rossi spent some time at Coole in August, his appreciation – translated as *Pilgrimage to the West* – published by the Cuala Press. He wrote some letters which gave Lady Gregory great pleasure, as did Yeats's reading poems in an Irish programme broadcast from Belfast. He ended up with a poem written to Lady Gregory's granddaughter Anne:

> ... only God, my dear,
> Could love you for yourself alone
> And not your yellow hair.[19]

In her journal, Lady Gregory recorded that though Yeats had broadcast he had never heard anything on the wireless until 9 October. And Mrs Yeats and Anne Yeats have related how for a long time he wouldn't have a wireless; when they did acquire one, he was listening to it the first evening it was turned on and he couldn't hear very well, so he put his hand to his ear and said, 'I beg your pardon?'

While at Coole, Yeats discussed the creation of an Irish Academy of Letters. Russell came there to help with drafting a constitution and in April Shaw agreed to be President, Yeats having met him in London when he was there to broadcast for the BBC. Lady Gregory was pleased that Yeats could be at Coole and delighted he was working well. He was reading Balzac, and Lady Gregory continued her habit of reading aloud in the evening. In May her journal records her pleasure in sitting outside with him, delighting in the fresh air and the greenness of spring. She now moved with great difficulty. The poem 'Coole Park and Ballylee, 1931' records this period; he stayed at Coole in August and during most of the autumn and winter:

> Sound of a stick upon the floor, a sound
> From somebody that toils from chair to chair;
> Beloved books that famous hands have bound,
> Old marble heads, old pictures everywhere;
> Great rooms where travelled men and children found
> Content or joy; a last inheritor
> Where none has reigned that lacked a name and fame
> Or out of folly into folly came.[20]

She became increasingly ill, was not sleeping and suffered considerable pain. Having to go to Dublin on theatre business, he did not
receive the message that she was sinking until late on the night of
23 May; when he arrived the next morning, it was to find that she
had died in the night. Later he wrote 'The Death of Lady Gregory',
a piece of prose he did not publish.[21] He had been continuously at
Coole for a year with the exception of brief periods away on business,
and she had been very thankful to him for staying so that she should
not be too much alone. His eloquent elegy was his essential tribute
to her:

> We were the last romantics – chose for theme
> Traditional sanctity and loveliness;
> Whatever's written in what poets name
> The book of the people; whatever most can bless
> The mind of man or elevate a rhyme;
> But all is changed, that high horse riderless,
> Though mounted in that saddle Homer rode
> Where the swan drifts upon a darkening flood.

Goats at Ballylee Castle, drawing by
Lady Gregory, 1895.

SEVENTEEN

1932–1935

In May 1932 the Yeatses took a thirteen-year lease on Riversdale at Willbrook outside Rathfarnham and moved there in July; it was a plain, creeper-covered eighteenth-century farmhouse at the foot of the Dublin mountains, with beautiful gardens approached by a bridge over a stream; there Yeats hoped to recreate the routine of Coole – not only had he lost one who, as he wrote to Mario Rossi, had been for nearly forty years his strength and his conscience, but he was heartbroken for the great rooms of Coole and its great woods – the only place where, he told Olivia Shakespear, he had ever had unbroken health. He became more content, however, once his pictures were hung on the walls of Riversdale. There was a croquet lawn; he enjoyed playing, being good if erratic.

In September the Irish Academy of Letters was launched and on 21 October Yeats sailed from Southampton on his fifth and last American lecture tour; he earned between £600 and £700 for himself and about the same for the Academy after a final lecture in New York. He wanted to create capital for the Academy to be able to offer a prize for the best Irish book by a writer under 35. He began by lecturing in New York and the North East, then moved to the mid-West, Detroit and Canada (the *Detroit News* reported him describing the Irish as not a nation of readers, but a people who sing songs and like to listen. That was why he had decided to devote his energies to the theatre), arriving back in Riversdale on 28 January 1933. His North American tours had occupied him for more than a year of his life, and sometimes people have queried why he did not meet, for instance, more writers and, particularly, poets, during that time. The obvious answer to such querists is to ask them if they have ever themselves been on a lecture tour; if they have not, they may find it hard to realise the exhausting nature of the experience; however stimulating the response to lectures may be – and in

America it is usually warm-hearted and encouragingly so – the lecturer is constantly aware of the need to perform, to earn the appreciation, to overcome the fatigue of travel, of changing accommodation, of meeting many hitherto unknown people, of adjusting to new climatic conditions and different kinds of audiences. Yeats performed admirably on his tours, but he found them exhausting as well as stimulating: 'too much excitement, too little exercise' he wrote on his second tour. He did find time, however, to attend séances there.

Words for Music Perhaps was published while he was in America in November. Many of its poems were written in 1929, others in 1930 and 1931. It contains the Crazy Jane poems, founded upon the talk of an old woman, Cracked Mary, who lived in a cottage near Gort and had 'an amazing power of audacious speech'.[1] Yeats thought the Crazy Jane poems and the love poems that followed them exciting and strange: 'Sexual abstinence fed their fire – I was ill and yet full of desire.'[2] These poems[3] express, in part, a glorification of sex in 'Crazy Jane and the Bishop', a wonder at the nature of creation in 'Crazy Jane Reproved' and of love in 'Crazy Jane on the Day of Judgment', an awareness of ghostly presences in 'Crazy Jane on God', a comment on the passing of beauty and the need for desecration in 'Crazy Jane Talks with the Bishop', while 'Crazy Jane Grown Old Looks at the Dancers' was prompted by a dream and expresses Blake's idea that sexual love is founded on spiritual hate. Blake's ideas inform other poems too, notably 'Girl's Song', 'Young Man's Song' and 'His Dream', while 'His Bargain' deals with the lover's choice overriding fate. 'Lullaby' contemplates the sleep of various lovers as an example to the beloved of the poem, while the charming 'Mad as the Mist and Snow' conveys a mood of disengagement from high seriousness. 'The Dancer at Cruachan and Cro-Patrick' reflects something sung by the Irish saint Cellach; 'I am of Ireland' derives from a fourteenth-century dance song; and 'The Delphic Oracle upon Plotinus' is based on the verse oracle Amelius received at Delphi when he sought to discover where the soul of Plotinus had gone after his death. Yeats was following Stephen MacKenna's translation very closely.

The last three poems reflect Yeats's reading, but some of the lyrics in *The Winding Stair* (1933) (in which *Words for Music Perhaps* was included) are more personal. 'Vacillation',[4] for instance, was written in 1931 in an attempt 'to shake off' Crazy Jane. It too returns to his interest in Blake's theories of contraries in its first section, while the second uses the image of the tree in *The Mabinogion*, which was half on fire, half in full leaf, as well as the Attis legend – probably taken from Sir James Frazer's *Attis, Adonis and Osiris*. The third section answers the query of the first, 'What is joy?', perhaps reflecting back on his own situation in his fortieth year, after Maud Gonne separated from John MacBride. The fourth section is a simple but highly effective recapturing of a moment of joy experienced when he was fifty-one and

> sat, a solitary man,
> In a crowded London shop,
> An open book and empty cup
> On the marble table-top.
>
> While on the shop and street I gazed
> My body of a sudden blazed;
> And twenty minutes more or less
> It seemed, so great my happiness,
> That I was blessèd and could bless.

The poem goes on to consider responsibility in its fifth section, emphasises transition in the sixth with the final lines of each stanza proclaiming with a certain indifference '"Let all things pass away"'. The seventh section contemplates the opposing views of Heart and Soul, with the Heart seeing reality in original sin, the final section considering the Christian views of Baron Friederich von Hügel, though Homer remains the poet's example 'and his unchristened heart'. This tension, this use of contrast was used to good effect in 'A Dialogue of Self and Soul', an earlier poem written between July and December 1927 in which in the first section, Self and Soul oppose their views; the poetic props of tower and Sato's sword with its silken embroidery drawing the attention of the Self to the Soul's unease. The Self, however, has the whole of the second section to itself and after some bitter images – the ignominy of boyhood, the distress of adolescence, the pain of the unfinished man at his clumsiness, the defiling and disfigured shape he thinks must be his shape – is content to live life again even if life involves pitching into the frog-spawn of a blind man's ditch. It is a great joyous affirmation, strengthened by the repetition Yeats had learned to use with such confidence:

> I am content to follow to its source
> Every event in action or in thought;
> Measure the lot; forgive myself the lot!
> When such as I cast out remorse
> So great a sweetness flows into the breast
> We must laugh and we must sing,
> We are blest by everything,
> Everything we look upon is blest.[5]

Repetition reaches its fullest point, its most effective cumulative power and variety in 'Byzantium'.[6] This poem originated from Sturge Moore's criticism (in a letter of 16 April 1930) of the fourth stanza of 'Sailing to Byzantium'. Yeats wrote to him that the letter had shown that the idea needed exposition. He drafted the poem in his 1930 diary thus:

Subject for a poem . . . Death of a friend . . . Describe Byzantium as it is in the system towards the end of the first Christian millenium. A walking mummy. Flames at the street corners where the soul is purified, birds of hammered gold singing in the golden trees, in the harbour [dolphins], offering their backs to the wailing dead that they may carry them to Paradise.[7]

Byzantium was an example of magnificence, excess, something beyond utility. It was the city where the Saints' wasted forms were shown against the background of gold mosaic, where the artificial bird sang and the ghosts, mounted upon dolphins, swam through the sensual seas to dance upon its pavements.

The parallelisms, the linkages, the repetitions, the intensifications, the echoes, the alliterations – all come together in a triumph of poetic art. In the atmospheric first stanza there are repetitions of 'The', of 'A', of 'All', of 'The' again. There are echoes: 'Night . . . night-walkers' 'starlit . . . moonlit'. Intensification occurs first in the second stanza:

> Before me floats an image, man or shade,
> Shade more than man, more image than a shade.

along with the paradox, the Heracleitean 'death-in-life and life-in-death'. The fury and mire become complexities of mire or blood, leave as complexities of fury and develop into the bitter furies of complexity broken by the dancing floor. The insistent alliteration blends with repetition in the fourth stanza:

> At midnight on the Emperor's pavement flit
> Flames that no faggot feeds, nor steel has lit,
> Nor storm disturbs, flames begotten of flame . . .

The poem deals in contrasts, the serenity of St Sophia's dome disdaining the complexities of human life; its taut rhyming binds together a rich and complex pattern of movement. It is like the moment of escape from nature, from externality, into a state where 'all fuel has become flame, where there is nothing but the state itself, nothing to constrain it or end it'. This is a state, Yeats thought, attained in creating or enjoying a work of art, though that was not an attainment of the whole being.

The eleven poems in *A Woman Young and Old*[8] were written between 1926 and 1929, but left out of *The Tower*. Plato's ideas may have lain behind 'Before the World was Made' and 'Chosen', a poem related to *A Vision*'s thirteenth cone, which 'may' deliver us from the twelve cycles of time and space. Of these poems 'Her Vision in the Wood' is a haunting, despairing treatment of the Adonis legend (with possible hints at the death of Diarmuid, the Irish hero also killed by a boar, on a Sligo mountain) in which a woman laments her lover, the man fatally wounded by the beast.

After writing the latest poems in *The Winding Stair*, Yeats began to wonder whether his imaginative life had dried up, since he had written no verse for some months after Lady Gregory's death. He had, however, other preoccupations. On 3 February 1932, he had written to Joseph Hone about an article in the *Irish Press* in which Aodh de Blacam was commenting on the attempt being made by certain Anglo-Irish leaders to bring back the eighteenth century; it was, he thought, 'the usual sort of thing – only the Gael or the Catholic is Irish . . .';[9] now, however, the Academy had to be defended against the attacks of Catholic Action. The Abbey Theatre, too, had to be defended. Yeats had cast his vote against de Valera's Fianna Fail party in the General Election of February 1932. Eamonn de Valera's victory disturbed many Irish Protestants who had found Cosgrave's government both constructive and conservative; they feared the new regime could be too radical. In May Yeats began to worry about whether the new government would continue the theatre's subsidy. By March 1933 he had decided to seek a meeting with de Valera about this and was impressed by both his simplicity and his honesty though the two men differed throughout the meeting: 'It was a curious experience; each recognised the other's point of view so completely.'[10]

There were also other political matters brewing. He told Olivia in April that he was trying – in association with an ex-cabinet minister, a lawyer and a philosopher – to work out a social theory which could be used against Communism in Ireland. The tempo began to change, and out of the excitement came 'Parnell's Funeral'.[11] The first section of the poem refers back to Parnell's funeral at Glasnevin in 1891, linking the shooting star seen there with a vision Yeats had at Tulira of a star shot by an arrow which he described in the Appendix to *Autobiographies*. Now he speculates about the significance of a falling star; is it the symbol of an accepted sacrifice? The poem puts the point made in the Introduction to *The King of the Great Clock Tower* (1934) that the accumulated hatred of years was now transferred from England to Ireland. Free discussion had come into being, a passion for reality, a satiric realism. The poem's second part compares de Valera, Cosgrave, his predecessor, O'Higgins, and 'even' O'Duffy with Parnell (the sacrificial victim whose heart is eaten), himself inspired by Swift, from whose views in the *Discourse of the Contents and Dissentions between the Nobles and the Commons in Athens and Rome* Yeats selected the idea that the health of the state depends upon a right balance between the One, the Few and the Many. In April he wrote to Olivia Shakespear to tell her how exciting Ireland was, that de Valera had said in private that within three years he would be torn in pieces; this was the Irish cult of sacrifice. By July he was telling her that Irish politics were growing heroic; he found himself urging that the despotic rule of the educated classes was the only end to Ireland's troubles. A fascist opposition was forming behind the scenes; he knew half a dozen men, any one of whom could be Caesar – or Cataline. He ended the letter by telling her that history was very simple; it was a constant alternation of the rule of the Many and the Few, and in small disturbed nations the tempo was racing.

On 23 July he wrote to Olivia to say the great secret was out. Captain Dermot MacManus – an Irishman who had served in the British Army, a well-read man, deeply interested in the supernatural – brought the leader of the 'National Guards' (the Blueshirts, originally a body of young men formed to keep meetings from being broken up), General O'Duffy – who had been head of the Garda Siochana for twelve years – to see Yeats, who did not however think

him a great man; rather a plastic man, he described him in a further
letter of 17 August, in which he wrote of the excitement in Ireland,
and the spread of the Blueshirt movement.

By September he was describing 'our political comedy' to Olivia,
and in November telling her he was suffering from blood pressure
and an attempt to write a new national song, three versions to the
tune of O'Donnell Abu, which were to be sung at the Abbey. These
were 'Three Songs to the Same Tune';[12] they first appeared in the
Spectator of 23 February 1934 and he wrote a note to go with them
to explain his 'one passion and one thought' in politics – rancour
against those who disturb public order and a conviction that public
order cannot last without the rule of able, educated men. This note
indicates disillusion with, detachment from the mood that had stirred
him into wanting to write what some crowd in the street could
understand and sing, a feeling that fanaticism was fuelling disorder.
It was a passionate mood which seized him 'with the violence which
profits the poet for all politics but his own'. He had realised he had
been misguided, and though he published a note on the Songs in
Poetry (Chicago) and in *The King of the Great Clock Tower*, dated
April 1934, saying that if any government was to break the reign of
the mob (and, if it did not, public life would move from violence to
violence or from violence to apathy, Parliament would disgrace and
debauch those who entered it and Irish men of letters live like
outlaws in their own country), to create unity of culture no less than
economic unity, it would need to weld to its purpose 'museum,
school, university, learned institution'. It would need force, marching
men; it would promise no particular measures but a way of life.
There was, he concluded, no such government or party; should
either appear, he offered it the song 'and what remains to me of
life'. A postscript dated August 1934 carried dissociation from the
Blueshirts further:

Because a friend [Captain Dermot MacManus] belonging to a political
party wherewith I had once some loose associations, told me that it had, or
was about to have, or might be persuaded to have, some such aim as mine,
I wrote these songs. Finding that it neither would nor could, I increased
their fantasy, their extravagance, their obscurity, that no party might sing
them.[13]

On the publication of *The Winding Stair* in September 1933,
Yeats had been particularly interested in what would be Olivia

Shakespear's reaction to the Crazy Jane poems and to three others, 'Three Things', 'Lullaby' and 'After Long Silence'.[14] He had written only twenty or thirty lines of verse in a year, he had told her in August, and with the publication of his *Collected Poems* in November he must have re-lived some of the moods his *Collected Works* had provoked in 1908. He became very conscious of his age; he saw an apparition at Riversdale seven times:

As I awoke I saw a child's hand and arm and head – faintly self-luminous – holding above – I was lying on my back – a five of diamonds or hearts I was [not] sure which. It was held as if the child was standing at the head of the bed. Is the meaning some fortune teller's meaning attached to the card or does it promise me five months or five years? Five years would be about long enough to finish my autobiography and bring out *A Vision*.[15]

This apparition appeared a tenth time in January, in broad daylight, 'an arm waving goodbye at the edge of a screen beside my door'. It was not seen again. Later more appeared in a poem 'The Apparitions':

> Because there is safety in derision
> I talked about an apparition,
> I took no trouble to convince,
> Or seem plausible to a man of sense,
> Distrustful of that popular eye
> Whether it be bold or sly.
> *Fifteen apparitions have I seen;*
> *The worst a coat upon a coat-hanger.*[16]

In 1933 he found it easier to meet Maud Gonne since her friend Charlotte Despard, a bitter revolutionary, the sister of the former British Field-Marshall Sir John French (who was Lord Lieutenant of Ireland from 1918 to 1921), had left Maud's house for Northern Ireland. She and Yeats disliked each other intensely. But a meeting with Maud arranged in the Kildare Street Club, then the stamping ground of the remains of the Anglo-Irish aristocracy, did not provide a suitable venue, however much Yeats enjoyed his membership. They had a brief quarrel, later composed. Despite the distractions of social life in Dublin and his preoccupation with politics, he had been working hard on the revision of *A Vision* and writing that part of his autobiography which appeared as *Dramatis Personae* in 1935; it dealt with the early days of the dramatic movement, largely with Edward Martyn, with Lady Gregory and with that 'preposterous

person' George Moore, who was amply repaid for his earlier comments on Yeats. There was no J.B.Y. now to say that one could
despise Moore but not hate him. The poet who had been described
by the novelist as, *inter alia*, a rook, a crane, a great umbrella
forgotten by some picnic party and the type of the literary fop, took
his long-delayed revenge, revealing that the novelist had no idea
how to use his braces to keep his underpants up, was someone who
spoke badly – and much – in a foreign tongue, read nothing and
was never to attain the discipline of style. In Paris he had been a
man carved out of a turnip looking at the world out of astonished
eyes. The mature autobiographer Moore, who had mocked Yeats's
social pretensions by remarking that the Yeatses were middle-class
merchants and millers, was characterised as a typical peasant sinner
in his behaviour. Many anecdotes in Moore's disfavour were woven
skilfully into the tapestry and told with relish. Moore, for instance,
having courted Mrs Craigie in vain, was accustomed to say 'Once
she and I were walking in the Green Park. "There is nothing more
cruel than lust," she said. "There is," I said. "What is that?"
"Vanity," and I let her go a step or two ahead and gave her a kick
behind.' (Yeats, however, missed Moore's later elaboration of the
incident in which the victim receives the assault 'nearly in the centre
of the backside, a little to the right'. 'It was inevitable,' he said, 'part
of the world's history' and he lost sight of all things but the track of
his boot on the black crêpe de Chine.) Yeats's prose was supple,
conversational, amusing; the ease with which he had expressed
himself in letters throughout his life marks his later autobiographical
writing and his essays. As he grew older he had less need to cite
authorities; there was less need of mystery in order to seem wise.
He could still be grandiloquent, still employ rhetorical flourishes,
for his prose was vigorous and emotive, intended at times to shock
his readers. He could give his sardonic humour its head, and
obviously enjoyed portraying Moore in Ely Place in Dublin.

When he arrived in Dublin, all the doors in Upper Ely Place had been
painted white by an agreement between the landlord and the tenants. Moore
had his door painted green, and three Miss Beams – no, I have not got the
name quite right – who lived next door protested to the landlord. Then
began a correspondence between Moore and the landlord wherein Moore
insisted on his position as an art critic, that the whole decoration of his
house required a green door – I imagine that he had but wrapped the green
flag around him – then the indignant young women bought a copy of *Esther*

Waters, tore it up, put the fragments into a large envelope, wrote thereon: 'Too filthy to keep in the house,' dropped it into his letter-box. I was staying with Moore, I let myself in with a latch-key some night after twelve, and found a note on the hall table asking me to put the door on the chain. As I was undressing, I heard Moore trying to get in; when I had opened the door and pointed to the note he said: 'Oh, I forgot. Every night I go out at eleven, at twelve, at one, and rattle my stick on the railing to make the Miss Beams' dogs bark.' Then I saw in the newspapers that the Miss Beams had hired organgrinders to play under Moore's window when he was writing, that he had prosecuted the organgrinders. Moore had a large garden on the other side of the street, a blackbird sang there; he received his friends upon Saturday evening and made a moving speech upon the bird. 'I enjoy its song. If I were the bad man people say I am, could I enjoy its song?' He wrote every morning at an open window on the ground floor, and one morning saw the Miss Beams' cat cross the street, and thought, 'That cat will get my bird.' He went out and filled his pocket with stones, and whenever he saw the cat, threw a stone. Somebody, perhaps the typist, must have laughed, for the rest of the tale fills me with doubt. I was passing through Dublin just on my way to Coole; he came to my hotel. 'I remembered how early that cat got up. I thought it might get the blackbird if I was not there to protect it, so I set a trap. The Miss Beams wrote to the Society for the Prevention of Cruelty to Animals, and I am carrying on a correspondence with its secretary, cat versus bird.' (Perhaps after all, the archives of the Society do contain that correspondence. The tale is not yet incredible.) I passed through Dublin again, perhaps on my way back. Moore came to see me in seeming great depression. 'Remember that trap?' 'Yes.' 'Remember that bird?' 'Yes.' 'I have caught the bird.'[17]

In February 1934, discussing his treatment of these autobiographical memories, he wrote to Olivia Shakespear that it was curious how one's life falls into definite sections. Apropos his friendship with Lady Gregory and his relations with the others who helped in the establishment of the dramatic movement, as well as his going for his first long visit to Coole, he added, 'In 1897 a new scene was set, new actors appeared.'[18] Now Coole had vanished from his life – a place where he had escaped from politics – he was perhaps shut out from his themes. He had nothing in his head; he wondered if the subconscious drama that was his imaginative life had ended with the death of Lady Gregory. He wrote little apart from 'Parnell's Funeral' and 'Meru',[19] a striking poem about man destroying what he creates, probably stimulated by preliminary work begun in August 1933 on the Introduction to Shri Purohit Swami's *The Magic Mountain* (1934); the hermits in the poem learn about the succession of

civilisations, the Swami having a friend who sought *Tuiya*, a greater
or conscious form of meditation, at Mount Kailas, the legendary
Meru. Yeats wrote *The King of the Great Clock Tower* in prose; this,
he thought, might perhaps force him to write lyrics for the characters.
He took the play with him when he and George went to Rapallo in
June 1934, to dispose of the Via Americhe flat there and have its
furniture sent to Dublin.

In Rapallo Yeats sought the advice of Ezra Pound:

> I am in my sixty-ninth year, probably I should stop writing verse. I had
> hoped he would ask me to read it but he would not speak of art, or of
> literature or of anything related to them . . . He took my manuscript and
> went away denouncing Dublin as 'a reactionary hole' because I had said
> that I was re-reading Shakespeare, would go on to Chaucer, and found all
> that I wanted of modern life in 'detection and the wild west'. Next day his
> judgment came and that in a single word 'Putrid'.[20]

Another friend was more encouraging; he tried two painters and a
poet, until he described himself as like Panurge consulting oracles
but rejecting everything that did not confirm his own desire.

Whereas 1933 had largely been preoccupied by politics and the other
distractions of Dublin, 1934 provided an apparent rejuvenation,
symbolised by a vasectomy operation which Yeats had in London in
April. He had been troubled by a waning in his sexual potency and
thought that this and his poetry were closely interrelated; he had
been told by a friend (to whom he had complained of this) about
the Steinach operation, read up the subject in Norman Haire's book
Rejuvenation (1924) and, believing this operation would renew his
sexual powers, had decided upon action. The effect of the operation
was psychological, but powerfully so. Some years later, in 1937, he
refused an invitation to go to India because of a practical difficulty
of a very personal kind. Though the operation revived his creative
power, it also had revived sexual desire, he wrote to Shri Purohit
Swami, and that was likely to last him till he died: 'I believe that if
I repressed this for any long period I would break down under the
strain as did the great Ruskin.'

Apart from feeling that his blood pressure had gone down after
the operation and realising that he was not irritable, the real effect
was indeed that he began to write new poems, those included in *A
Full Moon in March* (1935) expressing a most lively vigour.

'A Prayer for Old Age',[21] for instance, sets the tone of many subsequent poems in its last stanza:

> I pray – for fashion's word is out
> And prayer comes round again –
> That I may seem, though I die old,
> A foolish, passionate man.

In 'Church and State' of August 1934[22] he offers contradictory views of Church and State. The matter suitable for old age was

> Might of the Church and the State,
> Their mobs put under their feet.
> O but heart's wine shall run pure,
> Mind's bread grow sweet.

But was it?

> What if the Church and the State
> Are the mob that howls at the door!
> Wine shall run thick to the end,
> Bread taste sour.

The Blueshirts can be treated ironically now; indeed a lively letter to Olivia Shakespear recorded the doings of local ones:

Here is our most recent event. Next door is a large farm house in considerable grounds. People called —— live there, 'blue shirts' of local importance, and until one day two weeks ago they had many dogs. 'Blue shirts' are upholding law, incarnations of public spirit, rioters in the cause of peace, and George hates 'Blue shirts'. She was delighted when she caught their collie-dog in our hen-house and missed a white hen. I was going into town and she said as I started 'I will write to complain. If they do nothing I will go to the police.' When I returned in the evening she was plunged in gloom. Her letter sent by our gardener had been replied to at once in those words: 'Sorry, have done away with collie-dog' – note the Hitler touch – a little later came the gardener. In his presence, Mrs —— had drowned four dogs. A fifth had revived, when taken out of the water, and as it was not her own dog but a stray she had hunted it down the road with a can tied to its tail. There was a sixth dog, she said, but as it had been with her for some time she would take time to think whether to send it to the dogs' home or drown it. I tried to console George – after all she was only responsible for the death of the collie and so on. But there was something wrong. At last it came. The white hen had returned. Was she to write and say so? I said, 'No; you feel a multi-murderess and if you write, Mrs —— will feel she is.' 'But she will see the hen.' 'Put it in the pot.' 'It is my best layer.' However I insisted and the white hen went into the pot.[23]

This incident became part of the ironic chorus of the second of 'Three Songs to the Same Tune:[24]

> 'Drown all the dogs,' said the fierce young woman,
> 'They killed my goose and a cat.
> Drown, drown in the water-butt,
> Drown all the dogs,' said the fierce young woman.

This song became a mockery of the Irish historic heroic past, echoing the earlier mockery of 'Nineteen Hundred and Nineteen'. The third put the question firmly in terms of order, in a time

> When nations are empty up there at the top,
> When order has weakened or faction is strong . . .

it asked:

> Soldiers take pride in saluting their Captain,
> Where are the captains that govern mankind?

The scene was changing. A metaphysical poem, 'The Four Ages of Man', condensed, taut and intense, recorded this in July:

> He with body waged a fight,
> But body won; it walks upright.
>
> Then he struggled with the heart;
> Innocence and peace depart.
>
> Then he struggled with the mind;
> His proud heart he left behind.
>
> Now his wars on God begin;
> At stroke of midnight God shall win.[25]

He had, in effect, drafted the poem in a letter to Olivia Shakespear:

Waters under the Earth ⎱ The Earth ⎰	The bowels etc.	*Instinct*
The Water = The Blood and the sex organ		*Passion*
The Air = The lungs, logical thought		*Thought*
The Fire =		*Soul*

In *A Vision*'s thought the conflict was against the soul, to restore the body. He put the four elements into a historical shape later in his letter, Earth, Water, Air and Fire covering, respectively, every early nature-dominated civilisation; an armed sexual age (Froissart's *Chronicles*); the Renaissance to the end of the nineteenth century; and the present civilisation being purged away by hatred. In this letter he told her that he had a poem in his head ('Ribh at the Tomb of Baile and Aillinn'), where a monk reads his breviary on the tomb of long-dead lovers at midnight on the anniversary of their death, the night they are united above the tomb, their embrace a conflagration of the entire body that provides the light by which he reads: 'Strange that I should write these things in my old age, when if I were to offer myself for new love I could only expect to be accepted by the very young wearied by the passive embraces of the bolster.'[26]

The poems of *A Full Moon in March* are full of the conflict of the heart and mind; tensions set up by the rival claims of body and soul were still more deeply etching themselves into his art. He could stress these contrasts yet more deeply in what he called the second puberty that ensued after his operation – the ferment that had come upon his imagination.

He was living life to the full, enjoying a production of *The King of the Great Clock Tower* at the Abbey in July 'magnificently acted and danced', masks, choric attendants, climactic dance, and binding metaphors illustrating his theme of the ultimate victory of the poet over the Queen's 'virgin cruelty', art again triumphant over life. During August he was full of creativity. Then came a visit to Rome to speak at the fourth conference held by the Alessandra Volta Foundation in the Royal Italian Academy. He greatly enjoyed the personal – and highly dramatic – rows that developed there. His own subject was 'The Dramatic Theatre'; his audience included Maeterlinck, Pirandello and Gordon Craig.

These he had known before. Who were the new actors to come upon the stage? There was the Swami, who seemed to him a figure of wisdom, whose book *The Holy Mountain* appeared fundamental – a second experience of the Eastern wisdom initially conveyed by Mohini Chatterjee to him as a schoolboy in Dublin. In Ireland he saw more of F. R. Higgins, whose Rabelaisian conversation, like that of Gogarty, he greatly enjoyed, and who was to collaborate in the Cuala Press *Broadsides* with him. A new friend was W. J. Turner, the Australian poet and music critic, who disliked the abstraction of contemporary poetry and approved of the plans for the *Broadsides*. These took up an earlier idea, and were published in two series, 'the first with traditional Irish songs by modern Irish poets, the second songs by modern English and Irish poets with their music'.[27]

There were new actresses upon the scene too. Yeats had become very conscious of what he called the wasted nights of his youth, and wanted to make up for them. In September 1934 he met Margot Ruddock; this was her maiden name, her stage name being Margot Collis. In her teens she had married Jack Collis; divorced, she married Raymond Lovell in 1932. She was now twenty-seven, beautiful, with fine eyes and a rich contralto voice. She asked Yeats for help in creating a poet's theatre and to this end Frederick Ashton, Ashley Dukes, Dulac, T. S. Eliot and Rupert Doone of the Group Theatre were brought together with him. He introduced her to the Swami, encouraged her in her writing of poetry – altering and emending several of her poems – and saw her on his visits to London, where he now took a self-contained flat in Seymour Street which, he told her in a letter of 5 October, cost him 'little more than half' what the Savile Club charged. He wrote her several poems, among them the unpublished 'Margot' enclosed in a letter of 26 November:

I
All famine struck sat I, and then
Those generous eyes on mine were cast,
Sat like other aged men
Dumfoundered, gazing on a past
That appeared constructed of
Lost opportunities to love.

II
O how can I that interest hold?
What offer to attentive eyes?
Mind grows young and body old;
When half closed her eye-lid lies
A sort of hidden glory shall
About these stooping shoulders fall.

III
The Age of Miracles renew,
Let me be loved as though still young
Or let me fancy that it's true,
When my brief final years are gone
You shall have time to turn away
And cram those open eyes with day.[28]

In late December his friendship with the novelist Ethel Mannin began in London; the letters he wrote to her are less interesting than those to Margot Ruddock, as they tend to deal with his health or arrangements for meetings rather than with literary matters. He liked to entertain in the Ivy Restaurant and introduced Ethel Mannin – as he had Margot Ruddock – to the Dulacs and to Norman Haire.

After he returned to Dublin in January 1935 he developed congestion of the lungs, seemed to recover, then collapsed after a visit from a solicitor who read him 'document after document' for an hour. He had come from Lady Gregory's daughter-in-law. Margaret Gough, who had married Captain Gough from Lough Cultra in 1928, was obviously determined that Yeats should have as little to do with Lady Gregory's literary estate as possible (despite the codicil to her will, legally invalid because only witnessed by one person – an ironic occurrence in view of the fate of the Lane pictures – which stated that Yeats's verdict 'would be final'). She had rejected the tentative idea that he should write a Life of Lady Gregory; he could write what he liked after Lady Gregory's autobiography was published, she wrote, rejecting the terms of the codicil. Yeats, however, was more interested in the later Irish period of Lady Gregory's life and wrote to Margaret Gough to say he would write a life which was a study of the movement; this was *Dramatis Personae* which was unlikely to upset her plans; and, probably by July 1933 but certainly by November 1934 his relations with her seem to have become more friendly, as she became 'inexplicably' amicable.

His collapse led to spitting blood, shivering and panting. He was kept in bed, prescribed sleeping draughts and allowed no visitors and no work. With wry amusement he wrote to Olivia and to Ethel Mannin to say that several societies were preparing for his seventieth birthday in June: 'O Mrs Yeats,' said the secretary of PEN, 'don't let him slip away before June.' He read Balzac or *The Arabian Nights*, but after an hour or so his wife would substitute some Wild West fiction. He began to plan a visit to London, and by the end of February he was busy with the proof sheets of *Dramatis Personae. A Vision* was to follow; but there was a new exciting work to be begun.

In the autumn of 1934 he had agreed to edit the *Oxford Book of Modern Verse*. Why did he take on this onerous task? Making anthologies, of course, was no new venture. Making this particular one, apart from the attraction of the money involved, offered him a chance to evaluate modern poetry, to understand – as he put it in a letter to Margot Ruddock in February 1935 – for the sake of what he called in this letter his *Cambridge Book of Modern Verse*, 'the Auden Eliot school'. He decided that what he had read of the difficult poetry being written had the substance of philosophy but was not on the main road of poetry. We need, like Milton, Shakespeare, Shelley, he thought, vast sentiments, generalisations supported by tradition. He also thought that his own poetry might be stimulated by reading the younger poets; he might be reborn in his imagination.[29]

Illness interrupted his work again when he was in London in late March on Group Theatre business. He tried, as he had when young, to talk, walk and work it off, but Dulac realised how ill he was and sent a telegram to Mrs Yeats. Congestion of the lungs confined him to a ground-floor room, in 17 Lancaster Gate Terrace, for more than five weeks. He made another new friend; he had read Dorothy Wellesley's poetry and was introduced to her by Lady Ottoline Morrell; he first visited her house, Penns in the Rocks, in Sussex in early June. Then he arrived back in Ireland in time for his birthday celebrations and he also attended the PEN dinner planned in his honour. His breathing now only troubled him when going upstairs, and by July he felt well and began to work on the anthology of modern verse, asking his agent A. P. Watt to negotiate that its content should begin from Tennyson's death, which would let him work in Hopkins and some poets, such as Dowson, whom he regarded as modern.

George Russell died in Bournemouth, happy that a letter from Yeats had come. Yeats walked behind the hearse at the funeral of his oldest friend in Dublin and summed up their friendship to his new friend Dorothy Wellesley:

I constantly quarrelled with him but he never bore malice and in his last letter, a month before his death, he said that generally when he differed from me it was that he feared to be absorbed by my personality.[30]

Yeats thought Russell had no passions; the difference between them, as George had said to him, was that 'AE was the nearest to a saint you and I will ever meet. You are a better poet but no saint.' Her concern for his health and his poetry made her regard some of his new friendships as tiresome, but she said to him that after his death people would talk about his love affairs but she would say nothing of them, knowing how proud he was.

From 14 to 23 August he visited Dorothy Wellesley, bringing Anne with him. He was reading poetry at a great rate, buying books (from which he would cut out poems he liked), reading in the British Museum; on one visit, he told A. P. Watt, he 'read or smelt' forty-five books of poetry. By November he had completed his selection. Mrs Yeats had put a great deal of work into the book, typing poems, sometimes seeking later versions of texts, selecting fourteen of Yeats's own poems, arranging acknowledgments, paying authors and generally acting as more than a sub-editor. The material went to the Press in April 1936; like most anthologies, it was not entirely what the anthologist wanted. Some authors would not accept his choice of their work; and his choice of the work of others was in some cases curtailed by the high prices asked (by Kipling and Pound, for example). Some poems were not included as it was hoped the anthology would have a popular sale – and be read by schoolchildren. Apart from selecting poems, and often selecting parts of them, Yeats edited and rewrote some – notably those of Dorothy Wellesley and Gogarty. His Introduction, a fine piece of prose containing 'a little of my favourite thoughts', was not a survey of the poetry of the middle thirties, just as the anthology was not. It remains an eccentric book. Obviously, it was a highly individual response from someone who had reacted against Victorian rhetoric, who saw Masefield, Bridges, Binyon and Sturge Moore carrying on traditional themes, who disliked the change in continuity that came with the 1914–18 War, the realism, fragmentalism, obscurity and the emphasis on the contemporary.

Against this he set many Irish poets, thinking that they had kept their individuality and found in ballads a link to ordinary life – so, for example, Gogarty, now an unduly neglected minor poet, was represented by seventeen poems. Yeats was over-inclined to include work by his friends. Among English poets, Dorothy Wellesley was over-represented, and W. J. Turner also. The exclusion of Wilfred Owen caused a good deal of criticism; it was in keeping with Yeats's earlier attitude to the Great War. Owen, however, was excluded not only because Yeats thought passive suffering an unsuitable subject for poetry, but because he considered Owen a bad poet (though a good letter-writer). Every excuse could be made for him 'but none for those who like him'. He was 'all blood, dirt and sucked sugar stick'; he called poets 'bards', a girl a 'maid', and he talked about 'Titanic wars'.[31] Yeats caused great pain to the Irish poet Austin Clarke by omitting him, possibly because his earlier poetry had echoed Yeats's own Celtic period.

Despite its mixed reception the anthology sold very well: in spite of 'universal denunciation from both right and left,' he wrote to Mrs Llewellyn Davies, 'fifteen thousand . . . in three months.'[32] He was used to controversy and thought the vindictiveness of some critics showed he had got down to reality. And with the wisdom of seventy years he had earlier advised Dorothy Wellesley to be prepared for silly reviews until she was so old she was beyond caring; then they would take some other form of silliness. 'The more alive one is,' he concluded, 'the more one is attacked.'[33]

EIGHTEEN

1935–1939

After an operation on 16 October 1935 to remove a lump from his tongue, Yeats went to London a week later. There Nancy Price had arranged a Yeats Festival at the Little Theatre consisting of performances of *The Pot of Broth*, *The Hour-Glass* and *The Player Queen*. He attended the performance of *The Player Queen* on 28 October – praising Margot Ruddock for her performance, her precision and passion, as the true Queen but thinking she would have been better as the Player Queen. Four days after the publication of *A Full Moon in March* he set out for Majorca from Liverpool on 28 November – delighted to have finished the anthology, to be away from the problems of the Cuala Press, the Academy and the Abbey. His new plan was to spend four months of the year in some distant spot with nothing to do but write poetry. His imagination was on fire again, and at first all went well at the Hotel Terramar in Palma. He wrote in bed in the mornings, working on *The Herne's Egg*, founded upon Sir Samuel Ferguson's *Congal* but, he thought, as wild a play as *The Player Queen*, amusing but with more tragedy in it and philosophical depth. In the afternoons he worked with the Swami on a translation of the *Upanishads*. His heart had been somewhat irregular after four days of violent storm on the voyage from Liverpool and the Swami, voluminous in his pink robes, walked slowly in front of him when he went up or down stairs so that he should not strain it. But towards the end of January 1936 Yeats again became seriously ill. Summoned by telegram, Mrs Yeats flew out and found him extremely breathless, the Spanish doctor saying his heart was slightly enlarged and missing a beat.

By April he was better again – convalescent, his heart back to normal, but with a long list of things he was not to eat. The children arrived, the family staying at the Casa Pastor, from the balcony of which Yeats looked out over a wide stretch of very blue sea. He was reading Aldous Huxley and Vita Sackville-West, admiring the former immensely, the latter a little, and disliking both. He was still working with the Swami on the translation of the *Upanishads*. He wrote letters to Olivia Shakespear, Margot Ruddock, Dorothy Wellesley and Ethel Mannin. Though he could assert that only the wasteful virtues earn the sun, he was not at all wasteful in his correspondence, often using the same anecdotes or ideas or phrases in several letters to different recipients. As he got better, his wife's view that he should not go away without her or Anne did not suit him at all. As old age increased his chains, he told Olivia, his need for freedom grew:

I have no consciousness of age, no sense of declining energy, no conscious need of rest. I am unbroken. I repent of nothing but sickness.[1]

He certainly needed strength when Margot Ruddock walked in at 6.30 one morning, her luggage in her hand, a question on her lips: was her verse any good? Yeats had told her to stop writing as her technique was getting worse. He recounted the rest of the episode, encapsulated in the poem 'A Crazed Girl', to Olivia Shakespear:

I was amazed by the tragic magnificence of some fragments and said so. She went out in pouring rain, thought, as she said afterwards, that if she killed herself her verse would live instead of her. Went to the shore to jump in, then thought that she loved life and began to dance. She went to the lodging house where Shri Purohit Swami was, to sleep. She was wet through, so Swami gave her some clothes; she had no money, he gave her some. Next day she went to Barcelona and there went mad, climbing out of a window, falling through a baker's roof, breaking a kneecap, hiding in a ship's hold, singing her own poems most of the time. The British consul in Barcelona appealed to me, so George and I went there, found her with recovered sanity sitting up in bed at a clinic writing an account of her madness. It was impossible to get adequate money out of her family, so I accepted financial responsibility and she was despatched to England and now I won't be able to afford new clothes for a year. When her husband wrote it had not been to send money, but to congratulate her on the magnificent publicity. The paragraph you saw is certainly his work. Will she stay sane? It is impossible to know.

When I am in London I shall probably hide because the husband may send me journalists and because I want to keep at a distance from a tragedy where I can be no further help.[2]

In London, he stayed at the Savile Club and at Penns in the Rocks before returning to Ireland in late June. There he revised proofs of

the *Upanishads* and *A Vision*, often getting up at four in the morning
to work until about 5.30, then returning to bed and writing poetry
after breakfast until noon. It was a curious experience, he told Ethel
Mannin, to have an infirm body and an intellect more alive than it
had ever been, one poem leading to another as if he were smoking,
lighting one cigarette from another. But he declared himself an
invalid, being pushed by his wife or daughter in a wheeled chair,
often to Rathfarnham; on the way home from the village, his white
hair flowing in the wind, to the surprise of passing motorists, he
would eat an ice cream with relish. He decided to live on milk,
and peaches and grapes from the Riversdale garden, a diet which
obviously suited him.

Among the poems he wrote in the summer was 'Lapis Lazuli',[3]
which ends up with a description of a piece of lapis lazuli which
Harry Talbot de Vere Clifton had given him as a seventieth birthday
present. The poem sketches in the current fear of aerial bombing,
with phrases from 'The Battle of the Boyne', an Irish ballad, linking
such threats to the violence of King Billy (William of Orange)
and his bomb-balls. It moves from an idea suggested by Frank
O'Connor's worry over an Abbey actress weeping at the curtain
when playing the heroine of Lady Gregory's *Devorgilla* – something
which Yeats thought should never be done – to a contemplation of
tragedy, associated by him with cold passion and joy; he put the idea
in 'A General Introduction to My Work':

The heroes of Shakespeare convey to us through their looks, or through
the metaphorical patterns of their speech, the sudden enlargement of their
vision, their ecstasy at the approach of death: 'She should have died
hereafter,' 'Of many thousand kisses, the poor last,' 'Absent thee from
felicity awhile.' They have become God or Mother Goddess, the pelican,
'My baby at my breast,' but all must be cold; no actress has ever sobbed
when she played Cleopatra, even the shallow brain of a producer has never
thought of such a thing. The supernatural is present, cold winds blow across
our hands, upon our faces, the thermometer falls, and because of that cold
we are hated by journalists and groundlings. There may be in this or that
detail painful tragedy, but in the whole work none. I have heard Lady
Gregory say, rejecting some play in the modern manner sent to the Abbey
Theatre, 'Tragedy must be a joy to the man who dies.' Nor is it any different
with lyrics, songs, narrative poems; neither scholars nor the populace have
sung or read anything generation after generation because of its pain. The
maid of honour whose tragedy they sing must be lifted out of history with
timeless pattern, she is one of the four Maries, the rhythm is old and

familiar, imagination must dance, must be carried beyond feeling into the
aboriginal ice. Is ice the correct word? I once boasted, copying the phrase
from a letter of my father's, that I would write a poem 'cold and passionate
as the dawn'.[4]

The poem considers 'Old civilisations put to the sword', the brevity
of achievement such as that of the sculptor Callimachus:

> All things fall and are built again,
> And those that build them again are gay.

The Chinamen, carved in the lapis lazuli, stare on the tragic scene:

> Their eyes mid many wrinkles, their eyes,
> Their ancient, glittering eyes, are gay.

'Lapis Lazuli' is complemented by 'The Gyres',[5] written between
July 1936 and January 1937, which uses the shorthand of the gyres
to express the ruin of civilisation, coarsening of conduct and work,
and of the soul, all faced with the gesture of insouciance: 'What
matter?' The voice of the poem's 'Rocky Face' (a seer-like figure is
indicated), coming from a cavern, as the manuscripts of the poem
suggest, has only the one word 'Rejoice'; the keynote is 'What
matter?', since 'We that look on but laugh in tragic joy'.

There was cooperation with Dorothy Wellesley in a sequence of
poems 'The Three Bushes'; the correspondence shows the gradual
elaboration of the poem. The coarseness suggested in 'The Gyres'
lurks in 'The Three Bushes' and the three songs of the Lady, the
song of the Lover and the two songs of the Chambermaid.[6] This is
the story of the Lady disinclined for the physical side of love who
gets her maid to take her place at night:

> He shall love my soul as though
> Body were not at all,
> He shall love your body
> Untroubled by the soul.

The Lady is shamed by her love:

> What hurts the soul
> My soul adores,
> No better than a beast
> Upon all fours.

'The Chambermaid's Second Song' shows how much more explicit
Yeats had become since he wrote of the devil between his thighs in

1913;[7] now the devil has become the lover's 'rod and its butting head / Limp as a worm' and this 'From pleasure of the bed'.

His friendship with Dorothy Wellesley extended into further poetic collaboration; she was to write poems for the series of *Broadsides* planned for Cuala. In October 1936 he had been at Penns in the Rocks. Whether he saw the house with its elegance and comfort – a butler graced the establishment – as a possible re-creation of Coole's ambience, or whether he cast Dorothy Wellesley as an unattainable figure (she seems to have had lesbian tendencies) rather than a latterday Lady Gregory, the friendship became more intimate:

O my dear, I thank you for that spectacle of personified sunlight. I can never while I live forget your movement across the room just before I left, the movement made to draw attention to the boy in yourself.[8]

He spent a night in London to broadcast for the BBC, gave a dinner party for the Dulacs and Ethel Mannin at which he fell asleep. Back in Dublin in November, he described his bedroom to Dorothy Wellesley:

My dear Dorothy: I am writing in bed, the coverlet strewn with proofsheets of the *Upanishads*, on which I have spent the morning. In front of me, over the mantelpiece, is a large lithograph by Shannon, boys bathing, the most conspicuous boy drawn with voluptuous pleasure in back and flank, as always with Shannon. Under it a charcoal study by Burne Jones of sirens luring a ship to its doom, the sirens tall, unvoluptuous, faint, vague forms flitting here and there. On the other wall are drawings, paintings or photographs of friends and relatives, and three reproductions of pictures, Botticelli's 'Spring', Gustave Moreau's 'Women and Unicorns', Fragonard's 'Cup of Life', a beautiful young man and girl running with eager lips towards a cup held towards them by a winged form. The first and last sense, and the second mystery – the mystery that touches the genitals, a blurred touch through a curtain. To right and left are windows, one opening on to a walled garden full of fruit, one on a flower garden, a field and trees. When I came home I got the two shocks I always get – the smallness of my house, the bigness of my Persian cat. I have a longing to tell these things because our last talk has created a greater intimacy.[9]

But a better picture of the ageing poet in his last domestic setting came almost as an echo of an essay he had written in 1917:

A poet, when he is growing old, will ask himself if he cannot keep his mask and his vision without new bitterness, new disappointment. Could he if he would, knowing how frail his vigour from youth up, copy Landor who lived loving and hating, ridiculous and unconquered, into extreme old age, all lost but the favour of his Muses?

> The Mother of the Muses, we are taught
> Is Memory; she has left me; they remain,
> And shake my shoulder, urging me to sing.

Surely, he may think, now that I have found vision and mask I need not suffer any longer. He will buy perhaps some small old house, where, like Ariosto, he can dig his garden, and think that in the return of birds and leaves, or moon and sun, and in the evening flight of the rooks he may discover rhythm and pattern like those in sleep and so never awake out of vision. Then he will remember Wordsworth withering into eighty years, honoured and empty-witted, and climb to some waste room and find, forgotten there by youth, some bitter crust.[10]

The echo came in 'An Acre of Grass', a superb emanation of energy that bursts out after the poet describes his quiet life at Riversdale, his temptation quiet too, but then breaks into desire for an old man's frenzy, an old man's eagle mind:

> Myself must I remake
> Till I am Timon and Lear
> Or that William Blake
> Who beat upon the wall
> Till Truth obeyed his call.[11]

This poem came out of a re-reading of Nietzsche; so did 'What Then?', which he characterised as a melancholy biographical poem. I had telephoned him, as a schoolboy at his old school and editor of *The Erasmian*, to ask him for a poem, to which the answer was that he was not writing poems fit for a school magazine; but later he decided that 'What Then?' might be suitable. The poem employs its refrain impressively through the first three verses before its final and disturbing intensification:

> His chosen comrades thought at school
> He must grow a famous man;
> He thought the same and lived by rule,
> All his twenties crammed with toil;
> *'What then?' sang Plato's ghost. 'What then?'*
>
> Everything he wrote was read,
> After certain years he won
> Sufficient money for his need,

Friends that have been friends indeed;
'What then?' sang Plato's ghost. 'What then?'

All his happier dreams came true –
A small old house, wife, daughter, son,
Grounds where plum and cabbage grew,
Poets and Wits about him drew;
'What then?' sang Plato's ghost. 'What then?'

'The work is done,' grown old he thought,
'According to my boyish plan;
Let the fools rage, I swerved in naught,
Something to perfection brought';
But louder sang that ghost, 'What then?'[12]

Irish politics could still excite him. Henry Harrison, the author of
Parnell Vindicated, came to see him; the result was a ballad 'Come
gather round me, Parnellites' and 'Parnell', a historical footnote in
Essays 1931–1936. But then he got into a 'blind rage' on reading
Dr Maloney's *The Forged Casement Diaries* and wrote two furious
ballads, 'Roger Casement' and 'The Ghost of Roger Casement'.
Meeting Yeats shortly after he had written the first, Joseph Hone
was astonished at the ferocity of his feelings: 'he almost collapsed
after reading the verses and had to call for a little port wine'. In the
version of the poem published in the *Irish Press* on 2 February 1937,
he had attacked 'Alfred Noyes and all that troupe' for spreading
stories about Casement's homosexuality in order to prevent an
appeal against his being sentenced to death for treason in 1916.
Noyes was reported by Maloney as having described the Casement
diaries as 'filthy beyond all description'; but he wrote a disclaimer
to the paper and Yeats, in accepting his explanation, thanked him
for a 'noble' letter, agreeing with the suggestion that the diaries
should be examined by some tribunal – it is now generally accepted
that they are genuine. Yeats was presumably somewhat amused that
it was *The Irish Press* – pro-de Valera and pro-Fianna Fail in outlook
– and not *The Irish Times*, which had accepted the poem and devoted
a leader to him.

In December he was writing somewhat defensive letters to
Dorothy Wellesley and Ethel Mannin: 'Of course I don't hate the
people of England, considering all I owe to Shakespeare, Blake,
Morris – they are the one people I cannot hate.' These English
ladies could hardly be expected to understand the complexities of

Anglo-Irish attitudes to England, after all; but his real defence was what he had told Dorothy Wellesley and put in lines later called 'The Spur', a poem included in a letter of 11 December to Ethel Mannin:

> You think it horrible that Lust and Rage
> Should dance attendance upon my old age;
> They were not such a plague when I was young;
> What else have I to spur me into song?[13]

He also justified his Civil List pension to Ethel Mannin: it was given when Ireland was represented at Westminster and voted out of the taxes of both countries; it was not voted annually; it would not create a vacancy for anyone else if he surrendered it; he had refused it at first, but accepted it when the answer was 'yes' to his question if he was free to join an Irish insurrection; he considered it was earned by services to the people, not to government. Ethel Mannin was told she might some day understand what he saw in the Irish National movement and why he could be no other kind of revolutionist. He had belonged to the IRB as a young man; in many things he had been O'Leary's pupil:

Besides, why should I trouble about communism, fascism, liberalism, radicalism, when all, though some bow first and some stern first but all at the same pace, all are going down stream with the artificial unity which ends every civilization? Only dead sticks can be tied into convenient bundles.[14]

Though a broadcast from the Abbey stage in February 1937 seemed to him a fiasco – 'Every human sound turned into the groans, roars, bellows of a wild [beast]';[15] the accompaniment of hand clapping to the music was stirring in the theatre but came over the air like 'a schoolboy knocking with the end of a pen-knife or a spoon' – Yeats took well to studio broadcasting. In cooperation with George Barnes of the BBC, he arranged and took part in four programmes in 1937: 'In the Poet's Pub' (2 April); 'In the Poet's Parlour' (22 April); 'My Own Poetry' (3 July); and 'My Own Poetry Again' (29 October). His talks were conversational but possessed of an authority which came from his long meditation upon literary creation. And he had strong views about how poetry should be read, as ever: he put them in 'Modern Poetry: a Broadcast':

When I have read you a poem I have tried to read it rhythmically; I may be a bad reader; or read badly because I am out of sorts, or self-conscious; but there is no other method. A poem is an elaboration of the rhythms of common speech and their association with profound feeling. To read a poem like prose, that hearers unaccustomed to poetry may find it easy to understand, is to turn it into bad, florid prose. If anybody reads or recites poetry as if it were prose from some public platform, I ask you, speaking for poets, living, dead, or unborn, to protest in whatever way occurs to your perhaps youthful minds; if they recite or read by wireless, I ask you to express your indignation by letter. William Morris, coming out of a hall where somebody had read or recited his *Sigurd the Volsung*, said: 'It cost me a lot of damned hard work to get that thing into verse.'

His visits to London now included the pleasure of being a member of the Athenaeum – elected under Rule 2, which meant he did not have to pay an entrance fee. He told Dorothy Wellesley that he had always had a childish desire to walk up those steps and under that classical façade; he could entertain her – and Ethel Mannin – to lunch in the ladies' annexe. And he enjoyed working in the library where Maurice Bowra occasionally interrupted him, in cheerful conversations. He had made another new woman friend, Edith Shackleton Heald, a literary journalist who lived at The Chantry House, Steyning, Sussex. How far these friendships developed into sexual relationships or, if they did, how effective they were is not clear. Norman Haire, who had performed Yeats's vasectomy operation, thought them technically ineffective, for instance, citing conversations with Yeats,[16] who gave different impressions to others, writing to Ethel Mannin that she was right, the knowledge 'that I am not unfit for love' had brought him sanity and peace. Yet, he added, that was not altogether why 'I come from you with the feeling that I have been blessed.' His reactions led to excited contemplation and communication; these friendships stimulated his interest afresh in the matter of love and its infinite variations, and provoked him into poetry about the relationships of men and women.

As ever, work continued. In May he had finished the proofs of *A Vision*, and then was busy selecting poems for the Cuala Press *Broadsides*, F. R. Higgins singing the proposed two poems for each of the twelve numbers which were to be accompanied with music. He had wanted for his broadcasts not professionally trained singers but the sort of people who sing when they are drunk or in love; he advised Dorothy Wellesley to keep to the formula 'Music, the natural words in the natural order.' That formula enabled poets to go back to the people, while music would keep out contemporary ideas. He wanted to get back to simplicity and thought writing for Irish-style unaccompanied singing could do this best. In this he had some support from W. J. Turner, a large selection of whose work Yeats included in the *Oxford Book of Modern Verse*. Turner was enthusiastic about the *Broadsides*, which seemed to him to reinforce Yeats's idea that there was the remains of a folk tradition of music in Ireland where 'man's natural life' was not yet extinct. Dulac, very much the professional musician, distrusted any amateurism: he resented Yeats's preference for the unpredictable singing of Margot Ruddock over that of the disciplined Olive Groves. Turner, however, did not care whether Yeats knew if a singer was in tune or not, because he saw that Yeats was interested in expressiveness, and he did not think that trained musicians necessarily supplied what Yeats wanted . . . and that was the expression of something totally alien to current intellectual fashions, a sense of the spiritual imagination for which Yeats had, after all, been searching since the nineties, and which Turner believed was still alive in Ireland.

The proofs of *The Herne's Egg* were corrected by August and he had finished an essay and six poems and written a new poem. Among these may have been 'The Pilgrim', about the pilgrimage to St Patrick's Purgatory of Lough Derg in which Yeats had long been interested. About 1910, for instance, the Abbey had considered producing Calderon's play on the Purgatory. He read several books about it, notably one by Archdeacon St John Seymour; and he alluded to it in 'If I Were Four and Twenty', saying he would memorialise the bishops to open 'that cave of vision once beset by an evil spirit in the form of a long-legged bird with no feathers on its wings'. But the poem's vision is one of a sense of futility, with its refrain of *fol de rol de rolly O*.

The Irish Academy of Letters gave Yeats a banquet on 17 August 1937 and, prompted by a gift from an American Testimonial Committee formed by James A. Farrell – retired President of the United Steel Corporation – to express their admiration and to provide funds for an income for him, he began to form a poem in his head which he had promised to the subscribers in his speech at the banquet when the gift was made public.[17] This was in his grand manner, and his speech 'The Municipal Gallery Revisited' explained how when he went to the Gallery he was restored to many friends; after a few moments, overwhelmed with emotion, he sat down – surrounded by pictures painted by men now dead who had been friends and by pictures of his friends, and of aspects of modern Irish history. The poem conveys something of the emotion he felt in contemplating images of Ireland in spiritual freedom. He drafted it in prose and wrote the verses, a little over a verse a day, and the result is an affirmation not only of his own achievement and that of his friends, particularly Augusta Gregory and John Synge, but a testament of friendship:

> You that would judge me, do not judge alone
> This book or that, come to this hallowed place
> Where my friends' portraits hang and look thereon;
> Ireland's history in their lineaments trace;
> Think where man's glory most begins and ends,
> And say my glory was I had such friends.[18]

There were other moods to record. 'Are you content?'[19] reverts to the material of the Introductory Rhymes to *Responsibilities*, the ancestors who are called upon to answer whether he has been worthy of them, of his genetic inheritance. True, he now has himself passed this on to his children, but he is not content. It is a simple, elegiac and somewhat haunting poem. Another return to the past was 'The Curse of Cromwell'[20] with its image of the great house in which he is made welcome by his friends only to find on waking that it is an old ruin, something used in his plays *The King of the Great Clock Tower* and *Purgatory* as well as in the poem 'Crazy Jane on God', and probably a memory of Castle Dargan in Sligo. The poem, using imagery from Frank O'Connor's translation of *Kilcash* – 'The earls, the lady, the people beaten into the clay' – deals with the ebb and flow of civilisations and is meant to be spoken through the mouth of a wandering Irish peasant poet, through whom Yeats was confessing his rage against the intelligentsia – he regarded Cromwell as the Lenin of his day. 'The Circus Animals' Desertion' sees his inventions as the product of his embittered heart, his circus animals on show: Oisin and Niamh, the Countess Cathleen, Cuchulain's heroic fight with the sea balanced against banalities of the Fool and Blind Man. He seeks the source of his masterful images:

> A mound of refuse or the sweepings of a street,
> Old kettles, old bottles, and a broken can,
> Old iron, old bones, old rags, that raving slut
> Who keeps the till.

It is a despairing moment of truth:

> Now that my ladder's gone,
> I must lie down where all the ladders start,
> In the foul rag-and-bone shop of the heart.[21]

He could, however, extract sardonic humour from rehandling his circus acts. In 'News for the Delphic Oracle', the Immortals are 'golden codgers' now; the poem is closely related to MacKenna's translation of Porphyry's account of the Delphic Oracle on Plotinus. Gaelic mythology blends with the Greek; the fairy princess Niamh is characterised as a man-picker. The mockery continues as the last stanza describes Poussin's picture in the National Gallery of Ireland, now entitled 'Acis and Galatea' but when Yeats wrote the poem 'The Marriage of Pelius and Thetis'. Heightening the contrast between the lovers, with their delicate sensitivity and beauty, and the realities of sex, deliberately coarsens his language; this is the situation of Cuchulain the hero contrasted with Fool and Blind Man again:

> From where Pan's cavern is
> Intolerable music falls.
> Foul goat-head, brutal arm appear,
> Belly, shoulder, bum,
> Flash fishlike; nymphs and satyrs
> Copulate in the foam.[22]

There were poems such as 'Long-Legged Fly' with its vignettes:

> Our master Caesar is in the tent
> Where the maps are spread,
> His eyes fixed upon nothing,
> A hand under his head.
> *Like a long-legged fly upon the stream*
> *His mind moves upon silence.*[23]

This recaptured for one observer Eisenhower deciding in the light of adverse weather reports, whether or not to set the invasion of France in motion. But 'A Bronze Head'[24] worked out, in Yeats's mature manner, an idea tied tightly to imagery; this poem was prompted by the plaster cast, painted bronze, by Lawrence Campbell, of Maud Gonne in the Municipal Gallery of Modern Art in Dublin; it draws upon the ideas of the philosopher McTaggart about the rebirth of the soul; and it pays its tribute to Maud, 'a most gentle woman' but wild, her soul shattered with a vision of the terror it must live through. The poem, like so many others, contrasts past achievement and the present decline and fall: clown and knave mock heroic reverie.

In late June he was in London, erupting into a quarrel with Dulac at the BBC, though this was settled largely by Mrs Dulac; it arose from his general distrust of professional musicians. He found Margot Ruddock's ability to move from speech into song invaluable, though Barnes, like Dulac, considered her inability to reproduce effects consistently a decided disadvantage. V. C. Clinton-Baddeley, on the other hand, was able to read to Yeats's satisfaction, though it took a lot of effort to establish exactly the effect he wanted. A proposal for a radio debate between himself and James Stephens was rejected by Stephens; Dulac was impressed instead, but this debate did not take place. Yeats wanted to proclaim that 'all arts are an expression of desire – exciting desirable life, exalting desirable death'. The debate was abandoned; Yeats had to return to Ireland; when Professor Trench brought Professor Bose from India to call at Riversdale, he responded dramatically to a question – based on the different traditions of Hindus and Moslems – as to whether he could give India a message. Yeats's answer was prompt:

Let 100,000 men of one side meet the other. That is my message to India, insistence on the antinomy.[25]

Unsheathing Sato's sword which was on his desk, he shouted: 'Conflict, more conflict'.

From late September to November he was back in England, staying at The Chantry House with Edith Shackleton Heald and at Penns in the Rocks with Dorothy Wellesley as well as in London; the visit was mainly for his last broadcast on 29 October, in which he read early poems, except for 'Coole Park and Ballylee, 1931'. The second edition of *A Vision* was published in October. In this he replaced the earlier pretences of Giraldus and Kusta ben Luka with the obviously fantastic 'Stories of Michael Robartes and His Friends', while in 'A Packet for Ezra Pound' he told of his wife's automatic writing. In this section he put and answered the question – equivo-cally – of whether he believed in the existence of his circuits of sun and moon. He had it both ways: sometimes overwhelmed by miracle, he took the division of history into periods literally; but his reason soon recovered. He regarded them as stylistic arrangements of experience which helped him to hold reality and justice in a single thought. The revised version did not cover the problem of free will and determinism. If we are to judge by a letter to Ethel Mannin labelling the book as his 'public philosophy' and telling her he had a private philosophy, he was not wholly satisfied with it and had not, he told her, published it because he only half understood it. His ideas though often repetitive were not to be considered static and he was now thinking about the nature of 'individual mind'.[26]

Yeats left Dublin for Menton on 8 January 1938, to be joined by Mrs Yeats on 4 February at the Carlton Hotel; they later moved to the Hôtel Idéal Séjour on the hill above Cap Martin which had a charming garden and was quiet. He corrected the proofs of *New Poems*, subsequently published in May, wrote poetry and finished *On the Boiler*. This was intended to be the first in a series of bi-annual books to be published by the Cuala Press, a miscellany of his ideas '. . . an amusing thing to do – I shall curse my enemies and bless my friends. My enemies will hit back, and that will give me the joy of answering them.'[27] It was to be similar to Ruskin's irregularly published miscellany, *Fors Clavigera*, and was called *On the Boiler* because Yeats remembered a mad ship's carpenter called McCoy who used to make speeches from the top of an old boiler on Sligo Quay; a spirited drawing of him by Jack Yeats was part of the cover design of the book when the Cuala Press published it in 1939. This man used to denounce his neighbours, and Yeats remembered him being greeted by a shower of stones at a Rosses Point Regatta when he had sculled towards the shore to denounce general wickedness. Yeats spoke his mind freely: a crack at that 'cringing firbolg Tom Moore', criticism of Alfie Byrne (Dublin's Lord Mayor) for wanting to make himself popular among the common people, attacks on ignorance in schools, desire for an Irish system not political but moulded upon able men with public minds, some pondering over whether he had given too much time to the theatre, 'to the expression of other men's genius'. In the second section, headed 'Tomorrow's Revolution', he took a passage of Burton's *Anatomy of Melancholy* as text and considered the effects of heredity. He feared the multiplication of the uneducable masses, was in favour of what might be called eugenics. He exhibited his reading, his memories, and contrasted – in an Anglo-Irish way – Ireland and England:

The hero Finn, wishing for a son not less strong of body stood at the top of a hill and said he would marry the first woman that reached him. According to the tale two thousand started level; but should Jones of Twickenham bother?

This led him to a footnote, referring to an early version of 'The Courting of Emer', Cuchulain's wife. She was chosen for the strength and volume of her bladder, considered signs of vigour: 'a jealous woman of divine origin was murdered by jealous rivals because she made the deepest hole in the snow with her urine'. In 'Crazy Jane on the Mountain',[28] there is a parallel poetic use of the image; the poem arose from his having heard that George V had failed to persuade the English Prime Minister to bring the Russian Royal Family to England; in it Crazy Jane describes Emer as 'great-bladdered'. The poem laments lost heroism. In his prose Yeats returned to the differences between the islands, yet again begging our governments to exclude all alien appeal to mass instinct:

The Irish mind has still in country rapscallion or in Bernard Shaw an ancient, cold, explosive, detonating impartiality. The English mind, excited by its newspaper proprietors and its schoolmasters, has turned into a bed-hot harlot.

In his discussion of how social politics might affect Ireland he had deliberately decided to seek what he thought was 'the brutality, the ill breeding, the barbarism of truth'. He felt that he could affect Ireland's future nature. So much had changed already; he had lived through so much change himself that possibilities of further change could easily be considered. It is not perhaps something to be readily understood by those whose history has been clearly mapped out over the centuries in an orderly progress that has shaped them. Revolution and civil war, however, suggest and create a flux; the poet could put his vision, what he believed his shaping vision of what Ireland could and should be to his fellow countrymen and women – or, at least, to the intelligent among them. He moved into more varied matters – the Abbey, the Cuala Press *Broadsides*, the new designs for Cuala embroidery, a section which paraphrases the thought of a powerful, cryptic poem 'The Statues':[29]

There are moments when I am certain that art must once again accept those Greek proportions which carry into plastic art the Pythagorean numbers, those faces which are divine because all there is empty and measured. Europe was not born when Greek galleys defeated the Persian hordes at Salamis, but when the Doric studios sent out those broad-backed marble statues against the multiform vague, expressive Asiatic Sea, they gave to the sexual instinct of Europe its goal, its fixed type.

He went to England on 23 March, where he made two visits to Penns in the Rocks and two to The Chantry House, going up to London for rehearsals and a broadcast of his 'Poet's Pub' programme on 2 April. He decided against another broadcast, which was to have included Walter Starkie playing his fiddle. Out of the visit to Penns in the Rocks came 'Politics', in part a comment on a guest's 'panic-stricken' conversation, in part a reaction to Archibald Mac-Leish's praise of his poetry in an article in the *Yale Review* (the only article for years on his poetry which, he said, did not bore him) for its 'public' language; his reply to the article's comment that because of his age and relation to Ireland he was unable to use his public language on politics was the poem 'Politics' with its epigraph from Thomas Mann 'In our time the destiny of man presents its meanings in political terms.'

> How can I, that girl standing there,
> My attention fix
> On Roman or on Russian
> Or on Spanish politics?
> Yet here's a travelled man that knows
> What he talks about,
> And there's a politician
> That has read and thought,
> And maybe what they say is true
> Of war and war's alarms,
> But O that I were young again
> And held her in my arms![30]

At The Chantry House he began to write 'a scene of tragic intensity', the play *Purgatory*, planned when he was at the Hôtel Idéal Séjour. He continued work on it during the six weeks, from mid-May to early July, that he spent in Ireland. Then he was back in England again, staying with Dorothy Wellesley and Edith Shackleton Heald, until he returned to Ireland for the staging of *Purgatory* on 10 August; the settings of the play were by Anne Yeats, who also designed *On Baile's Strand*, performed the following night. The image of the ruined, uninhabited house suddenly lit up (like Castle Dargan) is a sombre background to a play possibly related to a ghost story he told at one of Ricketts's Friday evenings. *Purgatory* illustrates the degradation of the human stock and soul, leaving a question as to whether there is any ultimate way out of the situation; it has been argued by Professor Torchiana that Yeats symbolises life in the individualistic world: 'Eighteenth-century excellence fallen on evil days. A ruined house, ruined family and ruined tree suggest individual, familial and national failures.'[31] The play's intensity is impressive (its concentration can be superbly rendered when it is portrayed by puppets), its earth-bound ghost reminding us of the influence of the Nōh, the dreaming-back a continuous process. In an interview in the *Irish Independent*, Yeats said the play was founded upon a *mésalliance*; he thought the dead suffer remorse and recreate their lives, and in his play a spirit suffers because of its share, when alive, in the destruction of an honoured house, a destruction he saw taking place 'all over Ireland today'.

'The Man and the Echo' marked a new attitude to death: a moving poem with its repetition, alliteration and emphatic rhyming, it is set in the great rocky fissure on Knocknarea suggestive of Delphi, where the man shouts his question at the rock. He wonders about the effect of his *Cathleen ni Houlihan*:

> Did that play of mine send out
> Certain men the English shot?

of his words on Margot Ruddock's 'reeling brain' (she had to return to an asylum again after a period of normality when she read his poems for the BBC), wonders could his words have checked the ruin of a great house:

> Then stands in judgment on his soul,
> And, all work done, dismisses all
> Out of intellect and sight
> And sinks at last into the night.

After Echo's answer of 'Into the night' comes the cry of questioning of what happens after death, and the recognition that he simply cannot know. And this for him is a great honesty, a great stripping down to essential emotional truth; the effect of facing the question is mirrored in the final lines:

> Up there some hawk or owl has struck,
> Dropping out of sky or rock,
> A stricken rabbit is crying out,
> And its cry distracts my thought.[32]

He wrote the poem in July, and was revising it up to October. But in August his mind turned even more sharply to his own death: ideas of Rilke about death, he wrote to Dorothy Wellesley, had annoyed him when he read a book of essays, *R. M. Rilke, Some Aspects of his Mind and Poetry*. He wrote (though not on the margin of the book as he said) these lines:

> Draw rein, draw breath.
> Cast a cold eye
> On life, on death.
> Horseman, pass by.[33]

Seven days later, writing to Ethel Mannin,[34] he announced that he was arranging his burial place in the Irish country churchyard where his great-grandfather had been rector a hundred years before: just his name and dates and these lines (he omitted the first of the four previously quoted). To Edith Shackleton Heald, he reported in September that his sister Lily considered that he had broken with tradition by describing his own burial and tombstone in a poem; the Yeats family had not had a tombstone since the eighteenth century. However, he had probably been prompted by the example of his Pollexfen grandfather who had daily superintended the making of his tomb in St John's Church, Sligo. He completed the poem, 'Under Ben Bulben',[35] by 4 September. In it he links the monks living round the Mareotic Lake – itself a link with Shelley's Witch of Atlas, next invoked, who had glided down the Nile by Moeris and the Mareotic lakes – with superhuman forms seen on Knocknarea by George Pollexfen's servant Mary Battle; now they ride Ben Bulben's 'wintry dawn':

Some of them have their hair down but they look quite different, more like the sleepy-looking ladies one sees in the papers ... They are fine and dashing-looking, like the men one sees riding their horses in twos and threes on the slopes of the mountain with their swords swinging. There is no such race living now, none so finely proportioned.[36]

The poem goes to the two eternities of race and soul – his idea of the conflict of two states of consciousness, persons dying each other's life, living each other's death. The section suggests that clarity, even ease, comes to the mind in times of crisis, quoting John Mitchel's prayer for war, a parody of the daily order of the Church service's 'Give us peace in our time, O Lord' with its 'Send war in our time, O Lord'. The fourth section echoes the ideas of 'The Statues' about the role of images, created by the arts in imitation of

natural objects but yet themselves imitations going back, in terms
of Plotinus, to the Ideas from which Nature derives. The plea to
Irish poets is to select the best of the past – not only images of the
eighteenth century but of the past Gaelic civilisation, its lords and
ladies

> beaten into the clay
> Through seven heroic centuries.

Then comes the final and simple section about his own death and
burial:

> Under bare Ben Bulben's head
> In Drumcliff churchyard Yeats is laid.
> An ancestor was rector there
> Long years ago, a church stands near,
> By the road an ancient cross.
> No marble, no conventional phrase;
> On limestone quarried near the spot
> By his command these words are cut:
>> *Cast a cold eye*
>> *On life, on death.*
>> *Horseman, pass by!*

There was another journey to England in September; it involved
spending a day at Oxford, he and Edith Shackleton Heald later
lunching with R. A. Scott-James in Berkshire, en route to The
Chantry House.

In Ireland Maud Gonne came to visit him at Riversdale; she later
described how, as they said goodbye for the last time:

... he, sitting in his armchair from which he could rise only with great
effort, said, 'Maud, we should have gone on with our Castle of the Heroes,
we might still do it.' I was so surprised that he remembered, I could not
reply.[37]

He remembered more than she realised, and in the poem 'Beautiful
Lofty Things' had recently celebrated a moment in their relationship
which occurred nearly half a century before:

> Maud Gonne at Howth station waiting a train,
> Pallas Athene in that straight back and arrogant head:
> All the Olympians; a thing never known again.[38]

In early October he heard that Olivia Shakespear had died suddenly
at her home in London; she was seventy-five. For more than forty

years, he wrote to Dorothy Wellesley, she had been the centre of
his life in London and during all that time they had never had a
quarrel, 'sadness sometimes but never a difference'. He was himself
now suffering from kidney trouble, and confined to his room. Letters
to Ethel Mannin in October reveal him thinking more about death,
and planning a play on the death of Cuchulain. By the end of the
month he was in England again, drafting the play in prose at The
Chantry House; then he and his wife went to the Riviera, the winter
abroad financed by funds provided by the American Testimonial
Committee. They stayed at the Hôtel Idéal Séjour, finding the hotel
perfect with no other guests, the climate perfect too.

Michael came for the Christmas holidays and there was a good
deal of social life. Yeats acted as apparent magnet: Dorothy Wellesley
and her friend Hilda Matheson of the BBC were in a villa near
Beaulieu and W. J. Turner and his wife were staying with them;
Dermot O'Brien, the Irish artist, and his wife were at Cap d'Ail,
and Edith Shackleton Heald was to drive down in late January with
Evelyn Marriott, a neighbour at Steyning.[39] Though preparing
material for a second issue of *On the Boiler* and writing 'Cuchulain
Comforted'[40] left him enervated, for Michael's benefit he told stories
from the Indian monk's autobiography on Christmas Day when he,
his wife and Michael visited Dorothy Wellesley. He enjoyed the
company of his friends but, though this was a pleasant excitement,
he began to look forward to quiet in February, finding that the
conversation, the journeys to Beaulieu and chess with Michael made
him very tired.

The doctor thought his health had deteriorated, and though he
himself realised his time would not be long – writing to Lady
Elizabeth Pelham (a friend of the Swami with whom he had thought
of going to India) that he had put away everything that could be put
away so that he should be able to speak what he had to speak – he
was still buoyant with ideas. In two or three weeks, he thought,
having rested after writing much verse, he would begin to write his
most fundamental thoughts and the arrangement of them that he
thought would complete his studies. He told her he was happy, full
of an energy he had despaired of. It seemed he had found what he
wanted:

When I try to put all into a phrase I say, 'Man can embody truth but he
cannot know it.' I must embody it in the completion of my life. The abstract

is not life and everywhere draws out its contradictions. You can refute Hegel but not the Saint or the Song of Sixpence. . . .'[41]

He completed 'The Black Tower', a poem about political propaganda,[42] on Saturday 21 January, and read it to Mrs Yeats, Dorothy Wellesley, Hilda Matheson and the Turners. The next day he was visited by the O'Briens and told them he was feeling very happy, writing poetry again. But by Thursday he had failed considerably and was wandering in his speech; that evening he rallied and gave his wife corrections for *The Death of Cuchulain* and 'Under Ben Bulben'. On the next day he was given morphia for bouts of pain; he was very breathless and died on Saturday afternoon, 28 January.

His body was given temporary burial at Roquebrune. It was decided that his remains should be brought back to Ireland, the French government offering a destroyer to convey the coffin. The Dean of St Patrick's Cathedral suggested he should be interred in the Cathedral, close to the graves of Swift and Stella, but the family decided that his own plans for burial in Sligo should be followed. He had himself thought that if he died in France Roquebrune would be suitable; but, if it were convenient, they could 'dig him up later' and bring him to Sligo. Memorial services were held at St Patrick's in Dublin and in St Martin's-in-the-Fields in London.

The outbreak of war in the autumn meant that it was not until September 1948 that an Irish corvette, the *Macha*, brought his body back to Galway.[43] Mrs Yeats, Anne, Michael and Jack Yeats went aboard; the coffin was piped ashore and the funeral procession went by road to Drumcliff Churchyard, with a lying in State for an hour in front of the Sligo Town Hall. The cortege was met by Sean MacBride, then Minister for External Affairs, and other members of the government, the Mayor and Corporation of Sligo and a large number of Sligo citizens and visitors. There was a Church of Ireland Service in Drumcliff Churchyard where a stone inscribed as he had directed stands to show that this great poet intended his body to rest 'under bare Ben Bulben's head' in Sligo, his spiritual home in Ireland:

> Though grave-diggers' toil is long,
> Sharp their spades, their muscles strong,
> They but thrust their buried men
> Back in the human mind again.[44]

NOTES

These notes are intended to aid readers who may wish to pursue points raised in the text which are based on printed sources. In some cases, however, unpublished or oral sources of information are indicated, these would not normally be available to readers, or else those who supplied the information are now dead. In order to keep the notes within a reasonable compass they are selective rather than all-inclusive. To save space abbreviations are used for the titles which appear more than once in the notes. These are listed below.

Where the earliest version of a poem is quoted the source is given in these notes, but reference is also made to *CP* or *PNE*. Early versions of early poems are given because they were what Yeats wrote at the period of his life under discussion: later he often revised them so extensively they became very different poems.

Writings of W. B. Yeats

A	*Autobiographies* (1955).	L(K)	*The Collected Letters of W. B. Yeats*, I, Ed. John Kelly and Eric Domville (1986).
CK	*The Countess Kathleen and Various Legends and Lyrics* (1892).		
		L(W)	*Letters*, Ed. Allan Wade (1954).
CP	*Collected Poems* (1933; references are to 2nd edn., 1950, with later poems added).	Mem	*Memoirs*, Ed. Denis Donoghue (1972).
		M	*Mythologies* (1959).
C Pl	*Collected Plays* (1934; references are to 2nd edn., 1952, with additional plays).	PNE	*The Poems: A New Edition*, Ed. R. J. Finneran (1984).
CW	*Collected Works* (1908).	UP	*Uncollected Prose by W. B. Yeats*, I, Ed. John P. Frayne (1970); II, Ed. John P. Frayne and Colton Johnson (1975).
E	*Explorations* (1962).		
E&I	*Essays and Introductions* (1961).		

VP   *The Variorum Edition of the Poems of W. B. Yeats*, Ed. Peter Allt and Russell K. Alspach (1957).

V Pl   *The Variorum Edition of the Plays of W. B. Yeats*, Ed. Russell K. Alspach (1966).

Other Books

AREL   *A Review of English Literature.*

EPDS   *Ezra Pound and Dorothy Shakespear. Their Letters 1909–1914*, Ed. Omar Pound and A. Walton Litz (1985).

FD   Richard Ellmann, *Four Dubliners* (1986).

IER   *In Excited Reverie*, Ed. A. Norman Jeffares and K. G. W. Cross (1965).

JH   Joseph Hone, *W. B. Yeats 1865–1939* (1942; rev. edn. 1962).

LGF   *Lady Gregory Fifty Years After*, Ed. Ann Saddlemyer and Colin Smythe (1987).

LGJ   *Lady Gregory's Journals*, II, Ed. Daniel J. Murphy (1987).

LHS   John Butler Yeats, *Letters to His Son W. B. Yeats and Others*, Ed. Joseph Hone (1944).

LWBY   *Letters to W. B. Yeats*, Ed. Richard J. Finneran, George Mills Harper and William M. Murphy, 2 vols, (1977).

MAV   George Mills Harper, *The Making of Yeats's A Vision*, 2 vols, (1987).

PF   William M. Murphy, *Prodigal Father. The Life of John Butler Yeats (1839–1922)*, (1978).

SSY   *The Senate Speeches of W. B. Yeats*, Ed. Donald R. Pearce (1960).

YA   *Yeats Annual.*

YAE   Peter Kuch, *Yeats and A.E.* (1986).

Chapter 1

1 Information from Lily Yeats, whose memories, conveyed in lively conversation, supplemented the MSS she allowed me to consult: her scrapbook, draft scrapbook, another notebook and various letters.

2 *JH*, 9.

3 JBY, Letter to Lily Yeats, 15 Sept. 1916, *LHS* 229, describes his uncles Thomas and John as 'so clever and so innocent'.

4 JBY, Letter to WBY, 10 Feb. 1918; PF, 37.

5 JBY, Letter to John Quinn, 31 Dec. 1915; *PF*, 37.

6 Richard Ellmann, *Oscar Wilde* (1987), 12 *n*.

7 JBY, Letter to John Sloan, 17 July 1917, *PF*, 51.

8 Notably Agnes whom he called a 'termagant'; she later spent many years in an asylum, suffering mental imbalance.

9 JBY, Letter to Susan Yeats, 1 Nov. 1872, *JH*, 17.

10 Lily Yeats, MS material.

11 WBY, *A*, 9.

12 JBY, Letter to Lily Yeats, 15 Sept. 1916, *PF*, 94.
13 WBY, *A*, 14.
14 WBY, *A*, 27.
15 WBY, *A*, 11.
16 WBY, *A*, 18.
17 WBY, *A*, 19.
18 Lily Yeats, MS material.
19 WBY, *A*, 12.
20 WBY, *A*, 26.
21 WBY, *A*, 31.
22 WBY, *A*, 28.
23 WBY, *A*, 35.
24 WBY, *A*, 42.
25 WBY, *A*, 40.
26 WBY, *A*, 41.
27 JBY Letter to Edward Dowden, 11 May 1879, *PF*, 118.
28 WBY, *A*, 61.
29 WBY, *A*, 65.

Chapter 2

1 WBY, *A*, 58.
2 WBY, *A*, 60.
3 WBY, *A*, 64.
4 WBY, *Mem*, 72.
5 WBY, Letter to Katharine Tynan, *L* (K), 155.
6 WBY, Letter to Mary Cronin, *L* (K), 7.
7 WBY, 'What Then?', *CP*, 347; *PNE*, 302.
8 JBY, *Memoirs* (I), *PF*, 137.
9 WBY, *CP*, 10; *PNE*, 10. Text from *The Wanderings of Oisin and Other Poems* (1889).
10 WBY, *A*, 96.
11 WBY, *A*, 93.
12 WBY, *A*, 101.
13 WBY, *A*, 103.
14 JBY, Letter to Dowden, 8 Jan. 1884, *PF*, 134; WBY, *A*, 23; see also JBY, *Early Memories. Some*

Chapters of Autobiography (1923), 20.
15 WBY, 'The Poetry of Sir Samuel Ferguson', *UP*, I, 95.
16 Lollie Yeats, Diary, Nov. 1888, *PF*, 159.
17 WBY, Letter to K. Tynan, *L* (K), 15.
18 WBY, Letter to K. Tynan, *L* (K), 41.
19 WBY, Letter to K. Tynan, *L* (K), 98.
20 WBY, *CP*, 409; *PNE*, 355. Text quoted here is from the first edition of 1889.

Chapter 3

1 WBY, Letter to K. Tynan, *L* (K), 56.
2 WBY, *A*, 113.
3 WBY, *Mem*, 20.
4 Lollie Yeats, Diary entry, 18 Jan. 1888. Parts of this were published as 'A Scattered Fair', *The Wind and the Rain*, III, 3, 1946.
5 WBY, *A*, 128.
6 WBY, *A*, 134.
7 WBY, *A*, 146.
8 WBY, *A*, 135.
9 WBY, *A*, 136.
10 WBY, *Mem*, 31.
11 WBY, Letter to K. Tynan, 25 August 1888, L(K), 93.
12 WBY, Letter to K. Tynan, [18] Nov. 1890, *L* (K), 235.
13 WBY, Letter to John Quinn, 30 Sept. 1921; see B. L. Reid, *The Man from New York* (1968), 493.
14 WBY, Letter to K. Tynan, 6 Oct. 1890, *L* (K), 231.
15 WBY, *A*, 72.
16 WBY, 'The Lake Isle of Innisfree', *CP*, 44; *PNE*, 39. Text

taken from *The National Observer*, 13 December 1890.

17 WBY, *Mem*, 32. See *n. 3*.

18 WBY, *A*, 64.

19 WBY, *Mem*, 40; see also WBY, *A*, 123.

20 WBY, *Mem*, 42.

21 WBY, Letter to K. Tynan, 6 Oct. [1890], *L* (K), 231.

22 WBY, *A*, 166.

23 WBY, *A*, 171.

24 WBY, *Mem*, 46.

25 WBY, *Mem*, 49.

26 WBY, Letter to John O'Leary, [?25 November 1891], *L* (K), 272.

Chapter 4

1 WBY, *C Pl*, 50.

2 WBY, *C Pl*, 34. Text taken from *Poems* (1895).

3 WBY, 'The White Birds', *CP*, 46; *PNE*, 41. Text taken from *CK*.

4 WBY, 'To the Rose Upon the Rood of Time', *CP*, 35; *PNE*, 31. Text from *CK*.

5 WBY, 'Poetry and Tradition', *E&I*, 255.

6 WBY, 'The Rose of the World', *CP*, 41; *PNE*, 36. Text taken from *CK*.

7 WBY, 'To Ireland in the Coming Times', *CP*, 56; *PNE*, 50. Text taken from *CK*.

8 WBY, *Mem*, 59.

9 WBY, *Mem*, 81.

10 WBY, *A*, 342. The earlier version, in *UP*, I, 398, is less tightly written.

11 WBY, *A*, 342.

12 Geneviève Mallarmé, Letter to Stephane Mallarmé, 26 Feb.

1894, in Mallarmé, *Correspondence*, III, 235.

13 George Moore, *Ave* (1911), 45.

14 WBY, *A*, 283.

15 WBY, *A*, 266.

Chapter 5

1 WBY, *Mem*, 78.

2 WBY, *UP*, I, 359, 366, 375, 382. For the earlier 'The Thirty Best Irish Books', *United Ireland*, 16 March 1895, see *UP*, I, 355.

3 WBY, Introduction to *A Book of Irish Verse* (1895).

4 WBY, *A*, 322.

5 WBY, *Mem*, 157. He had noticed his own form of excitability in his sister Lollie, exaggerated by fits of profound gloom in her case. And he added that she had Mars in square with Saturn while he had Moon in opposition to Mars. See *Mem*, 156.

6 WBY, *Mem*, 85.

7 WBY, *Mem*, 85. It would be a courageous decision. His finances were parlous. In a letter of 16 July 1896 his father described him as 'wandering round like one of the disinherited for the last few days. He has no money. Just now I have made him quite happy and he is off to London. I have lent him 2/6. *Letters from Bedford Park: a Selection from the Correspondence (1890–1901) of John Butler Yeats*, Ed. William M. Murphy (1972).

8 WBY, *Mem*, 86.

9 WBY, *Mem*, 88.

10 WBY, *C Pl*, 152. Text from *The Shadowy Waters* (acting version) (1907).

11 JBY, Letter to Lily Yeats, [3 April 1896], *PF*, 192.
12 WBY, Letter to John O'Leary, 30 May [1897], *L* (W), 286.
13 WBY, 'Out of the Rose', *M*, 162; the text quoted, however, is from an earlier revised version, *CW*, IV (1908).
14 WBY, *M*, 155. Text taken from *CW* (1908).
15 WBY, 'He gives His Beloved certain Rhymes', *CP*, 71; *PNE*, 63.
16 WBY, *CP*, 90; *PNE*, 81.
17 WBY, *CP*, 46; *PNE*, 41. Text from *CK*.
18 WBY, *CP*, 319; *PNE*, 279.
19 George Russell, Letter to W. B. Yeats, [? April 1896], *YAE*, 110.
20 George Russell, Letter to W. B. Yeats, 2 June 1896, *YAE*, 110.
21 WBY, *M*, 271.
22 WBY, *M*, 287. Text taken from *The Savoy*, April 1896.
23 WBY, *M*, 294.
24 WBY, *M*, 310.
25 WBY, *V Pl*, 932.
26 WBY, *CP*, 73; *PNE*, 65. Text taken from *The Savoy*, April 1896.
27 WBY, *A*, 343.
28 WBY, *A*, 349.
29 WBY, *A*, 253.
30 WBY, *A*, 254.
31 WBY, *CP*, 77; *PNE*, 69. Text taken from *The Savoy*, September 1896.
32 WBY, *Mem*, 89.
33 WBY, *CP*, 68; *PNE*, 61. Text taken from *The Dome*, May 1898.
34 WBY, Letter to Olivia Shakespear, 6 Dec. [1926], *L* (W), 721.
35 WBY, *CP*, 251; *PNE*, 223.
36 WBY, *CP*, 250; *PNE*, 222.

Chapter 6

1 WBY, *Mem*, 112–113.
2 WBY, *Mem*, 125.
3 WBY, *Mem*, 126.
4 WBY, *Mem*, 160.
5 Their relationship is discussed by Elizabeth Longford, 'Lady Gregory and Wilfrid Scawen Blunt', *LGF*, 85–97, and in her biography *A Pilgrimage of Passion: The Life of Wilfrid Scawen Blunt* (1979). Lady Gregory's 'A Woman's Sonnets' are included in *LGF*, 102–113.
6 WBY, *A*, 377.
7 Lady Gregory, Diary entry, 30 Nov. 1897, cited by John Kelly, 'Friendship is the only House I have', *LGF*, 205.
8 WBY, *A*, 397.
9 WBY, *A*, 398.
10 WBY, *A*, 364.
11 WBY, *CP*, 79; *PNE*, 71. Text taken from *The Saturday Review*, 24 July 1897.
12 WBY, *Mem*, 132.
13 WBY, *CP*, 75; *PNE*, 68. Punctuation taken from text in *The Dome*, May 1898.
14 WBY, *Mem*, 134.
15 See Mary Lou Kohfeldt, *Lady Gregory: The Woman Behind the Irish Renaissance* (1985), 129.
16 George Pollexfen, Letter to W. B. Yeats, 24 Feb. 1899. See also *JH*, 156.
17 WBY, 'He wishes for the Cloths of Heaven', *CP*, 81; *PNE*, 73. Text from *The Wind Among the Reeds* (1899).

18 WBY, *E&I*, 194.
19 WBY, *E&I*, 157.
20 WBY, *E&I*, 161.
21 WBY, Introduction to *Oxford Book of Modern Verse* (1936), xi.

Chapter 7

 1 WBY, *A*, 401.
 2 WBY, *A*, 442. See also *JH*, 172.
 3 WBY, *E*, 86.
 4 WBY, *A*, 417.
 5 WBY, *E&I*, 15.
 6 From Cecil Salkeld's memories of Yeats's visit in September 1920 to Maud Gonne, then staying in the 'last cottage in the Glen', at Glenmalure, Co. Wicklow; these are included in *JH*, 326.
 7 It began with Eglinton's 'What Should be the Subjects of a National Drama?', *Daily Express* (Dublin), 18 September 1898, and ended with AE's (George Russell's) 'Nationality and Cosmopolitanism in Literature', *Daily Express* (Dublin), 10 December 1898. The controversy was published as *Literary Ideals in Ireland* in May 1899.
 8 WBY, Dedication (to Lady Gregory) in *Where There is Nothing* (1903), *V Pl*, 232.
 9 WBY, Appendix II to *Cathleen ni Houlihan*, in *CW* (1908) IV; see *V Pl*, 233. Lady Gregory, playing Cathleen in the Abbey in 1919, asked 'What is needed but a hag and a voice?'
10 Stephen Gwynn, *Irish Literature and Drama* (1936), 158.
11 WBY, 'The Man and the Echo', *CP*, 393; 'Man and the Echo', *PNE*, 345.
12 WBY, Letter to George Russell, 18 Oct. [1902], *L* (W), 381.
13 WBY, *CW* III; see *V Pl*, 712. See a later version of the note *V Pl*, 713 and see also *L* (W), 503.
14 WBY, *A*, 454.
15 WBY, Letter to Lady Gregory of 25 April [1900], *L* (W), 340. See also George Mills Harper, *Yeats's Golden Dawn*, (1974), 14–25.
16 WBY, Letter to George Russell (AE), [?May] 1900, *L* (W), 342. He was appealed to in later squabbles between Felkin and Miss Christina Mary Stoddard between 1918 and 1921, and, as an elder statesman, tried to keep the peace. He probably left the Order in 1922. (He was Imperator of the Amoun Temple of the Order of Stella Matutina in 1914).
17 WBY, *E&I*, 28. In July 1892 he had written to John O'Leary that it was absurd to consider him 'weak' to persist in a study which he had decided four or five years previously to make, next to his poetry, the most important pursuit of his life. If he had not made magic his constant study, he added, he could not have written his Blake book nor written *The Countess Kathleen*. See *L* (W), 210.
18 WBY, *CP*, 88; *PNE*, 80.
19 Maud Gonne MacBride, *A Servant of the Queen* (1938), 328.
20 WBY, *CP*, 465; *PNE*, 402.
21 WBY, MS.
22 Lady Gregory's Diary entries 14

February 1898. See John Kelly,
'Friendship is the only House I
Have', *LGF*, 199.

23 WBY, Letter in the *Freeman's
Journal*, 20 March 1900 (see *L*
(W), 335); Letter to the *Daily
Express* (Dublin), 30 March 1900
(See WBY, *UP*, II, 208); and the
essay 'Noble and Ignoble Loy-
alties', *The United Irishman*, 21
April 1900 (See WBY, *UP*, II,
211). See also a letter of 3 April
1900 to the *Daily Express*
(Dublin), *L* (W), 338.

24 WBY, Letter to Lady Gregory,
[3 Jan. 1903], *L* (W), 392.

25 WBY, *A*, 409.

Chapter 8

1 WBY, Letter to Lady Gregory,
[3 Jan. 1903], *L* (W), 393.

2 WBY, Letter to Lady Gregory,
[15 Jan. 1903], *L* (W), 396.

3 WBY, Letter to George Russell
(AE), 14 Mar. 1903, *L* (W), 402.

4 WBY, 'The Folly of Being
Comforted', *CP*, 86; *PNE*,
78.

5 WBY, *CP*, 455; *PNE*, 392.

6 *JH*, 189.

7 WBY, MS.

8 WBY, *CP*, 86; *PNE*, 78.

9 WBY, *CP*, 87; *PNE*, 79.

10 WBY, *E&I*, 213.

11 WBY, *E&I*, 64.

12 WBY, Letter to Lady Gregory,
[?16 Nov. 1903], *L* (W), 413.

13 WBY, Letter to Lady Gregory,
[?18 Jan. 1904], *L* (W), 422.

14 WBY, Letter to Lady Gregory,
[?28 Jan. 1904], *L* (W), 429.

15 WBY, Letter to Lady Gregory,
[?8 Feb. 1904], *L* (W), 431.

16 WBY, Letter to George Russell
(AE), [?] April 1904, *L* (W), 433.

17 WBY, Letter to John Quinn, 16
Sept. 1905, *L* (W), 461.

18 WBY, Letter to George Russell,
19 Sept. 1905. See *YAE*, 225,
and *Theatre Business*, Ed. Ann
Saddlemyer (1982), 38.

19 WBY, *C Pl*, 112.

20 WBY, *C Pl*, 141.

21 The account is from Joseph Holloway, *Joseph Holloway's Abbey
Theatre* (1967), 48. Holloway,
the architect who converted the
Mechanics   Institute   and
Morgue into the Abbey, was an
enthusiastic theatregoer whose
diary is a mine of information
about Abbey productions.

22 WBY, Letter to Frank Fay, [?20
Jan. 1904], *L* (W), 424.

23 WBY, Letter to Florence Farr,
[?] July 1905, *L* (W), 456.

24 WBY, Letter to Florence Farr,
[January 1906], *L* (W), 468.

25 WBY, Letter to Olivia Shakespear [? July/August 1904], *L*
(W), 436.

26 WBY, Letter to Olivia Shakespear [?8] August 1904, *L* (W),
439.

27 WBY, *CP*, 169; *PNE*, 150.

28 WBY, Letter to George Russell
(AE), [?8] Jan. 1906, *L* (W), 466.

29 JBY, Letter to W. B. Yeats, n.d.
[1906], *LHS*, 97.

30 WBY,   Letter   to   Stephen
Gwynn, 13 June 1906. See Joan
Coldwell, 'The Act of Happy
Desire: Yeats and the Little
Magazine' in *The World of W.
B. Yeats*, Ed. Robin Skelton and
Ann Saddlemyer (1965), 37.

31 Oliver St John Gogarty, Letter

to J. K. A. Bell, 12 Dec. 1904,
in Oliver St John Gogarty, *Many
Lines to Thee*, Ed. James F.
Carens (1971).
32 WBY, *C Pl*, 194.
33 WBY, *C Pl*, 189.
34 WBY, *C Pl*, 201.
35 WBY, *C Pl*, 201.

Chapter 9

1 In a letter to *The Irish Times*, 31
Jan. 1907.
2 J. M. Synge, Letter to Stephen
MacKenna, n.d., in *Irish Renaissance: A Gathering of Essays,
Memoirs and Letters from the Massachusetts Review*, Ed. Robin
Skelton and David R. Clark
(1965), 66.
3 WBY, *E&I*, 312.
4 WBY, 'Beautiful Lofty Things',
CP, 348; *PNE*, 303. See *LHS*,
214 for his father's account of
his speech; he began with remarks on Synge and continued,
'Of course I know Ireland is an
island of Saints but thank God
it is also an island of sinners –
and unfortunately in this country
people cannot live or die except
behind a curtain of deceit.' At
this point the chairman and his
son called out, 'Time's up,
time's up.' The papers said next
day that he was howled down
but he remarked it was worse,
he was pulled down!
5 See *LGJ*, 350; 501 for her memories of Yeats telling her what
they were saying of her.
6 A. E. F. Horniman, Letter to W.
B. Yeats, 3 Nov. 1907, in *LWBY*,
I, 194.

7 JBY, Letter to W. B. Yeats, 9
June 1909, *PF*, 330.
8 See Richard Ellmann, *Golden
Codgers* (1960), 108 n.
9 WBY, *CP*, 251; *PNE*, 223.
10 WBY, Letters to A. H. Bullen,
6 and 8 July 1907, *L* (W),
485–487.
11 See, for instance, WBY, Letter
to Miss E. M. Lister, 26 Sept
[1907], *L* (W), 493.
12 WBY, Letter to John Quinn, 4
Oct. 1907, *L* (W), 496.
13 WBY, Letter to John Quinn, 7
Jan. 1908, *L* (W), 502.
14 WBY, Letter to John Quinn, 27
April 1908, *L* (W), 509.
15 WBY, Letter to A. H. Bullen, [?]
March 1908, *L* (W), 504.
16 WBY, unpublished letter.
17 Maud Gonne MacBride, Letter
to W. B. Yeats, 26 June [1908],
LWBY, I, 200.
18 Maud Gonne MacBride, Letter
to W. B. Yeats, 26 July [1908],
LWBY, I, 201.
19 WBY, Letter to John Butler Yeats [27 Dec. 1908], *L*(W), 513.
20 WBY, *Mem*, 139.
21 WBY, *Mem*, 191.
22 WBY, 'All Things can Tempt
me', *CP*, 109; *PNE*, 97.
23 WBY, *Mem*, 157.
24 WBY, *Mem*, 157.
25 WBY, 'No Second Troy', *CP*,
101; *PNE*, 91.
26 WBY, *CP*, 100; *PNE*, 90.
27 WBY, *CP*, 101; *PNE*, 91.
28 WBY, unpublished letter.
29 WBY, *Mem*, 160.
30 WBY, *CP*, 109; *PNE*, 97.
31 WBY, *Mem*, 163.
32 WBY, *Mem*, 203.
33 See Corinna Salvadori, *Yeats and*

Castiglione (1965) for discussion of this.

34 WBY, *C Pl*, 243.

35 WBY, Letter to John Butler Yeats, 29 Nov. 1909, *L* (W), 539.

36 WBY, Letter to Lily Yeats, [?26 Sept. 1910], *L* (W), 551.

37 WBY, Letters to Lady Gregory, [28 and 29 Sept. 1910], *L* (W), 552–3.

38 WBY, 'In Memory of Alfred Pollexfen', *CP*, 175; *PNE*, 156.

Chapter 10

1 WBY, Letter to Edmund Gosse [10 Aug. 1910], *L* (W), 550.

2 WBY, *Mem*, 256.

3 From a letter to Joseph Hone, quoted *JH*, 225.

4 JBY, Letter to W. B. Yeats, 29 Nov. 1910. See *PF*, 37.

5 WBY, Letter to Sydney Cockerell, 6 March 1911, *L* (W), 557.

6 WBY, 'The Fascination of What's Difficult', *CP*, 104; *PNE*, 93.

7 WBY, Letter to John Butler Yeats, 21 Nov. 1912, *L* (W), 571.

8 Lady Gregory, Letters to John Quinn, [?16] March and 6 May, 1912, quoted in Daniel J. Murphy, 'Dear John Quinn', *LGF*, 129; 130.

9 WBY, *CP*, 103; *PNE*, 92.

10 WBY, *CP*, 103; *PNE*, 92.

11 WBY, *CP*, 136; *PNE*, 122.

12 A. E. F. Horniman, Letter to W. B. Yeats, 7 July 1907, *LWBY*, I, 184.

13 A. E. F. Horniman, Letter to W.

B. Yeats, 14 May 1908, *LWBY*, I, 199.

14 John Masefield, *Some Memories of W. B. Yeats* (1940).

15 WBY, Letter to Lady Gregory [10 Dec. 1909], *L* (W), 543.

16 WBY, 'Fallen Majesty', *CP*, 138; *PNE*, 123.

17 WBY, 'A Memory of Youth', *CP*, 137; *PNE*, 123.

18 Olivia Shakespear, Letter to Ezra Pound, *EPDS*, 153–4.

19 Dorothy Shakespear, Letter to Ezra Pound, 30 Jan. 1913, *EPDS*, 186.

20 WBY, *CP*, 140; *PNE*, 125.

21 WBY, *CP*, 123; *PNE*, 110.

22 WBY, Commentary on 'Parnell's Funeral', *VP*, 834.

23 WBY, Notes, *CP*, 530; *PNE*, 594.

24 WBY, *CP*, 119; *PNE*, 107.

25 WBY, *CP*, 120; *PNE*, 108.

26 WBY, *CP*, 122; *PNE*, 109.

27 Conor Cruise O'Brien, 'Passion and Cunning: Politics of W. B. Yeats', *IER*, 236.

28 WBY, *CP*, 120; *PNE*, 108.

29 WBY, Letter to Lady Gregory, [? July 1913]; see Lady Gregory, *Hugh Lane, His Life and Achievements* (1921), 137.

30 George Russell (AE), Letter to W. B. Yeats [5 Nov. 1913], *YAE*, 236.

Chapter 11

1 He also discusses the fat old medium in 'Swedenborg Mediums and the Desolate Places', *E*, 51, 65.

2 WBY, *Mem*, 264.

3 This is included in *Yeats and the*

Occult, Ed. George Mills Harper (1975), 141–171.

4 WBY, 'Beggar to Beggar Cried', *CP*, 128; *PNE*, 114.

5 WBY, *CP*, 174; *PNE*, 154.

6 WBY, *CP*, 115; *PNE*, 103. See *Mem*, 241.

7 WBY, Letter to Lady Gregory, 11 Feb. [1913], *L* (W), 575.

8 WBY, *CP*, 179; *PNE*, 159.

9 WBY, *CP*, 142; *PNE*, 127.

10 WBY, *Mem*, 196.

11 WBY, *CP*, 113; *PNE*, 101.

12 WBY, *CP*, 143; *PNE*, 128.

13 WBY, *CP*, 135; *PNE*, 121.

14 Ezra Pound, Canto LXXXIII.

15 JBY, Letter to Lily Yeats, 27 April 1915. See *PF*, 433.

16 See *YA*, No 1 (1982), the text edited and annotated by Steve L. Adams and George Mills Harper, 3–47.

17 WBY, 'The Manuscript of "Leo Africanus"' *YA*, No 1 (1982), 39.

18 WBY, Letter to John Butler Yeats, 12 Sept. [1914] *L* (W), 588.

19 'Did you ever throw a book at your daughter or your husband?' he asked a friend, embarrassed at Willie's account of having a book thrown at his head by his father as a child. 'If so, be careful. They may write their Memoirs.' JBY, Letter to Mrs Caughey, [?8] April 1916, *PF*, 446. In *Mem*, 19, WBY recorded a quarrel (probably in 1887) with JBY over Ruskin which 'came to such a height that in putting me out of the room he broke the glass in a picture with the back of my head'. On another occasion

JBY offered to box him; this quarrel was interrupted by Jack Yeats waking up in a rage, and urging his brother not to speak to JBY till he apologised.

20 W. T. Horton, letter to W. B. Yeats, 25 July 1914, *LWBY*, I, 295.

21 Ezra Pound, review in *Poetry* (Chicago), 11 May 1914, reprinted in *Literary Essays of Ezra Pound*, Ed. T. S. Eliot (1954) and in *W. B. Yeats. The Critical Heritage*, Ed. A. Norman Jeffares (1977).

22 WBY, *CP*, 172; *PNE*, 153.

23 WBY, *CP*, 170; *PNE*, 151.

24 WBY, *CP*, 168; *PNE*, 150.

25 WBY, *CP*, 169; *PNE*, 150.

26 WBY, *CP*, 174; *PNE*, 154.

27 WBY, *CP*, 168; *PNE*, 149.

28 WBY, *CP*, 174; *PNE*, 154.

29 WBY, *CP*, 164; *PNE*, 146.

30 WBY, *CP*, 172; *PNE*, 153.

31 WBY, *CP*, 167; *PNE*, 149.

32 WBY, *CP*, 163; *PNE*, 145.

33 WBY, *CP*, 164; *PNE*, 146.

34 WBY, *CP*, 166; *PNE*, 148.

35 WBY, Letter to John Butler Yeats, 14 June [1917], *L* (W), 626.

36 WBY, 'Fergus and the Druid', *CP*, 36; *PNE*, 32.

37 WBY, *Mem*, 151.

38 JBY, Letter to Lily Yeats, 15 Sept. 1916; a fuller version than that in *LHS*, 229 is given in *PF*, 455.

39 WBY, *M*, 331.

40 WBY, *M*, 331.

41 See 'Friends of my Youth', Ed. Joseph Ronsley, in *Yeats and the Theatre*, Ed. Robert O'Driscoll and Lorna Reynolds (1975),74.

42 WBY, *M*, 325.
43 WBY, *CP*, 175; *PNE*, 155.
44 WBY, Letter to Henry James, 20 August 1915, *L* (W), 599.
45 WBY, Letter to Olivia Shakespear, 8 March [1922], *L* (W), 679.
46 WBY, Introduction to *Certain Noble Plays of Japan, E&I*, 221.
47 See Masaru Sekine, 'Yeats and the Nōh', *Irish Writers and the Theatre*, Ed. Masaru Sekine (1987), 154.

Chapter 12

1 WBY, Letter to Lily Yeats, [10 December 1915], *L* (W), 603.
2 WBY, Letter to Lady Gregory, [11 May 1916], *L* (W), 612.
3 WBY, *CP*, 202; *PNE*, 180.
4 WBY, *CP*, 205; *PNE*, 182.
5 WBY, *CP*, 206; *PNE*, 183.
6 WBY, *CP*, 207; *PNE*, 184.
7 WBY, *CP*, 206; *PNE*, 183.
8 WBY, 'Visions and Beliefs', *E*, 64–8.
9 WBY, 'Dust hath closed Helen's eye', *The Celtic Twilight* (1902), 35.
10 WBY, Letter to Olivia Shakespear, 8 Nov. [1916], *L* (W), 615.
11 For details see A. Norman Jeffares, 'Poet's Tower', *The Circus Animals* (1970), 29 ff. and *Thoor Ballylee – Home of William Butler Yeats*, Ed. Liam Millar (1965).
12 JBY, Letter to W. B. Yeats, 14 December 1916, *LWBY*, II 328.
13 WBY, Letter to Lady Gregory, 8 Sept. 1917, *L* (W), 631.
14 WBY, Letter to Lady Gregory, 18 Sept. 1917, *L* (W), 632.
15 Information from Iseult Stuart.
16 WBY, Letter to Lady Gregory, 19 Sept. 1917, *L* (W), 633.

Chapter 13

1 WBY, 'Owen Aherne and his Dancers', I, *CP*, 247; *PNE*, 220.
2 WBY, 'Owen Aherne and his Dancers', II, *CP*, 248; *PNE*, 220.
3 WBY, Letter to Lady Gregory, 29 Oct. [1917], *L* (W), 633.
4 WBY, 'A Packet for Ezra Pound', *A Vision* (1937). The automatic writing was certainly not faked. Mrs Yeats began it to divert Yeats from his preoccupation with Iseult Gonne but found herself, as she later told Mrs Shakespear, 'seized by a superior power'. A recent biographer, Brenda Maddox (see Bibliography), has argued that the automatic writing was a means by which the young wife controlled her husband, notably in matters of sex. These theories distort the actuality of the process which helped Yeats to compel his original thoughts and those based upon his very varied reading into order as the script progressed through Mrs Yeats's mysterious, almost trance-like, agency. The exhausting, time-consuming automatic writing which began in 1917 was changed in 1920 into the 'Sleeps' transcribed by Yeats (see p. 184), which lasted until 1922, with another, significant one occurring on 21 March 1924. Denis Donoghue's review of the Maddox biography in

'The Fabulous Boys', *New York Review of Books*, 11 May 2000, sums up the case against its arguments well: 'It was Yeats, not George, who asked the questions and took charge of the themes. George was indispensable but she did not control the issues.'

5 WBY, Letter to Lady Gregory, 4 Jan. [1918], *L* (W), 643.
6 WBY, Letter to Lady Gregory, 16 Dec. [1917], *L* (W), 634.
7 WBY, *CP*, 210; *PNE*, 187.
8 WBY, *CP*, 183; *PNE*, 163.
9 WBY, Letter to Lady Gregory, 16 Dec [1917], *L* (W), 634.
10 WBY, Letter to John Quinn, 8 Feb. 1918, *L* (W), 645.
11 See F. P. Sturm, *His Life, Letters and Collected Work*, Ed. Richard Taylor (1969).
12 WBY, *CP*, 238; *PNE*, 211.
13 WBY, *Mem*, 230.
14 WBY, *CP*, 159; *PNE*, 141.
15 Colin Smythe, Afterword, *LGJ*, 640.
16 Lady Gregory, Diary entry, 1 August 1921.
17 WBY, *CP*, 155; *PNE*, 138.
18 WBY, *CP*, 199; *PNE*, 176.
19 WBY, *CP*, 164; *PNE*, 146.
20 WBY, *Four Plays for Dancers*, (1921). See *VLP*, 790.
21 WBY, *A*, 464.
22 WBY, *CP*, 154; *PNE*, 137.
23 WBY, Notebook entry, 8 October 1923. See *MAV*, I, discussion in Chapter 4, and for partial quotation, see II, 257.
24 WBY, *CP*, 214; *PNE*, 190.
25 WBY, *CP*, 148; *PNE*, 132.
26 WBY, *CP*, 152; *PNE*, 135.
27 WBY, *CP*, 190; *PNE*, 169.
28 WBY, *CP*, 157; *PNE*, 139.
29 WBY, Letter to H. J. C. Grierson, 14 Nov. [1912], *L* (W), 570.
30 WBY, 'To a Young Beauty', *CP*, 157; *PNE*, 139.
31 WBY, *CP*, 200; *PNE*, 178. See note in *VP*, 821.
32 WBY, *CP*, 209; *PNE*, 185.
33 J. O. Hannay, *The Spirit and Origin of Christian Monasticism* (1903) and *The Wisdom of the Desert* (1904).
34 WBY, *CP*, 189; *PNE*, 168.
35 WBY, Note on 'An Image from a Past Life', *Michael Robartes and the Dancer*, (1927) and in *VP*, 821.
36 WBY, *CP*, 208; *PNE*, 185. His dream of the Ben Bulben waterfall may have been suggested by their having been to see the waterfall at Powerscourt.
37 See *MAV*, II, 201.
38 WBY, *CP*, 208; *PNE*, 185.
39 WBY, *CP*, 191; *PNE*, 170.
40 WBY, *CP*, 192; *PNE*, 170.
41 WBY, *CP*, 191; *PNE*, 170.
42 WBY, *CP*, 158; *PNE*, 141.
43 *MAV*, II, 200.
44 WBY, *CP*, 207; *PNE*, 184.
45 WBY, *CP*, 206; *PNE*, 183.
46 WBY, *CP*, 211; *PNE*, 188.
47 Joseph M. Hassett, *Yeats and the Poetics of Hate* (1986), 88.
48 WBY, *CP*, 197; *PNE*, 175.
49 WBY, Letter to George Russell (AE), [? April 1919], *L* (W), 656.

Chapter 14

1 JBY, Letter to Lily Yeats, 13 Feb. 1920. See *PF*, 507.
2 WBY, Letter to Edmund Dulac, 22 March 1920, *L* (W), 662.
3 WBY, *CP*, 227; *PNE*, 202.
4 WBY, 'Meditations in Time of Civil War' I, *Ancestral Houses*, *CP*, 225; *PNE*, 200.
5 Grace M. Jaffe, 'Vignettes', *YA* No. 5 (1987), 145. See also her *Years of Grace* (1979) which deals with her memories of the Yeatses at Oxford and elsewhere at great length.
6 WBY, Letter to Olivia Shakespear, 25 July [1932], *L* (W), 800.
7 WBY, Letter to John Butler Yeats, 27 Oct. 1920, *PF*, 510.
8 WBY, Letter to John Butler Yeats, 9 Nov. 1920, *PF*, 510.
9 WBY, Letter to John Quinn, 30 Oct. 1920, *L* (W), 663.
10 WBY, *CP*, 242; *PNE*, 215.
11 WBY, *CP*, 256; *PNE*, 227.
12 This poem is not included in *CP*, nor in *PNE*, but can be read in *Poems of W. B. Yeats, A New Selection*, Ed. A. Norman Jeffares (2nd ed. 1988), 300.
13 See *PF*, 529 for letters to WBY of 24 June, 25 June and 30 June, 1921.
14 WBY, Letter to Olivia Shakespear, 9 April [1921], *L* (W), 667.
15 WBY, Letter to John Quinn, 25 Aug. 1921, *L* (W), 673.
16 WBY, Letter to Olivia Shakespear, 1 August [1921], *L* (W), 671.
17 WBY, *CP*, 232; *PNE*, 206.
18 WBY, *CP*, 61; *PNE*, 55.
19 See *MAV* I, 209–226.

20 WBY, *CP*, 210; *PNE*, 187.
21 WBY, Letter to Olivia Shakespear, 22 Dec. [1921], *L* (W), 675.
22 In a play written by John Butler Yeats (no text survives; the plot is given in a letter of his to Lily Yeats, 29 Nov. 1916) the hero is 'a celebrated young poet' and the scene 'is laid in Merrion Square', *PF*, 456; in a letter to WBY of 9 June 1909, *LWBY*, I, 216, he had characterised it as a haunt of the well-to-do.
23 WBY, Letter to Olivia Shakespear, 27 July [1922], *L* (W), 687.
24 WBY, *CP*, 225; *PNE*, 200.
25 WBY, Letter to Olivia Shakespear, 7 June [1922], *L* (W), 685.
26 WBY, Notes, *CP*, 534; *PNE*, 596; see also WBY, Letter to Charles Ricketts, 5 Nov. [1922], *L* (W), 692.
27 WBY, Letter to Charles Ricketts, 5 Nov. [1922], *L* (W), 691.
28 WBY, Letter to Olivia Shakespear, 18 Dec. [1922], *L* (W), 695.
29 WBY, Letter to Olivia Shakespear, 18 Dec. [1922], *L* (W), 694.
30 WBY, Letter to Olivia Shakespear, 28 June [1923], *L* (W), 698.
31 WBY, *On the Boiler* (1938), 12.
32 See W. B. Stanford, 'Yeats in the Irish Senate', *AREL*, IV, 3, July 1963, 71–80.

Chapter 15

1 WBY, *CP*, 109; *PNE*, 97.
2 *Irish Literary Portraits* (1972), 10.
3 WBY, 'The Bounty of Sweden', *A*, 544.
4 WBY, *The Cat and the Moon and Certain Poems* (1924). The note is reprinted in *VP*, 828–829.
5 WBY, *CP*, 519; *PNE*, 445.
6 WBY, *CP*, 241; *PNE*, 214.
7 WBY, 'Among School Children', *CP*, 242; *PNE*, 215.
8 WBY, *CP*, 218; *PNE*, 194.
9 *SSY*, 99.
10 George Russell, *The Irish Statesman*, 13 February, 1926.
11 *SSY*, 172. This was a speech made to the Irish Literary Society on 30 Nov. 1925.
12 WBY, *CP*, 242; *PNE*, 215.
13 WBY, *CP*, 217; *PNE*, 193.
14 WBY, *A Vision*, (1937), 279. Text taken from *A Vision* (1925), 191.
15 *The Irish Times*, 12 Feb. 1926.
16 Letter to Olivia Shakespear, 25 May [1926], *L* (W), 715.
17 WBY, Letter to Olivia Shakespear, 2 July [1926], *L* (W), 716.
18 WBY, *CP*, 254; *PNE*, 226.
19 WBY, Note in *New York Times*, 15 Jan. 1933, cited in *L* (W), 537 *n*.
20 *SSY*, 166.
21 WBY, Letter to Olivia Shakespear, 23 June [1927], *L* (W), 725.
22 WBY, *CP*, 267; *PNE*, 237.
23 WBY, *CP*, 264; *PNE*, 234.
24 WBY, *CP*, 263; *PNE*, 233.
25 WBY, in a letter to Eva Gore-Booth, 23 July [1916], referring to the roles of Casement and Constance Markiewicz in the late 1916 Rising, told her how he had written an appeal for clemency to the Secretary of State, and also told her how much he sorrowed over the misfortune that had come upon the Gore-Booth family: 'Your sister and yourself, two beautiful figures among the great trees of Lissadell, are among the dear memories of youth.' The letter is reproduced in *AREL*, IV, 3 July 1963.

Chapter 16

1 WBY, Letter to Olivia Shakespear, 29 Nov. [1927], *L* (W), 732.
2 WBY, *CP*, 278; *PNE*, 246.
3 WBY, Letter to Olivia Shakespear, 25 April 1928, *L* (W), 742.
4 WBY, Letter to Sean O'Casey [whom he still addressed as Casey], 20 April 1928, *L* (W), 740.
5 WBY, Letter to Olivia Shakespear, 12 August [1928], *L* (W), 745.
6 WBY, Letter to Olivia Shakespear, 29 March [1929], *L* (W), 760.
7 WBY, *CP*, 273; *PNE*, 242.
8 WBY, *A*, 395.
9 WBY, Letter to Olivia Shakespear, 24 August [1929], *L* (W), 767.
10 WBY, *CP*, 301; *PNE*, 265.
11 WBY, *CP*, 267; *PNE*, 237.
12 WBY, *Wheels and Butterflies* (1934), 10.
13 WBY, 'Swift's Epitaph', *CP*, 277; *PNE*, 245.

14 WBY, Letter to Olivia Shakespear, 27 Dec. [1930], *L* (W), 780.
15 WBY, *CP*, 239; *PNE*, 213.
16 The conversation, from John Sparrow's notes, is given in A. Norman Jeffares, *W. B. Yeats: Man and Poet*, (1949), 267–268.
17 Quoted *JH*, 422–423.
18 George Yeats, Letter to Dorothy Pound, 22 August [1931], *LGF*, 249.
19 WBY, 'For Anne Gregory', *CP*, 277; *PNE*, 245.
20 WBY, *CP*, 275; *PNE*, 243.
21 It is included in *LGF*, 633–638.

Chapter 17

1 WBY, Letter to Olivia Shakespear, [?22/23] Nov. [1931], *L*(W), 785.
2 WBY, Letter to Olivia Shakespear, 17 August [1933], *L* (W), 813.
3 WBY, *CP*, 290–306; *PNE*, 255–269.
4 WBY, *CP*, 282; *PNE*, 249.
5 WBY, *CP*, 265; *PNE*, 234.
6 WBY, *CP*, 280; *PNE*, 248.
7 WBY, *E*, 290.
8 WBY, *CP*, 308–315; *PNE*, 270–276.
9 WBY, *L* (W), 790.
10 WBY, Letter to Olivia Shakespear, 9 March [1933], *L* (W), 806.
11 WBY, *CP*, 319; *PNE*, 279.
12 WBY, *CP*, 320; *PNE*, 568.
13 WBY, *VP*, 835–8. Revised as 'Three Marching Songs', *CP*, 377; *PNE*, 333.
14 WBY, Letter to Olivia Shakespear, 20 September [1933], *L* (W), 815.
15 WBY, Letter to Olivia Shakespear, 11 November [1933], *L* (W), 817.
16 WBY, *CP*, 386; *PNE*, 344.
17 WBY, *A*, 444.
18 WBY, Letter to Olivia Shakespear, 27 Feb. [1934], *L* (W), 820.
19 WBY, *CP*, 333; *PNE*, 289.
20 WBY, Preface to *The King of the Great Clock Tower* (1934); in *VP*, 855.
21 WBY, *CP*, 326; *PNE*, 282.
22 WBY, *CP*, 327; *PNE*, 283.
23 WBY, Letter to Olivia Shakespear, 27 Feb. [1934], *L* (W), 820.
24 WBY, *CP*, 320; *PNE*, 568.
25 WBY, *CP*, 332; *PNE*, 288.
26 WBY, Letter to Olivia Shakespear, 24 July [1934], *L* (W), 823.
27 WBY, *On the Boiler* (1938), 35.
28 Included in *Ah, Sweet Dancer. W. B. Yeats, Margot Ruddock. A Correspondence*, Ed. Roger McHugh (1970).
29 See Jon Stallworthy, 'Yeats as Anthologist', *IER*, 171–192.
30 WBY, Letter to Dorothy Wellesley, 26 July [1935], *L* (W), 838.
31 WBY, Letter to Dorothy Wellesley, 21 December [1936], *L* (W), 873.
32 WBY, Letter to Mrs Llewellyn Davies, 19 March [1937], *L* (W), 885.
33 WBY, Letter to Dorothy Wellesley, 13 August [1936], *L* (W), 860.

Chapter 18

1 WBY, Letter to Olivia Shakespear, 10 April [1936], *L* (W), 851.
2 WBY, Letter to Olivia Shakespear, 22 May [1936], *L* (W), 856.
3 WBY, *CP*, 338; *PNE*, 294.
4 WBY, 'A General Introduction to My Work', *E&I*, 522.
5 WBY, *CP*, 337; *PNE*, 293.
6 WBY, *CP*, 341–346; *PNE*, 296–301.
7 WBY, 'Beggar to Beggar Cried', *CP*, 128; *PNE*, 114.
8 WBY, Letter to Dorothy Wellesley, [29 October 1936], *L* (W), 864.
9 WBY, Letter to Dorothy Wellesley, 8 Nov. [1936], *L* (W), 865.
10 WBY, *M*, 342.
11 WBY, *CP*, 346; *PNE*, 301.
12 WBY, *CP*, 347; *PNE*, 302.
13 WBY, *CP*, 359; *PNE*, 312. Text taken from *L* (W), 872.
14 WBY, Letter to Dorothy Wellesley, 30 November 1936, *L* (W), 869.
15 WBY, Letter to George Barnes, 2 Feb. [1937], *L* (W), 879.
16 See Richard Ellmann, *FD*, 25.
17 WBY, *A Speech and Two Poems* (1937).
18 WBY, 'The Municipal Gallery Revisited', *CP*, 368; *PNE*, 319.
19 WBY, *CP*, 370; *PNE*, 321.
20 WBY, *CP*, 350; *PNE*, 304.
21 WBY, *CP*, 391; *PNE*, 346.
22 WBY, *CP*, 376; *PNE*, 337.
23 WBY, *CP*, 381; *PNE*, 339.
24 WBY, *CP*, 382; *PNE*, 340.
25 *JH*, 459.
26 WBY, Letter to Ethel Mannin, 9 October [1938], *L* (W), 916.
27 WBY, Letter to Dorothy Wellesley, 11 November 1937, *L* (W), 900.
28 WBY, *CP*, 390; *PNE*, 582.
29 WBY, *CP*, 375; *PNE*, 336.
30 WBY, *CP*, 392; *PNE*, 348.
31 Donald T. Torchiana, *W. B. Yeats & Georgian Ireland*, (1966), 363.
32 WBY, *CP*, 393; *PNE*, 345.
33 WBY, Letter to Dorothy Wellesley, 15 August 1938, *L* (W), 913.
34 WBY, Letter to Ethel Mannin, 22 August [1938], *L* (W), 914.
35 WBY, *CP*, 397; *PNE*, 325.
36 WBY, *A*, 266.
37 Maud Gonne MacBride, 'Yeats and Ireland', *Scattering Branches*, Ed. Stephen Gwynn (1940), 25.
38 WBY, *CP*, 348; *PNE*, 303.
39 Information from Major Rowley Marriott.
40 WBY, *CP*, 395; *PNE*, 332.
41 WBY, Letter to Lady Elizabeth Pelham, 4 January 1939, *L* (W), 922.
42 WBY, *CP*, 396; *PNE*, 331.
43 At the time of her husband's burial in Roquebrune Mrs Yeats, whose French was excellent, made it clear to the French authorities when leasing a ten-year grave that her intention was to bring his body back to Ireland. The fact that Yeats's remains were moved to another part of the cemetery has prompted some confusion, but in May 1987 Professor Saddlemyer examined various documents in the Mairie

at Cap Martin and told delegates at a Yeats seminar at the Princess Grace Irish Library in Monaco that it had been fully understood that Yeats's body was to be reinterred in Ireland and that she was convinced his remains had been correctly brought to Sligo in 1948. Commenting on Diana Souhami's 1988 biography *Gluck* (of Hanah Gluckstein the painter, who became an intimate, domineering friend of Edith Shackleton Heald), which recounts a failure on the part of Edith Shackleton Heald, accompanied by Gluck on a visit to Roquebrune in June 1947, to find Yeats's grave, Mr Michael Yeats has remarked (*Irish Times*, 7 September 1988) that he himself possesses documentations proving his father is buried in Sligo.

44 WBY, *CP*, 398; *PNE*, 325.

BIBLIOGRAPHY

Some basic W. B. Yeats texts

Autobiographies (1955). This is Yeats's presentation of periods of his life, a selective and evocative ordering of experience.

Collected Poems (1933; editions after 1950 have extra poems added). This is a most attractive edition, its ordering of the poems originally suggested to Yeats by Macmillan. Changes in the texts of the poems can be followed in *The Variorum Edition of the Poems of W. B. Yeats*, ed. Peter Allt and Russell K. Alspach (1957).

Collected Plays (1934; editions after 1952 have additional plays). A companion volume to *Collected Poems* and, like it, a very useful edition. Changes in the texts of the plays can be followed in *The Variorum Edition of the Plays of W. B. Yeats*, ed. Russell K. Alspach (1966).

Essays and Introductions (1961). This contains *Ideas of Good and Evil, The Cutting of an Agate* and later essays and introductions.

Explorations (1962). This volume was selected by Mrs W. B. Yeats and has a collection of writings on the Irish Dramatic movement, 1901–19, as well as other writings not easily available, such as excerpts from *Wheels and Butterflies* (1934) and *On the Boiler* (1939).

Memoirs, ed. Denis Donoghue (1972). This contains the first draft of Yeats's autobiography and a journal begun in 1908. The two sections are very different; the autobiography is controlled and selective, the journal candid in its reactions to the day's events, and full of often insecure self-analysis.

Mythologies (1959). This collects *The Celtic Twilight; The Secret Rose; Stories of Red Hanrahan; Rosa Alchemica, The Tables of the Law* and *The Adoration of the Magi*; and *Per Amica Silentia Lunae*. It shows Yeats as a writer of fiction, as well as demonstrating the development of his early prose from simplicity to complexity.

The Poems: A New Edition, ed. R. J. Finneran. This annotated edition groups 125 poems as 'Additional Poems', many of them from the plays, others rejected by Yeats from his canon.

The Senate Speeches of W. B. Yeats, ed. Donald R. Pearce (1960). This illustrates Yeats's generally constructive and commonsense approach to public life.

Uncollected Prose by W. B. Yeats, I, ed. John P. Frayne (1970); II, ed. John P. Frayne and Colton Johnson (1975). These volumes demonstrate the range of Yeats's work as a literary journalist and are well annotated.

A Vision (1925; 2nd edn, (1937). The two versions are very different. The text of the first edition, which was privately printed for subscribers only in an edition of 600 copies and never re-issued, is now available in *A Critical Edition of Yeats's A Vision* (1925), ed. George Mills Harper and Walter Kelly Hood (1978).

A Vision and Related Writings, selected and ed. A. Norman Jeffares (1990). This edition brings together and annotates 'Swedenborg, Mediums, and the Desolate Places', *Per Amica Silentia Lunae*, the second edition of *A Vision*, parts of the first edition, *Pages from a Diary Written in Nineteen Hundred and Thirty* and eighteen relevant poems.

Yeats's Poems, ed. A. Norman Jeffares (3rd edn, 1996). This fully annotated edition contains a biographical summary, maps, diagrams from *A Vision*, a glossary of Irish people and places in the poems, the pronunciation of Irish words in the poems (by Loreto Todd), Yeats's notes on the 1949 edition of *The Poems of W. B. Yeats*, and an appendix by Warwick Gould on the Definitive Edition. The poems are placed in chronological order as Yeats had wished them to be in the proposed *Edition de Luxe* of his poems.

Correspondence

The Letters of W. B. Yeats, ed. Allan Wade (1954). An excellent selection, over 900 pages in extent, of Yeats's letters, chosen for their autobiographical content. Yeats was a prolific letter-writer, who expressed himself freely to his women friends, especially Mrs Shakespear, and these letters give a varied, vivid picture of his life.

The Collected Letters of W. B. Yeats:

Vol. I, 1865–1895, ed. John Kelly and Eric Domville (1986). A model of intelligent, balanced scholarship, this edition shows the rich pattern of Yeats's early life in Sligo, London and Dublin.

Vol. II, 1896–1900, ed. Warwick Gould, John Kelly and Deirdre Toomey (1997). This volume is particularly valuable, its Introduction tracing

Yeats's development from his leaving the family home to set up his own life in Woburn Buildings in 1896, when 'a new scene was set, new actors appeared'. These letters record the beginning of Yeats's relationship with Mrs Shakespear and his friendship with Lady Gregory, the unhappiness caused by his infatuation with Maud Gonne, the political activity involved in the Centenary Celebrations of the 1798 Rising and the problems within the Irish Revolutionary Brotherhood, his immersion in the energetic work which led to the Irish Literary Theatre, the heightened tensions in the affairs of the Order of the Golden Dawn and varied visionary activity. The Biographical and Historical Appendix is a mine of useful, detailed information.

Vol. III, 1901–1904, ed. John Kelly and Ronald Schuhard (1994). This volume records the 'coming down to earth' when Yeats, reshaping his style, left the role of Celtic poet and late romantic symbolist for that of modernist, faced the disaster of Maud Gonne's marriage to John MacBride, whom he regarded as a lout, and occupied much of his energy in playwriting and establishing the Abbey Theatre in Dublin as well as making his first successful visit to the United States.

Letters on Poetry from W. B. Yeats to Dorothy Wellesley (1940). These letters reveal Yeats's creative vitality, the power of his imagination and intellect in the last three and a half years of his life.

J. B. Yeats, *Letters to His Son W. B. Yeats and Others 1869–1922*, ed. Joseph Hone (1944). The artist's great conversational gifts can be guessed at from his lively original letters, which show his character clearly and make his relationship with his son more fathomable.

The Gonne–Yeats Letters 1893–1938, ed. Anna MacBride White and A. Norman Jeffares (1992). This book provides a fully documented account of their relationship, as far as is possible; it contains her letters to Yeats (as well as some of his to her), which he kept and which his widow returned to her. Anna MacBride is currently writing a two-volume life of Maud Gonne, who was her grandmother.

Some biographical studies

Terence Brown, *The Life of W. B. Yeats* (1999). This recent life is based upon criticism of Yeats written during the last forty to fifty years, setting his life and work within the historical background.

Richard Ellmann, *The Man and the Masks* (1948; 2nd edn 1979). This traces Yeats's development in a lively way; in *The Identity of Yeats* (1954) Ellmann discusses themes in Yeats's work, investigating the individuality of his writing.

R. F. Foster, *W. B. Yeats: A Life, Vol I. The Apprentice Mage* (1997). This
first volume of 'the first authorised biography of Yeats for over fifty
years', written by a distinguished Irish historian, is full, its details giving
particularly useful insights into the poet's political activities and their
backgrounds. This volume carries the story up to 1914, the year that
Yeats began to write his autobiography.

Lady Gregory, Fifty Years After, ed. Ann Saddlemyer and Colin Smythe
(1987), contains a brilliant essay by John Kelly on the friendship of Yeats
and Lady Gregory. *Lady Gregory's Journals*, ed. Daniel J. Murphy, I
(1978); II (1987), convey the flavour of Lady Gregory's mind well, illustrating not only life at Coole but the problems of the Abbey and the Lane
bequest.

Joseph Hone, *W. B. Yeats 1865–1939* (1942; rev. edn 1962). This very readable and, in effect, pioneering biography laid much of the ground work
for subsequent lives. It is full of information (occasionally inaccurate) and
rich in incident; it gives a convincing picture of Yeats.

A. Norman Jeffares, *W. B. Yeats: Man and Poet* (1996). Now in its third edition, this life has been continuously in print since 1949; it explores
Yeats's own writings set within a framework of his life rather than the
critical views of others, his own comments being particularly illuminating
and the conjunction between his verse and prose most stimulating.

Mícheál MacLiammóir and Eavan Boland, *W. B. Yeats and His World* (1971).
A balanced introduction, well illustrated.

Alasdair D. F. Macrae, *W. B. Yeats. A Literary Life* (1995). This short life
tackles the difference between the image of the poet as a detached seer-
like figure in a remote town and the man involved in so many disparate
public activities. It examines Yeats's fear of insecurity beneath the mask
of confidence he presented to the world, approaching the poet from a
number of angles to illustrate the complexity of his literary personality.

Brenda Maddox, *George's Ghosts: A New Life of W. B. Yeats* (1999). This
somewhat carelessly written book concentrates upon sex and the women
in Yeats's life so it is hardly to be regarded as a balanced biography. As
the author remarks in her introduction Yeats 'looks very different to a literary scholar than to a journalist, to a woman than to a man ...' While
putting forward theoretical interpretations of it, she regards Mrs Yeats's
automatic writing as fabrication (very wrongly in my opinion, but then,
unlike many recent biographers, I had the privilege of knowing, respect-
ing, admiring and liking Mrs Yeats) and trivialises Yeats's strength of
mind and Mrs Yeats's integrity and devotion to his poetry into an expression of feminist sexuality.

Augustine Martin, *W. B. Yeats* (1983). An excellent brief life giving a balanced view of the life and work.

Frank Tuohy, *Yeats* (1976). An enjoyable, discerning conversationable book, reinforced by salient quotations and illustrations.

Books about the Yeats family

Bruce Arnold, *Jack Yeats* (1998). An admirably full, critical biography of W. B. Yeats's artist brother which conveys his very idiosyncratic character convincingly and casts further light on the lives of John Butler Yeats and his Pollexfen wife, Susan.

Gifford Lewis, *The Yeats Sisters and the Cuala* (1994). This describes the enterprise, skills and achievements of Lily and Lolly, the skilled siblings of W. B. and Jack Yeats, in the establishment and continuance of the Cuala Industries as well as portraying their very different personalities.

William M. Murphy, *Prodigal Father: The Life of John Butler Yeats (1839–1922)* (1978). A fine study of the painter, it throws light on the Yeats and Pollexfen families and illustrates W. B. Yeats's relationships with the members of his family.

B. L. Reid, *The Man from New York: John Quinn and His Friends* (1968). A sympathetic biography of this often irascible lawyer and generous patron of the arts who was such a good friend to W. B. Yeats and, particularly, to J. B. Yeats.

Michael B. Yeats, *Cast a Cold Eye: Memories of a Poet's Son and Politician* (1999). Apart from detailing the political career of Michael as Senator, Cathaoirleach, MEP and Director on the Secretariat of the Council of Ministers, this book adds a new dimension to perception of the poet's domestic life.

Some books about and by Yeats's friends

John Harwood, *Olivia Shakespear and W. B. Yeats: 'After Long Silence'* (1989). An account of Yeats's relationship with Olivia Shakespear, written with sympathetic understanding of the intelligent cultivated woman with whom Yeats had his first experience of sex at the age of thirty. It deals with her family background and social life and tells of his first affair with her, the second, fourteen years later, and their long-lasting but not always untroubled friendship.

Peter Kuch, *Yeats and AE: 'The Antagonism That Unites Dear Friends'* (1986). This book traces the first twenty-three years of Yeats's friendship with George Russell, his oldest friend, whom he met in the Dublin School of Art in Kildare Street. It analyses skilfully the reasons for their

1

Maud Gonne MacBride, *A Servant of the Queen* (1938; 1994). Something of both the vitality and the 'stone doll' nature of Maud Gonne's approach to life emerge in this autobiography, some gaps in which are filled by Nancy Cardozo, *Maud Gonne: Lucky Eyes and a High Heart* (1979); little written material exists as many of Maud's papers were burnt during a raid on her Dublin house by troops, and some were lost in France. See, under *Correspondence* above, *The Gonne–Yeats Letters*.

Deirdre Toomey, *Yeats and Women* (1997). This volume contains two essays by Deirdre Toomey, a searching account of his relationship with Maud Gonne and an examination of his reactions to his mother. Other essays in the volume deal with aspects of Yeats's relations with Maud Gonne, Olivia Shakespear, Florence Farr, Lady Gregory, George Yeats, and 'the heterogeneous succession of women in his latter days'.

Some specialised studies

Drama

David R. Clark, *W. B. Yeats and the Theatre of Desolate Reality* (1965). This makes useful points about the plays and their meanings.

Liam Miller, *The Noble Drama of W. B. Yeats* (1977). A fine and enjoyable account of Yeats as a dramatist which links his plays closely to the theatre and is well illustrated.

Peter Ure, *Yeats the Playwright* (1963). An intellectual study of the plays and their meanings.

Helen Hennessy Vendler, *Yeats's Vision and the Later Plays* (1963). This offers subtle interpretations of the later work.

Kathleen Worth, *The Irish Drama of Europe* (1978). This examines the links between Irish and European dramatists in a stimulating way.

Yeats's methods of writing

Curtis Bradford, *Yeats at Work* (1965). An informative study of the manuscripts.

Jon Stallworthy, *Between the Lines* (1963). This detailed examination of some of Yeats's MS drafts shows the vast amount of work that went into his writing before (and after) publication.

Art

T. R. Henn, *The Lonely Tower* (1950; 2nd edn 1965). A study of the poetry in which there are useful discussions of Yeats's use of symbols (Ch. 9) and of his debt to painting (Ch. 14).

Frank Kermode, *Romantic Image* (1957). This contains some stimulating ideas.

Elizabeth Bergmann Loizeaux, *Yeats and the Visual Arts* (1986). This examines the links between Yeats's knowledge of art and his use of words; it has a good spread of illustrations.

Giorgio Melchiori, *The Whole Mystery of Art* (1960). An elegant examination of specific examples of Yeats's use of art.

Yeats's middle-aged interest in the less remote past of Ireland

Donald T. Torchiana, *Yeats and Georgian Ireland* (1966). A good examination of Yeats's interest in, especially, the eighteenth-century Irish writers such as Burne and Berkeley who influenced much of his political and philosophical thinking.

Religion, philosophy, magic, mysticism and the occult tradition

George Mills Harper, *Yeats's Golden Dawn* (1974). This supplies an analysis of the differences that occurred between the members of the Order and has useful detail in appendices.

George Mills Harper, *The Making of Yeats's 'A Vision': A Study of the Automatic Script*, 2 vols (1987). This contains a great deal of quotation from the scripts, which are very difficult to read; some of them cast new light on aspects of Yeats's life. There is, of course, much more in them than matter closely linked to *A Vision*. (See the section above on *Some basic W. B. Yeats texts* for a current annotated edition.)

Graham Hough, *The Mystery Religion of W. B. Yeats* (1984). This is an altogether admirable exposition of Yeats's beliefs; it avoids pedantry and over-detailed criticism and can be highly recommended for its skilful and sophisticated simplification of a complex subject.

Ellic Howe, *The Magicians of the Golden Dawn* (1972). A most informative book about the Order.

Virginia Moore, *The Unicorn: William Butler Yeats's Search for Reality* (1954). Sympathetic to Yeats's belief in the possibility of true vision, this study pays attention to his interest in philosophy as well as to the unusual sources which shaped some of his ideas. *A Vision* is well treated in it.

General introductions and detailed commentaries

Denis Donoghue, *Yeats* (1971). A generalised critical overview of Yeats's achievement.

James P. McGarry, *Place Names in the Writings of William Butler Yeats* (1976). A learned work giving English translations of Irish names, based upon unique local knowledge.

A. Norman Jeffares, *A New Commentary on the Poems of W. B. Yeats* (1984). This is intended to provide information on the sources of the poems, to help readers to understand their meanings and relate them to the circumstances in which they were written. Similar aims have prompted *A Commentary on the Collected Plays of W. B. Yeats* by A. N. Jeffares and A. S. Knowland (1975). A forthcoming third, expanded and revised edition of the *Commentary* on the Poems will include new material; it will be jointly edited by Jeffares, Warwick Gould and Deirdre Toomey. A similar third, expanded and revised edition of the *Commentary* on the Plays will also include new material (notably from the Abbey Theatre archives); it will be edited by A. N. Jeffares, Robert Welch and Anne McCartney.

INDEX